CLASSICAL

ARCHITECTURE

in

RENAISSANCE

EUROPE

1419-1585

By JOHN FITZHUGH MILLAR

Thirteen Colonies Press
Williamsburg, Virginia

1987

© Thirteen Colonies Press 1987
710 South Henry Street
Williamsburg, Virginia, 23185

No part of this book may be reproduced by any means except after written permission from the Publisher.

Library of Congress Catalogue Number 86-50560
ISBN 0-934943-06-0 *paperback*
        0-934943-07-9 *hardcover*

This book is set primarily in eleven-point Sabon, which is a modern, readable recutting of the sixteenth-century Garamond type. The paper is a smooth white approved by the Library of Congress for its long life.

Books of *Historical* interest, covering primarily from the Renaissance to 1800.

CLASSICAL ARCHITECTURE IN RENAISSANCE EUROPE 1419-1585

ABOUT THE AUTHOR

JOHN FITZHUGH MILLAR was educated in England and the United States. He received his A.B. from Harvard in 1966 and his M.A. in History from the College of William and Mary in 1981. He has taught history and architectural history at three colleges, and has spent a decade as a museum director in Rhode Island. He is active as an historical consultant and lecturer (anyone wishing to hire Mr. Millar for these purposes is invited to write to him in care of Thirteen Colonies Press). He lives with his wife Cathy in Williamsburg, Virginia.

His major published works include:

THE ARCHITECTS OF THE AMERICAN COLONIES, Barre Publishers, 1968 (out of print).

COLONIAL & REVOLUTIONARY WAR SEA SONGS & CHANTEYS, Folkways Records, FH 5275, 1975.

RHODE ISLAND: FORGOTTEN LEADER OF THE REVOLUTIONARY ERA, Providence Journal Books, 1975.

SHIPS OF THE AMERICAN REVOLUTION, Bellerophon Books, 1976.

AMERICAN SHIPS OF THE COLONIAL & REVOLUTIONARY PERIODS, Norton, 1978, (out of print).

ELIZABETHAN COUNTRY DANCES, Thirteen Colonies Press, 1986.

A COMPLETE LIFE OF CHRIST, Thirteen Colonies Press, 1986.

EARLY AMERICAN SHIPS, Thirteen Colonies Press, 1986

Forthcoming:

EARLY AMERICAN CLASSICAL MUSIC, Thirteen Colonies Press, 1987.

COLONIAL ARCHITECTURE, I: BRITISH, DANISH, DUTCH, FRENCH, GERMAN & RUSSIAN HIGH-STYLE IN AMERICA 1100-1790, Thirteen Colonies Press

COLONIAL ARCHITECTURE, II: EUROPEAN HIGH-STYLE IN AFRICA, ASIA & AUSTRALIA 1450-1790, Thirteen Colonies Press

TABLE OF CONTENTS

Foreword iii

Acknowledgements vi

The Renaissance 1

ITALY 5

FRANCE 55

THE GERMANIC COUNTRIES 87
    (Austria, Switzerland, West
    Germany, DDR, Belgium, Netherlands,
    Denmark, Norway & Sweden)

BRITAIN 121
    (England, Scotland & Wales)

EASTERN EUROPE 145
    (Yugoslavia, Romania, Hungary,
    USSR, Czechoslovakia & Poland)

SPAIN & PORTUGAL 167

Bibliography 209

APPENDIX 210

Biographical Information 212

Illustrated Glossary 223

Index 235

FOREWORD

I cannot claim that this book has been over twenty years in the making, but it does owe its existence to a seemingly chance event that occurred in 1963. Wendell Garrett, who is now the publisher of the magazine *Antiques,* was serving as a Fellow at Harvard while I was an undergraduate there. Over lunch one day he asked me if I would consider constructing models of buildings designed by the eighteenth-century American architect Peter Harrison in order to provide exhibition materials for the celebration of the 200th anniversary of a Harvard building that had been designed by Harrison.

I built a few models for the exhibition, but the research I had to conduct before my knife cut the first piece of wood convinced me to write a book about Harrison and his numerous contemporaries who designed hundreds of attractive buildings in early America. The book, *The Architects of the American Colonies,* was finished in 1966 and published less than three years later. As so often happens in the realm of publishing, no sooner had the book appeared than I began to grow dissatisfied both by its scope and its standard of accuracy. A new and greatly expanded version of the book began to take shape almost immediately, but its completion has been greatly delayed by many occupational, educational and publishing diversions along the way.

One of these diversions was actually related to the new book, whose title, incidentally, is to be *Colonial Architecture: British, Danish, Dutch, French, German and Russian High-Style in America.* The style of formal architecture in British America in the first half of the eighteenth century was clearly derived from the style used by Christopher Wren in England for over half a century, beginning in about 1660. Wren did not invent that style, but where were its roots? I was not satisfied with the usual answers that traced it to the Italian Renaissance via Inigo Jones and seventeenth-century French and Dutch architecture. Surely, I reasoned, classical buildings existed in England before Jones.

I started with the Royal Exchange, built in London in 1566; it was a gem that might almost have been erected in Italy a century earlier. When I discovered, not without difficulty, that the architect of the Exchange was Hendrik van Paesschen of Antwerp, it was not long before other details of his unusual career fell into place. The buildings he designed in Flanders, England, Wales and Scandinavia demonstrate that he outstripped his fellow architects and builders in northern Europe by as much as his almost exact contemporary, Andrea Palladio, dominated his rivals in Italy.

If that were not enough, a clear connection with Christopher Wren soon appeared. Wren, during his architecturally formative years, was resident professor of astronomy at Gresham College, London. Gresham College, which was only a stone's throw from the Royal Exchange, was itself an elegant classical design in brick and white marble by none other than Hendrik van Paesschen, and echoes of it can be detected in many of Wren's own subsequent works.

In Hendrik van Paesschen I had found a major architect of the Renaissance who had been almost totally ignored in all the standard texts on that subject; he is not listed, for example, even in the *Macmillan Encyclopedia of Architects* (1982). He was a man not only of his own day, for he had perpetuated some of his ideas through his influence on Wren a century later. Perhaps I should write a book on him.

My inclination to write a book-length biography of Hendrik van Paesschen was quickly deflected by conversations with several pessimistic publishers. "If no one has ever heard of this architect," said one publisher, "why do you suppose the public would buy a book about him?" Of course, he was right.

If the public were to be informed about Hendrik van Paesschen, what better way than to encounter him in a book about the major classical architecture of the Renaissance? In that way, if he were as worthy of notice as I thought, he would be able to stand on his own feet among his peers.

As my research into the classical architecture of the Renaissance continued it became evident that Hendrik van Paesschen was not the only part of the story that had been ignored in the standard reference works. Most books on Renaissance architecture acknowledge the spread of Italian ideas into France, the Iberian peninsula, Germany and the Netherlands, but leave the reader totally unprepared for the wealth of classical buildings in what is now called Eastern Europe. Even in Britain, where the study of architectural history is as advanced as can be found anywhere, no single book refers to more than a fraction of all the classical buildings built in England, Scotland and Wales through 1585.

Well-meaning friends have from time to time urged me to offer what I have learned in a university course, an undertaking that would appeal to me were it not for the fact that I could not recommend a handful of readily-available texts adequately to cover the subject. This book, then, is in part an attempt to fulfill that requirement.

I ought to make a few remarks about the format of this book. In the first place, I have found it practical to divide the subject into geographical categories. Thus Leonardo da Vinci, for example, appears both in the Italian section and in the French section, and Hendrik van Paesschen appears both in the chapter on northern Germanic countries and in the British section; this is perhaps regrettable but unavoidable, for Renaissance architects should be studied in the context of the regions where they worked.

I illustrated my first book, mentioned above, exclusively with elevation drawings executed specially for the book. For this book I have drawn my own elevations, and in a few cases ground plans, for three reasons. First, I feel that these sketches, in which I have tried to show buildings as they were designed to be rather than as they may now exist after possible alterations, can give the reader a truer picture of the buildings than can most photographs; this technique puts all the buildings on an equal footing for greater ease in comparison, especially since nearly all of them are drawn to the same scale. Second, the greatest value of this kind of a book lies in its accessibility to the public, which varies, in part, in inverse proportion to its price; acquiring and printing photographs is simply less economical than providing my own drawings. Third, executing the drawings teaches me more about each building than any other kind of prolonged study and reveals to me information about the architecture that I could never learn in any other way. Besides, elevation sketches of this type are necessarily the way such Renaissance architect-authors as Serlio and Palladio chose to illustrate their books. Of course, the criticism can always be made that no matter how carefully these sketches are measured and drawn they are subject to errors of interpretation, especially where I have had to imagine how an altered building may once have been intended to look. I can find no sure defense against such criticism other than to say that the positive reasons outlined above outweigh them.

No book of this type can stand alone. It depends on the research of hundreds of earlier scholars, including the authors of the standard texts whose adequacy I have questioned above. This book stands on the shoulders of giants and may before too long become itself the stepping-stone for others. I am grateful to the earlier scholars, and I am grateful to all those people who have helped me directly by answering queries by mail (I hope I have mentioned all of them in the section called

Acknowledgements), but there is one other group of people who deserve to be mentioned here. I would like to draw attention to all those in the Soviet Union and elsewhere who failed to answer my queries. Scholars who lack large foundation or government travel grants must do their research in libraries and by mail, and the research is liable to remain imperfect when letters are not answered. If the recipient of a query is too busy or otherwise unable to help he should at the very least send a simple post card to say so; I always try to respond to all enquiries that I receive, and I trust it will always be so with the majority of scholars and institutions.

Architectural history is in some ways akin to oral history: for many buildings the only surviving documentation about them is the buildings themselves; this is particularly true for an era such as the Renaissance, which is made remote from us by the passage of from four to six centuries. It was an era in which relatively few documents were produced in the first place, and only a minute fraction of those have reached our own day. Thus the surviving building, or an artist's view of a demolished building, provides prima facie evidence of a sort not usually available to most historians working in fields other than architecture. For that reason, I have made an effort to see a large percentage of the surviving Western European buildings in this book, and I am sometimes inclined to treat a building the way most historians treat a primary source. But in architectural history as in any other form of history the danger of relying too much on too few sources is apparent.

I apologise to the reader that I am not a draftsman. I am self-taught, and some of the drawings show it, but I believe that my shortcomings in this area will not prove a serious hindrance to the study of the designs, whose beauty often shines through regardless.

The selection of which buildings are included is a personal one and is by no means intended to be exhaustive. Some buildings have been omitted simply because they are too large to fit on the page at the scale I have tried to use in almost every drawing and because their design is not easily broken down into smaller components (like the Escorial, for example). The Cathedral of Saint Peter in Rome is omitted for that reason and also because its design history is so complicated that it can best be studied in a monograph of its own, although of course the evolution of its design is one of the more important stories of classical Renaissance architecture.

Finally, I would like to express my deepest thanks to my wife, Cathy, who has worked long and hard as a Registered Nurse at Williamsburg Community Hospital to support me in the mean time and has waited so patiently for this book to appear.

ACKNOWLEDGEMENTS

The following are thanked for their individual contributions to the writing of this book. James Ackerman, James Axtell, Jan Białostocki, Mette Bligard, Anthony Blunt, Cary Carson, Sir Colin Cole, Howard Colvin, Ethel de Croisset, Mr. & Mrs. Clifford Currie, Ann Davies, Luc Devliegher, Henri D'Origny, David Durant, Christian Eldal, Judith Ewell, Charling Chang Fagan, Pauline Fenley, John Fisher, Michel de Ganay, Mr. & Mrs. Jody Gibson, Mark Girouard, S. B. Halmann, Henry-Russell Hitchcock, Dale Hoak, Ralph Hyde, Sten Karling, Thomas Kaufmann, Bohumil Kejř, Carolyn Kolb, George Kubler, E. H. ter Kuile, Živan Kužel, D. T. LeFort, Carol Linton, Hakon Lund, Melle Massias, Josip Miliša, John Newman, Otto Norn, J. van Roey, John Schofield, Jiři Šimek, Joakim Skovgaard, Ejvind Slottved, Annabelle Studd, Sir John Summerson, Anne Lise Thygesen, J. S. Tickelman, Eric Truebenbach, and R. H. Harcourt Williams.

The following institutions kindly responded to requests for information. Antwerp Stad, Austria National Library, Barking Library, Burghley House, Clwyd County Record Office, Conway Library of the Courtauld Institute, Dendermonde Stad, East Sussex County Library, Edinburgh City Library, Gloucester County Library, Hamburg Statsarchiv, Hamburg Wertpapierbörse, Munich Residenz, National Library of Wales, National Monuments Record of Great Britain, State Institute for Preservation of Historical Monuments and Nature Care (Prague), Victoria & Albert Museum, Vienna Burghauptmannschaft, and Yugoslav Press & Cultural Center.

THE RENAISSANCE

The Renaissance (French for "rebirth") was a most remarkable multi-cultural movement that took place at the end of the Middle Ages. Its chief characteristic was an emphasis on reality that often inspired its adherents to a level of brilliance seldom seen before or subsequently. Genius seemed to thrive on the joy and excitement of the first years of awareness of the freedom from formalism and freedom from dependence on higher authority that was available through education.

It is impossible to state with any certainty when or where the Renaissance began, but it is possible to describe some of the conditions that gave it birth and nourished it. In the first place, after many centuries of a rough standard of living, life was becoming by the end of the fourteenth century comfortable enough that some people could think of more than mere survival; one often-underestimated factor in this must surely have been the invention of a practical chimney.

Along with comfort, wealth was being accumulated by the likes of bankers and merchants, who thus could afford to become patrons of the arts; it is axiomatic that artists flourish under the influence of patronage. Inventions that led to this wealth were the importation of Arabic numerals, which revolutionized banking and accounting; the development of knitted cloth; the proliferation of clocks for regulating life; and the many improvements in ship design and equipment, including the compass card, the stern rudder, the combining of square and lateen sails in the same ship and the melding of the best characteristics of hull design of the Mediterranean caravels with the North Sea carracks.

One of the first applications of the new-found wealth was in the spread of universities throughout Europe. It is true that the primary purpose of universities was to train men for the clergy, but it was inevitable that other students and disciplines would quickly become important parts of the universities. Universities gradually became interested in seeking for truth rather than in passing on by rote the theories of the past.

Finally, the relatively small kingdoms, duchies and city-states of Europe seemed to be continuously in political turmoil, which meant that no single power could be strong enough to protect the status quo and eradicate those who sought change. In fact, the very turmoil of Europe encouraged a search for improvement in many fields as part of the general competition for advantages over neighboring states. Quite the reverse was true in contemporary Ming China, a country that had hitherto led the world in technological development but where the ruling dynasty perceived that its future lay in upholding the status quo; the irony was perhaps completed by the fact that the Chinese invention of gunpowder was being combined with the European invention of the gun by the end of the fourteenth century, which made all previous concepts of fortifications and siege warfare obsolete, and thus fostered further change.

Under ordinary circumstances, the Roman Catholic Church would have been strong enough to discourage free enquiry, but it had been weakened by the removal of the papacy to Avignon (known as the Babylonian Captivity) and then paralyzed by the resulting papal schism of 1378 to 1417, in which two popes were proclaimed at the same time, one at Avignon and the other at Rome, each excommunicating the other. This was apparently the very opportunity the Renaissance required for building a solid foundation.

Although perhaps the most obvious characteristics of the Renaissance are the changes that were wrought in the various arts, such a successful movement required first of all an intellectual ground. Hence, while the first Renaissance artists, sculptors, architects and composers did not develop the new styles until after 1400, the literary fathers of the Renaissance were at work up to half a century earlier. Their writings took many forms. Some scholars suddenly took the trouble to learn Greek, a language that had been almost completely ignored for about six centuries in Italy. With this Greek, they were able to read early texts of the Bible and make new and more accurate translations of the Bible into Latin; this was somewhat threatening to the Church, because it put into question all the "facts" based on the previous, inaccurate translations. The Greek scholars also found themselves reading classical Greek literature that had been unknown for so many centuries, and thus led the way for sculptors and architects in their subsequent "back to the classics" movement. These scholars considered themselves "humanists," from the Latin word "humanitas," a loose translation for which is "education." Humanism is not, as some believe, summed up in the remark by the Greek philosopher Protagoras, "Man is the measure of all things," but rather that through education man is enabled to find the measure of all things—a significant difference. Renaissance architect Alberti was closer to the mark with "A man can do all things if he will."

The first herald of humanism—some have called him the first humanist, which may be a slight exaggeration—was Francesco Petrarcha (1304–1374), or Petrarch as he is known in English. Born of a Florentine family in exile, Petrarch was so highly regarded for his Latin epic poetry that he was invested as Poet Laureate of Rome. He was the first to write sonnets in Italian, a language not then considered suitable for higher literature.

Petrarch's good friend, Giovanni Boccaccio (1313–1375) is perhaps a better candidate for the title of "first humanist." Not only was he the first to write prose in Italian (some of which was borrowed and translated by Chaucer in England), but, unlike Petrarch, he took the trouble to learn fluent Greek and was thus able to study the classics, which he then reflected in his own works. He too was a Florentine.

Sixteenth-century art historian, Giorgio Vasari, attempted to explain why so many of the early Renaissance masters were found at Florence. It was "the spirit of criticism," he said; "the air of Florence making minds naturally free, and not content with mediocrity." Certainly, the republican government of that powerful and wealthy city-state fostered the right amount of intellectual freedom to stimulate creativity. Some of the other early Florentine writers include Gian Francesco Poggio Bacciolini (1380–1459), who was a scholar and copier of ancient manuscripts; Gianozzo Manetti (1396–1447), who wrote a treatise called *On the Dignity & Excellence of Man,* an influential work; Count Baldassare Castiglione (1478–1529), the author of the widely-admired book *Il Cortegiano* (the Courtier); and, after Florence had changed its form of government away from being truly republican, Niccolò di Bernardo dei Machiavelli (1469–1527), known chiefly for his great book on statecraft, *The Prince.*

But the rebirth was not confined to Florence. In England, a priest named John Wycliffe (ca. 1320–1384) became the first writer of English prose. He also attempted to reform the Church and eliminate many of its more obvious abuses. He was the first to translate the Bible into English, so that the English could see for themselves what it said, and he preached the necessity of a personal, inward religion as opposed to the formalism of the day. Strangely, he was not persecuted in his lifetime, although his followers, known as Lollards, were, and Wycliffe's bones were exhumed and publicly burned in 1428.

One of his followers was John Hus of Bohemia (ca. 1369–1415), who achieved such a following in central Europe that he was given a safe-conduct pass to appear before a Church council to explain himself, and was then treacherously seized and executed. His followers, including clergy, nobility and people, next revolted and formed their own sect, the Moravian Church, which still functions today as the only pre-Reformation Protestant church.

An English contemporary of Wycliffe was Geoffrey Chaucer (ca. 1340–1400), who wrote the first poetry in the English language. Somewhat later, another Englishman or Welshman, John Lloyd of Bristol, led an expedition that rediscovered America in 1483, almost a decade before Columbus. Little is known about his visit to Newfoundland, because the news of the voyage was suppressed when Henry Tudor defeated and killed Richard III, the sponsor of the voyage, in 1485. Nevertheless, the Tudors made England such an attractive place for intellectuals that no less a person than Desiderius Erasmus of Rotterdam (1466–1536) chose to settle for many years in Cambridge. Erasmus is widely regarded as the greatest of the humanists.

Florence may justly be regarded as the mother of the Renaissance in terms of literature, sculpture and architecture, but music and painting were developed elsewhere—the two fields for which no evidence had by then come to light regarding the forms they had taken in classical Rome. For some reason, Renaissance music was developed largely in northern Europe. The earliest of these composers was John Dunstable of England (ca. 1370–1453). He recognised that formal music for the voice did not have to have a religious text, and that music could be written for instruments alone without voice. Whether or not it was written by Dunstable, one piece of music of his era reflects the new ideas that he developed; this same piece is known in one form as the great Palm Sunday hymn, "All glory, laud and honour to thee, Redeemer, King," and in another form as the country-dance "Sellenger's Round," which is still danced today.

Other notable composers in the new polyphonic styles included Guillaume Dufay of Cambrai (ca. 1400–1474), who was technically English for part of his life because Cambrai was an English possession; Johannes Ockeghen (ca. 1430–1495); Conrad Paumann (1410–1473); Josquin des Prez (1450–1521); and Paulus Hofhaimer (1459–1537).

The earliest painters of the Renaissance came from the Low Countries, where they found ample patronage in the great mercantile city of Bruges/Brugge. The brothers Hubert Van Eyck (ca. 1370–1426) and Jan Van Eyck (ca. 1385–1440) worked together on the same paintings until Hubert died. Without classical Roman prototypes to follow they nonetheless introduced a lively realism to their paintings, in strong contrast to the symbolic stereotypes found in painting of the previous age. They paid particular attention to the effects of light on colors. The works of the brothers Van Eyck were so obviously different from those of their predecessors that these Flemings can be called without reservation the founders of Renaissance painting. In addition, the fifteenth-century invention or re-invention of harmony in music had its parallel in the rediscovery of perspective in the graphic arts.

Among those who followed the early lead were Rogier van der Weyden (ca. 1400–1464), Tommaso di Cristoforo Fini Masolino of Florence (1383–ca. 1447), Tommaso Guidi Masaccio of Florence (1401–1428), Paolo Uccello di Dono (1397–1475), Fra Filippo Lippi (1406–1469), Domenico Veneziano (ca. 1410–1461), Alessandro Filipepi Botticelli (1444–1510), and others too numerous to mention.

Florence made up for its not owning the first painters of the Renaissance by sponsoring the first sculptors in the classical style. Since much of the early sculpture was not free-standing but in low relief panels, the relationship to painting was much closer than it otherwise would have been. The first sculptors were Nanni di Banco (ca. 1390–1421) and Lorenzo Ghiberti (1378–1455), who executed the celebrated gilded panels on the bronze doors of the Baptistery of the Cathedral of Florence, after winning a competition with Brunelleschi. However, historians accord the title of "founder of modern sculpture" to Donato di Batto Bardi, otherwise known as Donatello (ca. 1386–1466). He was a close friend of Brunelleschi, and the pair of them made several trips to Rome to study ancient sculpture. Brunelleschi made a great contribution by his re-invention of the theory of perspective.

Sculpture could be created in a variety of media; it could be cast in metal, like Ghiberti's bronze reliefs, and it could be carved out of stone, such as the bulk of Donatello's work. One family developed modelling in clay and plaster to a high art: Luca della Robbia (ca. 1400–1482) and his nephew Andrea della Robbia (1435–1525).

The story of Renaissance architecture is rather different from that of sculpture, although many of the architects were first painters or sculptors. Classical architecture is the style that is generally identified with the Renaissance, and yet to the architects themselves the paramountcy of the classical style was by no means assured. Strictly speaking, even the classical style produced buildings that would have baffled the ancient Romans, for in many cases they used the classical vocabulary—what Sir John Summerson has called the Classical Language of Architecture—to create entirely new forms, which are then called classical for the lack of anything more precise to call them. The Renaissance architects themselves called their work "all'antico."

In architecture, far more than in the other arts of the Renaissance, the old gothic ideas persisted, even in Italy, with remarkable tenacity. In northern Europe, the old styles continued to the middle of the seventeenth century with hardly any slackening of pace, and even achieved some notable advances. Perhaps because England and the Low Countries receive relatively small amounts of sun, one of the aims of the perpendicular gothic style in those countries was to increase the proportion of glass areas to masonry areas in a wall; King's College Chapel, Cambridge is a well-known example of this trend, the culmination of which was Hardwick Hall, Derbyshire, 1591 ("Hardwick Hall, more glass than wall," as a bit of shameless doggerel put it). Half a century later, the style exemplified by Hardwick Hall had been totally defeated by the classical work of men like Inigo Jones and Christopher Wren, but it was to rise again triumphant in the second half of the nineteenth century.

A more accurate characterization of Renaissance architecture would be "experimental" rather than "classical." Even such stalwarts of the classical style as Alberti and Bramante designed non-classical buildings, as witness the former's church of Santa Maria Novella in Florence and the latter's experimental church of Santa Maria delle Grazie in Milan. Lesser architects produced experimental designs like the Certosa at Pavia.

As part of the experimental mood must be the Mannerist movement in Italy. Approximately a century after the beginning of Renaissance realism in art, many prominent artists rebelled against what they had been taught. The painter Tintoretto and his followers distorted their pictures from pure reality in order to show the stress of emotions, while Michelangelo often preferred to eschew the realism of an ugly face for the idealism of perfection in his sculptures. Raphael and Giulio Romano explored the grotesque (theoretically, what one would expect to find in a grotto, hence the modern British slang "grotty," from which is derived the American slang "grody"), and Rosso invented what is known as strapwork: wood, stone or stucco decorations carved to resemble curling pieces of leather.

Mannerism had its counterparts in architecture. In Italy, spelled with a capital M, Mannerists like Vasari had been well trained in the theories of classical design and composition, but preferred to disobey the rules on purpose. In northern Europe, mannerists (spelled in this book with a small M) were native architects who only imperfectly understood the classical style and how to relate it to local requirements, and thus deviated from the classical by knowing too little rather than too much. Some of these, starting about 1550 and continuing for almost a century, picked up strapwork and developed it as their own form of Renaissance architectural decoration.

The course of the development of Renaissance art was influenced by advances in other areas. Generally, it was spurred forward by the work of people like Laurens Janszoon Coster of Haarlem, who invented printing from movable type about 1420, and Johannes Gutenberg, who refined the invention some thirty years later. Even the fall of Constantinople to the Turks in 1453 had a positive effect: Portuguese navigators had discovered the Azores by 1439, but with the Turks sitting astride the traditional trade routes to the Orient a stronger stimulous existed to venture further on the sea. By 1500 the Spanish were busy carving out an empire in the Americas and the Portuguese were establishing seaborne trade routes to the Orient around the Cape of Good Hope. Meanwhile, the rest of Europe set up an elaborate network of bourses, banks and fairs to help spread the Iberian silver and gold around the continent, thus providing more wealth for patronizing the arts.

In Italy, more than paradoxical coincidence may have tied the rise and fall of genius in classical architecture to the ebb and flow of the fortunes of the papacy. The papal schism ended in 1415 with Rome being declared the undisputed seat of papal power, and only four years later Brunelleschi produced his first classical architecture. When Brunelleschi died, Alberti became the reigning giant. After a lull of a few years, Bramante carried the banner as leader of the movement. However, at the death of Bramante in 1514, the movement appears to have lost confidence about a century after it had begun. While there was no shortage of architects at that time, none of them stood out in the way Brunelleschi, Alberti and Bramante had done. At the same time, all was not well with the papacy; it faced corruption at home and Protestant revolt in most of the countries of Europe. The nadir came in 1527 with the sack of Rome by the soldiers of Emperor Charles V and in 1532 when Henry VIII withdrew the Church of England from allegiance to Rome; at this point, over half of Europe was in the hands of the Protestants. The tide was reversed in 1534 with the election of Pope Paul III, a wise, if corrupt, member of the powerful Farnese family. In 1540 he licensed the Jesuit order and then launched the Counter-Reformation at the Council of Trent in 1545, with amazing results. Just as the papacy began to recover, Palladio appeared to give direction to Italian architecture; although he died shortly before the end of the period covered by this book, his influence has lingered for centuries.

While painting, music and literature of the Renaissance seem to have appeared spontaneously in many parts of Europe, classical architecture began in Florence in 1419. It spread initially by Florentines carrying it to other centers, including Rome (which must have been like carrying coals to Newcastle), then by Florentines and other Italians carrying it beyond the borders of Italy, and finally also by foreigners visiting Italy to study. By 1470, the style had reached Milan, Venice, Rome and Italian colonies in Yugoslavia. By 1500, it had appeared in Moscow, France and Spain and nearly all of Italy, as well as Hungary and Czechoslovakia.

Barely a decade later it had reached Rumania, Poland, southern Germany and, in the form of sculpture at least, the British Isles. In the 1530s, well over a century after the first paintings of the brothers Van Eyck, Renaissance classical architecture reached the Low Countries, north Germany, England, Scotland and Portugal. In the 1560s, Scandinavia and Wales were added. By 1585, the last year covered by this book, hardly any corner of Europe remained untouched by some variation of the new style, but it was by no means a pervasive influence: far more buildings were being built in other styles, and in some places, such as Moscow and Rumania, the seed had withered soon after sprouting, for a variety of local reasons.

Any observer of Renaissance architecture has to be subjective in defining which of it is classical and which is merely mannerist. The Italian architects themselves called their style "all'antico," meaning that they had studied ancient Roman examples and believed that they were designing buildings that would not have looked out of place to the ancient Romans. In spite of the surprising variety of ancient Roman architecture (as, for instance, shown by Margaret Lyttleton in *Baroque Architecture in Classical Antiquity,* most of whose examples would not have been available to the Renaissance antiquarians), the Renaissance architects were actually creating a new style that used a classical vocabulary and was bound by some of the same rules as the ancients. The circumstances, however, were different, and new forms had to be invented or adapted; the best that can be said for some of the new forms is that they appear to be in harmony with the principles laid down by the ancients, whether in surviving buildings or in the treatises of Vitruvius. Whether this qualifies examples of the new style to be called classical or not is as much a subjective decision as anything else.

For the most part, this book treats the definition of classical with latitude. Buildings are included with the merest pretension to classical design, whether through a rigid adherence to symmetry and proportion, or through a more-or-less correct use of classical details, such as the orders and pediments and arcades. These are subjective judgments; for example, while many writers emphasize how proportions in classical architecture are governed by observable mathematical ratios, and offer examples as proof, the truth is that good proportion is far more a subjective decision by a knowing eye than the result of a mathematical formula. Few symmetrical designs, whether classical or not, can not be broken down into relatively simple mathematical ratios in one way or another, regardless of whether the designer had those ratios in mind.

The human mind often prefers to compartmentalize and categorize things that have at best blurred boundaries. Readers will have to make up their own minds about the classicism demonstrated by the Renaissance architecture in this book.

ITALY

Although the Florentine sculptor and architect, Filippo Brunelleschi (1377–1446), was the subject of a handful of biographies written during the Renaissance, many facts about his life are uncertain. For example, it is likely that he designed other buildings before 1419, but only two of them are known with any certainty, both on the south bank of the river: the chapel of Schiatta Ridolfi in the church of San Jacopo sopr'Arno (1418) and the chapel of Barbadori in the church of Santa Felicita (1418).[1] Neither is readily accessible to the public nor particularly impressive. The Barbadori Chapel is a small, square room with pairs of Ionic quarter-columns in each corner supporting spandrels that are linked under a saucer-dome. In such a fashion did classical architecture quietly appear in the Renaissance.

Ospedale degli Innocenti, Florence PLATE 1

Because it was far more impressive and influential, the Spedale degli Innocenti (1419ff; Foundling Hospital) has usually been hailed as the first building of the Renaissance. The front of this building faces the Piazza of Santissima Annunziata, a two-storey structure at the top of a flight of steps, of which most of the lower storey consists of a nine-bay arcaded loggia on composite columns. At first glance, it would seem that nothing more than degree of refinement separates the Innocenti loggia from that of its slightly earlier neighbor, the Hospital at Lastra a Signa just outside Florence, but a second look confirms that the latter is still a product of the Middle Ages.[2] But the Innocenti is not a copy of anything known from ancient Rome, where Brunelleschi had spent months studying ruins of classical architecture; it is the beginning of a new era of architecture.

The Innocenti is also the beginning of a new era of city planning, for it turns one of its arcades to the outside as part of a new city square, whereas the previous era's loggias were confined to cloisters inside a building.

The Innocenti was never completed as planned, according to ample documentation.[3] Pilasters and entablature were omitted from the upper storey (they have been supplied for the drawing in this book), and the roundels containing the charming della Robbia figures of foundling children were intended to have been left plain; a section of vertical architrave was added by an ignorant builder, and an extra bay was added. Much later, a third floor was added under a monitor roof. Fortunately, later builders continued the motif of the loggia around two other sides of the square.

Old Sacristy & Church of San Lorenzo, Florence PLATES 1 & 2

Brunelleschi's next two commissions were from the parish of San Lorenzo, both the same year (1419). He was required to build a sacristy (which is now known as "the Old Sacristy") next to the church, and in his solution he was the first to attempt what would become a theme popular with many Renaissance architects: the centrally-planned chapel or church. In this he was no doubt influenced by small round and square ancient temples he found in Rome. The interior is the Sacristy's glory: Corinthian pilasters support an entablature from which spring spandrels under a sixteen-ribbed dome; each panel of the dome contains a round window. The dome is not expressed on the exterior, for the inner dome is roofed by a simple hipped roof.

Brunelleschi was also given the task of building an entirely new church next to the Old Sacristy. This was designed with a Latin cross plan and a basilical section with flat, coffered ceiling, not unlike some early Christian churches then still standing in Rome. At the crossing is a round dome expressed only on the interior. The crossing is framed by giant Corinthian pillars, whose entablature also rests on the tops of the arches of the nave in much the same way as the loggia of the Innocenti supports its lower entablature. The nave arches are supported by Corinthian columns with flying entablatures; this last can be credited as one of Brunelleschi's many inventions, although in this case the entablatures have rather squashed proportions. The interior has been altered by the addition of a series of side chapels along the outside of the aisles. The exterior was never completed. A painting dated ca. 1450 shows the entrance to have been once hidden behind a one-storey loggia of five high bays and two lower bays, but this has since been swept away. The parish sponsored a competition early in the sixteenth century in which many prominent architects submitted drawings for adding an heroic façade to the church, but no construction was ever done.

Palazzo di Parte Guelfa, Florence PLATE 2

Another Brunelleschi building that was never finished was the Palazzo di Parte Guelfa, begun about 1420. Perhaps reflecting the turbulent street politics of the day, the ground floor consists of a plain wall with a few small windows and no other trim. The upper two storeys are four bays contained within a pair of giant-order Tuscan pilasters, each bay being a large compass-headed window under a round window. The archivolts of the round windows were never completed and the workmen also omitted the entablature, which has been included in this book.

Pazzi Chapel, Florence PLATE 2

Perhaps the best-loved of Brunelleschi's buildings is the Pazzi Chapel at the church of Santa Croce, begun in 1430. Unlike most chapels of big churches, this one is intended to be entered from outside the church. In plan, the chapel has a twelve-ribbed dome with carved shells in its spandrels with transepts and a small chancel. Instead of a nave it has an entrance porch the whole width of the building. The front of the porch is composed of six Corinthian columns supporting an entablature with an arch breaking it in the middle; this appears to be an early version of a Venetian arch, but it is copied directly from a portion of the interior of the old Roman

1. Giovanni Fanelli, *Brunelleschi*, Florence, Becocai, 1977, pp. 4–5.
2. Peter Murray, *Renaissance Architecture*, New York, Harry Abrams, 1971, pp. 10–11.
3. Charles Randall Mack, "Brunelleschi's Spedale degli Innocenti re-articulated," *Architectura*, Munich, 1981, Vol. 11 no. 2, pp. 129–146.

Ospedale degli Innocenti, Florence

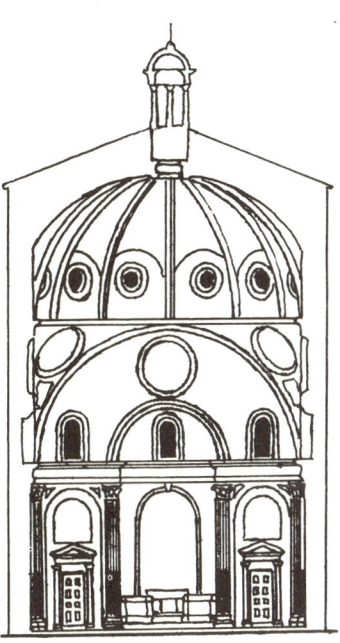

Section of Old Sacristy, Church of San Lorenzo, Florence

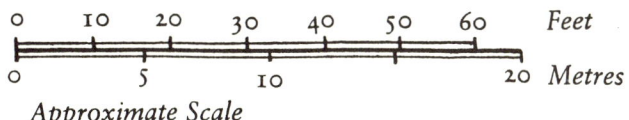

Approximate Scale

PLATE I

Original entrance, Church of San Lorenzo, Florence

Section of the Nave, Church of San Lorenzo, Florence

Part of Longitudinal section   Church of San Lorenzo, Florence

PLATE 2

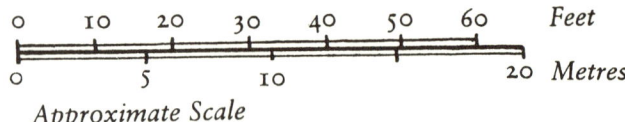
Approximate Scale

Palazzo di Parte Guelfa, Florence

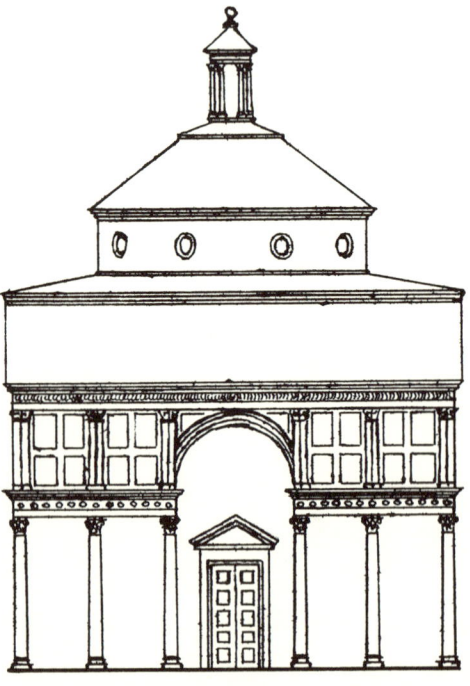

Pazzi Chapel, Florence

Section of Pazzi Chapel, Florence

Cathedral of Saint Peter in Rome. Some of the detail of the upper portion of the porch was added by Giuliano da Maiano, who completed it after Brunelleschi's death. Some time after the Chapel was built, part of the roof was raised to leave an opening above the porch. Brunelleschi probably designed the loggia at Santa Croce, built by Rosselino.

Church of Santo Spirito, Florence PLATE 3

Starting in 1434, Brunelleschi was hired to design another large church, Santo Spirito on the south bank of the river. This is very similar to San Lorenzo in design and detail, although it is larger. It has semi-circular chapels projecting outward from each bay of the aisles, and its dome is expressed on the exterior, perhaps the first time for a classical dome in the Renaissance. Like San Lorenzo, the entrance façade was never completed to a formal design, but its surface is smooth in contrast to the rough stonework of San Lorenzo.

Church of Santa Maria degli Angeli, Florence PLATE 3

In many ways, the most remarkable of Brunelleschi's designs is a small, central-plan church close to the Piazza of Santissima Annunziata. This is Santa Maria degli Angeli, begun in 1434 and never finished. Originally, a T-shaped entrance vestibule was to feed into the main church, which consisted of an eight-ribbed dome lit by round windows and eight oval spaces around the periphery, six of which were to serve as chapels. As the building stands today, the dome is hidden under a hipped roof, but according to an early painting an octagonal dome was intended to be seen on the outside, and each of the round windows led through a long tunnel to a pediment on the outside. A large, compass-headed niche stood on the exterior to mark each division between the interior chapels.[4] Doubtless, the painting was executed by someone who had seen the plans, for the church was never completed to that design.

Palazzo Pitti, Florence PLATE 4

Two further buildings should be mentioned in connection with Brunelleschi. The Pitti Palace, which was altered greatly by Cosimo di Medici starting in 1549, was built about a century earlier. Even in its original size it was an enormous building whose massive scale is reinforced by the giant courses of rusticated masonry. Originally, it was three storeys tall under a hipped roof and stood seven bays wide. Each of the upper storeys was marked by a large cornice, on which stood a continuous, projecting balcony, which gave sanction to later builders of towers with such balconies (such as the Royal Exchange in London and the Hanseatenhuis in Antwerp), and the roof itself was raised above its cornice to make room for another balcony, as was later done at the Raadhuis in Antwerp. There is some question as to Brunelleschi's share on the design, because he died before any construction was begun, and it must be admitted that the Pitti Palace is quite different from any of his other known designs. Its original design is known from an early seventeenth-century copy of an earlier painting.[5]

The last Brunelleschi project to be mentioned is the Cathedral at Florence. This had been under construction for centuries, and in a burst of civic pride had been built to such large dimensions that no builder dared to attempt building the planned dome across the gaping crossing. Brunelleschi thought of a method for doing this that would not require wooden centering or staging to support it during construction, for there were no trees large enough in the region. He also added attractive details to the upper parts of the body of the Cathedral around the drum of the dome. Although these details and the lantern atop the dome are in the classical idiom, the dome itself is an eight-ribbed gothic design that made use of the most advanced weight-saving technology of the day.

It should be pointed out that although Brunelleschi avidly studied the remains of ancient sculpture and architecture in Rome for many months at many stages of his life, the historical record was not then well enough established for him to be certain of the difference between ancient Roman architecture and romanesque buildings, like the Baptistery at the Cathedral and the church of San Miniato, and so he made indiscriminate use of details from both periods. However, his eye seems to have been sharp enough that the only romanesque details he employed blended harmoniously with the classical details.

Tempietto capriccio PLATE 3

Brunelleschi was apparently on good terms with many of the other Florentine artists of his day, such as the sculptor Donatello and the painter Masaccio. Tommaso Guidi Masaccio is regarded as the first major Florentine painter of the Renaissance (1401–1428). His draughtsmanship obviously benefitted from Brunelleschi's re-invention of the theory of perspective, and it is possible that in his short life he never learned much about classical architecture. In any case, he painted a fresco of Christ crucified on the wall of the church of Santa Maria Novella about 1425; the frame and background of the painting are a classical architectural composition, designed to look as if the painting were the entrance to a barrel-vaulted chapel projecting beyond the walls of the church. One expert on Brunelleschi has asserted that Brunelleschi drew out the perspective and the architectural elements for his young friend, but no record of such collaboration has yet appeared.[6]

Church of Santa Annunziata, Florence PLATE 5

Another Florentine associate of Brunelleschi was Michelozzo de Bartolomeo (1396–1472). A metal-caster by training, he slipped easily, like so many Renaissance masters, from one discipline to another. He designed buildings in a variety of styles: gothic, romanesque and classical, and sometimes an amalgamation of all of them. His earliest classical building, which no longer

4. Fanelli, *Brunelleschi,* p. 63.
5. Fanelli, *Brunelleschi,* p. 76.
6. Fanelli, *Brunelleschi,* p. 63.

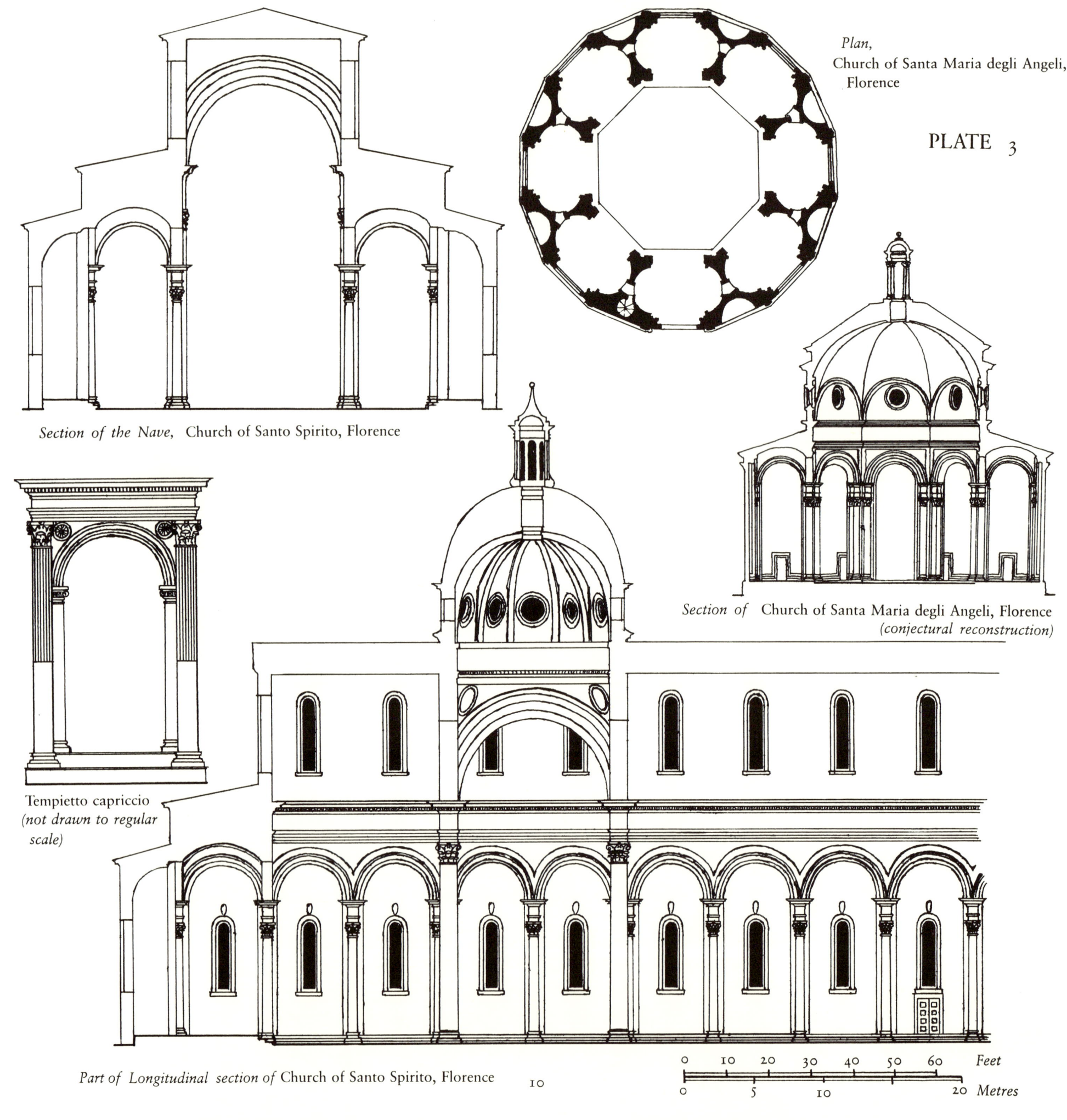

PLATE 3

Plan, Church of Santa Maria degli Angeli, Florence

Section of the Nave, Church of Santo Spirito, Florence

Tempietto capriccio (not drawn to regular scale)

Section of Church of Santa Maria degli Angeli, Florence (conjectural reconstruction)

Part of Longitudinal section of Church of Santo Spirito, Florence

PLATE 4

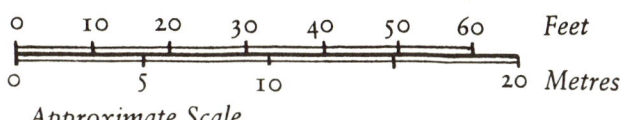

Palazzo Pitti, Florence

Medici Bank, Milan

Approximate Scale

Courtyard, Palazzo Medici-Riccardi, Florence

PLATE 5

Altar end, Church of Santa Annunziata, Florence
(conjectural reconstruction)

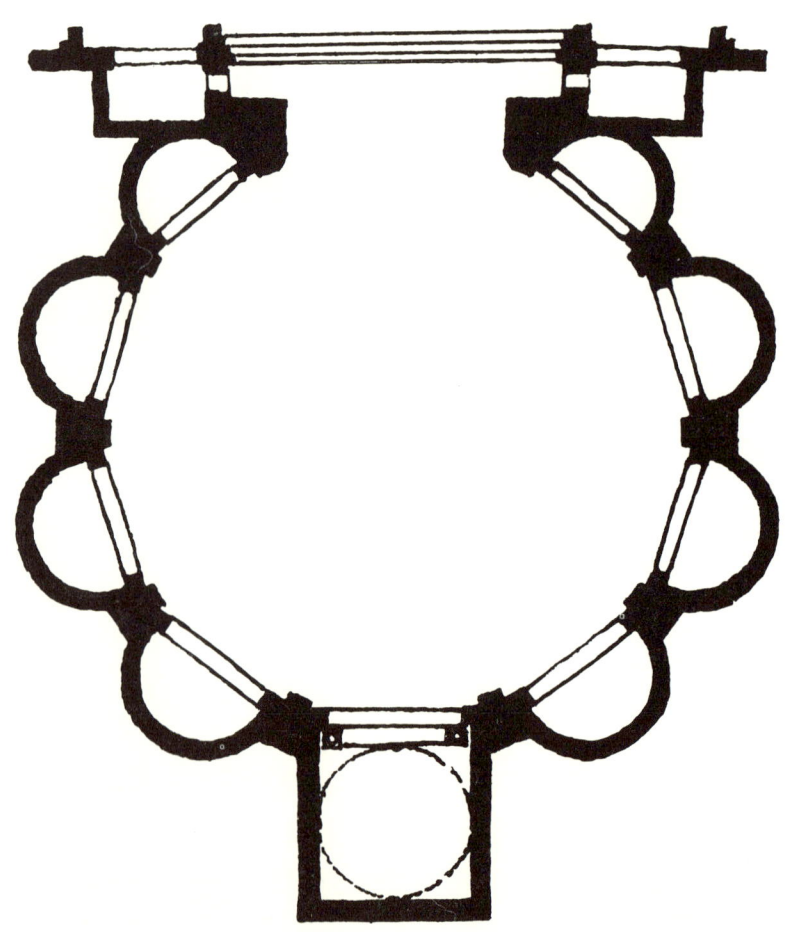

Plan, Church of Santa Annunziata, Florence

stands the way he designed it, was the large domed rotunda at the altar end of the church of Santissima Annunziata that formed a side of the same piazza as Brunelleschi's Innocenti. The design is known from a variety of early views of Florence, and it dates from 1444. The rotunda had ten openings around its perimeter: the entrance from the main church, a square, domed chapel behind the high altar, and four semi-circular chapels each crowned with a half-dome on each side.

Palazzo Medici-Riccardi, Florence PLATE 5

The same year, Michelozzo designed a palace for the Medici family; Brunelleschi had previously designed a palace for the Medici, but the model had not suited and so Brunelleschi had destroyed it. Michelozzo's Palazzo Medici-Riccardi has the typically forbidding exterior of most Florentine palaces of the day, presumably intended to discourage street-mobs from attacking and sacking such seats of power at the behest of some rival nabob, but inside it contains a charming little courtyard. The lowest level of the courtyard is a three-bay arcaded loggia on Corinthian columns. Like Brunelleschi's similar courtyard loggias, the straight loggia of the Innocenti has simply been bent around corners. The corners are therefore awkward with two archivolts colliding at right-angles, a problem that was to be solved by future architects. Above the loggia is a storey of curtain-wall pierced by three arched windows, above which is a colonnaded loggia with no arches.

Medici Bank, Milan PLATE 5

Before he moved to Yugoslavia in 1461, Michelozzo designed a handsome bank building for the Medici family in Milan. This was a two-storey building of rusticated stonework, completely within the classical idiom with two exceptions: the upper storeys windows—the piano nobile—had pointed, gothic arches and were twelve in number, while classical designers usually tried to arrange buildings into an odd number of bays. The building is known to us from a drawing by Filarete at the National Library, Florence, and from the original doorway, preserved at a museum in Milan. The Medici Bank was clearly the inspiration for the Medinaceli Palace in Spain, 1492.

Palazzo Rucellai, Florence PLATE 6

Like Michelozzo, Leon Battista Alberti (1404–1472) was not always wedded to the classical style (for example, the eclectic façade of the church of Santa Maria Novella in Florence), but he was its first great theorist, for he wrote extensively about architecture. He also had influential ideas on city planning.

Like Michelozzo, Alberti did not appear to mind designing a classical building with an even number of bays. The Palazzo Rucellai in Florence (1446) is eight bays wide in three storeys. The ground floor is in the usual impregnable form, but has two doors because there is no central bay. The bays of the ground floor are articulated with Tuscan pilasters and the two upper floors with their compass-headed windows are articulated with a form of Corinthian pilaster. The building was never completed. It served as inspiration for the Palazzo Piccolomini at Pienza (1469), usually attributed to Bernardo Rossellino, who had been the building contractor for the Palazzo Rucellai; Rossellino had died five years before the Pienza building was begun, although he was responsible for the town plan and other buildings there. The two palaces have quite different proportions.

Benediction Loggia, Vatican, Rome PLATE 6

Alberti may have picked as his model for the Palazzo Rucellai the articulation of the Colosseum in Rome. He used a variation on the same theme for his first building in Rome, the Benediction Loggia in the Vatican, built about 1460. This triple-decked arcaded loggia was only four bays wide (to fit between existing buildings) and the proportions of the lower section appear to have been excessively elongated. The railings were surprisingly added above the bases of the arches, rather than incorporated into the areas below, which were presumably solid masonry. Alberti was the first to introduce the all'antica style to Rome, the place that had given birth to the original idea.

Tempio Malatestiano, Rimini PLATE 6

Alberti is perhaps best known for three unusual churches. The earliest is the Tempio Malatestiano at Rimini, 1446. This was intended as a memorial chapel to members of the wealthy family with the unfortunate name of Malatesta. The lower part of the façade was patterned after a Roman triumphal arch, while the upper part, never finished, was an unsuccessful solution to a long-standing problem of how to disguise a basilical silhouette behind a classical façade and yet still integrate the two. The church was to have had a large dome, which, however, was never built.

Church of San Sebastiano, Mantua PLATE 6

The small church of San Sebastiano at Mantua (ca. 1460) has the façade of a six-columned Corinthian temple from ancient Rome, except that the entablature is broken in the middle to allow the insertion of a large, compass-headed window. In addition, the columns of the temple have been replaced with pilasters for this church.

Church of Sant'Andrea, Mantua PLATES 6 & 7

Very much larger is the church of Sant'Andrea in Mantua (ca. 1470), whose facade is modelled on a tetrastyle temple with the shape of an arch filling the central space. Above the pediment protrudes a strange form whose function is mostly to light the end of the ceiling of the nave. The nave consists of a large, coffered barrel-vault, whose entablature rests on pairs of Corinthian pilasters. Instead of side aisles, three chapels fill the spaces on either side of the nave, each chapel lit by a Diocletian window. In this design, Alberti demonstrated that he had learned to increase scale when building a large church, in contrast to Brunelleschi, who used a relatively small scale in his large churches. Brunelleschi

Unfinished front, Palazzo Rucellai, Florence
(conjectural reconstruction)

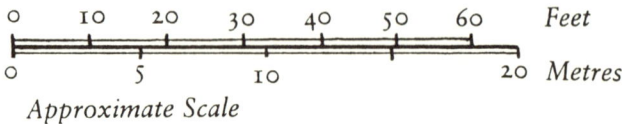

Approximate Scale

Benediction Loggia, Vatican, Rome

Church of San Sebastiano, Mantua

PLATE 6

Tempio Malatestiano, Rimini

Church of Sant'Andrea, Mantua

probably felt the need to relate his churches more to the scale of a human, while Alberti must have learned that the separate parts of a building should most of all be related to the totality of the building.

The Rossellino family produced two architects among its many sons. Bernardo, the elder of the two, is also the more famous, because he extended his concept of classical architecture to cover the arrangement of several buildings together, as in his work at Pienza. Architecturally, the Pienza buildings are not outstanding, but they were designed to relate to each other. Bernardo had worked as Alberti's assistant at the Palazzo Rucellai at Florence, and used almost the same design for the Palazzo Piccolomini at Pienza. The younger brother, Antonio, may have had a better grasp of classical architecture. His finest work is the Chapel of the Cardinal of Portugal at the Church of San Miniato, Florence, built 1461–1466. The square room is made into a cross by shallow coffered arches. Small, L-shaped Corinthian pilasters mark the angles. Above an entablature that runs completely around the square, a dome rests on pendentives. This concept was echoed in Italy and Eastern Europe for many funerary chapels during the next century. No Rossellino work is shown in this book.

Church project for Sforzinda PLATE 7

An extraordinary contemporary of Alberti was Antonio Averlino Filarete (ca. 1400–ca. 1470). He attached himself to the patronage of the powerful Sforza family and proposed that the family make a major investment by building an ideal city from scratch, to be called Sforzinda, and to be designed, of course, by Filarete. It was never built.

Two of the possible buildings to be included in Sforzinda are shown here; their plans were probably drawn about 1455. A domed church with a central plan and no fewer than four campaniles or bell-towers—one at each corner—and a base that contained an arcaded loggia, would probably be considered a major development in the history of the design of centrally-planned churches, were it not for all the extraneous features, such as the bell-towers and the loggia. In later years, one of the characteristics of mannerist architecture is that the designer, not sure of his basic proportions for the whole building, seeks to impress the viewer by adding many needless excrescences and other trim, somewhat as Filarete has done here.

Palace project for Sforzinda PLATE 8

For a palace at Sforzinda, Filarete designed a building with the same kind of faults as the church: the basic building is a worth-while design with an arcaded loggia on the ground floor and the next two storeys articulated by giant Ionic pilasters. However, above the upper cornice stand three decorative towers that detract from the dignity of the building. The piano nobile is divided into ten bays—again, the use of an even number—but the loggia that Filarete drew for the ground floor has eleven bays. For this book, half the drawing has been reproduced as Filarete drew it with ten over eleven, and the other half as he may have intended it with ten over ten bays.

Ospedale Maggiore, Milan PLATE 8

While much of Filarete's work was theoretical, for he wrote many treatises on architecture in addition to planning Sforzinda, one major design of his was built, and it still stands today, although with many alterations. This is the Ospedale Maggiore at Milan, begun in 1456. Perhaps as a result of some new theory that fresh air was helpful in curing the sick, the hospital was well equipped with airy, arcaded loggias in two storeys, the lower on Ionic columns with four-sided capitals and the upper on Corinthian columns. Only a relatively small part of Filarete's enormous, multi-courtyarded scheme for the hospital was actually carried out, but it remains one of Milan's handsomest examples of architecture from any period.

Palazzo Ducale, Urbino PLATE 9

Surely one of the most civilized places in Renaissance Italy was at the court of Duke Federigo Montefeltro at Urbino. He was the leader of the pope's army, and he built a heavily-fortified palace high in the mountains. Once the palace was made safe from attack the duke made every effort to beautify it. His architect for the finest parts was apparently Luciano Laurana (ca. 1420/5–1479), who came from Yugoslavia. He began work at Urbino in 1466. His design for one exterior façade, which has since been altered, anticipated some Mannerist ideas, for he staggered three doors on the lower floor in the gaps between four windows above. The lower floor is textured with channelled stone, while the upper wall is smooth.

The arcaded courtyard of the palace was perhaps as close to the ideal as any Renaissance architecture, although it has been altered by the addition of other storeys. An arcade of Corinthian columns stands under a series of windows separated by Corinthian pilasters, and the corners are reinforced by large pilasters to avoid the problem that Michelozzo encountered at the Medici Palace.

Church of San Michele in Isola, Venice PLATE 9

Classical architectural ideas came slowly to Venice; Venice had been prosperous and independent for years, and had developed its own blend of Byzantine romanesque and gothic with which it was quite satisfied. The first to employ classical ideas in Venice was Mauro Coducci (ca. 1440–1504) who had worked under Laurana. Most of his buildings can be seen as variations on the old Venetian style, perhaps in obedience to the wishes of his clients, but one of his earliest buildings, the diminutive church of San Michele in Isola (1468), is basically a classical composition. The lower part of the façade is articulated by four Ionic pilasters, of which the middle two support short shafts that terminate in fur-

Longitudinal section of the Nave, Church of Sant'Andrea, Mantua

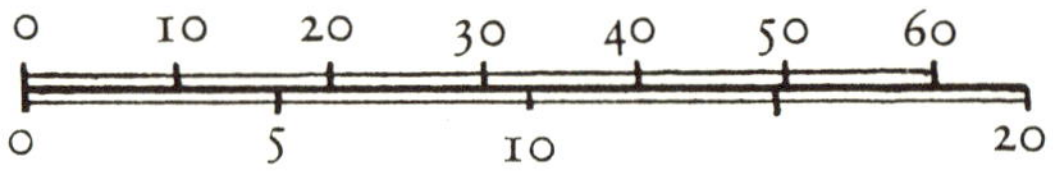

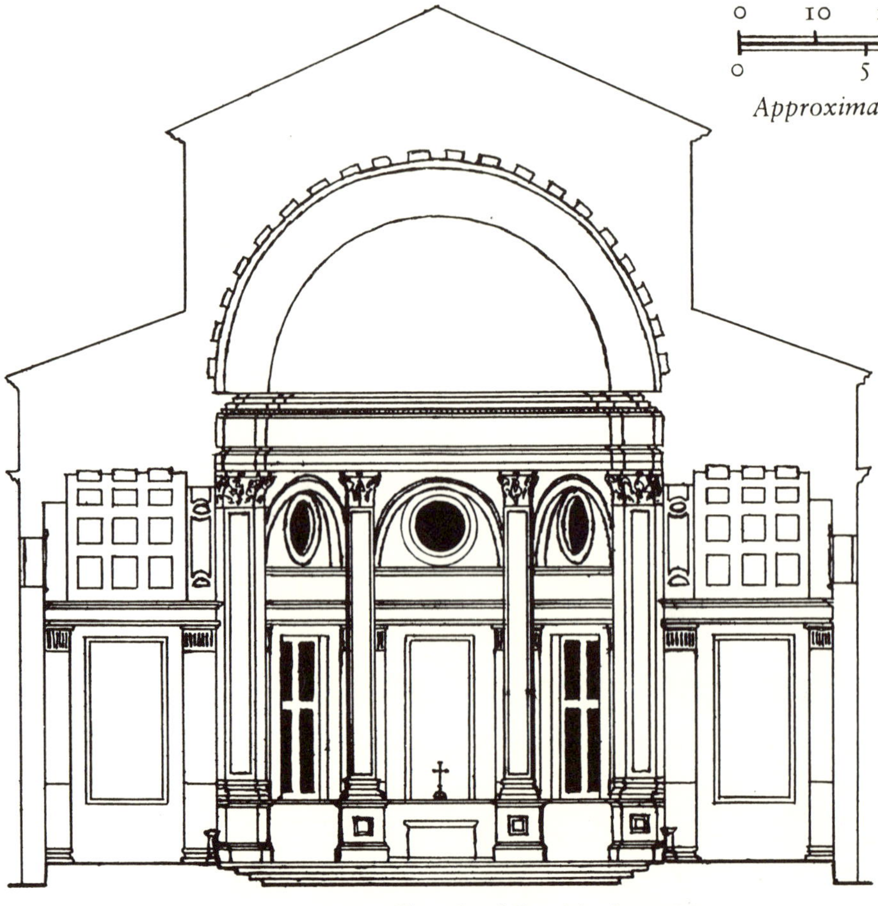

Section of the Nave, Church of Sant'Andrea, Mantua

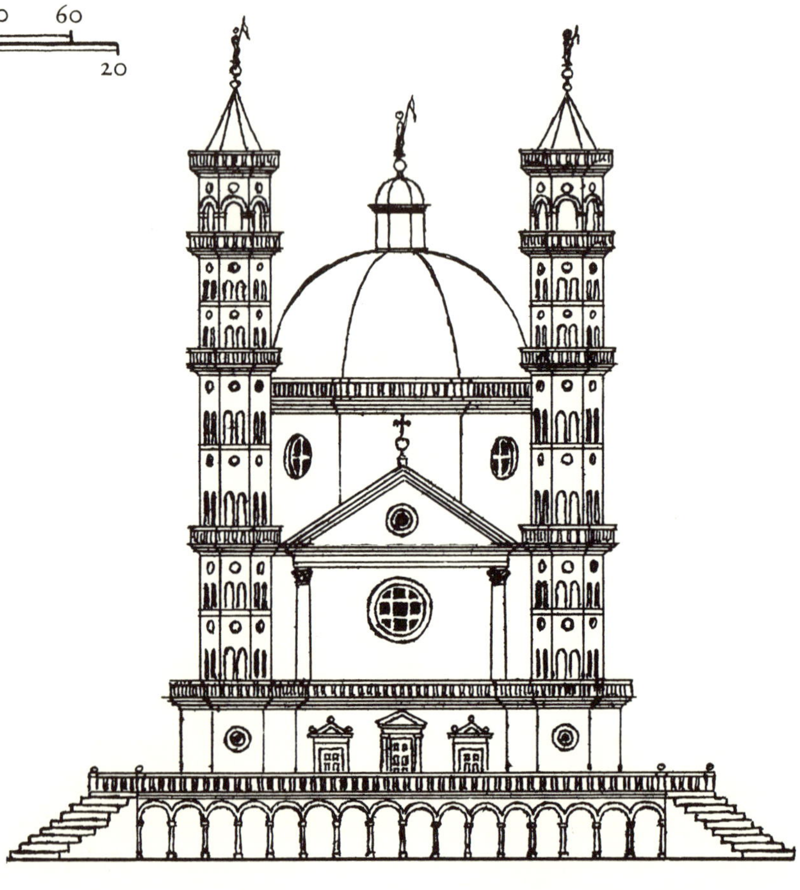

Church project for Sforzinda

PLATE 7

Palace project for Sforzinda

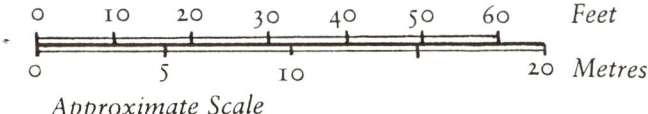

PLATE 8

Courtyard, Ospedale Maggiore, Milan

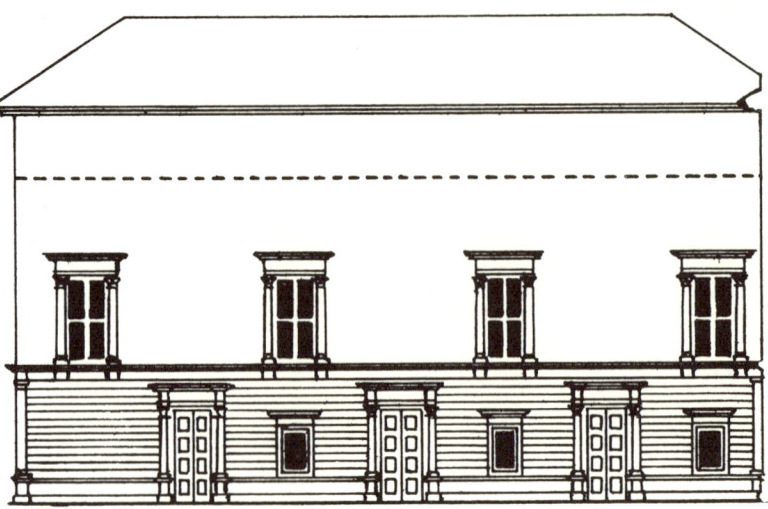
Palazzo Ducale, Urbino

Courtyard, Palazzo Ducale, Urbino

Approximate Scale

Church of San Michele in Isola, Venice

Palazzo Loredan-Vendramin-Calergi, Venice

PLATE 9

Courtyard, Palazzo Venezia, Rome

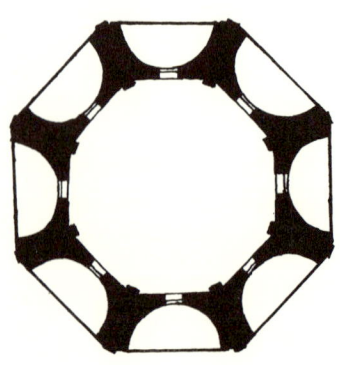

Plan & elevation, Tempietto project

18

ther Ionic capitals under an entablature and semicircular pediment. The shape of the pediment is echoed in the rounded half-pediments over each wing of the lower section. Although the design is slightly clumsy it is altogether a creditable attempt to marry a classical façade to the basilical form of church. This solution is echoed in the much larger cathedral at Sibenik, Yugoslavia.

Palazzo Loredan-Vendramin-Calergi, Venice
PLATE 9

San Michele was a product of the beginning of Coducci's career, and it is necessary to skip to the end of his career to find something equally as classical. The large Palazzo Loredan-Vendramin-Calergi along the Grand Canal was built in 1502. It has three storeys, each with full entablatures completely around the building. The half-columns towards the outside of the facade are grouped in pairs while those in the middle are single, which shows that Coducci had a good understanding of rhythm and balance. However, the arches of each bay, which were once open to the weather but are now glazed, contain smaller arches in the Byzantine manner—sometimes called Venetian soap-bubble tracery—, which suggests that Coducci was still unable to cut the ties with the Venetian past.

Palazzo Venezia, Rome   PLATE 9

At almost the same time that Coducci began his career in Venice, Giuliano da San Gallo (ca. 1445–1516) was designing a building for Venetians in Rome, the Palazzo Venezia (1469ff). The courtyard contains a double-decked arcaded loggia, different from any others hitherto (except Alberti's Benediction Loggia). Inspired, no doubt, by the Colosseum, San Gallo used his Tuscan and Corinthian half-columns purely for decoration, for the arches of the loggia spring from solid piers and not from the columns.

Tempietto project   PLATE 9

In the files of the Uffizi Gallery in Florence are drawings by many architects, including San Gallo. One of San Gallo's drawings shows his idea for an octagonal church or tempietto that seems distantly related to Brunelleschi's Santa Maria degli Angeli. The interior is a simple octagon with a pilaster at each angle, under a dome, but the exterior is richly sculptured; the lower part of each face is cut away into a niche with a carved shell at the top of the arch. The dome, which is expressed on the exterior, is crowned with a large lantern, presumably the only source of light for the interior.

Church of Santa Maria delle Carceri, Prato
PLATE 10

San Gallo was a died-in-the-wool Florentine, so it is perhaps no surprise that he was deeply influenced by the work of Brunelleschi, a man he had never met. None of San Gallo's works exemplifies this more than his church of Santa Maria delle Carceri at Prato (1484). This small, cruciform church has a twelve-ribbed dome expressed only on the interior, bullseye windows between the ribs of the dome, and the simple interior with Corinthian pilasters of the type associated with Brunelleschi.

Project for façade of Church of San Lorenzo, Florence   PLATE 10

At the end of his life, San Gallo took part in the competition to design a façade for the church of San Lorenzo in Florence. He submitted at least two designs, neither of which is particularly successful in relating the basilical silhouette to a classical front. One uses two storeys of large-scale pilasters to produce a rectangle with pediment above the middle; the outer parts of the upper storey are merely a curtain-wall to give the impression that the aisles are the same height as the nave. The other design, based on the theme of a Roman triumphal arch, uses smaller half-columns in pairs on high pedestals; the unusually high pedestals of the upper storey are continued all the way across the front in order to hide the slope of the roofs of the aisles. Both designs are decorated by an excessive number of statues perhaps in a fruitless attempt to gain favor when the otherwise bland designs failed.

Poggio Reale, Naples   PLATE 10

The classical style took over half a century to arrive as far south as Naples. The Florentine architect, Giuliano da Maiano (1432–1490), who had finished the construction of the Pazzi Chapel with a few minor changes of his own after Brunelleschi's death, designed a small palace for Prince Alfonso, starting about 1476. The palace, known as the Poggio Reale, was influential on later architects, such as Peruzzi and Serlio, but that did not prevent it from neglect and eventual destruction in the nineteenth century. Its appearance is known from drawings made by both Peruzzi and Serlio, which however are not as accurate as could be desired. The palace appeared to have three storeys on the exterior. The plan was a rectangle with blocks projecting from each corner; these were the actual living quarters, for the walls connecting the corner blocks concealed no more than a double-decked, arcaded loggia around all four sides of the courtyard. The arches sprang from square Tuscan pillars. The courtyard itself was sunken at the bottom of several steps. Reflections of this design can be seen in the Villa Chigi (by Peruzzi) and the Château of Ancy-le-Franc (by Serlio).

Palazzo dei Diamanti, Ferrara   PLATE 11

Forms of classical architecture from the hands of lesser architects began to appear in many small towns in the north of Italy by this time. One such architect was Biagio Rossetti (ca. 1447–1516) of Ferrara. He was engaged to lay out the town plan of a new section of Ferrara and he found himself designing many of its new buildings. He designed the church of San Francesco there (1494) with its ungainly volutes, and about 1482 he began work on a palace for the d'Este family, the so-called Palazzo dei Diamanti or Palace of Diamonds. The reason for the name is easily apparent: not content with

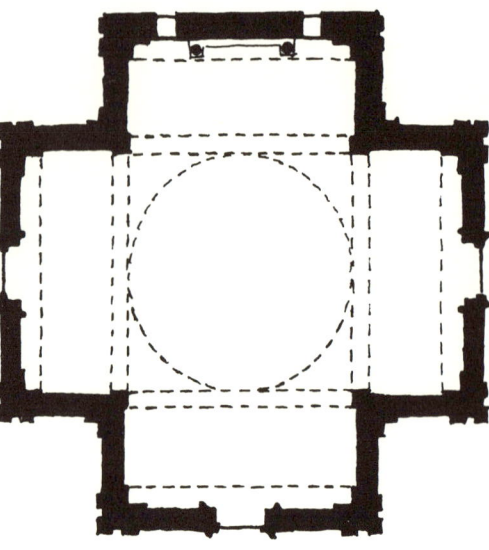
Section & plan,
Church of Santa Maria delle Carceri, Prato

Project I for façade of Church of San Lorenzo, Florence

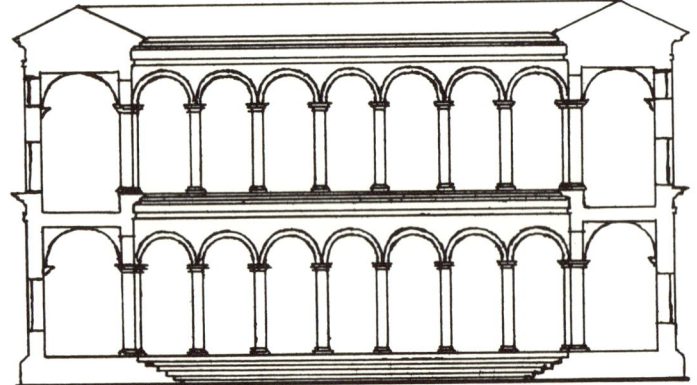

Courtyard Section   Poggio Reale, Naples

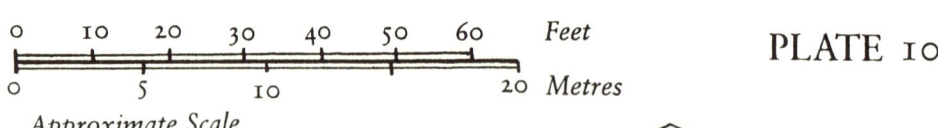

Approximate Scale

PLATE 10

Poggio Reale, Naples

Project II for façade of Church of San Lorenzo, Florence

20

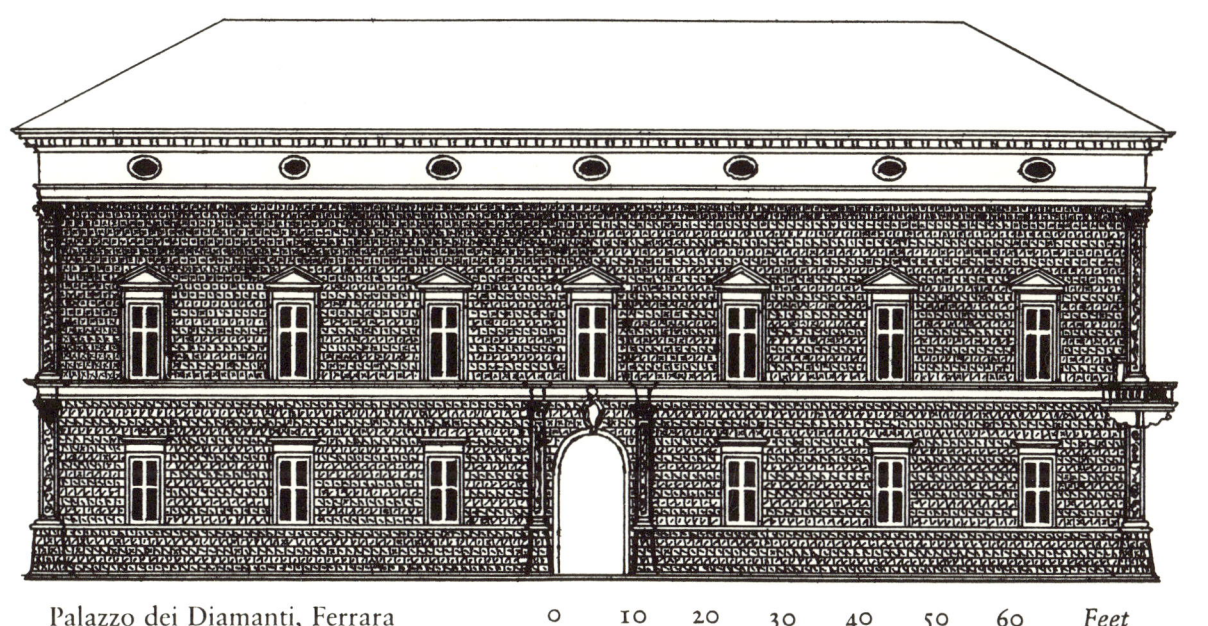

Palazzo dei Diamanti, Ferrara

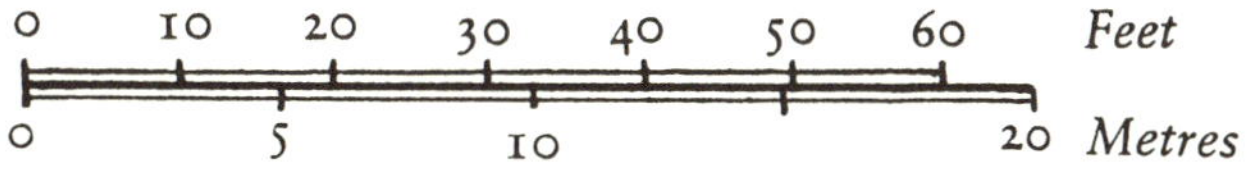

0 10 20 30 40 50 60 Feet
0   5   10   20 Metres
Approximate Scale

Church project I

PLATE 11

Part of courtyard loggia,
Sforza Castle, Milan

Church of Santa Maria del Calcinaio, Cortona

Tempietto project

Church project II

rustication for the texture of the outside walls he had each small block of marble carved into a faceted shape (like its near contemporary, the Palace of Facets in Moscow). When viewed from an angle the walls look like herringbone tweed cloth. The front of the palace is divided into three storeys of seven widely-spaced bays. The windows of the middle floor are crowned with pediments, while the oval windows of the top floor stare out through an exceptionally wide frieze in the heavy entablature. The corners of the building are marked by large, decorated pilasters, and a balcony curls around the right-hand corner about a third of the way up the wall, reminiscent of the encircling balconies of the Pitti Palace.

Church of Santa Maria del Calcinaio, Cortona   PLATE 11

To replace Laurana at Urbino, the Sienese artist and engineer Francesco di Giorgio Martini (1439–1501) was hired to decorate the palace there. However, his best work was at Cortona, where he designed the small church of Santa Maria delle Grazie al Calcinaio in 1484. Designed in the form of a Latin cross with a dome expressed above a high drum, this church was in some ways out of date when it was built. In plan and silhouette, the design is relatively successful, but it fails in its details; the corners, for instance, are expressed by thin pilaster strips that appear too weak to belong to the rest of the otherwise-robust design.

Church project   PLATE 11

Two centrally-planned church designs whose details are well matched to the proportions of the buildings appear in one of the many sketch-books of Leonardo da Vinci (1452–1519).[7] Because the particular book is not closely dated the drawings could have been done any time between 1489 and 1509, but they are likely to have been drawn close to the earlier of the two dates. Each church is designed around the theme of a central square with a semi-circular projection in the middle of each side, a drum and dome on top and a small dome or cupola at each corner; both make use of the giant Corinthian order. This same general form in more refined shape was actually built: the church of Santa Maria della Consolazione at Todi, begun 1504, and therefore Leonardo's two sketches (among many others) were doubtless his ideas for that church. The smaller of the two designs groups the giant pilasters in pairs at the corners, while the larger employs six pilasters a side, well spaced. The smaller design has a smooth, round dome, while the larger has an octagonal, slightly pointed dome that recalls Brunelleschi's work on the Cathedral at Florence.

Church of Santa Maria della Consolazione, Todi   PLATE 12

The actual church at Todi, often attributed to Cola di Matteuccio da Caprarola who carried out some of the construction, is larger, more dignified and more polished than Leonardo's two projects, but, in substituting a small order for the giant order in the projects, the church as built sacrifices some of the grandeur it could have had. The semicircular projections have been given two storeys up to the main entablature and an attic storey under the roof, and they are so enlarged that they almost completely obscure the central block. The four cupolas have been replaced by a simple balustrade and the drum of the dome made much higher with rich sculptural decoration afforded by pairs of pilasters and windows alternating with niches not unlike the eventual drum at Saint Peter's, Rome. Bramante was developing plans for a grand replacement for the Cathedral of Saint Peter in Rome at about this time, and it is possible that he was looking over Leonardo's shoulder to see how such a large centrally-planned church would work; in the event, the Todi church has more of a sense of its own scale than did Bramante's model for the Cathedral.

Sforza Castle, Milan   PLATE 11

Leonardo was a philosopher, a scientist, an engineer and a painter and only occasionally an architect. Relatively few of his designs were ever built, and even fewer remain unaltered to this day. One of his executed designs that has been almost totally swept away is the arcaded courtyard of the Sforza Castle in Milan, built about 1490. The arcaded loggia is supported on Corinthian columns. The middle storey consists of a row of simple windows, each surrounded by an architrave, above which is a cornice band. In the narrow space between the cornice band and the principal cornice is a row of round windows.

Tempietto project   PLATE 11

One of Leonardo's smallest projects was for a fountain or tempietto, dated about 1497.[8] The structure is square in plan with a simple arch facing all four directions. The corners are reinforced with pilaster strips that terminate above the cornice in pinnacles, while above each arch is an awkward pediment. The structure is crowned with a ribbed dome with lantern. The architectural forms of this design are somewhat abstract, which could have been Leonardo's intention or merely the result of leaving the design in the form of a quick sketch.

Tall Villa project
Low Villa project   PLATE 12

Two projects for villas by Leonardo can be dated to the first decade of the sixteenth century. The single-storey project is divided into five bays by pairs of Corinthian pilasters, but only the outer two bays contain windows, which are set in pedimented aedicules.[9] The central bay contains the doorway, while the interim bays feature niches. The corners of the building are emphasized by windowless round towers, on top of which are colonnaded lookout stations under conical roofs. Presumably Leonardo used these for symbolic protection rather than in the expectation of enemy attack. Behind the façade stands a narrow, taller block, as at Wollaton. The taller of the two villas has a three-

7. Institut de France, Paris, Ms. "B". A useful work on Leonardo as architect is Carlo Pedretti, *Leonardo Architect*, New York, Thames & Hudson, 1985.
8. *Codex Atlantico*, fol. 346r-b.
9. In the Royal Collection, Windsor Castle.

Plan, Church of Santa Maria della Consolazione, Todi

Low Villa project

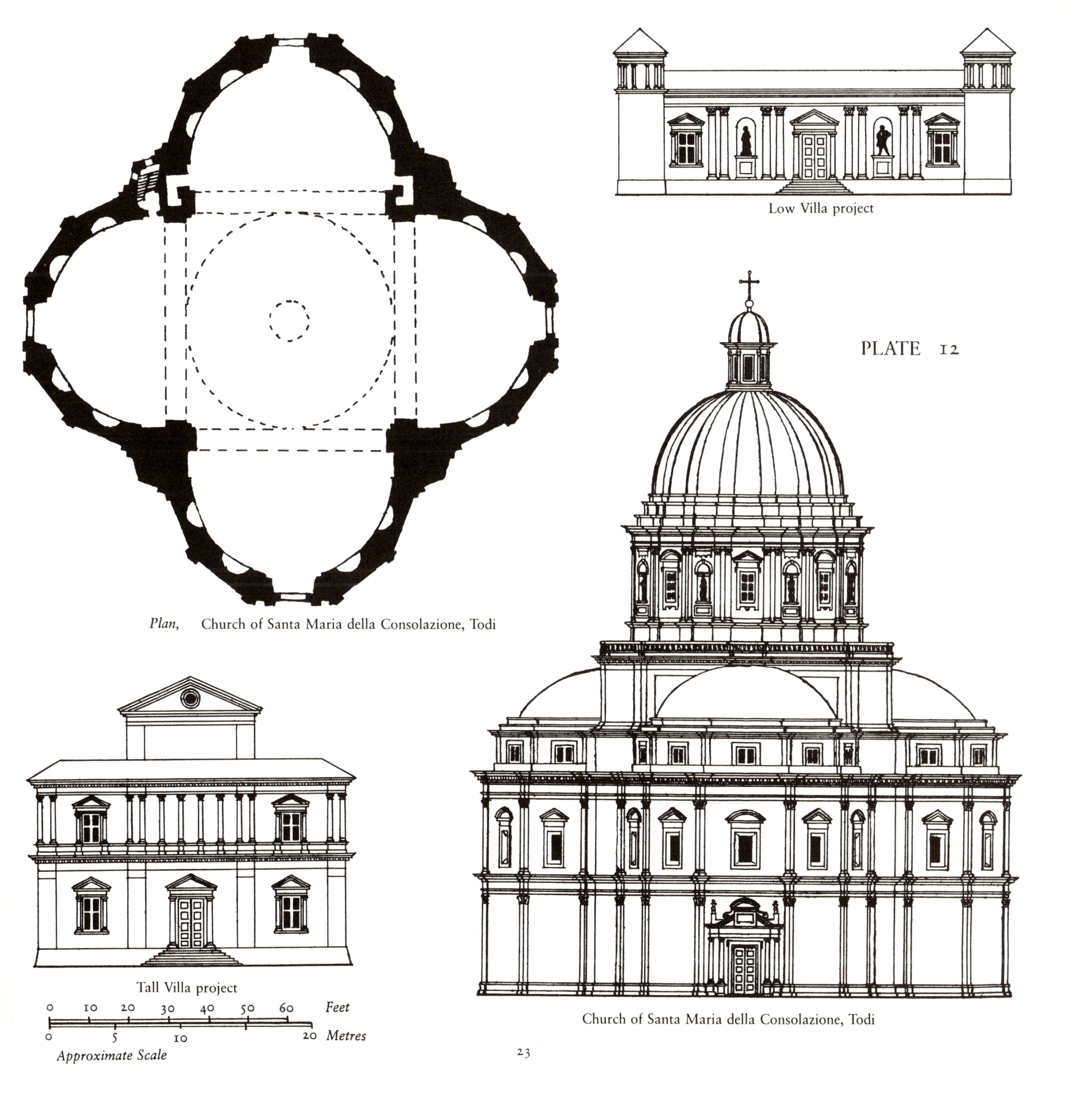

PLATE 12

Tall Villa project

Church of Santa Maria della Consolazione, Todi

Approximate Scale

bay front with windows in pedimented aedicules, while above the doorway is an open Corinthian colonnaded loggia, behind which a windowless block with a pediment projects high above the front roof.[10] The design is quite unlike any buildings by any other architect of the Renaissance, and yet in its own way it is a classical design. One might expect to see such a design from the hand of one of the neo-classical architects like Chambers or Soane.

Trivulsio Chapel project, Church of San Nazaro, Milan PLATE 13

Leonardo received a commission about 1507 for a centrally-planned church design for the funerary chapel of the Trivulzio family at the church of San Nazaro, Milan. Unlike most such chapels, it was to serve also as the entrance vestibule for the nave of the main church. He designed a two-storey, square exterior with hipped roof and lantern, whereas the interior is octagonal and contains a dome. The chapel was never quite completed—for example, the lower entablature and pediment were omitted—but Leonardo's intentions are clear even without resorting to his designs, preserved in the Trivulzian Library.

Project for a Church façade PLATE 13

Many leading architects of the day were attracted to the competition to design a classical façade for Brunelleschi's church of San Lorenzo in Florence. None of the entries to the competition was ever executed, although Brunelleschi's own façade was peeled off to lay bare the rough stone to which any new front would be bonded. Leonardo did not take part in the competition, but it obviously consumed some of his thoughts because he drew two different designs for San Lorenzo. One of these, dated 1515, is in the background of an illustration he did of the Visitation.[11] As a piece of background scenery, the design is plausible, for no suggestion is made as to how large the building is intended to be. However, if one enlarges the picture to the correct scale to represent the large church of San Lorenzo, it is immediately clear that Leonardo's design is absurdly out of scale; the doors, for example, are enormous. The design would be far more appropriate to a small church or tempietto. As absurd as Leonardo's first design may be, his other could have been a winner had he entered the competition.[12] It is the first serious expression of the design concept that was refined by Vignola half a century later for the church of the Gesù in Rome. In this design, Leonardo successfully integrated the basilical silhouette with the classical idiom. The façade is divided into two storeys with pilasters of the Ionic order over those of the Tuscan order. The upper part is narrower than the lower part, the difference between them being bridged by a large volute on either side (an improvement might have been made if the volutes were smaller and if they rested on a base the same height as the pilaster bases). The width of the upper part is expressed in the lower part by a breakfront of the same width, thus giving the design dynamic tension in both directions.

Project for a Square Building PLATE 13

One final design from Leonardo's sketchbooks is shown here, a drawing for an odd square building whose middle section rises high above the roofs of the lower part. It is not clear what use such a building could have, other than perhaps the display of statues in the nineteen niches around its base and the further eleven in the upper part; the interior could serve as the meeting facilities for a town council, but precious little else.

Donato Bramante (ca. 1444–1514), said Serlio, "was the inventor and light of all good architecture, which had been buried until his time." Palladio felt the same way: "Bramante," he said, "a keen student of ancient buildings, erected some most beautiful buildings in Rome . . . [and] was the first to bring back to the light of day the good and beautiful architecture that had been hidden since the time of the ancients." Both statements, illustrative of the esteem in which Bramante was held by his contemporaries, are perhaps extreme, for they ignore the important contributions of Brunelleschi, Alberti and a host of lesser men who came before Bramante. In spite of this, until recently no scholarly evaluation of Bramante and his works has existed.[13]

Doric Cloister, San Ambrogio, Milan PLATE 14

Bramante began his career at Urbino, where he presumably learned the basics of architecture from Laurana. He designed many works in both Milan and Pavia that show that he had not yet hit his classical stride. By 1497, however, he was employed to build a series of four cloisters and other improvements to the church of San Ambrogio in Milan, perhaps in partial imitation of the nearby hospital by Filarete. In the event, only two cloisters were actually built, the so-called Ionic and Doric Cloisters. The Doric Cloister has eleven arches a side resting on Tuscan columns with flying entablatures. The storey above is diminutive in height when compared with the lower arches, and contains windows within arches, two for each one arch of the lower storey. This arrangement was imitated a few years later at the Royal Hospital at Santiago de Compostela in Spain.

Building project & Tower project PLATE 14

About this time, Bramante drew an imaginary street scene, either of an ideal city or of how he thought an antique city would have looked.[14] Two buildings in the drawing are shown in this book: a companile in the background and a two-storey palazzo in the foreground. The campanile has been included because it shows that some Renaissance architects saw nothing wrong in locating a balustrade over the outer edge of a cornice, rather than squarely over the body of the tower; this precedent was followed over sixty years later in London and Antwerp by Hendrik van Paesschen. The palazzo has been included because it is a rare example of a large loggia made from a colonnade rather than from an arcade. The proportions of the building are also unusual, for it is higher than might be expected. A similar building with lower proportions had appeared a few

10. In the collection of the Biblioteca Reale, Torino.
11. *Golden Book of Laodamias de' Medici,* British Library, Yates Thompson Ms. 30, fol. 20v.
12. Gallerie dell'Accademia, Venice.
13. Arnaldo Bruschi, *Bramante Architetto,* Rome, ed. Lateran, 1969, and *Bramante,* New York, Thames & Hudson, 1977.
14. An engraving based on the drawing is in the British Library.

Project for a Church façade

PLATE 13

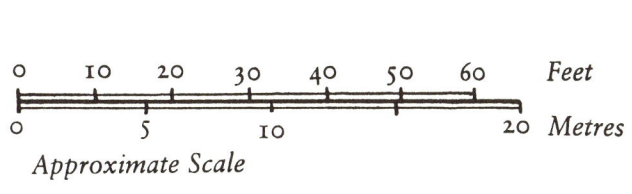

Trivulsio Chapel project, Church of
San Nazaro, Milan

0 10 20 30 40 50 60 Feet
0   5   10   20 Metres
Approximate Scale

Project for a Square Building

Project for a Church façade

25

Doric Cloister, San Ambrogio, Milan

Tower project

Building project

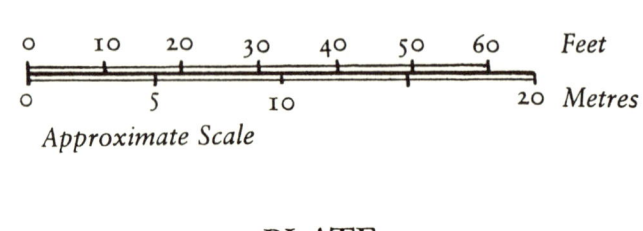

Approximate Scale

PLATE 14

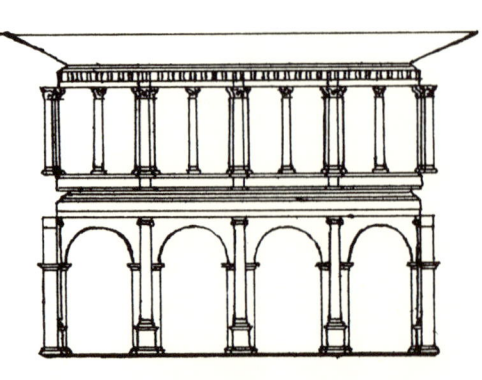

Courtyard loggia,
Convent of Santa Maria della Pace, Rome

Tempietto of San Pietro in Montorio, Rome

Palazzo Caprini (House of Raffaello), Rome

years earlier in a painting of an ideal street scene attributed to Piero della Francesca, and it is quite likely that Bramante knew the work.[15]

Palazzo Caprini (House of Raffaello), Rome
PLATE 14

From about 1500 onwards, Bramante was based in Rome. No exact chronology of his works from the early years at Rome is known, so the order used here is arbitrary. One of the buildings from this period was the Palazzo Caprini, often called the House of Raphael, in the Via Alessandrina. From the exterior, the palace would appear to have had two storeys, the lower a heavily rusticated five-bay arcaded loggia and the upper a row of tall, pedimented windows between pairs of Doric columns under a proper Doric cornice. It is just the sort of design that was commonly used in eighteenth-century England and America for a town hall over a market. In fact, it was not many years before the ground floor of the Palazzo Caprini was turned over to commercial purposes and a mezzanine inserted with windows in the arches. Further alterations (one assumes they were not part of the original design, for they do not appear in a 1549 picture of the building) included the opening of windows for an attic storey inside the metopes of the Doric frieze. This building, like many of Bramante's, was unusually sophisticated for its date. It was destroyed in the 1930s.

Convent of Santa Maria della Pace, Rome
PLATE 14

The earliest work by Bramante at Rome for which we have a precise date is the cloister of Santa Maria della Pace, 1500. This consists of a small, square courtyard with a four-bay arcaded loggia on each side. The arches, which spring from piers, look naked with no archivolt mouldings. Ionic pilasters on pedestals stand in front of the piers. On the upper storey, clusters of Composite pilasters stand above the Ionic pilasters, and Corinthian columns stand in the interstices, helping to form an upper loggia.

Tempietto of San Pietro in Montorio, Rome
PLATE 14

Two years later, Bramante designed his most famous work, the Tempietto of San Pietro in Montorio. It was intended to be part of a much larger shrine on the traditional site of the crucifixion of Saint Peter, but the rest of the project was not realised. The actual Tempietto is enclosed in a small courtyard, which is an impediment to viewing and properly appreciating the perfection of its design. The Tempietto, which has served as model and inspiration for countless domes, large and small, is a round drum capped by a dome with finial, and around the base is a loggia of Doric columns. This arrangement is a refined version of an imaginary tempietto shown in the anonymous painting, "The Miracle of the Man Wounded by a Stake," from the Nicchia di San Bernardino at the Galleria Nazionale dell'Umbria, 1473; in fact, it is entirely possible that a much younger Bramante was the artist of the eight panels of the Nicchia. Serlio assisted in the spread of knowledge of the hidden Tempietto by including somewhat inaccurate woodcuts of it in the fourth chapter of his third book, which was widely read for centuries.

Palazzo della Cancellaria, Rome PLATE 15

From about the same period comes an enormous palace, the Palazzo della Cancellaria. No documentary evidence connects its design with Bramante, but it is often attributed to him. The principal front of the building is asymmetrical, and only the symmetrical part on either side of the entrance is shown in this book. In contrast to the Palazzo Pitti in Florence, with its brutally giant scale emphasized by large, rough rusticated blocks of stone, the Cancellaria is composed through the careful repetition of relatively small-scale elements. A texture is established on most of the surface by rustication of smooth stonework. Contrasting with the rustication are bands of smooth stonework, such as at the level of the basement windows, a belt-course under the ground floor windows and the various entablatures, cornices and pedestals of the upper floors. The upper two storeys are articulated by pairs of Corinthian pilasters spaced more widely than is normal for pairs. Very similar to the Cancellaria is the smaller and less sophisticated Palazzo Corneto-Giraud-Torlonia, which is the only building of this period that Vasari positively ascribes to Bramante; if the Palazzo Corneto was by Bramante's hand, surely at least the front elevation of the finer Cancellaria must also be his design.

Loggia di San Damaso, Vatican, Rome
PLATE 15

Bramante also designed a large structure in the Vatican known as the Loggia di San Damaso. The building was later enlarged and altered. As first built, it was a four-storey open loggia with some of the ground-floor arches replaced by windows and doors. The next two storeys, obviously inspired by the Colosseum, consisted of arches springing from piers with Tuscan and Ionic pilasters standing in front. The top floor was a Corinthian colonnade. The original purpose for this structure was simply to serve as an impressive exterior for the pope's palace, but it eventually became no more than the west flank of an awkward courtyard. It was constructed only a few metres from Alberti's Benediction Loggia, which was designed around the same theme but with different proportions.

Loggia, Belvedere, Vatican, Rome PLATE 16

Bramante designed other loggias for the Vatican, two of which were part of an impressive landscaping project known as the Belvedere, 1503. Parts of the project still stand, but in greatly altered form. For the upper court of the Belvedere, Bramante designed a single-storey loggia of 14 arches with pairs of pilasters between the arches and niches between the pilasters; Serlio later used a variation of the same theme in the courtyard of the Château of Ancy-le-Franc. Down the hill, in the lower court of the Belvedere, Bramante designed a massive

15. Galleria Nazionale delle Marche, Urbino.

Part of entrance front, Palazzo della Cancellaria, Rome

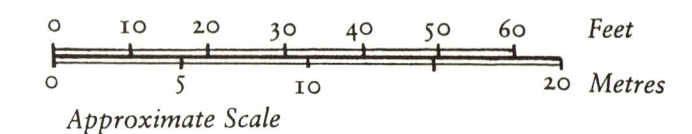

Approximate Scale

PLATE 15

Loggia di San Damaso, Vatican, Rome

Part of 17-bay Lower Court Loggia, Belvedere, Vatican, Rome

Plan, Chapel of San Biagio, Palazzo dei Tribunali, Rome

PLATE 16

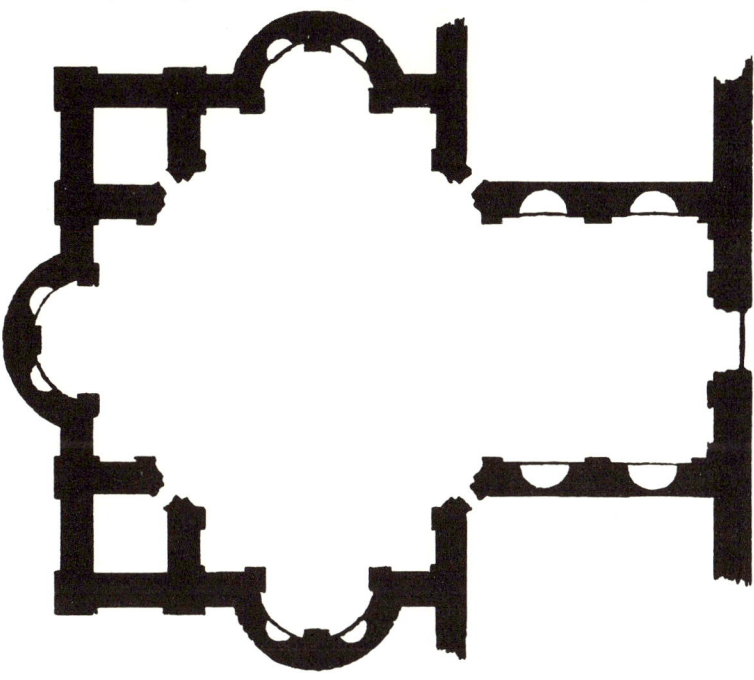

Part of Upper Court Loggia, Belvedere, Vatican, Rome

Approximate Scale

Longitudinal section of
Chapel of San Biagio, Palazzo dei Tribunali, Rome

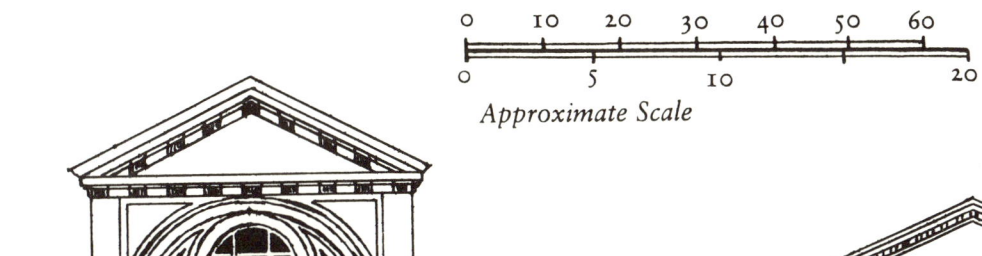

Church project

Church, Roccaverano

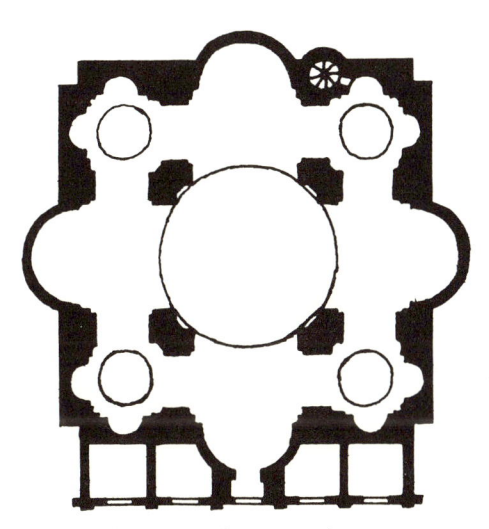

Church of Santi Celso e Giuliano, Rome

three-storey loggia that was impressive but not as well composed as that of the upper court. The arches of the ground floor sprang from piers, in front of which stood Doric pilasters on pedestals. The middle floor had windows with pediments, alternately triangular and segmental, flanked by small niches and clusters of Ionic pilasters on pedestals. The top floor was an open loggia with squat Corinthian columns on pedestals reaching up to the entablature, but pairs of smaller Tuscan columns in between, holding up panels below the entablature. The original intention for the Belvedere was that it should be an outdoor theatre for staging spectaculars and for displaying the papal collection of sculptures, but subsequent popes had little or no interest in recreating the grandeur of ancient Rome, so parts of the project remained uncompleted and others were demolished to make way for new buildings.

Church project PLATE 16

The churches Bramante designed after his move to Rome were far more mature than his early works, and it is to be regretted that many of his early churches still stand while no trace remains of his later churches. Bramante produced three different solutions to the old problem of how to marry a basilical interior to a classical exterior. One project of about 1505, and in the collections of the Louvre in Paris, is said by some to have been a new façade for the church of Santa Maria presso San Satiro in Milan. The lower part is divided into two storeys of five bays set between four giant Corinthian pilasters. The clerestory rises above the main entablature and contains a large round window set inside the archivolt of a blind arch. This is a more refined version of the theme first encountered at Coducci's church of San Michele in Isole, Venice.

Church, Roccaverano PLATE 16

The second was the parish church at Rocaverano, built about 1507 and now lost. Several diverse themes were woven into this design. The height of the nave was treated as the principal thrust of the façade. The nave was outlined by a pair of giant Corinthian half-columns on pedestals, supporting the entablature and pediment of the clerestory, as if it were a classical temple with two columns. The aisles were screened by a lower motif whose entablature was supported on Tuscan pilasters at the outer corners and piers at the inner corners, as if the aisles were part of a lower temple placed slightly behind the higher one. The archivolt for a giant blind arch rested on the entablature of the aisles to give the impression of an arch in the nave, while each aisle also contained a smaller arch underneath its entablature. A fairly close copy of this arrangement was built for the church of Santa Maria detta le Sagra at Carpi (date unknown), but the most important descendants of this design were some of Palladio's Venetian churches.

Project for Church of Santa Maria, Loreto
PLATE 17

The third cleverly eliminated the question of how the aisles would look next to the nave by hiding them behind twin campaniles. This was probably the first time this solution was employed in classical architecture, although it had been used many times in gothic churches. The design was for the church of Santa Maria at Loreto in 1509, and it is known to us through its image on the foundation medal struck that year.[16] The design also included a large dome with unusually large lantern on top. The proportions of the composition suggest that Bramante was using it was one of his many experiments in search of the optimum design for the new Cathedral of Saint Peter.

Chapel of San Biagio, Palazzo dei Tribunali; Church of Santi Celso e Giuliano, Rome
PLATE 16

Two other Bramante churches that may have been similar experiments were the chapel of San Biagio della Pagnotta in the Tribunali Palace, Rome (1508) and the church of Saints Celso and Giuliano, Rome (ca. 1509). Both reflect his interest in reconciling the traditional cruciform plan with the more interesting and classical central plan. The dome (not shown in the drawings in this book) of San Biagio stood over a square plan tipped to its diagonal axis, so that the apse stood at one corner of the square and similar apsidal shapes marked the corners of the square that formed the transepts.[17] The fourth corner was omitted in favor of a two-bay, barrel-vaulted nave, which was something the processional-minded clergy would have needed far more in a cathedral than in a chapel. Michelangelo drew a plan for Saint Peter's that seems to have been based on San Biagio. A further feature of San Biagio that was to be echoed at Saint Peter's was the use of giant-order Corinthian pilasters supporting a massive entablature from which the barrel-vaults sprang. Bramante placed one of these pilasters in the center of each apse, thus making each apse in elevation appear to have two bays rather than the more correct classical three (or other odd number).

While San Biagio formed a Latin cross, Santi Celsi e Giuliano was a pure Greek cross, set in a square.[18] It had a central dome and four smaller domes, one in each corner. A semicircular apse broke the plane of each side, including the entrance side. The two surviving copies of the plan disagree in minor details, in particular the articulation of the exterior with pilasters. Bramante's plans for two projects for Saint Peter's are clearly related to the plan of this smaller church.

Tegurio, Cathedral of Saint Peter, Rome
PLATE 17

One of Bramante's most unusual projects—in fact, an unusual commission for any architect—was the tegurio at Saint Peter's Cathedral, 1513. This was intended to be a temporary shelter for the papal altar and visual focus during the demolition of the old Cathedral and the construction of the new. It was dismantled in 1592. It

16. Vatican collection.
17. *Codex Coner*, Sir John Soane's Museum, London.
18. *Codex Coner*, and Ms. A-4037, Gabinetto dei Disegni e Stampe, Uffizi Gallery, Florence.

Project for Church of Santa Maria, Loreto

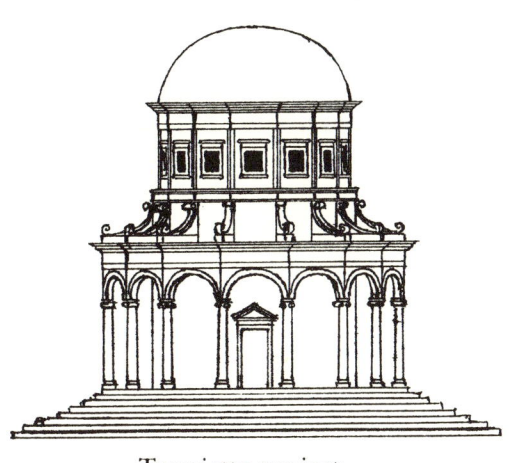

Tempietto project

Palazzo Bresciano, Rome

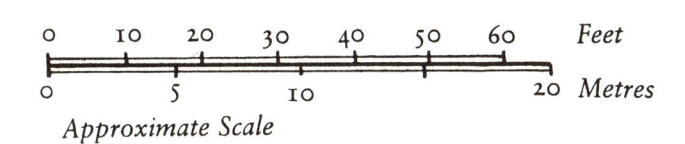

Approximate Scale

PLATE 17

Tegurio, Cathedral of Saint Peter, Rome

External loggia,
Villa Madama, Monte Mario, near Rome

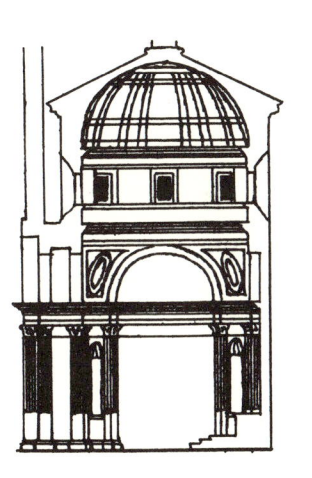

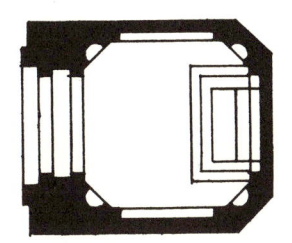

Plan & section of Chigi Chapel,
Church of Santa Maria del Popolo, Rome

resembled an ancient Roman triumphal arch or three equal arches, articulated with engaged Doric columns and surmounted by a panelled attic storey and pediment. The tegurio was surprisingly large, but it was intended to shelter the entire papal court when the pope came to say Mass. It was Bramante's last major work, and it was left to Peruzzi to complete it after Bramante's death.

Tempietto project   PLATE 17

Closely associated with Bramante for part of his career was Raffaelle Sanzio (1483–1520), often known as Raphael. Raphael is better known as a painter than as an architect;[19] in fact, more than one of his biographers have ignored his architectural contributions. His earlier designs followed the new orthodoxy established by Bramante, but some of his later designs tended towards Mannerism, a trend more or less echoed by his paintings. An early design was never built but formed the background for his painting of the Marriage of the Virgin, 1504. The building is a 16-sided tempietto with a domed top. The ground floor was composed of the central drum surrounded by an arcade resting on Ionic columns. Above the arcade a series of volutes buttressed the drum, whose surface was pierced by rectangular windows set inside panels. Raphael's tempietto was obviously a tribute to Bramante's Tempietto of San Pietro in Montorio in Rome, built just two years earlier, but it was a refreshingly original design that was not in any way a copy of the Bramante building.

Villa Madama, Monte Mario, near Rome   PLATE 17

About 1516 Raphael designed a two-storey garden building at Villa Madama, Monte Mario, just outside Rome. The garden façade of this building, now known only through an engraving by Serlio (folio 120-1), was apparently inspired by Bramante's smaller Belvedere Loggia at the Vatican. The ground floor had three arches separated by Ionic pilasters, while the upper floor had three pedimented windows with Corinthian pilasters. Narrower bays at each end of the front contained niches. Serlio used this design as part of his Villa Trissino at Cricoli, near Vicenza.

Chigi Chapel, Church of Santa Maria del Popolo, Rome   PLATE 17

In 1513 Raphael designed the funerary chapel for the powerful Chigi family, attached to the church of Santa Maria del Popolo in Rome. This little chapel, which still stands intact, is square in plan with clipped corners containing niches. The angles of the ground floor are articulated by Corinthian pilasters, above whose entablature are blind arches with spandrels between them to convert the lower (square) plan into the round drum of the clerestory. Above the clerestory with its rectangular windows is a coffered dome under a low hipped roof. The chapel is contemporary with similar chapels in Poland, Hungary and France as well as in Italy.

Palazzo Bresciano, Rome   PLATE 17

Two years later, Raphael designed the four-storey Palazzo Bresciano in Rome for the wealthy Jacopo da Brescia. For practical reasons, the lower two floors, set apart by channelled stonework, consisted of shop-fronts with a mezzanine over them. The piano nobile above the mezzanine had five windows with alternating triangular and segmental pediments, and between the windows were clusters of Doric pilasters (a device used by Mannerists) on high pedestals. Above the Doric entablature was an attic storey with rectangular windows with shouldered architraves on a surface textured by panels.

Fondaco dei Tedeschi, Venice   PLATE 18

The classical style had been strongly entrenched in parts of Italy for many years before it appeared in other areas in Europe. This is particularly true of the Germanic countries, where the earliest classical building was built in 1509. Nevertheless, it was not the earliest classical building designed by a German. A German architect known only as Hieronymus (in Italian he was called Gerolamo Tedesco, Tedesco being the Italian word for German) was brought by German merchants to Venice, where they had him build them a commercial palace, known as the Fondaco dei Tedeschi (which means no more than Commercial Palace of the Germans) in 1505. By Venetian standards, the Fondaco is not a noteworthy piece of classical design, but it becomes noteworthy because its architect was not Italian, perhaps the first non-Italian to design a large classical building in Italy. The six-storey palace approaches classicism through its symmetry and its five-bay loggia in the center of the ground floor. Its double windows, both rectangular and round-headed, are more in keeping with earlier Venetian architecture.

Michelangelo Buonarroti (1475–1564) is undoubtedly one of the most widely known of all the architects of the Italian Renaissance. In fact, he was already 45 years old before his first building was built, and even in the rest of his life he designed very little architecture. Michelangelo was primarily a sculptor, not an architect. Notwithstanding, he successfully modified the designs of his predecessors and completed most of Saint Peter's Cathedral in Rome, including the dome.

Project for façade of Church of San Lorenzo, Florence   PLATE 18

His earliest architectural design was part of the competition to produce an entrance façade for Brunelleschi's church of San Lorenzo in Florence. Michelangelo's design was executed in a wooden model, which the judges apparently liked, but nothing ever came of it.[20] The design is rather sterile; its wide, flat wings are a less successful solution than Leonardo's for classicizing the disparity of heights between nave and aisles. The design is divided into two storeys, both articulated with the Corinthian order. The lower storey employs engaged columns and deeply sculptured breakfronts, while the

19. Christoph L. Frommel, *Raffaello Architetto,* Milan, Electa, 1984, and *Raffaello e l'Architettura a Firenze nella Prima Metà del Cinquecento,* Florence, Sansoni, 1984, both exhibition catelogues.

20. Preserved at Casa Buonarroti, Florence. Useful works on Michelangelo are James S. Ackerman, *The Architecture of Michelangelo* (second edition), Cambridge, MA, MIT Press, 1985, and Linda Murray, *Michelangelo, His Life, Work and Times,* New York, Thames & Hudson, 1984.

Fondaco dei Tedeschi, Venice

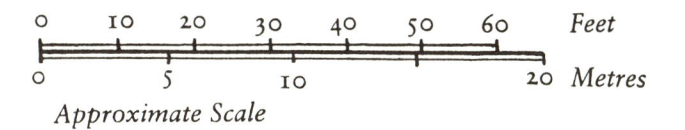

Project for façade of Church of San Lorenzo, Florence

PLATE 18

Palazzo dei Conservatori, Rome

upper storey, in less relief, uses pilasters standing on exceptionally high pedestals. The competition was judged in 1516.

Palazzo dei Conservatori, Rome   PLATE 18

In sharp contrast to the dry, small-scale model for San Lorenzo stands the enormous Palazzo dei Conservatori on the Capitoline Hill in Rome (1538–1561). Michelangelo was hired to design a complex of three large buildings for the Capitol: in the center is the Palazzo Senatorio and in the front on either side, but not at right-angles to it are the matching forecourt buildings, the Palazzo Capitolino and the Palazzo dei Conservatori. These last are each composed of seven large bays articulated by truly giant Corinthian pilasters supporting an unusually heavy entablature with balustrade above. The lower storey is open in front to form a loggia with Ionic columns. The upper storey contains six large, rectangular windows in Corinthian aedicules with segmental pediments with Mannerist shells in the tympana, and one large opening in the middle of the façade, a whimsical piece of pure Mannerism under a triangular pediment. The Mannerist elements are perhaps unexpected in such otherwise sober buildings, but they serve to lighten the effect of massive scale and bulk. Mannerist ideas appear in more profusion in many of Michelangelo's other buildings, such as the Library and New Sacristy at San Lorenzo in Florence and the Porta Pia in Rome, but inasmuch as they point in a direction away from classicism they are not included in this book.

Sansovino had won the 1518 papal competition to design the new Church of San Giovanni dei Fiorentini in Rome, defeating entries by Peruzzi, Raffaello and Antonio da San Gallo II. San Gallo was hired to execute Sansovino's design, but Pope Leo X died before the foundations were more than partially built, and the project failed to interest his non-Florentine successor, so all work ceased. In 1559, Duke Cosimo of Tuscany hired Michelangelo to draw new elevations to stand on the foundations. The plan that he drew is at the Casa Buonarroti, Florence, and his elevation and section were engraved and published by Valérien Regnart (reproduced in Heydenreich & Lotz, *Architecture in Italy 1400–1600*). For some reason, Michelangelo's designs, which are of high quality, did not win approval, and the church was eventually built to boring designs by della Porta. Michelangelo's drawings are not shown in this book. They called for a dome standing over a square building with rounded corners.

Project for Villa Chigi delle Volte, near Sienna   PLATE 19

The powerful Chigi family gave architectural commissions to Bramante's assistants. Raphael designed the Chigi Chapel in Rome, but Baldassare Peruzzi (1481–1536) was hired to design most of the many buildings erected for this family. In 1505 Agostino Chigi commissioned him to build the immense Villa Farnesina in Rome (not to be confused with the enormous pentagonal Villa Farnese at Caprarola, near Viterbo, which Peruzzi began, but which was later finished by Vignola). About ten years later, Agostino Chigi built the Villa Chigi delle Volte near Siena on a more modest scale, and presumably Peruzzi was its architect.[21] It shared with the Farnesina a U-shaped plan. In the middle was a two-storey arcaded loggia on panelled pillars, four bays wide rather than the more classical five bays. The relative importance of each storey was indicated by the height of its windows: ordinary for the ground floor, large for the piano nobile and small for the attic storey. Peruzzi was the teacher of both Serlio and Alessi, and the partner of Antonio da San Gallo II in furthering the construction and design of Saint Peter's Cathedral. In his own time, he was widely regarded as the greatest architect of the day and a universal man. Subsequent critics, relying more on his known works than on the man himself, have not seen fit to praise him as highly, perhaps because he had the misfortune to have been working in an age of genius.

Project for Pilgrimage Church of the Madonna of San Biagio, Montepulciano   PLATE 19

Antonio da San Gallo I (ca. 1453–1534), brother of Giuliano and uncle of Antonio II, was a Florentine who worked with Raphael and Peruzzi in Rome, including at Saint Peter's Cathedral. His most famous building is the Pilgrimage Church of the Madonna of San Biagio at Montepulciano (1518). The plan is a central one, a modified Greek cross with a dome; a single-storey, semi-circular chapel projects from the altar arm of the cross, and a pair of handsome steeples were planned to stand independently in the Italian companile tradition on either side of the entrance arm. In fact, only the left steeple was ever built. The body of the church is divided on the exterior into two storeys, the lower being Doric and the upper Ionic on the towers and plain on the church itself. The drum of the dome is decorated with Ionic pilasters while the upper stages of the towers and steeples are trimmed with Corinthian and Composite columns and pilasters.

Loggia Cornaro, Padua   PLATE 19

Giovanni Falconetto (1468–1535), an architect of lesser importance, was a follower of Bramante, and helped to introduce Bramante's style to the Padua area. His best-known building is the Loggia Cornaro at Padua. This five-bay, two-storey structure is classically correct with its engaged Doric columns standing on high pedestals between the arches of the ground floor and Ionic pilasters between the pedimented windows of the upper floor. However, some Mannerist ideas are evident in the design, such as the pieces of flying entablature over most of the columns and pilasters, the pedestals under the windows and the fact that the central arch is slightly distorted so as to make it wider than its fellows while not rising any higher than them.

21. The villa is known through a wash drawing preserved at the Vatican Library.

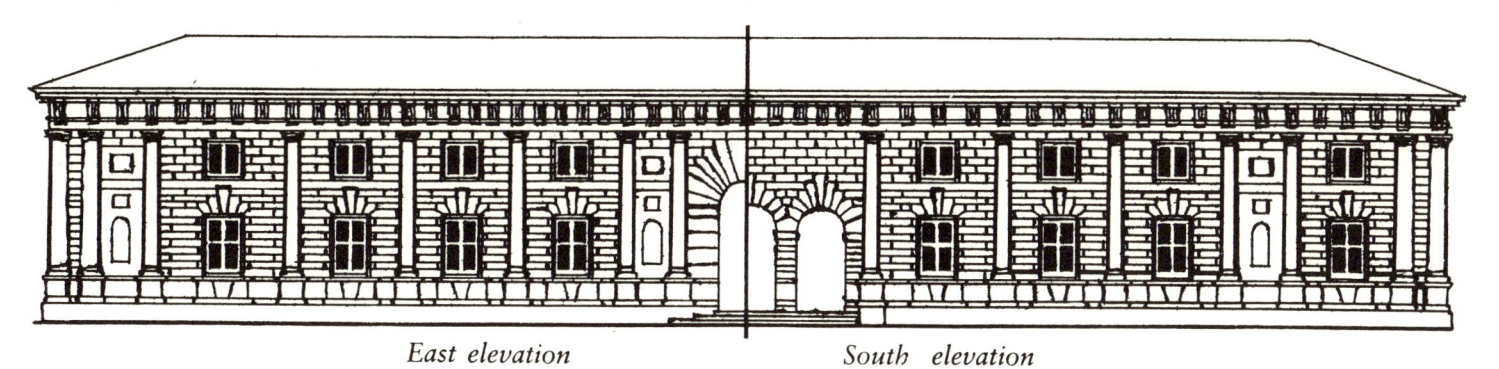

East elevation   *South elevation*
Palazzo del Te, Mantua

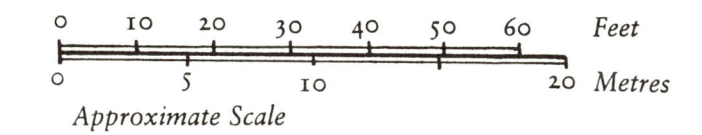

Approximate Scale

Project for Villa Chigi delle Volte, near Sienna

PLATE 19

Project for Pilgrimage Church of the Madonna of San Biagio, Montepulciano

Loggia Cornaro, Padua

35

Palazzo del Te, Mantua PLATES 19 & 20

Giulio Pippi, better known as Giulio Romano (ca. 1492/9–1546), studied painting with Raphael when he was young and later worked as his assistant.[20] He was therefore in a good position to extend Raphael's experiments with Mannerism and the grotesque. Romano, in turn, trained Primaticcio, who assisted with some of the grotesque designs at the French court. When Raphael died, Romano moved to the ducal court at Mantua to design buildings for the Gonzaga family. Among these are the austere Cathedral of Mantua, whose interior resembles somewhat an early Christian basilica, and the massive gate of the Citadel. His most famous work is undoubtedly the Palazzo del Te, begun in 1525 as a pleasurable retreat outside Mantua. Most of the exterior of this nearly square palace is heavily rusticated with giant Doric pilasters to provide a vertical contrast to the rough stonework. The triglyphs of the Doric frieze are spaced irregularly, a hint of the Mannerism to be seen inside. The west side of the palace, finished in smooth stonework, is pierced by a series of Venetian arches in two different sizes and spaced irregularly; the central three arches are contained in a pedimented breakfront. On the courtyard side of the west range the exterior of the entrance front is echoed by more rustication articulated with giant Doric pilasters, but here the windows are all blind, and occasional triglyphs of the cornice have been located a noticeable distance below their normal station (a Mannerist conceit intended to suggest that the palace was an ancient Roman ruin that had been rehabilitated). The palace was never actually completed, but enough of it was built, along with painted interior decorations, to qualify it as one of the most important buildings of its era in Italy.

Rustica, Cavallerizza/Estivale/Cortile della Mostra, Palazzo Ducale, Mantua PLATE 20

At the Ducal Palace at Mantua itself, Romano was hired to do various minor works, but he began one significant addition to the palace that was never finished according to the architect's original intent, the courtyard with a variety of names: the Rustica, the Cavalierizza, the Estivale and the Cortile della Mostra. Frederick Hartt has carefully reconstructed on paper Romano's original intentions, and has documented when the various parts were actually built—most of it long after Romano's death. At one point, the duke wanted to stage a spectacular in front of a partially-built wing, and so, in the finest Hollywood tradition, he erected a wood and canvas screen and had theatre-scenery-painters paint the missing building on the screen at full size! Romano's design is actually a great deal more massive than it looks. The ground floor, heavily rusticated, is composed of seven elliptical arches. Above them is a wide band of relatively smooth masonry with projecting pedestals for columns. The engaged columns standing in front of the upper rusticated wall are barley-sugar twists of the Doric order with an oversized entablature above. Romano, who designed the seven bays with randomly different widths (for the sake of clarity they have been drawn as if equal in this book), clearly intended to use this building as a means of poking fun at rustic builders, but later architects and builders, not understanding this, felt the need to "improve" upon the design, and so the other sides of the courtyard are somewhat different. The Rustica was begun in 1538.

Abbey Church of San Benedetto Po, Polirone PLATE 20

In 1539, Romano's attention was diverted to the ancient gothic Abbey Church of San Benedetto Po at the nearby village of Polirone. He was asked to convert the church into the classical style, a task made complicated by the unequal spacing of piers in the interior. The lower part of Romano's exterior casing, composed of modified Venetian arches, somewhat related to Bramante's smaller Belvedere loggia, introduces the motif to be seen inside, where Venetian arches run between the piers of the nave and screen the nave from the aisles. The upper part of the entrance front is an exuberant piece of fantasy that prefigures some of the baroque churches of Nicholas Hawksmoor in London. A heavy attic storey with unclassical cornice running almost completely around the church hides from view the remaining masonry vaulting of the medieval building.

Basilica of San Bernardino, L'Aquila, Abruzzi PLATE 20

Nicola di Filotesio dall'Amatrice, in spite of his impressive name, is considered to be a minor architect. His design for the façade of the Basilica of San Bernardino at L'Aquila in the Abruzzi area (1525) seems to be a development of Michaelangelo's wooden model in the competition for San Lorenzo in Florence. Where Michelangelo used two storeys, dall'Amatrice used three, articulated with the Doric, Ionic and Corinthian orders. Raised at the top of a flight of steps this nearly-square block makes an impressive show, perhaps more appropriate to a Roman theatre than to a church. It is unfortunate that the façade gives no hint of what lies behind it, no suggestion that the nave is higher than the aisles.

Villa Rovere, Pesaro PLATE 21

Another minor architect of this period was Girolamo Genga of Urbino (1476–1551). He presumably learned from Luciano Laurana and Francesco di Giorgio Martini, and probably passed his secrets to Diogo da Torralva, one of the leading architects in Portugal. Genga worked most of his life for the delle Rovere dukes. His most impressive building is the Villa Rovere or Imperiale at Pesaro, about 1530. This courtyarded building with towers at each corner is large enough to be called a palace rather than a villa. The courtyard elevation is divided into two levels articulated by Tuscan and Ionic pilasters, and each level contains two storeys. Unusual features of the building include the segmental stair-towers that project from each corner of the courtyard,

22. Frederick Hartt, *Giulio Romano*, Northford, CT, Elliots Books, 1958.

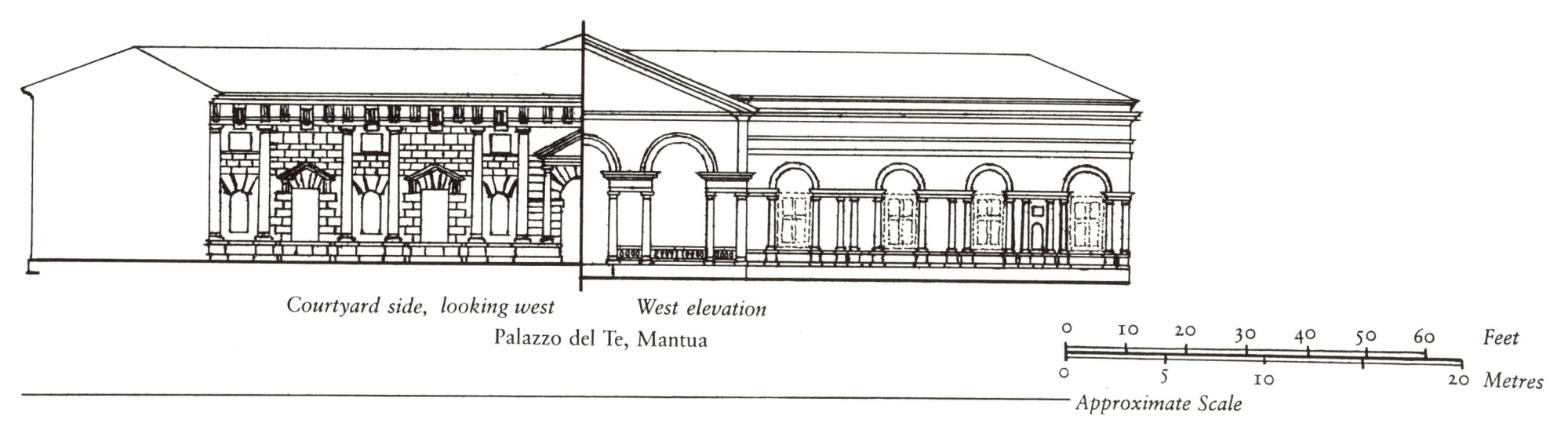

Courtyard side, looking west   *West elevation*
Palazzo del Te, Mantua

Rustica, Cavallerizza/Estivale/Cortile della Mostra, Palazzo Ducale, Mantua   *(drawing regularized)*

Longitudinal section of the Nave,
Abbey Church of San Benedetto Po, Polirone

PLATE 20

Basilica of San Bernardino, L'Aquila, Abruzzi

Main entrance,   Abbey Church of San Benedetto Po, Polirone

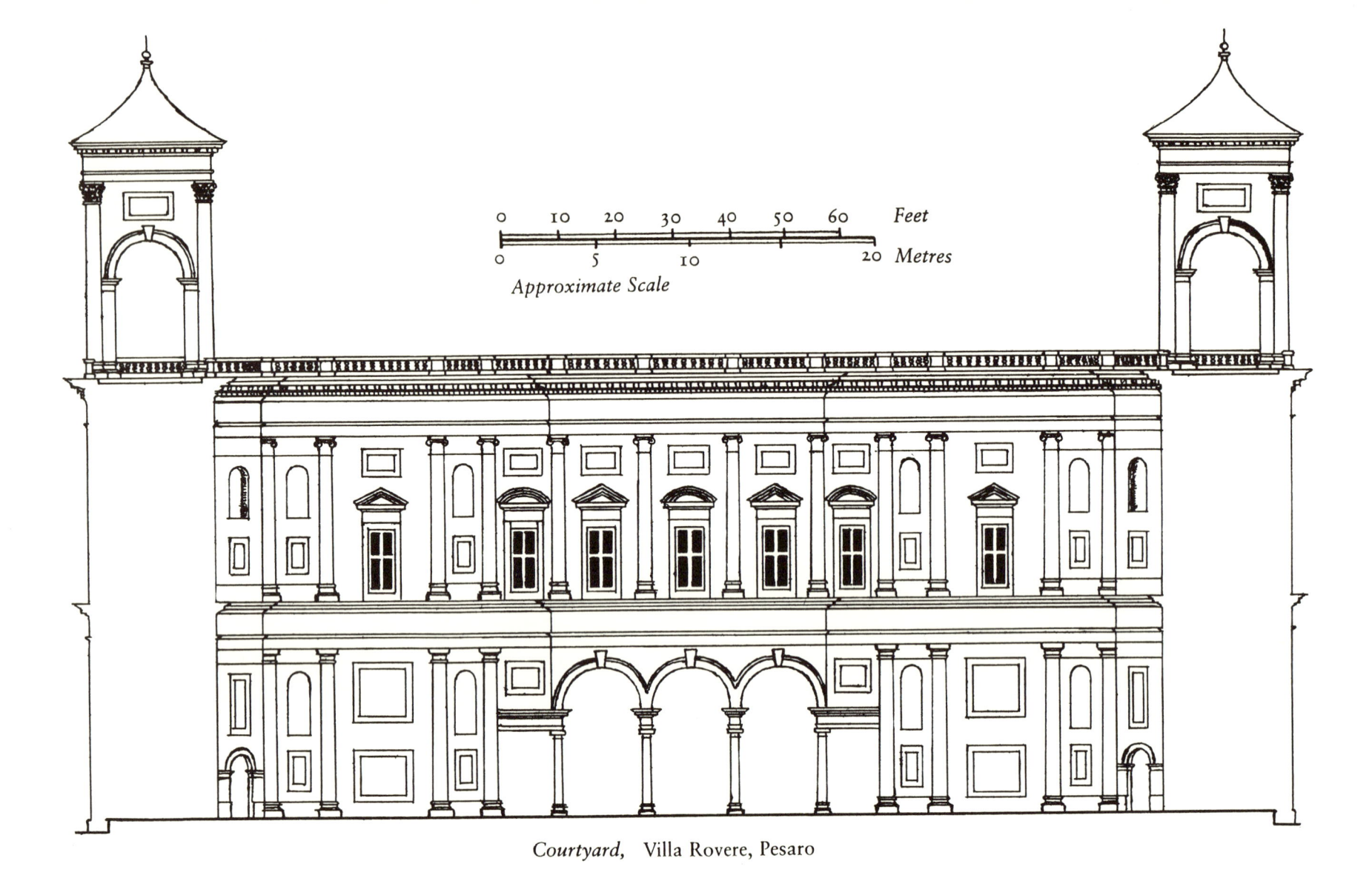

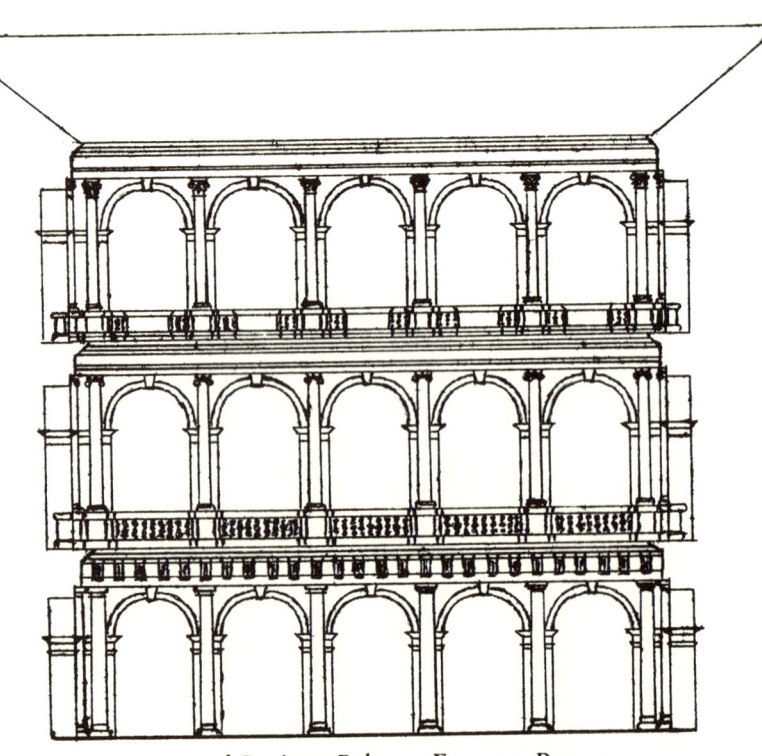

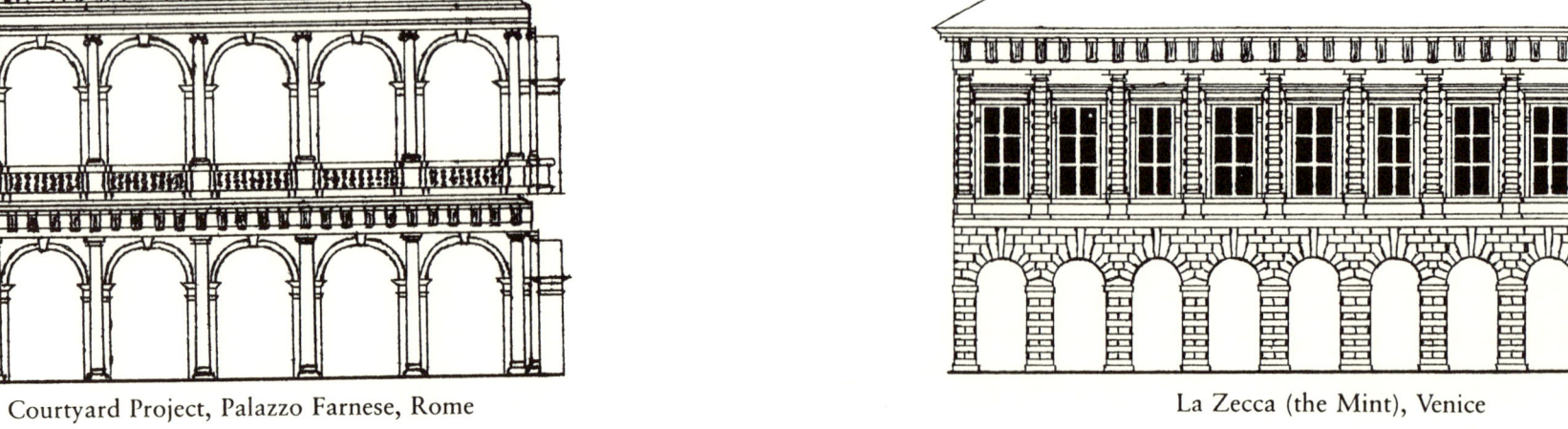

Courtyard, Villa Rovere, Pesaro

PLATE 21

Courtyard Project, Palazzo Farnese, Rome

La Zecca (the Mint), Venice

and that foreshadow the similar structures at the Convent of Christ at Tomar, Portugal by Diogo da Torralva; also unusual is the arcaded entrance, in which Tuscan columns support flying entablatures under three arches in the middle, flanked by a trabeated opening on each side in the manner of a Venetian arch.

Courtyard Project, Palazzo Farnese, Rome
PLATE 21

Antonio da San Gallo II, nephew of both Antonio I and Giuliano (1483–1546), was trained by his two uncles, and learned further by working with Raphael and Peruzzi in Rome. He, in turn, was one of the teachers of Alessi. His most important building was the immense Farnese Palace in Rome. He received the commission for this in 1517, but radically altered his initial design later. His altered design was under construction by the 1530s, but remained unfinished at San Gallo's death.[23] Michelangelo was asked to finish the project, but he decided not to follow San Gallo's plans, and his upper storey gives the building a totally different character from what San Gallo intended. The courtyard elevation of San Gallo's project, shown here, is yet another variation on the theme of the Colosseum. It has three storeys of arcades with half-columns and pilasters of the Doric, Ionic and Corinthian orders.

Pope Leo X, a Florentine, announced in 1518 that he was holding a competition for the design of the new Church of San Giovanni dei Fiorentini at Rome. Peruzzi, Raffaello (design now lost) and others entered the competition. Sansovino was declared the winner, but Antonio da San Gallo II was hired to do the actual construction of Sansovino's design. In the event, the pope died in 1523, so work ceased after only part of the foundation had been laid. The church was later completed to a boring design by della Porta after Michelangelo had been hired to draw new elevations to stand on the foundation. Arguably, the best of the original competition designs was by San Gallo (see fig. 62 in Heydenreich & Lotz, *Architecture in Italy 1400–1600*). The body of the church was to be circular with sixteen chapels contained inside the buttress-piers that supported the dome. The flying-buttresses that held back the thrusts of the dome were in the shape of volutes. The drawings are at the Uffizi, Ms. 199, but are not shown in this book.

La Zecca (the Mint), Venice   PLATE 21

The Florentine architect, Jacopo Tatti Sansovino (1486–1570) entered the famous competition to design a façade for the church of San Lorenzo in Florence. After the sack of Rome in 1527 he sought security in Venice, where he quickly became the leading architect. His first notable building there was the Zecca (from which is derived the monetary denomination known as the Ducat) or Mint, 1535. This is a heavily rusticated building with a plain arcade for the ground floor and nine rectangular windows above standing between rusticated Doric half-columns with a heavy Doric entablature. A matching Ionic storey above (replacing an earlier alteration of a monitor roof) has since been added by another architect, which detracts from Sansovino's carefully balanced design.

Library of the Church of San Marco, Venice
PLATE 22

Two years later, Sansovino built the ornate Library of the Basilica of San Marco next door to the Mint. Saint Mark's Library, which may have been an inspiration to Wren for his Trinity College Library, Cambridge, is composed of two storeys of arcades with engaged columns standing in front of the piers—Doric on the ground floor and Ionic above, with heavy entablatures. The balustrade around the hipped roof is decorated with pinnacles and statues. The Library is twenty-one bays long, but only three bays wide, on the side facing the harbor. Although the Library and the Mint are separated by only two years and a few centimetres, it would be difficult to imagine that they had been designed by the same architect.

Project for Church of Santa Maria della Misericordia, Venice   PLATE 22

Among Sansovino's many designs is a project, never executed, for the church of Santa Maria della Misericordia in Venice. Palladio was interested enough in the design to record it in one of his sketchbooks. The three-bay, two-storey façade was capped by a giant pediment, but without the pediment the design would just as easily have served for a palazzo along the Grand Canal; indeed, with its pairs of fluted Corinthian columns, it recalls Coducci's Palazzo Loredan of about four decades earlier. We are left to guess how the interior would have related to the front, if at all.[24]

Church of San Geminiano, Palermo, Sicily
PLATE 22

Sansovino spent most of his life in northeastern Italy, but he also managed to design a church in the southwest corner, San Geminiano at Palermo, Sicily in 1557. This church, which has long since been destroyed, is known to us only through a painting. The front is divided into two storeys articulated by pairs of pilasters, Ionic over Tuscan, with portions of entablature breaking forward over the pilasters, in contrast to the previous church where the entablatures were unbroken. Above the Ionic entablature, a central pedimented block with a pair of volutes hid the roof, in a manner that foreshadowed the Jesuit façade, but the general proportions were awkward because of the excessively high pedestals on which stood the Tuscan order of the ground floor.

Church project   PLATE 22

An earlier church design that prefigured the Jesuit façade was an unexecuted project by Sebastiano Serlio (1475–1554) that he published in one of his many books of architecture.[25] The design, which appears to be related to one of Leonardo's projects for the façade of San Lorenzo in Florence, would be a masterpiece if only the central part of the lower storey were defined by a breaking forward of the main entablature.

23. Ms. A-627, Gabinetto dei Disegni e Stampe, the Uffizi Gallery, Florence.
24. Collection of the Museo Civico, Vicenza.
25. Sebastiano Serlio, *The Fourth Book of Architecture*, London, 1611 edition of ca. 1537 book, fol. 51. The Palazzo project in the next paragraph was actually built to an altered and smaller design as the Palazzo Civena, Vicenza.

End elevation, Library of the Church of San Marco, Venice

Project for Church of Santa Maria della Misericordia, Venice

Church of San Geminiano, Palermo, Sicily

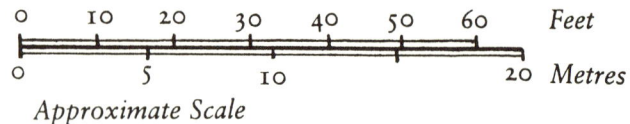

0 10 20 30 40 50 60 Feet
0 5 10 20 Metres
Approximate Scale

PLATE 22

Church project

Palazzo project

Palazzo project PLATE 22

Ten years later, written about 1545, Serlio's *Seventh Book of Architecture* included a project for a palazzo of two and a half storeys. The ground floor was a large, rusticated arcade of seven bays, while the next storey contained windows with alternating segmental and triangular pediments; like the church project, the palazzo had pairs of pilasters, although they were of the Ionic order, while both storeys on the church were Corinthian. A row of dormer windows with segmental pediments pierced the roof; this feature had scarcely been seen in Italy, if at all, and must reflect Serlio's experience in France.

Villa project PLATE 23

Also in the *Seventh Book,* Serlio drew a villa that would have been completely at home in England in the Jones-Wren-Gibbs period, one and two centuries after Serlio's own time. This is not surprising, for Serlio's books were among the most influential architectural texts in the western world. The villa, probably never executed, was five bays wide and two and a half storeys tall. The ground-floor windows were compass-headed and the upper windows were rectangular, and both of them had a piece of cornice projecting above each window. The dormers had pediments that were alternately triangular and segmental. Giant-order Corinthian pilasters delineated each bay under a full entablature.

Few of Serlio's designs were ever built, and even fewer remain standing today. In fact, only two villas presently in Italy can be identified with any certainty as being by Serlio's hand. Even in France, where he spent some of his most productive years, only two buildings and one gateway survive. Nevertheless, Serlio is regarded as one of the architectural giants of his time, not so much for the quality of his work—which was above average but generally not outstanding—as for the fact that he was the first apologist for the classical style to disseminate designs for buildings of all kinds and details of buildings in several books with copious woodcut illustrations. These books underwent several editions and were translated into many languages at quite an early date. So great was his fame that a further book that remained unpublished until recently was yet known and consulted in its unpublished forms by architects and others for years.[26] Serlio wrote about eight books on architecture, and the numbering of them often does not agree from one edition to another, so *caveat lector.*

Michele San Micheli (1484–1559) was a respected contemporary of Serlio who lived and worked in Verona, not far from Venice. Unlike most other architects, who also did painting and sculpture, he was an architect and nothing else. Like Serlio and Sansovino, he returned to the Veneto after the sack of Rome in 1527, and he worked in his native Verona as an official of the Venetian Republic; he was also sent by the government all over the Mediterranean to inspect fortifications. San Micheli's first commission after his return to Verona was the Pellegrini Chapel at the church of San Bernardino. This is round and has a coffered dome under a hipped roof with a lantern on top; it is very much the same sort of building as Raphael's Chigi Chapel. The Pellegrini Chapel is not shown in this book because it was left to be finished by other designers, who, according to Vasari, ruined it, and it is therefore not possible to draw the building as San Micheli designed it.

Palazzo Canossa, Verona PLATE 23

The most handsome of San Micheli's palazzos is the Canossa Palace, Verona (about 1536). This is divided into two levels of two storeys each: the lower level is rusticated in varying weights of stone, and the upper level is delineated by close pairs of Corinthian pilasters. The lower level contains an entrance of three large arches and a mezzanine over, while the upper level contains the piano nobile and a mezzanine-like storey over it. Above the entablature is a heavy balustrade holding up a series of large statues. The windows of the piano nobile are distinguished from the others not only by their size but also by their having compass heads.

Church of Madonna di Campagna, Verona PLATE 23

San Micheli's last design was for the church of the Madonna di Campagna, begun in 1559 after the report of a miracle there. It was not finished until many years after the architect's death and is known to have been altered, particularly by lowering the Tuscan peristyle around the base (conjecturally restored in this book). The basic theme of the church is an echo of Bramante's Tempietto: a domed drum surrounded by a colonnade, but the proportions are quite different from those of Bramante's masterpiece—with not unfortunate results.

While Sansovino, San Micheli and Serlio were at the height of their careers in the Veneto, young Andrea di Pietro Palladio (1508–1580) was just beginning his in the same area. Some of his designs could hardly be distinguished from theirs, while other designs broke new ground. He was born in Padua and worked for many years as a mason until a wealthy patron took him to Rome to study architecture in 1545. The trip bore almost immediate fruit.

Villa Saraceno, near Vicenza PLATE 23

His first design was probably for the Villa Saraceno, near Vicenza (1546), and it exemplified a trait often associated with the best of Palladio's designs: it simplified the building so that its proportions spoke for it rather than any columns or pilasters or statues or rustication. Indeed, the villa has none of these. The two-storey, hip-roofed building has a pedimented breakfront in the center, containing three arches on the ground floor and a single small window upstairs. On either side of the breakfront is a tall pedimented window and a small window above a belt course. The pediments are about the only clues to the building's classical heritage, other than its proportions.

---

26. Myra Nan Rosenfeld, *Sebastiano Serlio on Domestic Architecture,* Cambridge, MA, MIT Press, 1978. This book was intended by Serlio to be his *Sixth Book,* but his unnumbered *Libro Extraordinario* was posthumously renamed as the *Sixth Book.* The First Book, about geometry, was published in 1545, the same year as the *Second Book,* which is about perspective. The *Third Book* was published earlier, in 1540, and shows ancient Roman and early Renaissance architecture. The *Fourth Book,* the first to be published, appeared about 1537 and shows Roman orders, Venetian palaces and ceiling & garden ornaments. The *Fifth Book,* 1551, is about churches. *The Sixth Book/Libro Extraordinario,* about doorways and gateways, appeared in 1551, and the *Seventh Book,* published posthumously in 1575, is about houses for rich and poor. The eighth book (that Serlio intended as his *Sixth* and that Rosenfeld has edited), about more houses for rich and poor, is known in three different forms: a manuscript at Munich, another manuscript at Columbia University, and a series of woodcut blocks at Vienna.

Villa project

Palazzo Canossa, Verona

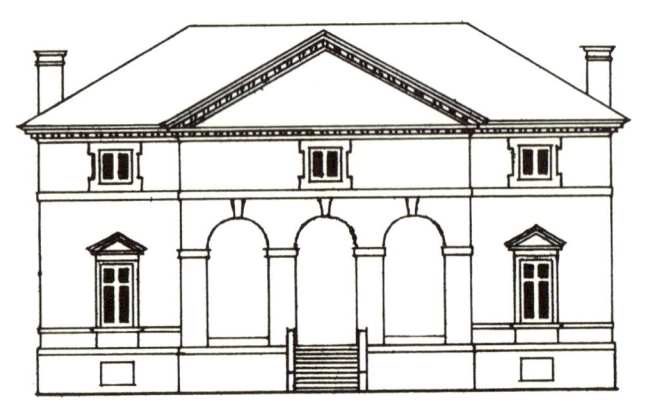

Villa Saraceno, near Vicenza

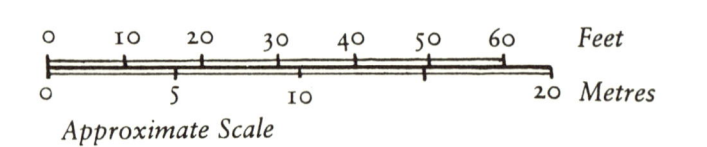

PLATE 23

Approximate Scale

Palazzo Iseppo-Porto, Vicenza

Church of Madonna di Campagna, Verona

Palazzo Iseppo-Porto, Vicenza PLATE 23

It would be a mistake to assume that Palladio followed this rule of simplicity in all his designs. In fact, some of his designs were as encrusted with classical details as the work of many mannerists. An example of this is the Palazzo Iseppo-Porto at Vincenza, built about 1551. With its rectangular windows set in blind arches in the rusticated base and its pedimented windows between Ionic columns in the piano nobile, this palace could have been the work of any number of Palladio's predecessors. Even the attic storey above the piano nobile is not an innovation. The design of the courtyard (not shown in this book) is more innovative; it is lined with giant-order Composite columns and seems to be unrelated to the themes expressed on the façade. Palladio's own drawings for this building survive at the Royal Institute of British Architects in London.

Basilica, Vicenza PLATE 24

One of Palladio's best-known buildings is the Basilica at Vicenza (1549). Here, he was hired to encase and buttress a nondescript older municipal building (here, the word basilica reverts to its original, classical meaning of a government building rather than its more recent meaning of a church) in a classical exterior. The core of the building is surrounded by an impressive, double-decked loggia that owes more than a little in inspiration to Sansovino's Library of San Marco in Venice. Each bay of the loggia is delineated by a half-column, Doric below and Ionic above, and each bay is filled with a Venetian arch, Tuscan below and Ionic above. The arches vary in size to fit the irregular dimensions of the building, the end bays being narrower than the rest. It is no doubt this profusion of Venetian arches that has caused many people to call that kind of arch a Palladian arch, even though the Venetian arch had been in existence long before Palladio. The Basilica combines great size with fine details (such as the cushion frieze of the upper storey) by including orders in two different scales in order to bridge the chasm between size and detail, and is a fitting focus for the civic pride of Vicenza. It was not finished until after Palladio's death.

Villa Pisani, near Padua PLATE 24

The Villa Pisani, near Padua, was built in 1552, and although it contains columns, sparingly used, it is essentially one of Palladio's simpler designs. It is included here because it exemplifies a theme often used by Palladio, a house with a portico made of two decks of colonnades. In many of his others, Palladio used six columns at each level, but in this case he used four, Ionic over Doric, and a pediment over the top. This device has been copied many times, particularly in England and America where Palladian ideas attracted a strong following in later centuries. The rest of the house has but a single bay on either side of the portico, expressed in four storeys by a tall window under a mezzanine and then another tall window for the piano nobile under a small window included in the Ionic entablature. Although the villa stands solitary today, according to the woodcut of his design in his book *I Quattro Libra dell' Architettura* (1570), Palladio intended that it should be attached to dependency buildings on either side by means of a hyphen with an arch in it. This (not shown in this book) exemplifies another of Palladio's most notable contributions to the development of classical architecture. Many of his impressive villas were in reality no more than country farmhouses with a classical design. He reasoned that if the lowly farmhouse can have a classical design so should other farm buildings, and if such buildings should also be classical then they should be linked to the main house in some sort of unified design. Many architectural critics have termed a building (neo-)Palladian merely because its dependencies were grouped around it in a formal pattern, such as was first called for at Villa Pisani.

Convent of Santa Maria della Carità, Venice PLATE 24

Palladio allowed himself to be influenced, as so many other architects have been, by the Colosseum in Rome; this is reflected in the courtyard of the convent of Santa Maria della Carità in Venice, 1560. The convent, which still stands in altered form (a particularly noticeable alteration is the glassing in of the arches of the loggias), consists of two storeys of arcades with Doric and Ionic half-columns standing in front of the piers, and another storey above with Corinthian pilasters standing between rectangular windows. Palladio was apparently not afraid to flout convention, for he gave the principal front an even number of bays rather than the more classically correct odd number.

Villa Barbaro, Maser PLATE 25

One of Palladio's most important patrons was Daniele Barbaro. Barbaro sponsored the publication of a new edition of Vitruvius with some drawings and commentary in it by Palladio, and accompanied Palladio on one of his research trips to Rome, out of which came one of Palladio's books, *Le Antichità di Roma*. At Maser, Barbaro commissioned Palladio to build him a house in about 1556. The Villa Barbaro is one of Palladio's most admired designs and has been copied many times.[27] The central house is a two-storey, tetrastyle temple with the entablature cut in the middle. Matching dependencies on either side are linked to the center by arcaded loggias that stand in front of a row of rooms. Such a sprawling arrangement of rooms is well suited to comfortable living in hot weather, which is when the villa was intended to be used, but would be difficult to heat in the often sharp winters of the Veneto.

Church of San Giorgio Maggiore, Venice PLATE 25

One of Palladio's most admired designs is that of the façade of the church of San Giorgio Maggiore on the island of San Giorgio, Venice (1565). The façade was not actually erected until 1597, long after Palladio's death, and some have even suggested that the builders altered the original design; however, even though the

27. One particularly successful adaptation is the waterfront villa built for Sir Ronald Tree at Heron Bay, Barbados. The local coral stone is a dramatic medium for Palladian designs.

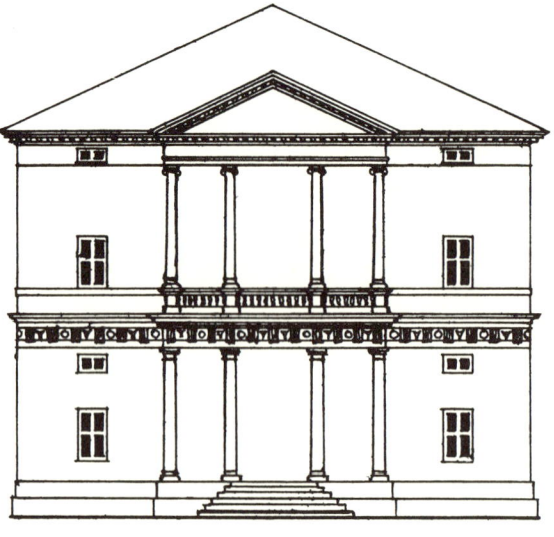

Villa Pisani, near Padua

Courtyard, Convent of Santa Maria della Carità, Venice

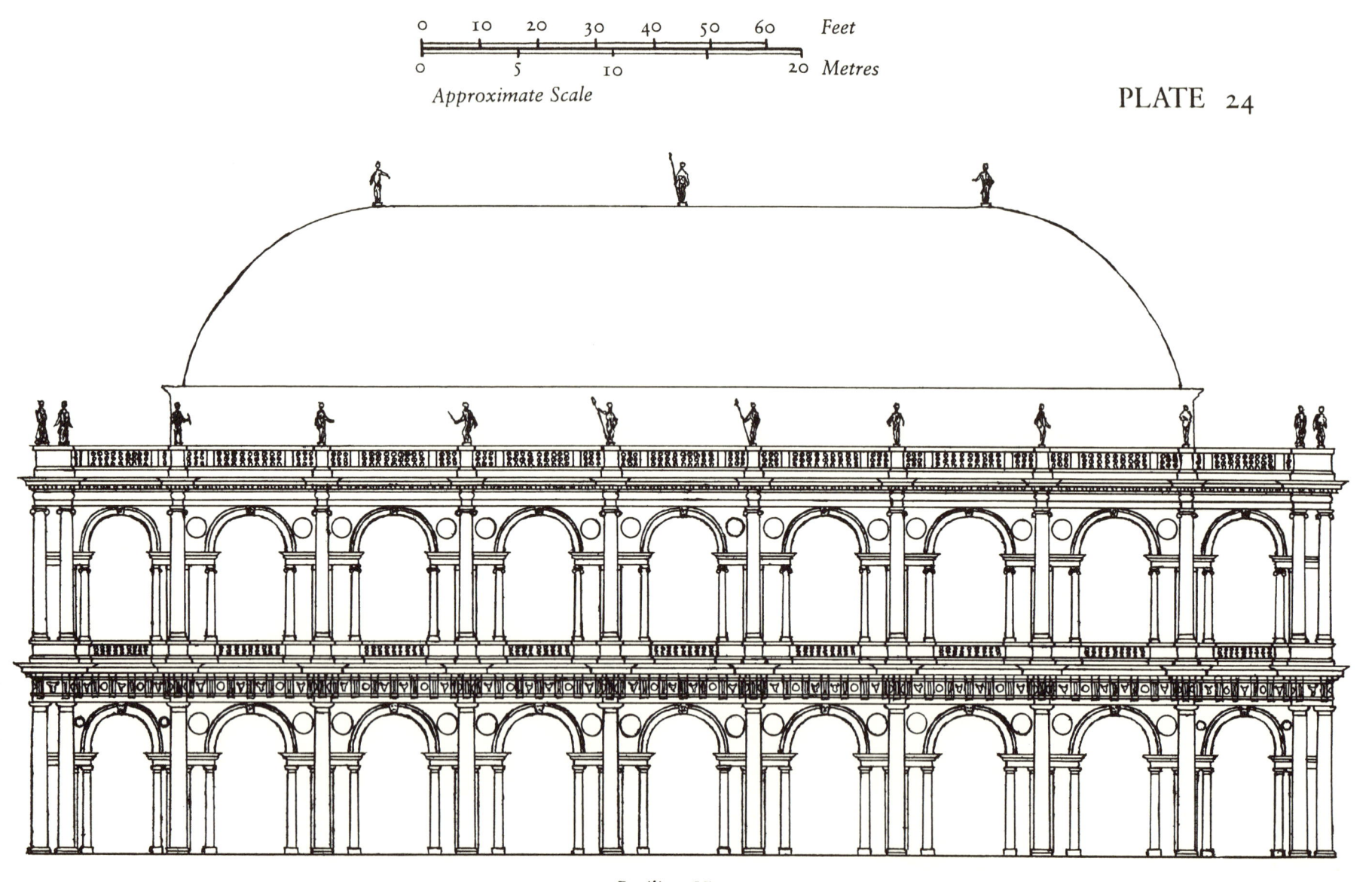

Approximate Scale

PLATE 24

Basilica, Vicenza

Villa Barbaro, Maser

Courtyard, Monastery of San Giorgio Maggiore, Venice

PLATE 25

Approximate Scale

Church of San Giorgio Maggiore, Venice

Loggia del Capitaniato, Vicenza

original design no longer survives, it is unlikely that the builder made any substantial changes to it.[28] This design, often copied by later architects, was one of several similar solutions that Palladio devised to the problem of how best to relate the mass of the aisles to that of the nave in a classical building; two of his others are the church of the Redentore (Redeemer) and the church of San Francesco della Vigna (the rest of this church had been designed by Sansovino), both in Venice. The center is expressed as a tetrastyle Roman temple with engaged Corinthian columns, while the aisles are expressed by a smaller order of Corinthian pilasters supporting half-pediments as if they were part of a lower and wider temple hiding behind the central one.

The motif of the two different sizes of Corinthian orders is maintained on the interior of the church to frame the nave and the side-chapels that take the place of the aisles. Over the crossing is a simple dome, which is scaled perfectly to suit the façade, whereas the mass of the transepts would tend to overpower the façade, were it not for the fact that they are executed in brick and the façade in marble.

Monastery of San Giorgio Maggiore, Venice PLATE 25

The plan of the church is somewhat unusual, in that an extra choir projects beyond the altar; this was for the use of the monks of the monastery of San Giorgio, which is located adjacent to the church just to the south. The loggia of the monastery cloister extends for sixteen bays (once again, an even number rather than the more classically correct odd number) on each side of the courtyard. The lower storey consists of a row of arches on Ionic columns spaced more closely than usual, while the upper storey has closely spaced rectangular windows capped with alternately triangular and segmental pediments; because of the even number of bays, Palladio has given each of the two windows in the middle a triangular pediment. A bold modillioned cornice under a low parapet decorates the top of the wall.

Loggia del Capitaniato, Vicenza PLATE 25

In the seventeenth and eighteenth centuries in England and America, many towns had some sort of civic building with an open loggia on the ground floor and a council chamber upstairs for municipal government. Many Italian cities had similar structures in the sixteenth centuries, among them Vicenza. When the old building had deteriorated by 1571, Palladio was commissioned to build a new one, known as the Loggia del Capitaniato. However, the money ran out before construction had progressed very far, and so the building, which was presumably intended to be five bays or even seven bays wide, is now only three bays wide. Four giant-order Corinthian half-columns stand between the arches of the ground floor and rise between the rectangular windows of the council chamber. Above the large entablature is a balustrade and an attic storey. The side elevation (not shown here) contains a Venetian window motif with niches in the side openings. Both front and side elevations have most of their surfaces covered with a variety of carvings (not, as usual, shown in this book).

Project for Villa Rotonda/Capra/Almerico, near Vicenza PLATE 26

The fourth of Palladio's buildings that is known around the world is the Villa Rotonda, or Villa Capra or Almerico, as it was also called, on the outskirts of Vicenza. Its date is uncertain, and it has been claimed to be as early as 1550 and as late as 1566. The Villa Rotonda is different from Palladio's other villas; it was not a country farmhouse for a gentleman-farmer but rather a suburban retirement villa on a hill with views in all four directions for an important clergyman. Thus, it had no need of any dependency buildings, and it could be built with an almost identical front on all four sides to take advantage of the siting. In fact, Palladio was so impressed by the opportunities for symmetry on more than one axis that he carried the idea over into the interior: the floor-plan is exactly symmetrical on both axes.

As Palladio conceived it, the Villa Rotonda has a most unusual plan for a house. The four Ionic hexastyle porticos with their flights of steps form a cross, upon which is superimposed a square for the bulk of the house, and in the middle of the square is a circle representing the dome—itself an unusual component for a house. The dome is known from Palladio's own designs, published in one of his books, but his assistant, Vincenzo Scamozzi, replaced the external dome in execution with a low, conical roof.[29] The elevation of the house is divided into three storeys: a high basement under the piano nobile, whose windows are decorated by pediments resting on brackets, and an attic storey above the entablature. Palladio planned a remarkably similar design for the Villa Trissino in Meledo, but with the addition of a pair of forecourt dependencies linked to the main house by colonnaded quadrants; however, construction work on this interesting building never progressed very far, and the projected appearance is therefore known to us only through Palladio's illustrations of it in one of his books.[29] The Villa Rotonda has been widely imitated in England and America; Thomas Jefferson drew similar designs for two of his most important projects.

Project for Ducal Palace, Venice PLATE 26

By no means all of Palladio's designs are admired by critics, and it is at least instructive to include here one of his less successful designs. Nor were all his poorer designs the result of inexperience, for at least one of them dates from near the end of his life. The palace of the Doge (Venetian language for Duke) in Venice suffered a disastrous fire, and Palladio was asked to submit drawings for rebuilding it. Since the palace was, as it is now once again, in the Venetian gothic style—that curious blend of gothic, Turkish, Byzantine and Romanesque—Palladio thought that the rebuilding would be a suitable time for enhancing the prestige of the Doge by encasing the ruins in a classical building. He produced

28. Rudolf Wittkower, *Palladio and English Palladianism*, New York, Thames & Hudson, 1983, pp. 11, and 207.
29. Andrea Palladio, *I Quattro Libri dell'Architettura*, Venice, 1570.

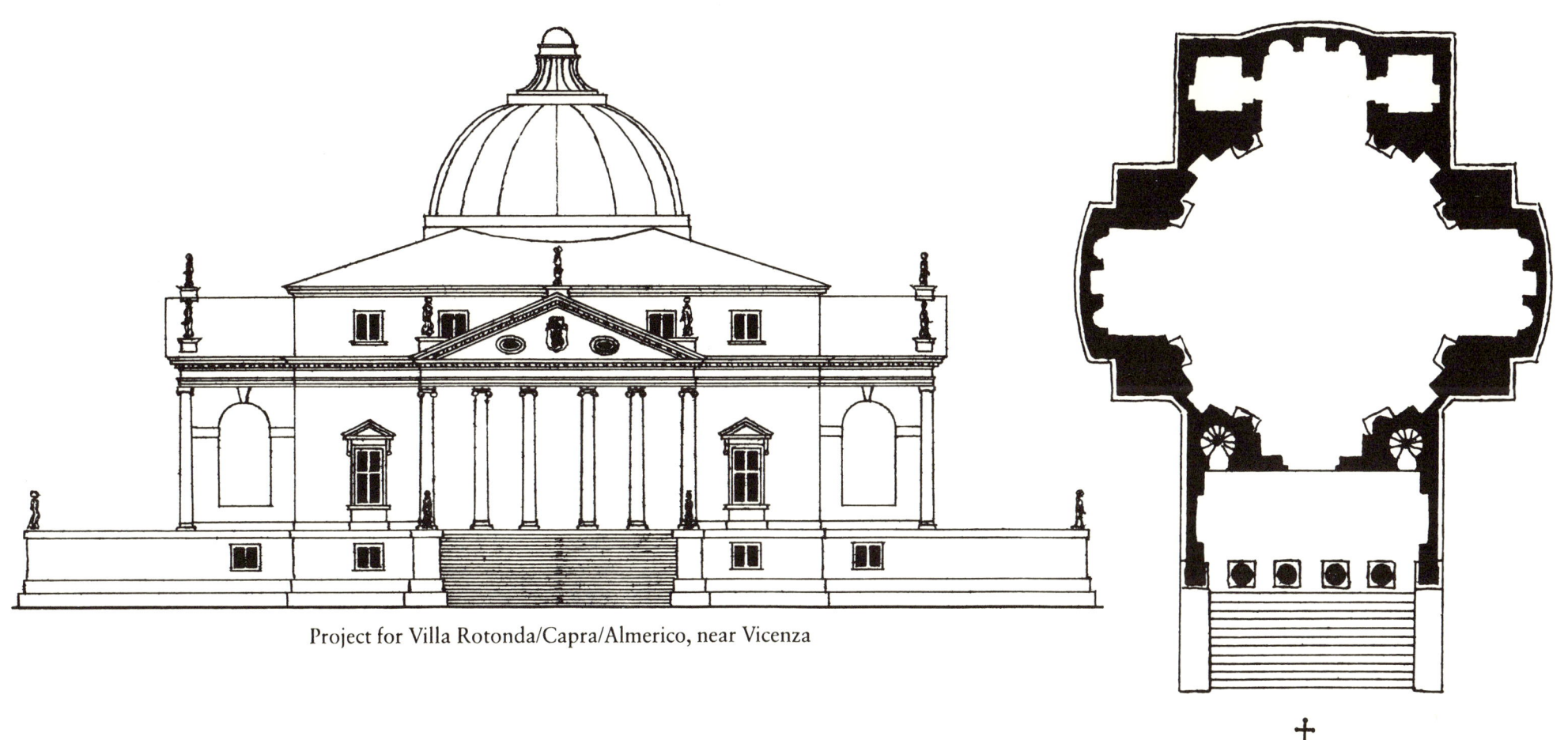

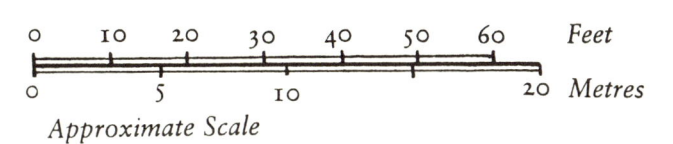

Project for Villa Rotonda/Capra/Almerico, near Vicenza

PLATE 26

0 10 20 30 40 50 60 Feet
0   5   10   20 Metres
Approximate Scale

Project for Ducal Palace, Venice

Plan & elevation, Tempietto Barbaro, Maser

47

an extraordinarily weak design in 1578.[30] The building was to be eleven bays wide and three storeys tall. The central bay on each storey was an arch flanked by two pairs of half-columns (Ionic on the bottom, then Corinthian and Composite) and a pediment at roof level, but the resulting triumphal arch motif was not set off from the rest of the building by the entablature breaking forward except on the ground floor. The rest of the ground floor was an arcaded loggia with Ionic pilasters or half-columns standing in front of the piers. The middle storey had rectangular windows contained in aedicules between Corinthian pilasters, and the top storey had windows in shouldered architraves with alternating segmental and triangular pediments (also alternating with the aedicules on the floor below) between Composite pilasters. The busy design, which does not convey adequately the dignity of the office of the Doge, can be compared with another of Palladio's unexecuted designs, that for a classical façade for the large gothic church of San Petronio in Bologna, dated 1572.[31]

Tempietto Barbaro, Maser PLATE 26

By contrast, one of Palladio's most successful designs is the detached chapel he built at Maser for Daniele Barbaro's villa in 1580, his last building. This tempietto, which obviously owes much to the example of the Pantheon in Rome, has a cruciform plan on which is superimposed the large circle of the dome. Palladio had previously designed a similar plan, but without the transepts, for the church of San Nicola di Tolentino, which is known to us only through his drawing for it.[32] The principal feature of the entrance front of the tempietto is a large hexastyle Corinthian portico, whose pediment is surmounted by a pair of bell turrets. The portico achieves additional dignity because the columns at each end are square, not round. One aspect of Palladio's career that needs further exploration is the extent to which he borrowed ideas from his contemporaries. Many of his earlier buildings repeat themes of Sansovino, San Micheli, Serlio and Guilio Romano, but this tempietto strongly suggests that Palladio was familiar with the tempiettos built by Philibert Delorme in France a few years earlier, particularly the chapel at the Château of Anet. Palladio's assistant, Scamozzi, is known to have possessed a copy of one of Delorme's books.[33] If Palladio thus borrowed from Delorme it must surely be the first time that an Italian Renaissance architect accepted ideas from a contemporary in another country.

Many of Palladio's buildings survive in more or less original condition, and they are indeed a feast for the eye. However, his greatest contribution to the advancement of architecture, akin to Serlio's, lies in the publication of his book, *I Quattro Libbri dell' Architettura*, in 1570. This book has been republished in many editions and translated into many languages. Some people have used it as a mine of architectural designs, and others have valued it for Palladio's frankly-expressed theories of the philosophy behind architecture. However, it should be pointed out that following Palladio's theories would not by itself produce fine architecture; what really counts is surely a fine eye, and with a fine eye an architect has little or no need of complicated theories.

Palladio may have been the towering architectural genius of his age, but he was by no means the only good architect. One of his contemporaries was Giacomo Barozzi da Vignola (1507–1573). Like Palladio, he wrote an influential book on architecture, *Regola delli Cinque Ordini d'Architettura*, published in Rome in 1562. He was born near Bologna and studied first as a painter. He worked in France for two years under Primaticcio, after having trained with Peruzzi and Antonio da San Gallo II. Upon his return to Italy, he was given the valuable patronage of the Farnese family and took over the responsibility for the gradual construction of the Cathedral of Saint Peter in Rome. In fact, because Michelangelo, the most important other architect in Rome at the time, had such personal and unpredictable views about architecture, Vignola received many commissions that would probably otherwise have gone to Michelangelo. Vignola's first major work was the completion of the Farnese villa at Caprarola that had been begun by Peruzzi and Antonio da San Gallo II.

Church of Sant'Andrea in Via Flaminia, Rome PLATE 27

One of Vignola's earlier designs was for the church of Sant'Andrea in Via Flaminia in Rome (1550). At first glance, this would appear to be a variation on the theme of the Pantheon: the entrance through a pedimented block decorated with six Corinthian pilasters leads into a high, domed cell. However, the cell turns out not be round but rectangular with an oval dome—probably the first instance of an oval dome, an idea that formed part of many architectural experiments in the baroque and rococo eras. In this case, the oval shape was an attempt to blend the idea of a central plan and dome with the liturgical requirements of a church that was longer than its width.

Giulio Farnese Tempietto, near Viterbo PLATE 27

Another variation on the Pantheon theme is the Giulio Farnese tempietto at Bomarzo, near Viterbo (1565). Here, the cell is octagonal, the high octagonal dome sits on a drum lit by three round windows. The entrance portico of Tuscan columns that form a Venetian arch is continued around the sides and back of the cell with engaged columns somewhat awkwardly following the outline of the octagon. The tempietto is an ideal feature of the garden in which it sits.

Gate, Farnese Gardens, Rome PLATE 27

Vignola was engaged in designing other garden ornaments: in 1568 he built the two-storey gateway to the Farnese Gardens in Rome. The lower storey, heavily rusticated and trimmed with the Doric order, is reminiscent of a Roman triumphal arch, while the upper storey

30. Collection of the Dukes of Devonshire, Chatsworth House, Derbyshire.
31. James S. Ackerman, *Palladio*, Harmondsworth, Penguin Books 1966, p. 142.
32. Ackerman, *Palladio*, p. 140.
33. Scamozzi's annotated copy of Delorme's *Architecture* (1567) is in the British Library.

Church of Sant'Andrea in Via Flaminia, Rome

Giulio Farnese Tempietto, near Viterbo

Gate, Farnese Gardens, Rome

Garden elevation, Villa Cambiaso, Genoa

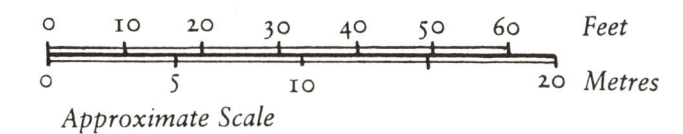

0 10 20 30 40 50 60 Feet
0   5   10   20 Metres
Approximate Scale

PLATE 27

Project for Church of Il Gesù, Rome

Courtyard, Palazzo Sauli, Genoa

49

with its baroque decoration and curved buttresses recalls the elevation Vignola designed for the great church of the Gesù that same year.

Project for Church of Il Gesù, Rome
PLATE 27

The church of the Gesù, headquarters for the Jesuit Order, was commissioned by Cardinal Farnese. The cardinal set forth his views on the shape such a church should take: "The church is not to have a nave and two aisles, but is to consist of one nave only, with chapels down each side.... The nave is to be vaulted, and is not to be roofed in any other way in spite of any objections they may raise, saying that the voice of the preacher will be lost because of the echo. They think that this vault will cause the echo to resound, more than is the case with an open timber roof, but I do not believe this...."

In an effort to stem the tide of the Reformation, which depended more on preaching and reading the Bible than on mystery, the Council of Trent had called for more and better preaching, and the Jesuits were founded to do just that. The mother church of the Jesuits, then, ought to set an example of the best design for a church in which the congregation could easily hear the preacher, and so Vignola was careful to make the nave short and wide in order to accommodate the maximum number of worshippers within the sound of the preacher's voice.

Although Vignola was a painter, the interior of the church was devoid of decoration, so it looked quite different from the lavish prospect afforded today. If Vignola's intentions for the interior have been thwarted by the more recent addition of decoration, his design for the entrance façade had a worse fate: it was never built. Vignola's assistant, Giacomo della Porta, after Vignola's death, supplied his own design, which, though vaguely similar, is not as successful. The two designs have been extremely influential around the world, for each offers a satisfactory solution to the problem of how to relate the bulk of the nave to the lower aisles in a classical front. Similar solutions had been proposed first by Leonardo (plate 13) and Serlio (plate 22), but Vignola's design was more fully developed and had the advantage of being the favored design of the Jesuit Order as it expanded around the world.

The last major architect in Italy covered in this book is Galeazzo Alessi (1512–1572), who devoted most of his life to the area around Genoa. He was taught by Antonio da San Gallo II and Baldassare Peruzzi, and is credited with reviving the more emotional Lombard style that had gone out of favor as a result of works by Bramante and his followers. He was thus attracted to Michelangelo and became one of his followers, but he had enough of an open mind to borrow ideas from Bramante.

Villa Cambiaso, Genoa   PLATE 27

Following the Sack of Rome, Genoese officials swore allegiance to Charles V and thus forestalled Spanish tampering with their internal politics or the garrisoning of Spanish troops in Genoa. Genoa and her fleet became the crucial link between Spain and the rest of the Empire whenever France was hostile, and Genoese bankers quickly assumed a key role in Charles' finances. Genoa grew in prosperity and population, two developments that paved the way for a blossoming of architecture from the hand of Alessi and others.

One of Alessi's earliest buildings in Genoa is the Villa Cambiaso (1548). This building, whose plan is like a shallow H, is, like so many other buildings of its type, divided into four storeys expressed architecturally as two storeys. The entrance floor and its mezzanine are enclosed by engaged Doric columns grouped in a way reminiscent of the church of San Biagio at Montepulciano by Antonio da San Gallo I. The three central bays are an arcaded loggia on the garden front. The piano nobile is expressed by large rectangular windows, above which brackets support alternately triangular and segmental pediments. The piano nobile is linked to its mezzanine by fluted Corinthian pilasters under a heavy entablature that includes a decorated cushion frieze. Above the entablature is a balustrade, which puts the seal on the pretentious but boxy monumentality of the building.

The artist Rubens travelled in Italy in the early seventeenth century, and the ostentatious villas and palaces of Genoa struck his fancy. He felt that they should be emulated by the wealthy merchants of Flanders and the Netherlands. He wrote: "We see that in these parts the mode of architecture which is called barbarian and Gothic is gradually falling out of use, and that some extremely fine minds are introducing the true symmetry...."

Palazzo Sauli, Genoa PLATE 27

We are indebted to Rubens for having sketched, among others, the lavish Palazzo Sauli, designed by Alessi about 1555. The courtyard façade, once again four storeys disguised as two, is composed of an interesting collection of Venetian arches. Those of the ground floor are Doric, but are blind arches pierced by windows and doors. The arches of the piano nobile are Ionic and the three central bays form an open loggia. Above the entablature with cushion frieze is a balustrade around a high, hipped roof. The idea of combining a row of Venetian arches with shared rectangular openings was by no means new with Alessi, for it had been used previously by Giulio Romano and Serlio, among others, but the arches at the Palazzo Sauli were particularly influential on subsequent buildings.

Church of Santa Maria in Carignano, Genoa
PLATE 28

Alessi's *chef d'oeuvre* at Genoa is the church of Santa Maria in Carignano, begun in 1552. This church has an almost square plan that derives from some of Bramante's work in Rome. Superimposed on the square is the outline of a cross, and each of the four angles thus formed is filled with a small dome. A much larger dome stands over the middle; its drum is pierced by more Venetian arches with squared rectangular openings. The

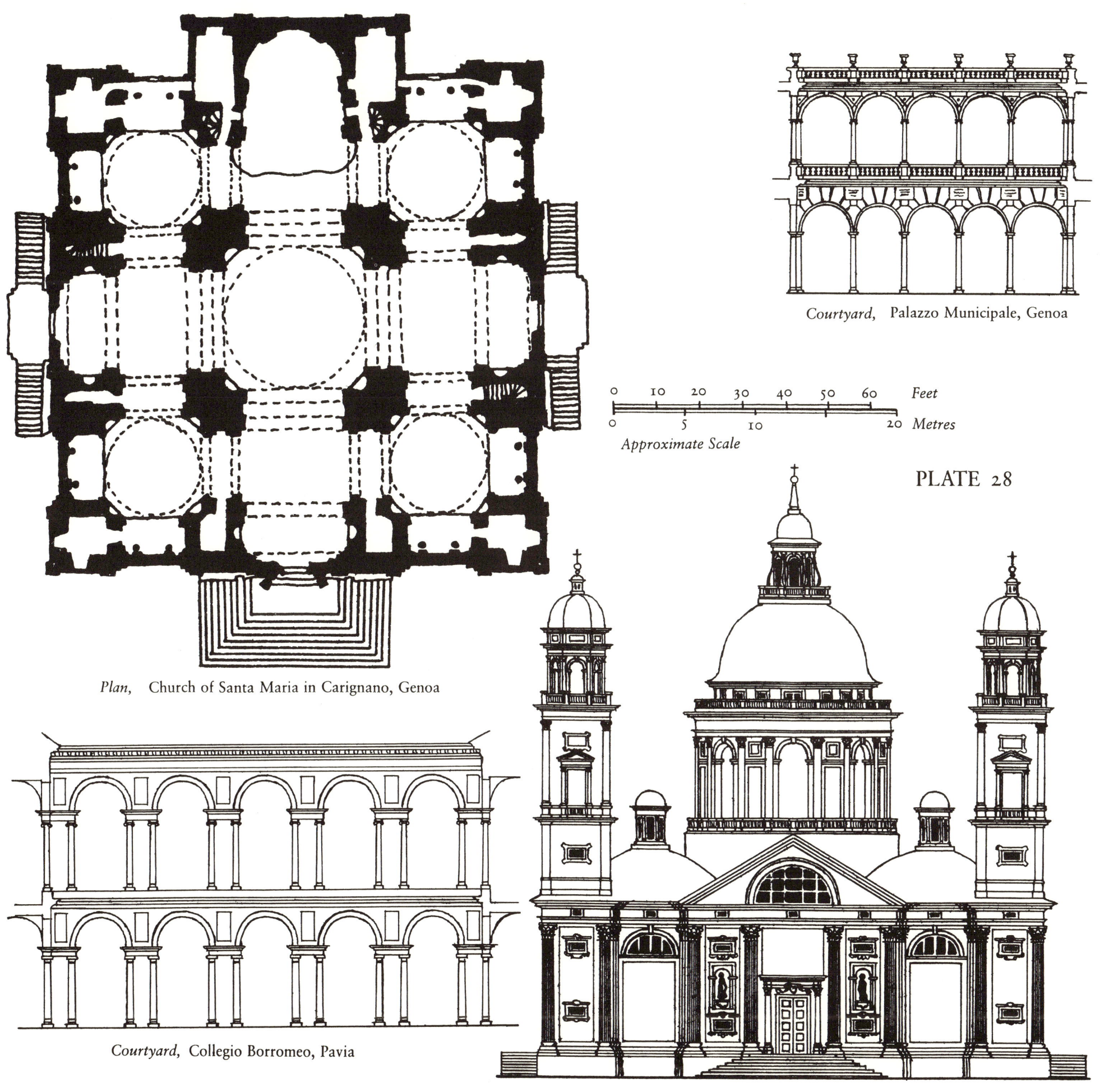

Plan, Church of Santa Maria in Carignano, Genoa

Courtyard, Palazzo Municipale, Genoa

PLATE 28

Courtyard, Collegio Borromeo, Pavia

Church of Santa Maria in Carignano, Genoa

51

dome was impressive enough that Alessi was consulted at length about the design for the church at the Escorial in Spain, whose dome bears more than a passing resemblance to that of Santa Maria. The entrance elevation is relatively too wide and too low for the height of the dome, a fault that Alessi tried to alleviate by placing an unusually tall campanile at each end of the front and an abnormally high pediment in the center of the façade. The body of the church is framed by fluted Corinthian pilasters, and many of the decorative surrounds of the windows and niches are in imitation of Michelangelo; marrying Michelangeline decorations to a Bramantesque plan is a bold stroke that is not altogether successful. Light for the interior is all from above: what does not come from the five domes floods in through a series of thermal windows (beloved of Palladio) high in the walls.

Collegio Borromeo, Pavia   PLATE 28

Alessi's influence can be seen at the Collegio Borromeo at Pavia, on the road to Milan from Genoa, built in 1563 by Pellegrino Tibaldi (1527–1596), who also went by the grandiose title of the Marchese de Valsolda. Pellegrino, who was initially a follower of Michelangelo, had worked at Fontainebleau and the Escorial as a painter, but most of his work was concentrated in the area around Milan. The courtyard elevation of the college is composed of two storeys of arcaded loggias each made of five Venetian arches with shared rectangular openings; the lower storey is Tuscan and the upper is Ionic.

Palazzo Municipale, Genoa   PLATES 28 & 29

Another follower of Alessi was Rocco Lurago (1501–1590). His greatest work is what is now the Palazzo Municipale at Genoa, built for Nicolò Grimaldi in 1564. This palace is even more pretentious than most in Genoa. Because it is built on the side of a hill, its entrance front is given more height than usual: a high basement under the entrance floor with its obligatory mezzanine are framed by rusticated Tuscan pilasters; then the piano nobile with alternating triangular and segmental pediments over its large windows, and the next storey above are framed by fluted Tuscan pilasters, and finally the windows of yet another storey peep out from between the brackets of the entablature. The extra height is balanced by additional width: the main house is nine bays wide, and the front is further extended by an arcaded screen of three bays at each end of the façade. In the middle of the palace is a relatively simple two-storey arcaded loggia around the courtyard.

Auberge d'Italie, Valletta, Malta   PLATE 29

No discussion of Italian architecture of this period would be complete without some mention of Malta, the island fiefdom of the Knights of Saint John.[34] The first evidence of classical architecture in Malta dates from about 1530, but what little survives is unrecognizable. The Knights had been driven out of their previous stronghold on the island of Rhodes by the Turks; they had then taken a vow to fight the Turks upon any occasion, and the Turks, in an attempt to forestall being attacked, decided to capture Malta first. Therefore, most architecture built for the Knights in the first few decades on Malta took the form of fortifications. Because the architects present in Malta were primarily fortification engineers, much of the non-military construction in the sixteenth century had somewhat the look of military buildings.

Such is the case with the Auberge d'Italie (Lodge of the Italian Knights), built in Valletta in 1574 by Gerolamo Cassar. Cassar was a native Maltese (1520–1586) who had received his training at the hands of two engineers, one Maltese and the other Italian. He was given the most important commissions when the city of Valletta was built, but unfortunately nearly all of his designs have been destroyed or unrecognizably altered. The Auberge d'Italie has been altered by the addition of an extra storey in the seventeenth century and other details, but its basic lines are still discernible. The rusticated arched doorway and corner piers, together with the horizontality of the building, strongly suggest a small fort. The windows are grouped into five bays in the center and an extra bay at each end of the façade. The windows of the main storey have heavy sills and cornices resting on brackets, and the square windows of the storey above have shouldered architraves. A parapet used to hide the flat roof; Malta, although an island, has remarkably little rainfall, so a flat roof would not be a great liability.

Church of Santa Maria in Trivio, Rome
PLATE 29

Giacomo del Duca (ca. 1520–1604) came from Sicily to Rome, where he worked under Michelangelo. The church of Santa Maria in Trivio in Rome (1575) is an example of how a small church can use an adaptation of the Jesuit façade. A closer look reveals Mannerist details in the style of Michelangelo in the surrounds of the niches and windows, and in the pediment over the front door—a curious mixture of a triangular with a split and scrolled segmental pediment.

Church of Santa Maria dei Monti, Rome
PLATE 29

Giacomo della Porta (1532–1602) came to Rome from the region of Genoa. He worked for Michelangelo on the dome of the Cathedral of Saint Peter, and he assisted Vignola with the church of the Gesù; after Vignola's death, he produced his own variant design for the façade, which although not as good as Vignola's was accepted. His façade of the small church of Santa Maria Dei Monti in Rome (1580) echoes the better features of the Gesù, and is more like Vignola's work—a belated tribute to the master.

At this point, the Italian Renaissance in architecture, which had already begun to lose momentum with the advent of Michelangelo and the Mannerists, ran out of steam and produced little of value until the next great

34. A useful study of Malta's historic architecture is J. Quentin Hughes, *The Building of Malta,* London, 1956.

Palazzo Municipale, Genoa

Church of Santa Maria in Trivio, Rome

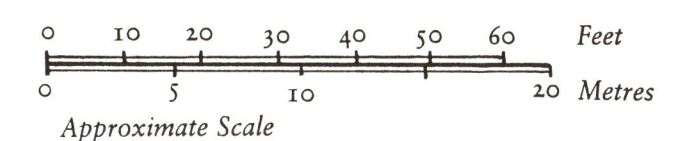

Auberge d'Italie, Valletta, Malta

Church of Santa Maria dei Monti, Rome

PLATE 29

movement of the Baroque era. In the remarkably short space of just over a century and a half, Italian tastesetters decided they wished to emulate classical ancient Rome and then, using the vocabulary of ancient Rome, evolved a style of architecture that uniquely answered the questions of their own day, not of ancient Rome.

Other useful references to Italian renaissance architecture include: Stefano Borsi, *Giuliano da Sangallo: i disegni di architettura e dell'antico*, Rome, Officina, 1985; Renato de Fusco, *L'Architettura del Cinquecento*, Turin, UTET, 1981; Wolfgang Lotz, *Studies in Italian Renaissance Architecture*, Cambridge, MA, MIT Press, 1977; Paolo Portoghesi, *Rome of the Renaissance*, New York, Phaidon, 1972; Ludwig Heydenreich and Wolfgang Lotz, *Architecture in Italy 1400–1600*, Harmondsworth, Penguin Books, 1974; John McAndrew, *Venetian Architecture of the Early Renaissance*, Cambridge, MA, MIT Press, 1980.

FRANCE

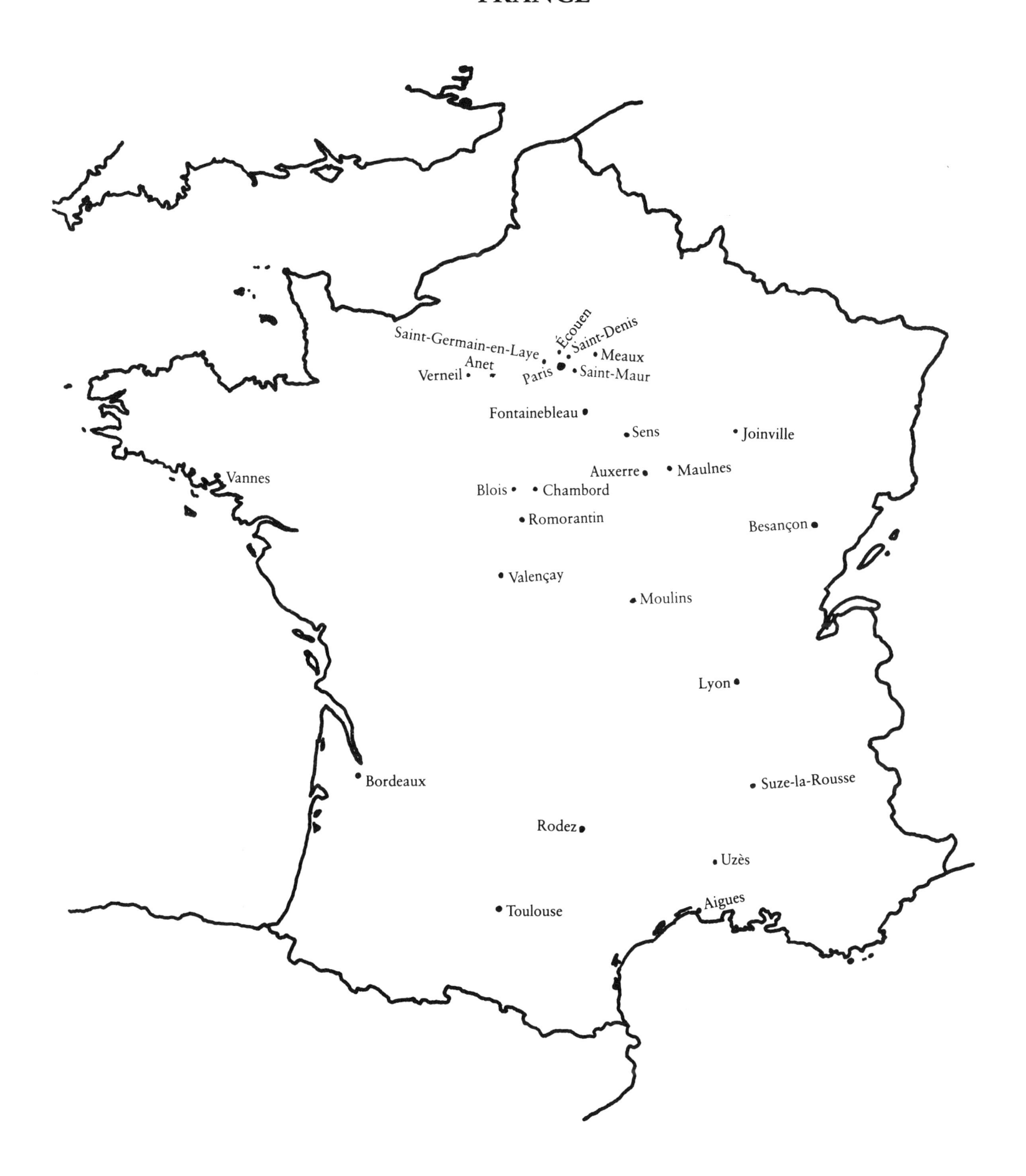

The history of classical architecture in Renaissance France begins with a non-event. In 1496, the Florentine architect Giuliano da San Gallo followed his patron, Cardinal della Rovere, into exile in France and met the French king at Lyon. There he offered him a model for building a new palace. Charles VIII, who lived only another two years, apparently took no advantage of his possession of a model by one of the foremost followers of Brunelleschi and the model itself has long since disappeared. Thus, France missed a golden opportunity to acquire a Florentine palace of the latest style.

Château of Moulins (Allier) PLATE 30

That same year, an anonymous architect made some vaguely classical additions to the Château at Moulins in central France for Princess Anne, daughter of Louis XI and co-regent of France. When Charles VIII returned from Italy with various Italian workmen she managed to borrow some of them, including one called Pietro di Napoli, but there is no evidence that Pietro designed the new parts of the château. These new parts consisted of a seven-bay loggia whose central bay projected forward and was capped by a tower with ogee-shaped roof, and a chapel; the chapel, which was destroyed by fire in 1755, had classical engaged columns and cupola, but its ceiling was gothic.

Loggia, Château Bury, near Blois PLATE 30

About 150 kilometres northwest of Moulins the Château of Bury was built for Florimond Robertet between 1514 and 1524, just west of Blois. The château, which was in ruins by the beginning of the nineteenth century, was built for the most part in a late gothic style, but at least two wings around its principal courtyard were decorated by Corinthian pilasters between the large, rectangular mullioned windows. The pilasters were continued around the entrance side of the courtyard, where they stood in front of the piers of a handsome thirteen-bay arcaded loggia of the finest Italian design. For many years, the name of Fra Giocondo (Giovanni da Verona, ca. 1433/5–1515) was associated with the design of the Château of Bury, but it now appears that he was not its architect; Fra Giocondo, who came to France in 1495 and worked at Amboise, Paris and Blois, returned to Italy in 1506 and became one of Raphael's assistants in Rome. The Bury loggia must be considered the earliest known French building in the pure classical style.[1]

Project for Royal Palace, Romorantin
PLATE 30

If Fra Giocondo was not even in France when Bury was built, at least one other Italian was working only a short distance from Bury at Romorantin in 1519: Leonardo da Vinci. He had moved to France in 1506 to serve Louis XII and later François I. His royal employment would probably have prevented him from providing designs at Bury, but his hand there can not be ruled out completely. At Romorantin, Leonardo was asked to design a palace or palaces near the river, and several different projects were sketched to this end, but nothing that may have been built to Leonardo's plans has survived.[2] Most of the sketches are difficult to interpret, but one elevation is completed enough that it is possible to hazard an interpretation.[3] Near the elevation is a sketch for a building with an octagonal plan, but whether or not the plan is to be connected with the elevation is debatable; the elevation offered in this book is drawn as if the building were rectangular, not octagonal, because of the spacing of the arches. Thus interpreted, the front is divided into three storeys and three sections. The lower floor, of channeled masonry, was pierced only by an arched entrance. The upper storeys consisted of arcaded loggias, the central section five bays wide and the outer section three bays each. Giant Corinthian pilasters separated the sections. No roof was shown above the heavy Corinthian entablature, but since the Loire region is subject to considerable rain and snow a flat roof would not have been possible. Leonardo's death in 1519 may have prevented any execution of his ideas.

Project for the Keep, Château, Chambord
PLATE 30

Domenico Bernabei da Cortona, known in France by his nickname "Boccador," (ca. 1470–1549) arrived in France in 1495 along with his teacher, Giuliano da San Gallo. His activities over the next two decades are but partially known—he could have designed the loggia at Bury, for example—but by 1519 he was in the service of François I, for whom he designed a palace at Chambord, in the region of the Loire. The Château of Chambord as it stands is undoubtedly altered from Boccador's original design, for much of it is late gothic in execution. However, the plan is likely to be more or less as designed. The outer part is a large rectangle with a round tower at each corner, and, nestling against one side of the rectangle, is the square "donjon" with a round tower at each corner. Boccador built a wooden model of how he intended the donjon to look, and the drawing shown in this book is based on that model (whose appearance is known through drawings by Félibien). The bulk of the donjon was to be three storeys, of which the ground floor was to be an arcaded loggia that extended even around the towers. The loggia motif was repeated on the upper two floors, but with blind arches pierced by windows where needed. The model did not show what Boccador intended for the roofs; the present roofs are high, after the French tradition.[4]

Hôtel de Ville, Paris PLATE 30

Boccador's other major work in France was the Hôtel de Ville or City Hall in Paris, begun in 1529. Just as he did at Chambord, he built a wooden model of it, which is now lost. As at Chambord, it contained many arches. Boccador died long before the building was finished—it was in fact still under construction well into the seventeenth century, at which time a proposal was made to build a series of copies of it around the edge of a large

1. Philippe de Cossé Brissac, *Châteaux de France Disparus,* Paris, Éditions Tel, 1947, pp. 25–27.
2. Carlo Pedretti, *Leonardo da Vinci, the Royal Palace at Romorantin,* Cambridge, MA, Harvard/Belknap Press, 1972, figs. 111, 114, 136, 139, 143, 149, 160.
3. Codex Atlanticus, 217 v-b.
4. François Gebelin, *Les Châteaux de la Renaissance,* Paris, Les Beaux Arts, 1927, pp. 68–74.

Courtyard loggia, Château of Moulins (Allier)

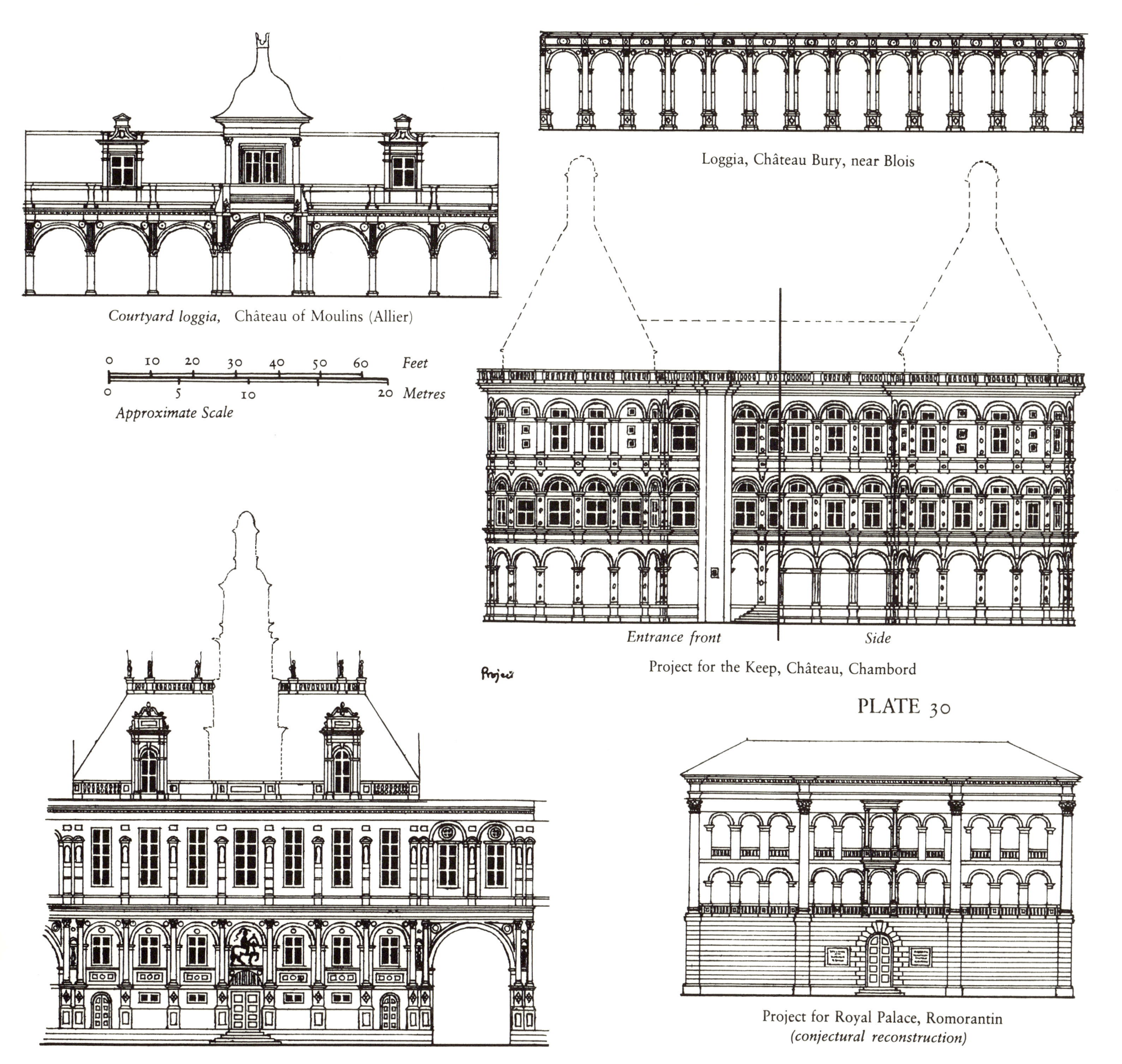

Loggia, Château Bury, near Blois

Approximate Scale

Entrance front   *Side*

Project for the Keep, Château, Chambord

PLATE 30

Part of Hôtel de Ville, Paris

Project for Royal Palace, Romorantin
(conjectural reconstruction)

57

crescent, but nothing ever came of that—and its design was substantially altered over the years; the building was destroyed in 1871 by angry revolutionaries, but a facsimile of the old building was erected as the core of a larger new City Hall. The drawing in this book shows the central part of the building, which is divided into two major storeys. The lower storey is articulated by a series of seven blind arches with Corinthian columns on high pedestals standing in front of the piers. This was as high as was built at the time of Boccador's death. The upper storey, as built, consists of seven large rectangular windows standing between pedimented buttresses with niches in them, although it is likely that the original design called for another tier of blind arches with Corinthian columns instead of the buttresses.[5]

After the wars in Italy, that ended with the sack of Rome, many influential Frenchmen returned home enthusiastic about the new style of architecture they had encountered in Italy. As a result, many châteaux were built in the Loire region, near Lyon and around Paris that reflected the new Italian style. For the most part, the reflections were at first clouded, and Italian cognoscenti would have been hard put to recognize the French architecture as being at all related to the Italian Renaissance. In many cases, the Italian inspiration took the form of the addition of one or more tiers of arcaded loggias grafted onto an existing building, but the proportions and rules were poorly understood by the local builders. This is the case with the Château of La Rochefoucauld, altered in the Charente region about 1528, for the arches of the triple-decked loggia are less than semi-circles (not shown in this book).

Chapel of the Holy Sacrament, Cathedral, Vannes PLATE 31

The Roman Catholic Church was one of the avenues for dissemination of Renaissance ideas to remote parts of Europe, for many of the more important clergy were not locals but place-men sent out from Rome. This is probably the explanation of how the gothic Cathedral of Saint-Pierre at Vannes (near Lorient, Brittany) received the addition of the little round chapel of the Holy Sacrament in 1537. This chapel is, if one makes allowances for somewhat crude execution by local builders, a counterpart to such Italian funerary chapels as the Chigi Chapel by Raphael some two decades earlier. It is two storeys high. The lower floor is decorated with Doric half-columns on high pedestals and niches in aedicules with alternately triangular and segmental pediments, while the upper floor has Ionic pilasters and compass-headed windows with mouldings that look more romanesque than Renaissance. Although a number of small, centrally-planned chapels appeared in France in the next few decades, none appears to have been influenced by the chapel at Vannes and its anonymous architect.

At the other side of France at Annecy in the Alps near Lake Geneva, another anonymous architect fitted to the Cathedral there a façade that was intended to echo Italian Renaissance ideas (not shown in this book). The lower part of the front is divided into three sections by four panelled Tuscan pilasters. Each section contains a pedimented doorway, the one in the middle being larger than the others. The upper level, above the main entablature, contains a central gothic rose window with a pilaster on either side, but the pediment above the upper entablature had to be much steeper than classical pediments in order to mask the gothic roof behind it. The aisle roofs are masked by half-pediments that are left unfinished, as if the builder were unable to construct the volutes that would have suited the design better. The attempt thus fails to give France an early classical church façade, but almost a century would elapse before the construction of anything closer to the mark.

Granvelle Palace, Besançon PLATE 31

A short distance to the north of Annecy is the ancient city of Besançon, now part of France, but in the sixteenth century a part of the Empire with close ties to Flanders. Nicolas Perrenot, Sieur de Granvelle, chief minister to Emperor Charles V, lived in Besançon, and in the mid-1530s decided to build himself a palace there worthy of his station. He hired architect Onorato Magena from Italy to design it and Richard Maire and probably Jean Delorme to be in charge of construction. The principal façade, three storeys tall, contains obvious classical elements, such as occasional columns and pedimented windows, but these are arranged in an irregular way. The courtyard inside the palace is more regular and more classical; it is six bays in one direction and seven in the other. The lower floor is an arcaded loggia of basket (flattened) arches on short Tuscan columns. The basket arch may not be classical, but it is not incompatible. The upper floor is composed of pedimented windows and Ionic pilasters. A nineteenth-century painting of the courtyard by Edouard Bérard (student of Viollet-le-Duc) shows an additional short open storey above, with a balustrade, but this feature, if it was ever more than in the artist's fertile imagination, has disappeared without a trace. Granvelle had 14 children, of whom one was Antoine Cardinal Granvelle, who followed his father as chief minister to Charles V and later to Philip II; like his father, he was a builder of palaces. The Granvelle Palace at Besançon is now an impressive museum.

Château Mesnières (Seine Inférieure) PLATE 31

The Château of Mesnières (Seine Inférieure) was built 1540–1546. Much of the U-shaped structure is typical of the period, a late-medieval castle with strong round towers. However, the south face of the courtyard has an arcaded loggia on the ground floor with fluted Ionic columns on high pedestals standing in front of the piers, and more Ionic columns decorating the upper storey. The exceptionally high roof is pierced with dormer windows, framed by more Ionic columns, this time arranged in pairs. The architect is unknown.

5. Louis Hautecoeur, *Histoire de l'Architecture Classique en France*, Paris, Picard, 1963, vol. I, pp. 259–263.

Chapel of the Holy Sacrament, Cathedral, Vannes

Courtyard, Granvelle Palace, Besançon

Approximate Scale

Courtyard, Château Saint-Maur-les-Fossés (Ile de France)

Courtyard, Château Saint-Maur-les-Fossés (Ile de France)

Main entrance, Château Saint-Maur-les-Fossés (Ile de France)

Courtyard, Château Mesnières (Seine Inférieure)

PLATE 31

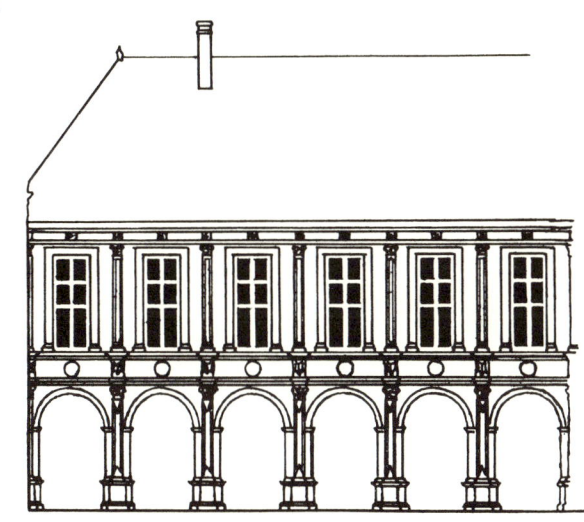

Archbishop's Palace, Sens

Courtyard side, Château of Valençay (Indre)

Château of Valençay (Indre) PLATE 31

Another castle with large round towers is the Château of Valençay (Indre), built over a period of decades from about 1540 onwards. Its most famous resident was Charles Maurice de Talleyrand-Périgord, Napoleon's scheming minister who had formerly been a Roman Catholic bishop before he had fallen from grace. The château as it stands today reflects many enlargements made in the seventeenth and eighteenth centuries, but one small section in the courtyard is a delightful flight of Renaissance fancy. The ground floor has an arcaded loggia with elliptical arches and Doric pilasters standing in front of the piers. Above are fluted Ionic pilasters amid panels and large windows under an outsized and elaborate entablature. Its architect is anonymous.

Archbishop's Palace, Sens PLATE 31

Another anonymous work is the so-called Henri II wing of the Archibishop's Palace at Sens, built in the 1540s. The ground floor is an arcaded loggia with panelled Corinthian pilasters standing in front of the piers and more attenuated Corinthian pilasters on the floor above, standing between large windows.

Château Saint-Maur-les-Fossés (Ile de France) PLATE 31

The first giant among the architects of the Renaissance in France was Philibert Delorme (sometimes spelled de l'Orme), ca. 1505/1510–1570.[6] He was France's first native architect to understand fully the classical ideas of the Renaissance. He studied in Rome in the 1530s and began working in the service of the pope, but Cardinal Jean Du Bellay persuaded him to return to France. The cardinal commissioned him to design a villa a short distance east of Paris in 1540, the Château Saint-Maur-les-Fossés; since the cardinal had but little money this would be a small building that would demonstrate the highest of taste. The entrance front uncompromisingly announced its Italian inspiration; the front was seven bays wide and the great windows of its piano nobile were crowned alternately by triangular and segmental pediments. Most of the building had a flat roof, but pedimented corner towers anchored the ends of the front. The corner bays were further emphasized by quoins and rusticated pilasters, while the rest of the front was articulated with fluted Corinthian pilasters.

Inside the courtyard, whose floor was considerably elevated above the level of the ground outside, the walls, sometimes containing arches, sometimes windows, were decorated with pairs of Corinthian half-columns. When Henri II came to the throne in 1547, Du Bellay fled back to Rome. In 1563, Catherine de Medici took over the château and planned to enlarge it. She hired Delorme to rebuild it, but he died after doing only a few drawings. By 1579, it was greatly enlarged in a garish style established years earlier by François I, but it remained unfinished well into the seventeenth century. It was rebuilt again to a different design about 1670 and demolished in 1796.

Chapel, Villers-Cotterets PLATE 32

Delorme's next projects include a string of centrally-planned chapels with domes, only one of which remains standing. For the Château of Villers-Cotterêts (Aisne), he built a chapel in the park about 1548 with a most unusual plan that seems to reflect slightly the plan of an ancient temple that Serlio published. The chancel and transepts were in the form of semicircles that projected from the central drum, while the entrance was through a portico of banded pairs of Corinthian columns on the fourth side of the drum; the plan thus resembled a three-leafed clover. Although much of the château still stands, the chapel is long since gone.

Chapel, Château, Anet (Eure et Loire) PLATE 32

The one Delorme chapel that remains is at the now much-diminished Château of Anet (Eure et Loire), begun 1549. Much attention has been focussed on the château itself, its three-tiered entrance (now removed to the École des Beaux Arts in Paris) and its elaborate gateway; the château was not actually a successful design, for it was cluttered with many mannerist conceits and its proportions were not admirable. It was built for Diane de Poitiers. Delorme apparently hoped that the chapel would be free-standing, as at Villers-Cotterêts, and he designed an impressive façade for it that was recorded by Du Cerceau. However, Diane insisted that the chapel be attached to the château and that is how it was built, although since much of the château has been demolished the chapel is now free-standing but minus Delorme's façade. The plan is a Greek cross set in a square, the ends of the arms of the cross being slightly curved. Palladio later used a remarkably similar plan for his chapel at Maser, and it is likely that he took inspiration from Delorme's masterpiece. When Delorme was faced with burying his chapel in the bulk of the château, he managed to draw attention to the entrance of the chapel by placing a pair of tall, square steeples in front of the dome, a device that looks odd now that the chapel stands alone, but must have been impressive inside the courtyard of the château. The dome is crowned with a large lantern, which helps to illuminate the rich tracery of intersecting arcs on the inside of the dome.

Chapel, Château, Saint-Léger PLATE 33

The chapel at the Château of Saint-Léger was also attached to one range of the château, and, characteristically, Delorme fitted this chapel with a pair of tall, square steeples to mark the entrance. The bulk of this chapel, which was built in 1550, was in the form of a tall, square block illuminated by high bullseye windows; above the block was a dome that was perhaps too small for the building. Segmental apses protruded from the central block to mark the altar and the vestigial transepts.

6. Anthony Blunt, *Philibert de l'Orme*, London, Zwemmer, 1958, is the most complete account of Delorme's life and works. Some of his individual buildings are the subjects of monographs, such as Françoise Boudon & Jean Blécon, *Philibert Delorme et le château royal de Saint-Léger-en-Yvelines,* Paris, Picard, 1985.

Side elevation, Chapel, Villers-Cotterets

Chapel, Villers-Cotterets

Plan, Chapel, Villers-Cotterets

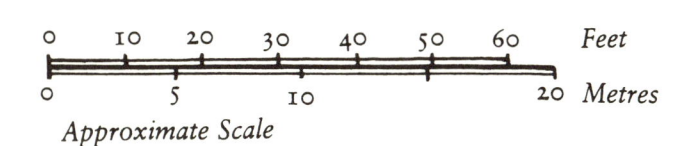

Approximate Scale

PLATE 32

Project for entrance, Chapel, Château, Anet (Eure et Loire)

Side elevation,
Chapel, Château, Anet (Eure et Loire)

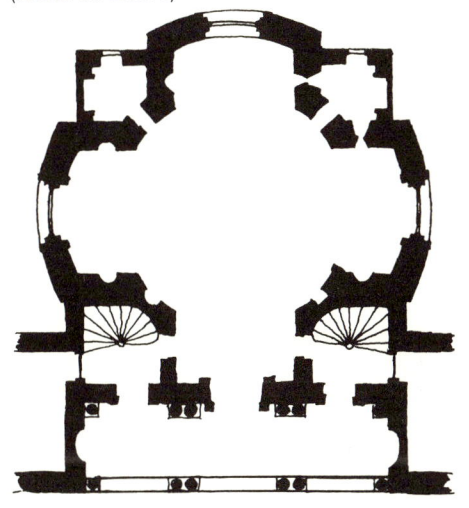

Plan, Chapel, Château, Anet (Eure et Loire)

Altar end,
Chapel, Château, Anet (Eure et Loire)

61

Plan, Chapel, Château, Saint-Léger

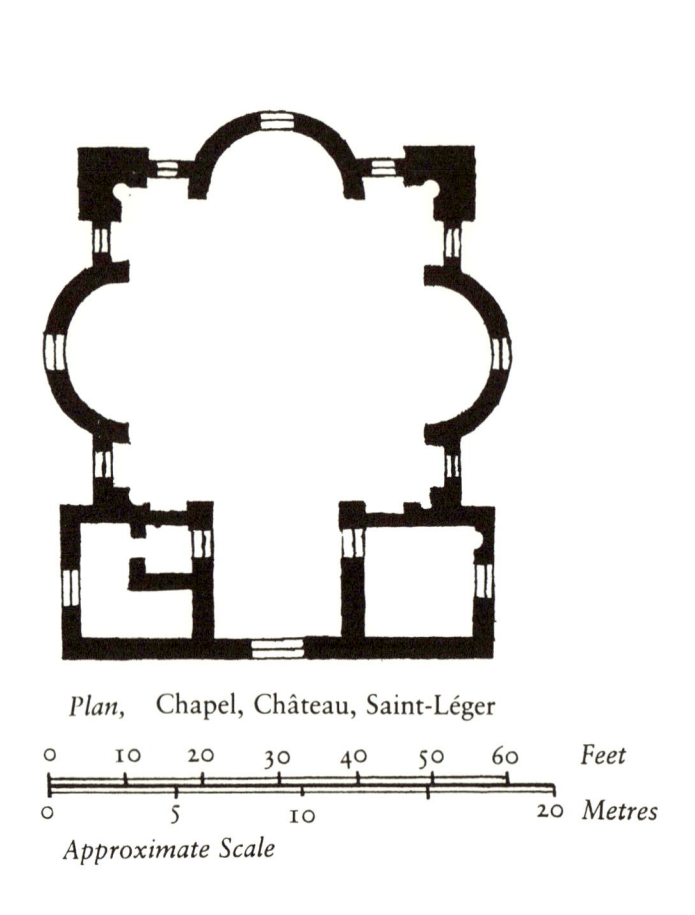

Side elevation, Chapel, Château, Saint-Léger

PLATE 33

Side elevation, Chapel, Saint-Germain-en-Laye

Chapel, Saint-Germain-en-Laye

Plan, Chapel, Saint-Germain-en-Laye

Chapel, Saint-Germain-en-Laye PLATE 33

Delorme built a free-standing chapel for the royal Château of Saint-German-en-Laye about 1557, now known to us only through Du Cerceau's drawings preserved at the British Library. The body of the chapel was a hexagon, from the sides of which protruded alternately semicircles and rectangles that were presumably used as locations for one principal altar and four secondary altars. The entrance portico had but two Tuscan columns. The hexagonal dome was in the shape of a basket arch—a rather baroque touch—and it had a small lantern on top.

Château-Neuf, Saint-Germain-en-Laye PLATE 34

The ancient Château of Saint-Germain-en-Laye had been modernized by François I in garish style (François probably did much of the design himself) and it still stands. Henri II asked Delorme about 1557 to design a lodge near the old château on a steep hillside, a place he hoped would be suitable for theatrical entertainments. The lodge, known as the Château-Neuf, was a simple villa of one and a half storeys in the shape of a U, and eleven-bay arcades stretched out from either side to provide a sheltered place for strolling. Down the hill, he designed elaborate terraced gardens, allegedly the first such in Europe. Inevitably, the theatrical Château-Neuf, whose construction was not the most durable because of its frivolous purpose, was adapted for more serious purposes and subsequently enlarged; it then fell into ruins, and only some of the terracing remains of the gardens of this pleasure-palace that was a worthy contemporary to Palladio's Villa Barbaro.

Project for Tuileries Palace, Paris PLATE 34

While other architects were employed to enlarge and replace parts of the Louvre Palace in Paris, Delorme was engaged to design a totally new palace next door to the Louvre: the Tuileries Palace, so called because it was on the site of an earlier tile factory.[7] Queen Catherine de Medici was behind the commission, but she quickly lost interest in it, so it was not completed according to the original designs. Delorme's plan called for a large central courtyard with a narrower courtyard on each of two sides. The principal elevation was to consist of five two-storey pavilions with high hipped roofs, linked by two-storey hyphens with low roofs. The two hyphens on either side of the central pavilion (the part shown in this book) stood behind one-storey arcaded loggias of eleven bays apiece; banded Ionic columns stood in front of the piers of the arches. In the seventeenth century the central pavilion was completed with a dome instead of Delorme's hipped roof, and under successive regimes the palace was altered and enlarged unrecognizably. The palace was ritually sacked every time the French government changed hands in a less than peaceful manner, until it was finally destroyed by a vengeful mob in 1871. However, parts of it were saved: the central pavilion was re-erected at Ajaccio, Corsica, and a few of the arches of Delorme's loggias stand in the Tuileries Gardens.

Project for Delorme's House PLATE 34

Rarely does the design survive for a house designed by a Renaissance architect for his own use, but Delorme published drawings of his own house in his *Architecture* (folios 253–255). The house was divided into two blocks, the rectangular, gable-roofed entrance and the U-shaped main house at the back of a small, arcaded courtyard. The elevations of the two blocks were in the Mannerist taste and were decorated extensively by quoins and niches. The house was not really a classical exercise, but it is included because it presumably represented Delorme's unfettered architectural ideas at one moment.

House Project PLATE 34

Another design for a house published in *Architecture* (folio 252) shows the use of giant Corinthian pilasters across the front, and the central bay composed of a series of twin arches, a motif that was echoed in Bullant's design for part of the alterations to the Château of Écouen.

Gate, Hôtel des Tournelles, Paris PLATE 34

An important feature of life in Renaissance Paris was the Tournelles or jousting tournament, in which leading nobility and even royalty took part; in fact, Henri II died from a wound suffered at the Tournelles. It is not surprising, therefore, that Delorme should be asked to design an impressive entrance gateway for the Tournelles, the design for which appears in *Architecture* (folio 247). This is in the manner of a Roman triumphal arch, but Delorme added an unprecedented swan-necked pediment to the top, along with statues and trophies. Although the arch no longer survives, the anonymous architect of the south door of the church of Saint-Nicolas-des-Champs in Paris (late sixteenth century) copied it closely there with only a few alterations.

According to Blunt, the only original Delorme building in Paris still standing is the church of Saint-Eloi, but it is so much altered as to be unrecognizable (not shown in this book). Delorme designed at least two enormous buildings for erection in Paris that were never built, and he has preserved their designs in *Architecture* (folios 303 and 306 respectively). The first was for a Basilica or giant meeting room for Henri II. This was to have covered an area approximately 73 metres long by 46 metres wide with a single curved wooden roof, starting low to the ground in the manner of a Quonset Hut, and it was to have a loggia running along the ridge, from which Henri could presumably look down in secret on his assembled subjects.

The other large building was intended as a replacement for the Convent of Notre Dame de Montmartre, which had burned down early in 1559. Delorme produced a revolutionary design for the nuns when he learned that Henri would pay for it. This was a rotunda

7. André Devèche, *The Tuileries Palace and Gardens*, Paris, La Tourelle-Maloine, 1981.

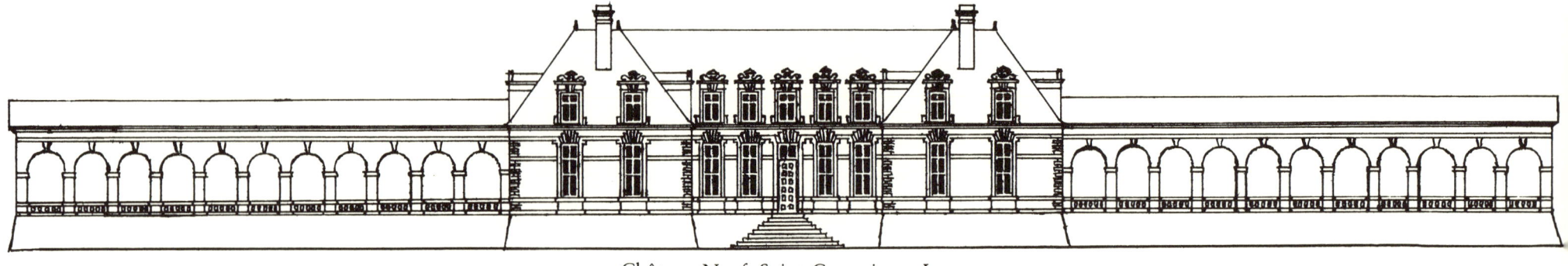

Château-Neuf, Saint-Germain-en-Laye

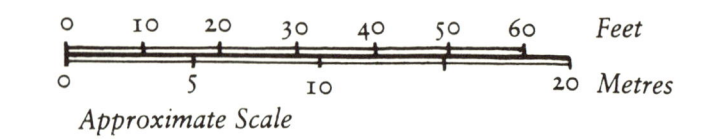

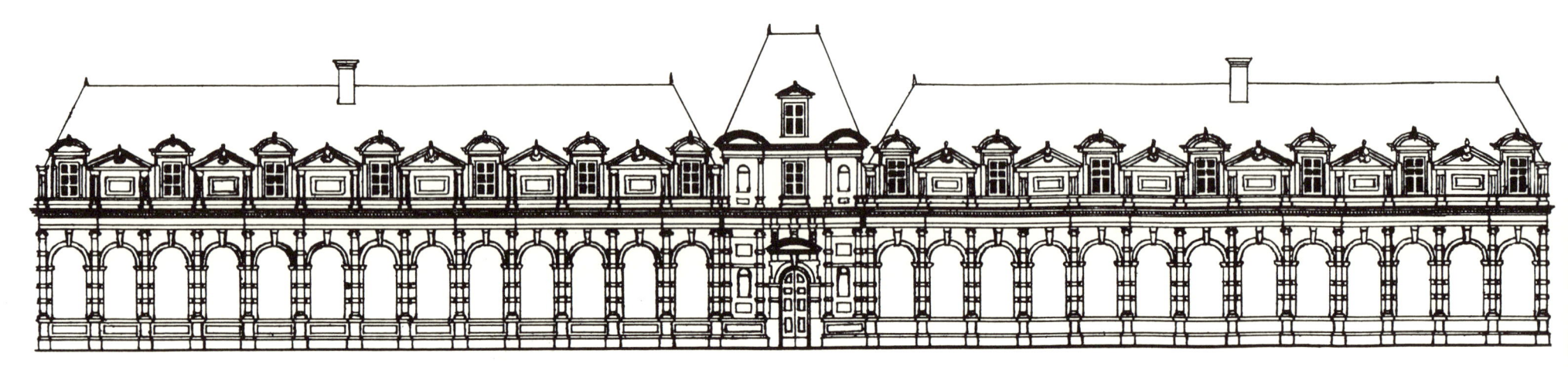

Project for Tuileries Palace, Paris

PLATE 34

Project for Delorme's House

House Project

Gate, Hôtel des Tournelles, Paris

about 55 metres in diameter with three storeys of nuns' cells around the edge and two superimposed Ionic colonnades under a dome made of metal over a wooden frame. The interior was lit by a large lantern atop the dome, the top of which was to be about 90 metres above the ground. Unfortunately, Henri's death occurred before either of these bold schemes could be put into motion, and Henri's successors initially disliked Delorme.

Since so few of Delorme's buildings remain standing his greatest impact must be found elsewhere. On one level, his impact was on paper, whether through his book (full title: *Le Premier Tôme de l'Architecture,* 1567) or through the admiring portraits of his buildings by Du Cerceau, but on another level, less easy to measure, his impact was on the artistic spirit of France through his clear demonstration that native French architects were capable of creating masterpieces without the need to import talent from abroad; no matter that Delorme himself had learned the rules of his profession while on a trip abroad. One unfortunate later result of the new French self-confidence in architecture was Louis XIV's invitation to the great Italian architect Bernini to come to Paris to design a wing for the Louvre in 1663; although Bernini's designs were of the highest quality, Louis ostentatiously spurned them in favor of plans by a Frenchman, Claude Perrault, and it is believed that Louis had intended to do that from the beginning.

Louvre project, Paris PLATES 35 & 36

An earlier Italian who was asked to prepare designs for the Louvre was a contemporary of Delorme, Sebastiano Serlio (1475–1554).[8] François I invited him in 1541, one year after Delorme had begun the Château Saint-Maur. Serlio's project for the palace was so vast that only the central two-fifths of the principal façade can be included in this book. The front was to be divided into three storeys; in his first design, Serlio indicated that the lower two storeys be articulated with two levels of Tuscan pilasters and one of Ionic, while in his alternative design the orders were Tuscan, Ionic and Corinthian. Both designs called for the ground floor to be divided into a full storey plus a mezzanine, and for the piano nobile to be accented by pedimented windows. The first design had a relatively low roof with a single layer of pedimented dormers, while the alternative drawing had a high roof with three additional storeys of dormer windows over the pedimented dormers. Behind the façade, Serlio planned an extensive system of courtyards of different shapes and sizes. The principal courtyard was to be square with a two-storey arcaded loggia, of which the lower level was rusticated and the upper level was decorated with panelled pilasters in front of the piers. A smaller, octagonal courtyard also had two storeys of arcaded loggias, the lower storey of which had an odd Mannerist device of only the top third or so of the Tuscan half-columns appearing on the piers above a heavy moulding. A round courtyard had a loggia only on its ground floor with Tuscan columns grouped in threes to form a variation on the Venetian arch motif. Corinthian pilasters on the other two storeys were also grouped in threes. For whatever reason, François decided not to embrace Serlio's costly scheme, but hired him to work at Fontainebleau instead.

Bourse, Lyon PLATE 36

Serlio's first months in France were spent mainly at Lyon, an important mercantile center. There, he designed an entire block of commercial buildings, now lost, and an Exchange or Bourse. His first design for the Bourse showed a three-storey building whose ground floor was an arcaded loggia of rusticated arches decorated with panelled pilasters; the floors above were decorated by Doric and Ionic pilasters that stood singly between windows but in pairs at each end of the five-bay façade. The hipped roof contained a row of pedimented dormers plus an extra row of small dormers above. As built, the design was altered slightly: the dormers were all given circular windows under segmental pediments, and the windows of the piano nobile were emphasized by the addition of alternating triangular and segmental pediments. The Bourse has long since been destroyed, but the plan of the block and the elevation of the Bourse both appear in Serlio's *Seventh Book* (folios 185 and 195 respectively).

Ballroom project, Royal Palace, Fontainebleau PLATE 37

At Fontainebleau, it is difficult to distinguish Serlio's work from the work of other talented artists working there at the same time, such as Delorme, for the account books are not clear. Furthermore, both Serlio and Delorme had to contend with workmen who thought they knew better than the architects. Such a workman was Gilles Lebreton, who had worked at Chambord, and he radically altered, for the worse, Serlio's drawings for what became the Ballroom at Fontainebleau. A seven-bay version of the original design for what was supposed to be merely a two-storey open loggia appears on folio 97 of the *Seventh Book,* although the design was presumably intended to be eleven bays wide on the courtyard front. It looked particularly French with its channelled stonework and high-roofed pavilions at each end of the façade. Lebreton made the design much lower and chose to use smooth stone. He decorated both storeys with the Corinthian order, but the upper pilasters are made diminutive in order to make room for a row of roundels, except for the pilasters at each end, which are full height. The arches were glazed in order to make the loggias into rooms, the upper of which became a ballroom. Serlio began work on this project about 1541.

Royal bath-house project, Fontainebleau PLATE 37

Also at Fontainebleau, but never built, was Serlio's project for the King's Bath-house. This was to be a heavy square block of rusticated stone crowned by an

8. Myra Nan Rosenfeld, *Sebastiano Serlio on Domestic Architecture,* Cambridge, MA, MIT Press, 1978.

Part of Louvre project, Paris

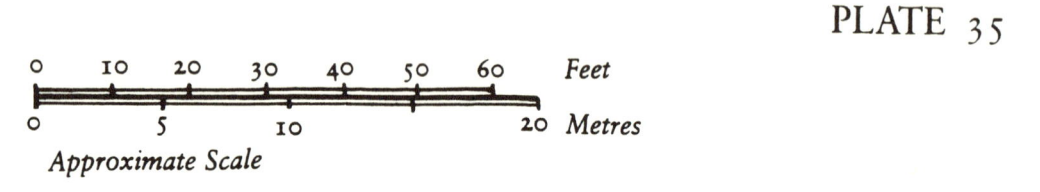

PLATE 35

Approximate Scale

Part of Alternative Louvre project, Paris

Principal courtyard, Louvre project, Paris

Bourse project, Lyon

Octagonal courtyard, Louvre project, Paris

Bourse, Lyon

Circular courtyard, Louvre project, Paris

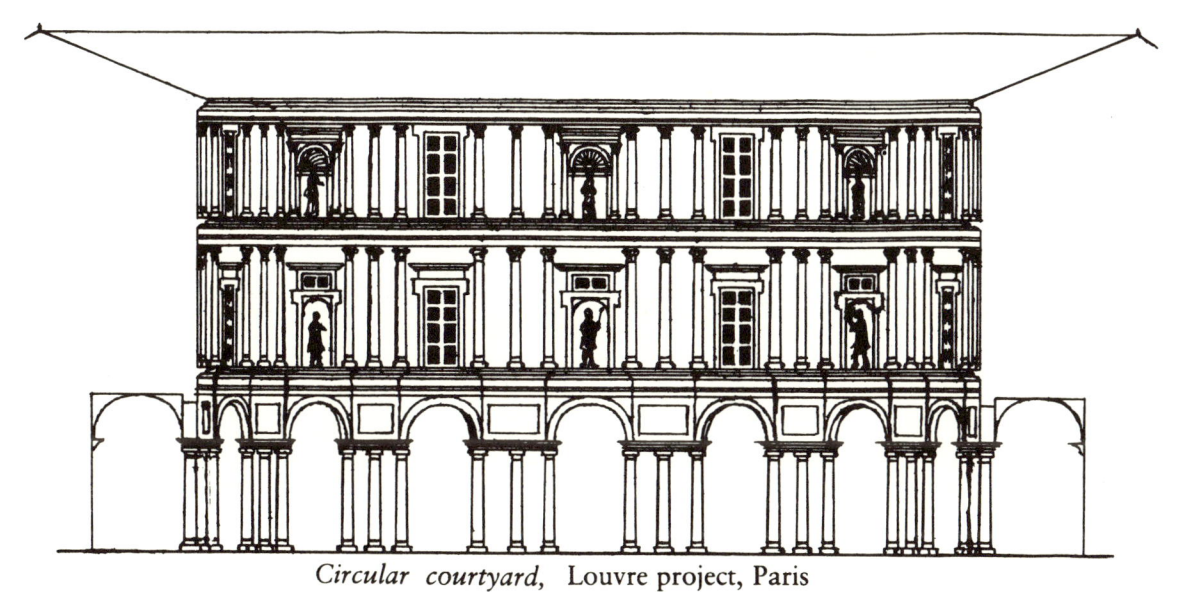

PLATE 36

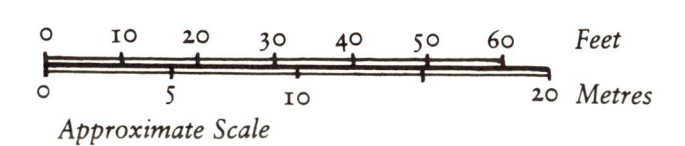

Approximate Scale

Ballroom project, Royal Palace, Fontainebleau

Ballroom (as built), Royal Palace, Fontainebleau

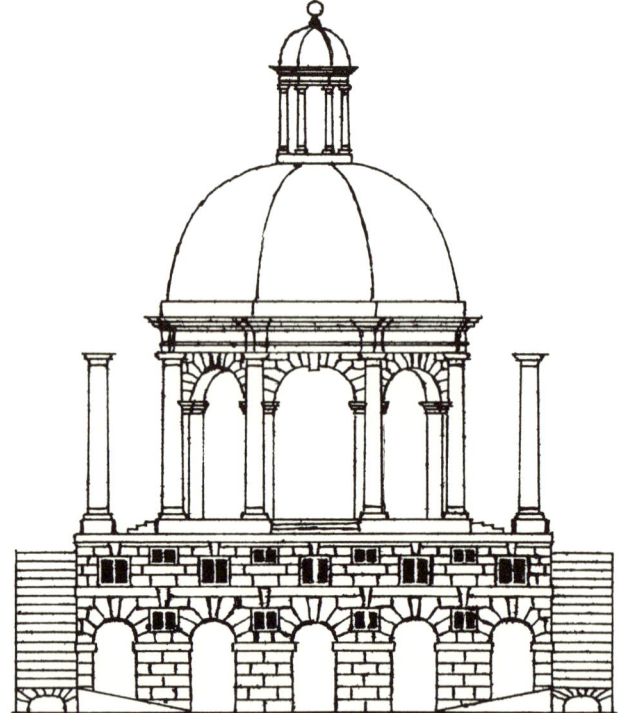

Royal bath-house project, Fontainebleau

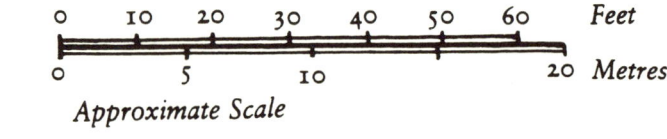

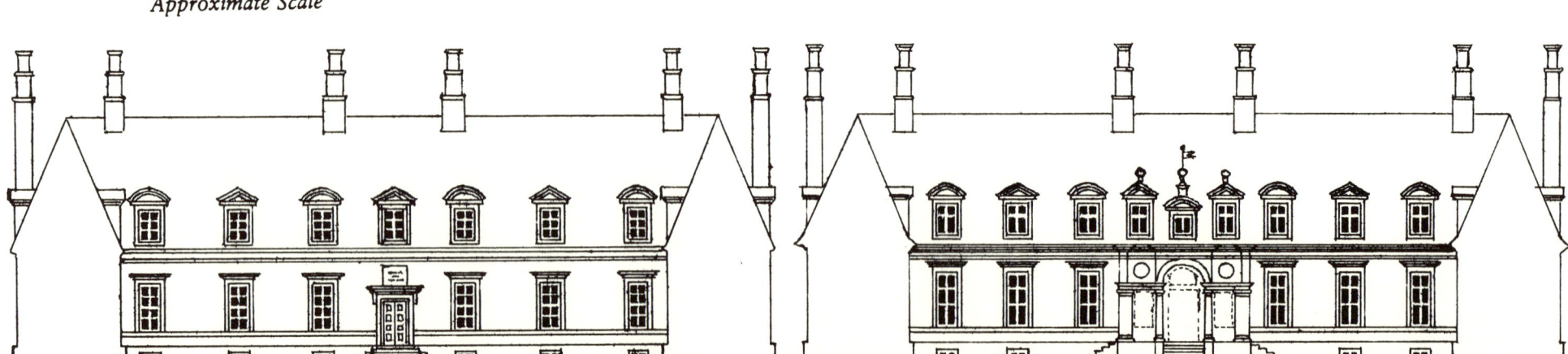

PLATE 37

Project for House for Cardinal d'Este, Fontainebleau

House of Cardinal d'Este of Ferrara, Fontainebleau

arcade under a large dome. Free-standing Tuscan columns stood at each corner, perhaps to balance the masses of the outside staircases.

House of Cardinal d'Este of Ferrara, Fontainebleau PLATE 37

While he was working at Fontainebleau, Serlio was persuaded to design a house for Cardinal Ippolito d'Este of Ferrara, who was an advisor to François. Serlio's first effort, a U-shaped building of a storey and a half with a high French roof, was apparently not grand enough for the Cardinal, so Serlio revised it to include an entrance in the form of a Venetian arch (perhaps the first one built in France) and windows closer together. Unfortunately, the house was destroyed long ago, but its gateway still stands.

Project for a Royal Lodge PLATE 38

Serlio drew at least two other projects for the king, neither of which was apparently built. One was a square hunting-lodge with a large dome. The body of the building was five bays wide with giant Doric pilasters. The lower storey had pediments over all the windows and the upper storey was but a shallow mezzanine. The central dome was surrounded by eight small domes and four truncated obelisks.

Project for a Royal Palace PLATE 38

The other was a small royal palace of three storeys with a central dome that could only be seen from opposite the middle of the four sides, for it was hidden at other angles by high hipped roofs over the corners of the building. The ground floor was screened by a rusticated arcade of seven arches. While the hunting lodge was clearly an Italian work that might have been designed by Giulio Romano, the palace was just as clearly a French work, both because of its massing and because of its French roofs.

Château Ancy-le-Franc, near Auxerre (Yonne) PLATES 38 - 40

The massing of the palace was vaguely echoed in the eventual design of Serlio's most impressive extant building, the Château of Ancy-le-Franc (Yonne), begun 1546. For this château, evidence exists for three distinct stages of design, two of which appear in plates in various of Serlio's books. All three designs shared essentially the same ground plan of a rectangular, arcaded courtyard block attached to a tower block at each corner on the exterior. The first two designs were evidently too Italian for the owner, so the final design has markedly French characteristics. The two early designs, making substantial use of rustication, appeared massive and bold, almost oppressively so, but the final design lacks any sign of rustication and looks surprisingly delicate under its high French roofs. Each of the tower roofs was originally crowned with a cupola, but these have long since disappeared. The exterior elevations are articulated by Tuscan pilasters for each bay on all storeys, but the courtyard elevation elegantly borrows the theme of Bramante's Belvedere Cortile at Rome, a happy rhythm of arches, niches and paired, fluted Corinthian pilasters. The two preliminary designs called for attic storeys that detracted from the design, but the attic is now contained under the high roof and is lit by handsome dormers.

Château Rosmarino PLATE 40

Even if his client at Ancy was apparently dissatisfied with the Italian nature of the earlier designs for the château, Serlio liked them enough to try them out in modified form at the Château of Rosmarino (which despite its Italian name was in France), built about 1549 but no longer surviving. The building stood atop a high rusticated basement, and access to the front door was obtained by means of a long, shallow ramp on each side. The windows of the principal storeys were separated by pilasters, arranged singly in the middle and in pairs on the towers. The middle had an attic storey under a low, Italian roof, but the towers had high roofs with a cupola on each.

Château Maulnes-en-Tonnerois (Yonne) PLATES 41 & 42

Not far from Ancy, near the village of Cruzy-le-Châtel, stand the ruins of the most extraordinary château built in sixteenth-century France, the Château of Maulnes-en-Tonnerois (Yonne). No documentary evidence survives connecting Serlio to this pentagonal structure built for the Duc d'Uzès, but, knowing that Serlio was closely connected with Peruzzi, who had designed the pentagonal villa of Caprarola near Rome, one could safely assume that Serlio designed Maulnes. Maulnes was surrounded by a deep moat that was normally treated as a sunken garden, but that could be flooded in time of war, and access to the château was gained across a drawbridge from an attractive Y-shaped forecourt of arcaded stables. Maulnes was completed in the 1570s, but must have been begun before Serlio's death in 1554. Its ruinous state today must be regarded as a national scandal in art-conscious France; an unofficial explanation was given that in spite of its high French roof, it is essentially an Italian building, and therefore of a low priority for preservation![9]

The unofficial attitude of twentieth-century French officialdom towards sixteenth-century architecture by an Italian in France had its counterpart in sixteenth-century France. Some French kings felt that the only buildings worth having had to be designed by Italian architects, at which point the stars of Serlio and Primaticcio rose at court; other kings would have nothing to do with any foreign architects, at which point Delorme and Lescot basked in the sunshine of royal pleasure. François I (reigned 1515–1547), although he had initially hired Serlio and other Italians, did prefer French architects, and he tried his own hand at designing palaces. The extent of the king's authorship in each case is not known, but it is thought that he contributed to the design of four. The Château du Bois de Boulogne in Paris (later renamed Château de Madrid) was begun in

9. Brissac, *Châteaux*, pp. 67ff.

Project for a Royal Lodge

Center of main front, Project for a Royal Palace

PLATE 38

Courtyard, Project for Château Ancy-le-Franc (Yonne)

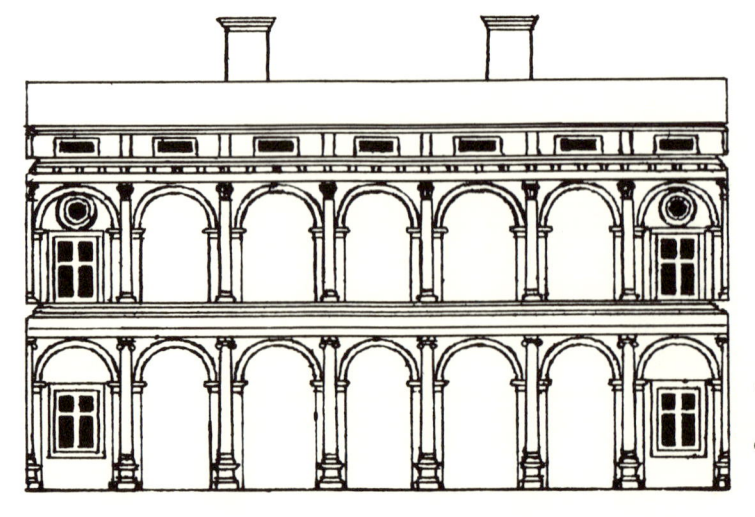

Courtyard, Project for Château Ancy-le-Franc (Yonne)

Courtyard, Château Ancy-le-Franc, near Auxerre (Yonne)

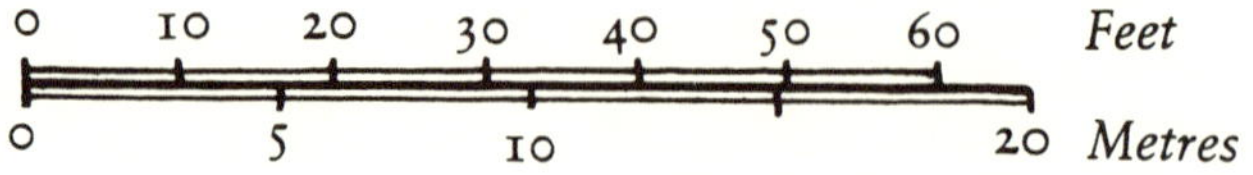

Approximate Scale

70

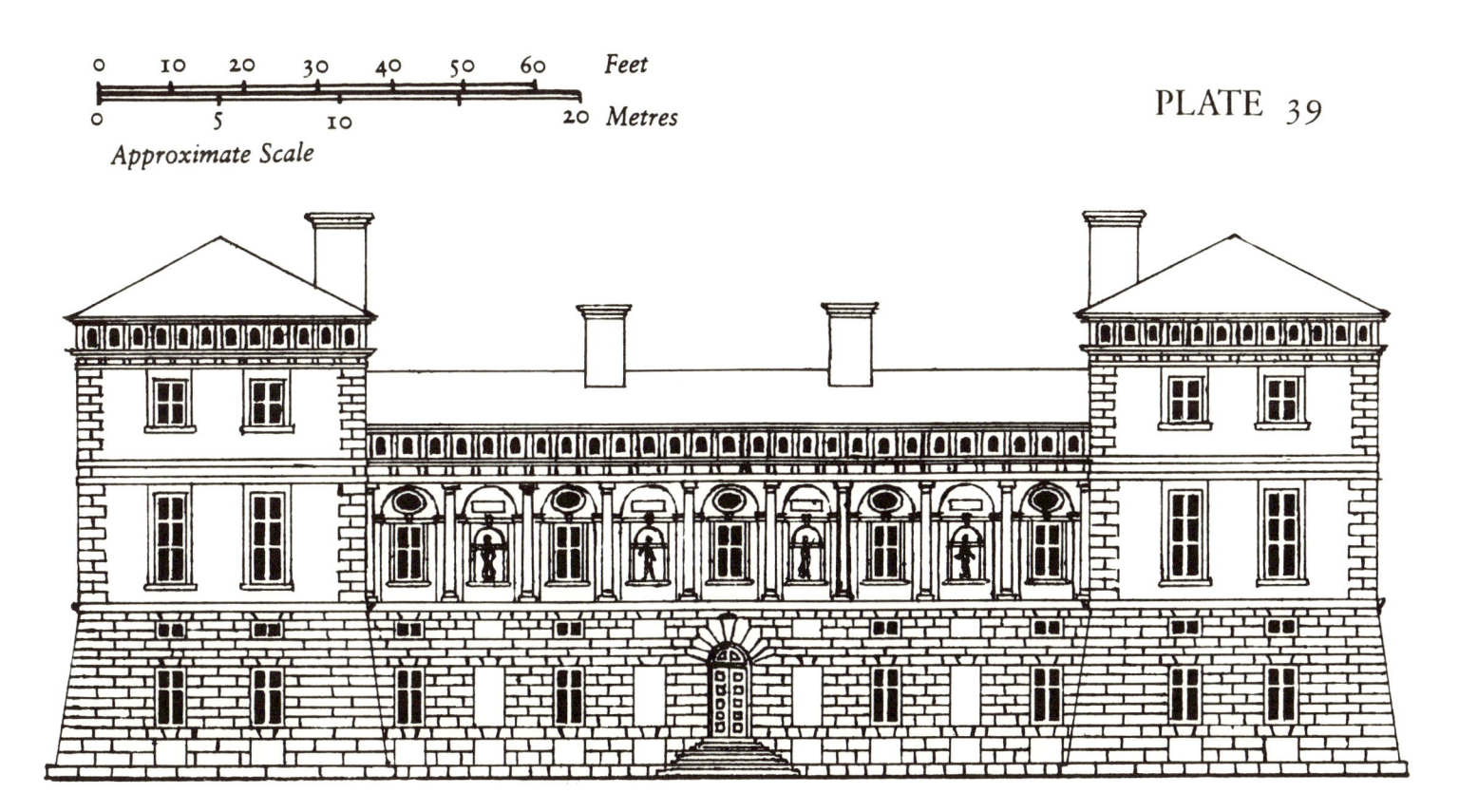

Project for Château Ancy-le-Franc (Yonne)

PLATE 39

Project for Château Ancy-le-Franc (Yonne)

front   Side
Château Ancy-le-Franc, near Auxerre (Yonne)

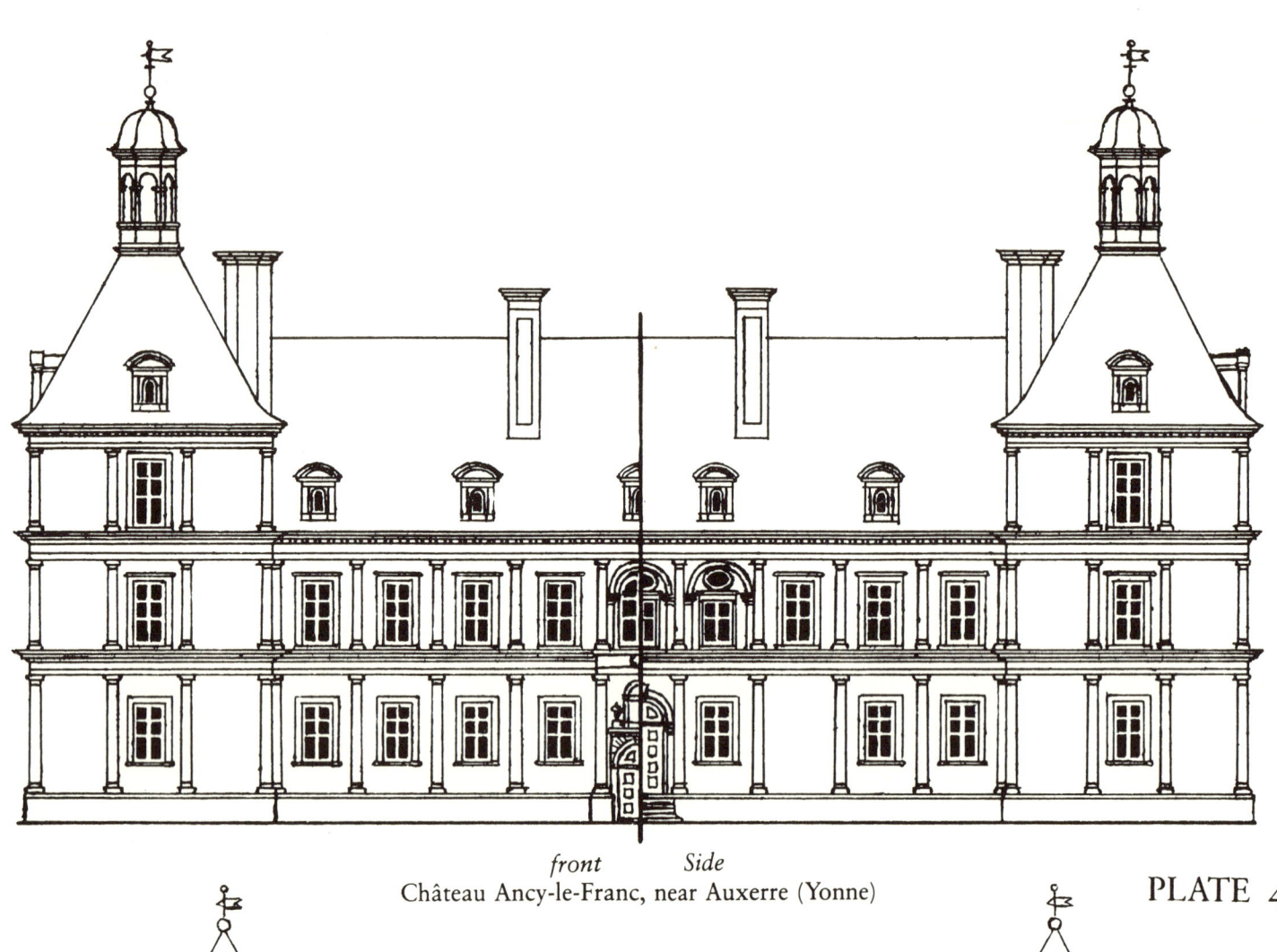

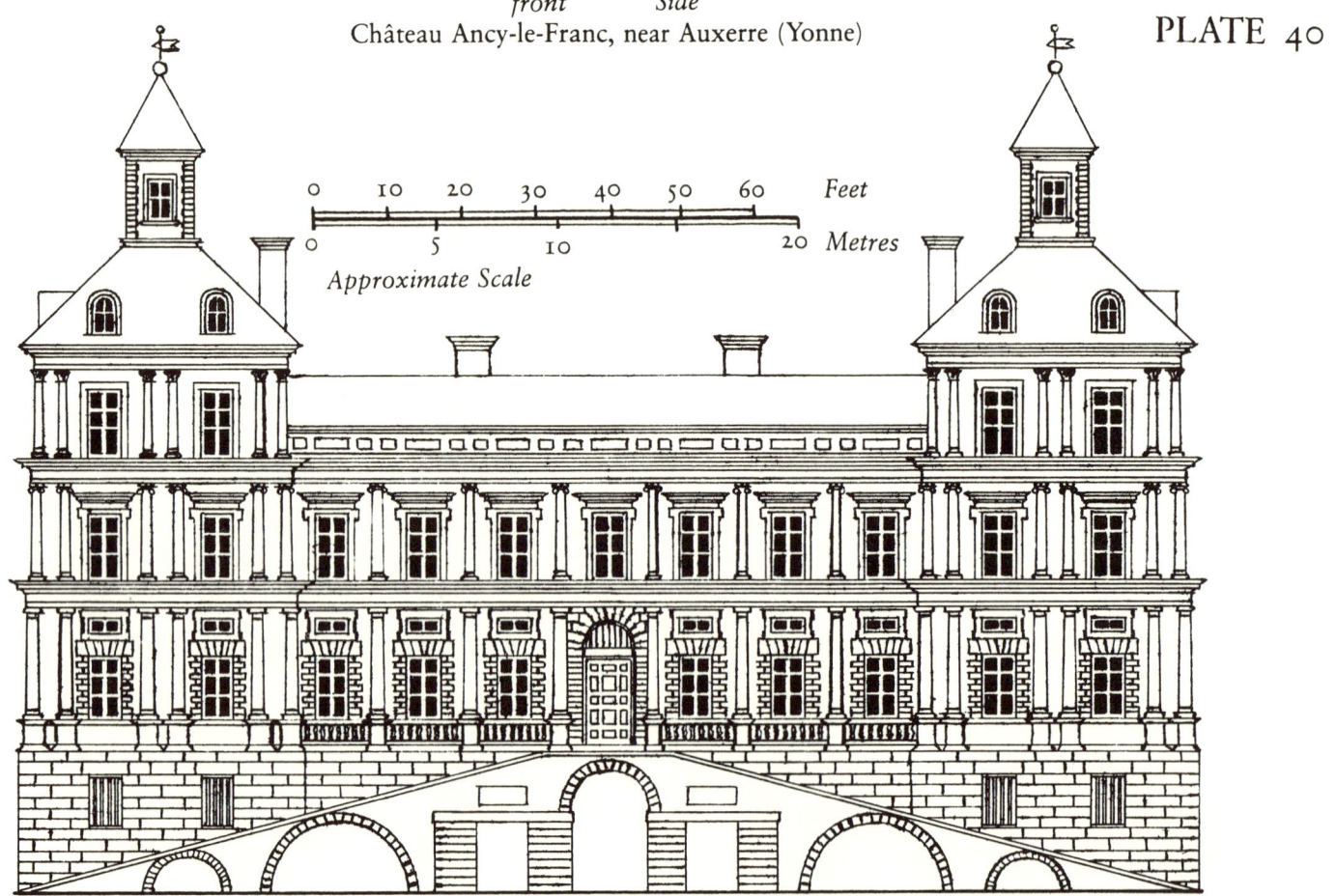

PLATE 40

Château Rosmarino

Forecourt Buildings, Château Maulnes-en-Tonnerois (Yonne)

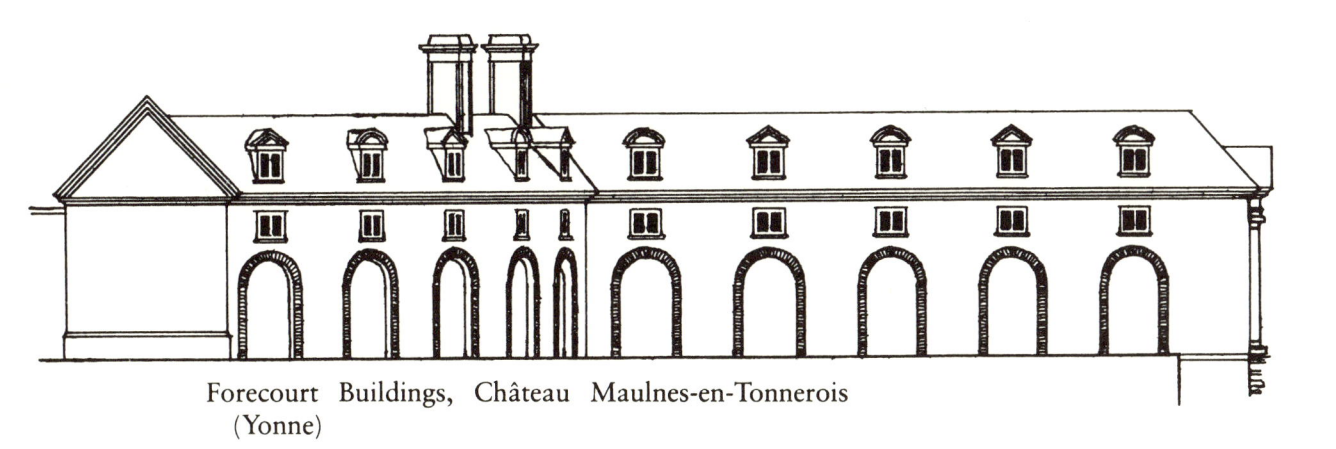

PLATE 41

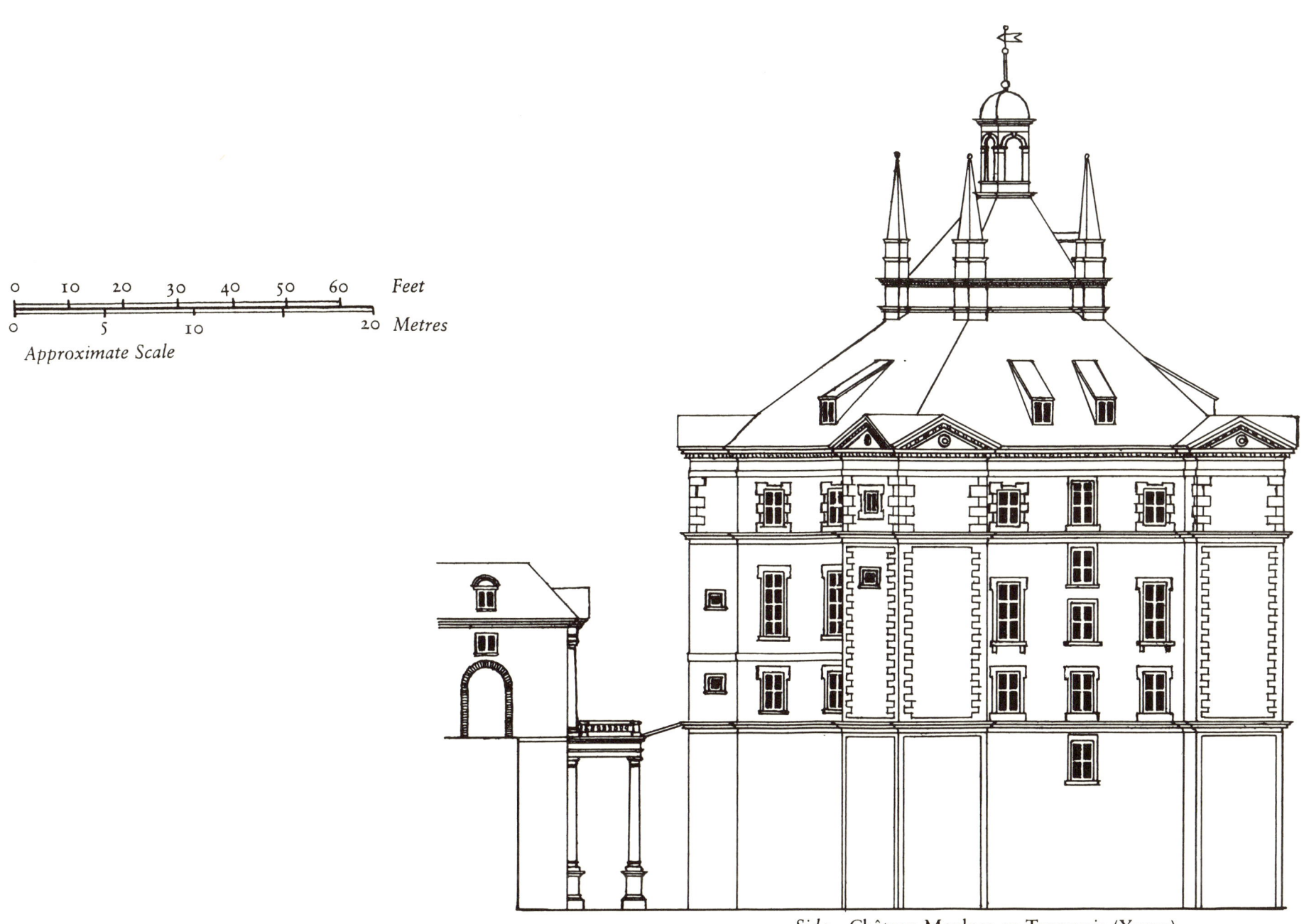

Side Château Maulnes-en-Tonnerois (Yonne)

Forecourt Buildings, Château Maulnes-en-Tonnerois (Yonne)

PLATE 42

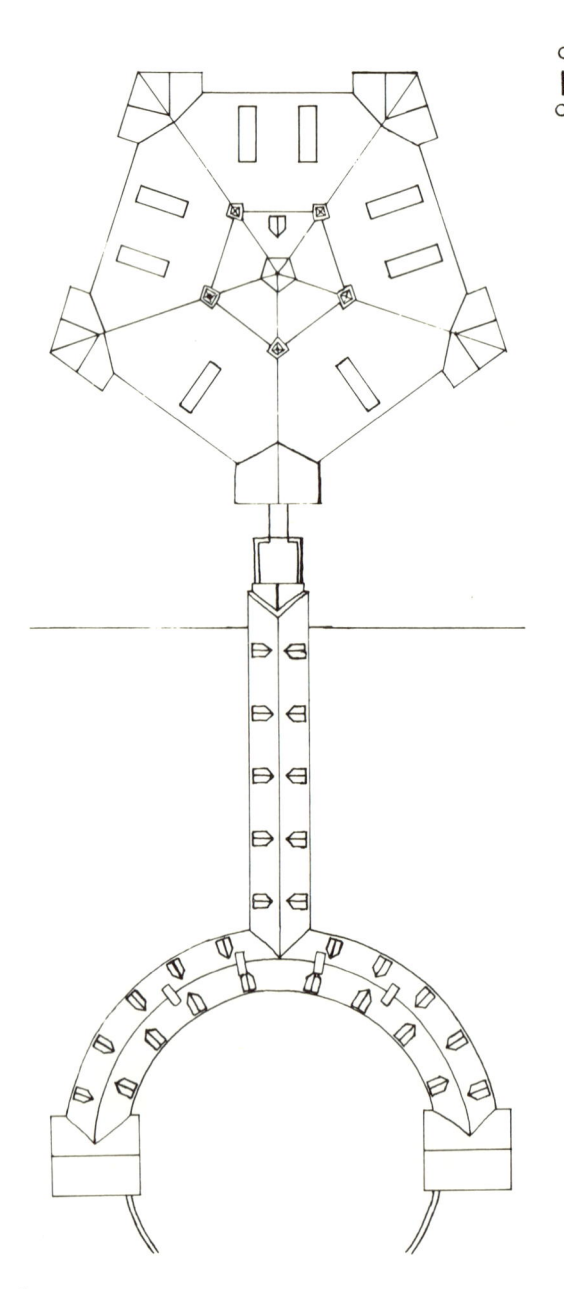

Plan, (drawn to 50% of regular scale)
Château Maulnes-en-Tonnerois (Yonne)

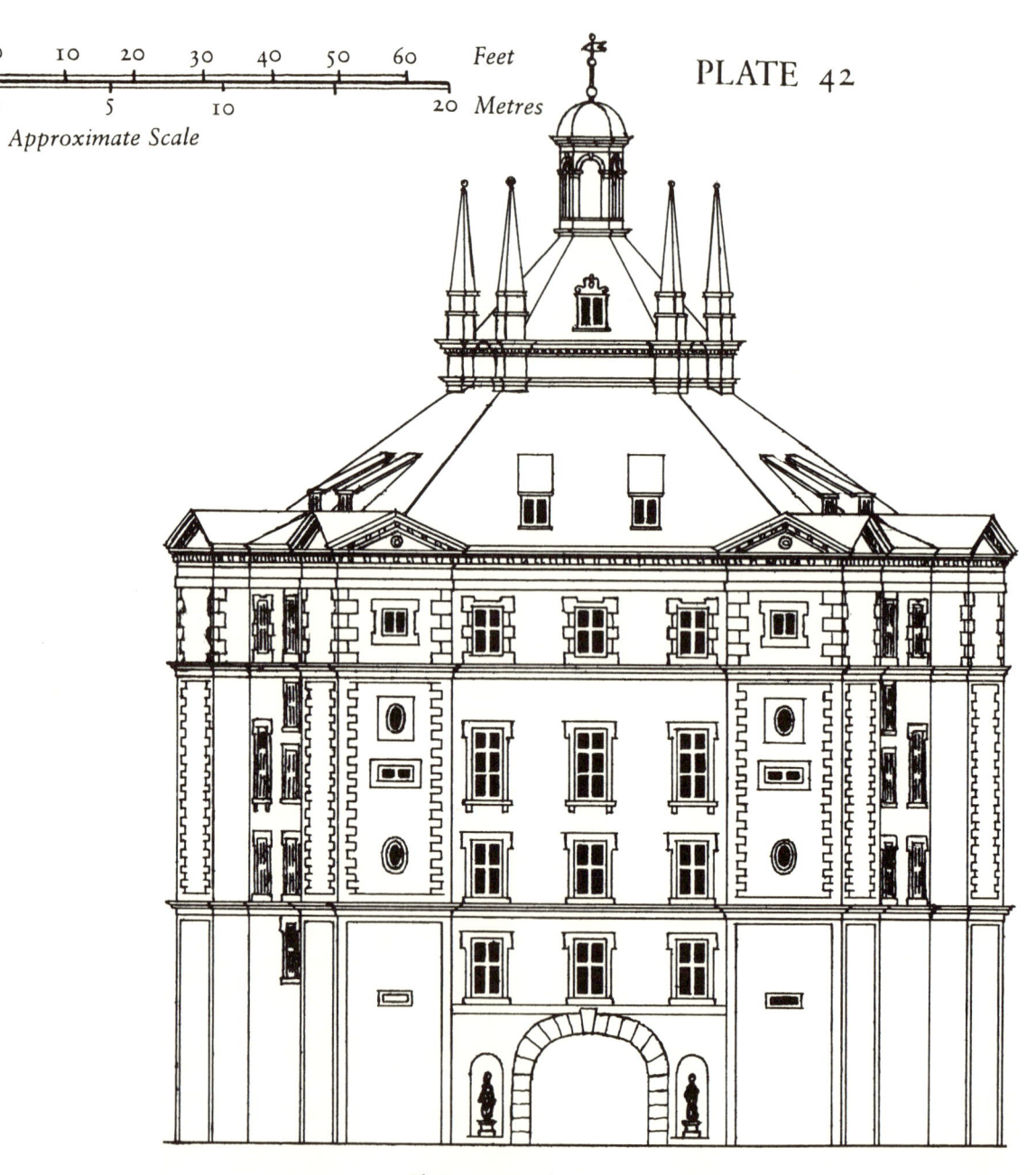

Château Maulnes-en-Tonnerois (Yonne)

1529 and not finished until 1570. Pierre Gadier, Gaten François and Girolamo della Robbia all worked on it, and like the other three it was a curious mixture of classical forms and a partial classical plan with French medieval forms. It was demolished 1792. The old Château of Saint-Germain-en-Laye, Paris, was rebuilt with some classical details 1539–1544 under Pierre Chambiges I, and it still stands. Chambiges was also in charge of the last two, the Château of la Muette, built in 1542 in the forest six miles north of Saint-Germain, and the Château of Saint-Ange at Challuau (Seine-et-Marne), built about the same time. The latter was demolished in the nineteenth century, while the former was so poorly constructed that it was already ruinous by 1650 and the site was cleared in 1789. None of these buildings is shown in this book, but they constitute an important component in the struggle for the direction of French renaissance architecture.

Hôtel de Ligneris/Carnavalet, Paris
PLATE 43

One of the last acts of François I before he died was to appoint the French architect Pierre Lescot to design parts of the Louvre Palace in Paris where Serlio's projects had never been executed. Lescot, in partnership with the sculptor Jean Goujon, had already begun to make a name for himself with his work at the Hôtel de Ligneris (since renamed Carnavalet) in Paris, begun about 1544. Much of the building echoes earlier forms, but a four-bay loggia of the Tuscan order shows clear understanding of classical forms, reminiscent of Bramante's cloister at Santa Maria della Pace in Rome.

Louvre, Paris PLATE 43

Lescot and Goujon worked on two parts of the Louvre from 1546 to 1556. These were the King's Pavilion, an awkward four-storey tower on a high basement (long since destroyed), and the southwest wing of the Square Courtyard. The latter was designed as a two-storey building with the ground floor partially comprised of an arcaded loggia, but it was completed as a three-storey building, as it stands today. The façade is articulated with Corinthian pilasters, well disposed for the large scale of the building. The upstairs windows have alternately triangular and segmental pediments. Segmental pediments also accent the three projecting portions of the front above the cornice. In 1549, Henri II ordered that the rest of the Louvre be designed by others.

Fountain of the Innocents, Paris PLATE 43

Lescot's finest achievement, however, must be the little Fountain of the Innocents, Paris, 1547. This has the appearance of a four-sided Roman triumphal arch on a pedestal, crowned by a dome. Each side has four fluted Corinthian pilasters. The fountain was unfortunately altered in the eighteenth century. Once again, Goujon was involved in the execution.

Château Vallery (Yonne) PLATE 43

Two works outside Paris in the 1550s are often attributed to Lescot, and they appear to be related to each other through their use of brickwork trimmed with rusticated stone. Vallery (Yonne) was begun for the military commander Jacques d'Albon de Saint-André. Both Lescot and Primaticcio are mentioned in contracts, so it is difficult to know who was responsible for what. The east wing contained a five-bay arcade in which each arch was surmounted by a little pediment to match the pediments over the ground-floor windows. The high roof was pierced by many larger dormers. In the eighteenth century, much of the château was demolished in order to sell the building-materials, and the remaining portions were badly altered so as to be unrecognisable.

Château Fleury-en-Bière (Seine et Marne)
PLATE 44

The Château of Fleury-en-Bière (Seine-et-Marne) is attributed to Lescot in collaboration with the mason Gilles LeBreton. This 15-bay building built for Cosme Clausse is large. Although it has been altered and enlarged over many centuries (for example, windows have been made taller) its original flavor remains remarkably intact. With its seventeenth-century farm courtyard, Fleury is well maintained by the Ganay family.

Château Joinville (Haut-Marne) PLATE 44

Domenico Fiorentino (Domenico the Florentine) was the architect and sculptor at the Château of Joinville (Haut-Marne) in 1546. This large, apparently single-storey building divides its seven-bay front with pairs of giant Corinthian pilasters. The steep, high roof once had seven elaborate dormers, but only three remain today. Towers that once stood at each end of the building have now vanished.

Unidentified Fountain & Loggia (Bourgogne) PLATE 44

A manuscript that once belonged to Palladio (but was not drawn by him) showed a fountain and a garden loggia built in Burgundy at an undisclosed location. The structures were apparently built by an Italian architect in the second quarter of the sixteenth century. The fountain was a simple square of four arches resting on Corinthian columns with a high hipped roof over the entablature. The loggia was similar, but with Tuscan columns and a low roof; it was seven bays wide.[10]

Château La Tour d'Aigues (Provence)
PLATE 44

Early in the second half of the sixteenth century, a large U-shaped château was built at Vaucluse in the south of France; because it had a prominent tower in the middle it was called the Château of La Tour d'Aigues. It is thought to have been designed by its owner, Jean Nicolas de Bouliers, Seigneur of Cental. Most of the building was of brick trimmed with rusticated stone in a style reminiscent of Fleury and Vallery. The château

10. Destailleur Codex, destroyed at Leningrad in World War II.

South West wing, Cour Carrée, Louvre, Paris

Pavillon du Roi, Louvre, Paris

PLATE 43

Fountain of the Innocents, Paris
(*not drawn to regular scale*)

Courtyard,
Hôtel de Ligneris/Carnavalet, Paris

Part of East wing, Château Vallery (Yonne)

Château Fleury-en-Bière (Seine et Marne)

PLATE 44

Entrance,
Château La Tour d'Aigues (Provence)

Château Joinville (Haut-Marne)

Unidentified Fountain & Loggia (Bourgogne)

Approximate Scale

77

burned down in 1782, but much of it remained standing for the next two centuries. Not enough information about it survives to show a complete reconstruction in this book, but the distinctive entrance portal combined features of Roman temples and triumphal arches, both of which still stand in the south of France, such as the temple at Nîmes and the arch at Orange.

Château Suze-la-Rousse (Drôme) PLATE 45

The elegant courtyard of the Château of Suze-la-Rousse (Drôme) is dated 1551, but the architect is unknown—perhaps in part due to the building's remote location in the south of France. The three-storey courtyard is seven bays long and three bays wide. The arches of the ground-floor loggia are separated by Tuscan piers, and the mullioned windows of the upper floors are separated by fluted Ionic pilasters and fluted Corinthian half-columns respectively. The arches of the arcade are slightly elliptical.

Hôtel d'Assézat, Toulouse PLATE 45

Little is known about the architect Nicolas Bachelier, who was born in Arras in northeastern France but worked principally in and around Toulouse in southwestern France. His most impressive design is the Hôtel d'Assézat, built in the early 1550s. It contains two different classical elevations in its courtyard. The main building has three storeys of arches (subsequently filled with windows) separated by pairs of columns in the typical order of Tuscan, Ionic and Corinthian. The arches of the top floor are narrower than the others, and are expressed as if they were part of Venetian windows. The other elevation is a four-bay loggia of arches separated by Tuscan half-columns, with an upper storey of arched windows dressed to look like miniature Venetian arches with alternately triangular and segmental pediments on top—a novel and attractive conception.

Château Écouen (Seine et Oise) PLATE 45

Jean Bullant II has been widely praised as one of France's greatest architects, but an examination of his known work shows that he was probably inferior to Bachelier and Philandrier, for example, who are probably less well known than Bullant because they worked so far from Paris in southwestern France. Because France was at war for so much of the second half of the sixteenth century, Bullant found more call for the two books he had written about architecture than he did for large buildings to be built; those were *Reigle Générale d'Architecture* (1563) and *Petit Traicté de Géometrie et d'Horologiegraphie* (1564). Bullant had studied in Rome, but his style of architecture was more mannerist fantasy than classical, for the most part. Bullant's best-known work is at the Château of Écouen (Seine et Oise) just north of Paris, where he was hired from 1556 on to add some classical details to the otherwise late-gothic château, some of whose early work was by the sculptor Jean Goujon for Anne de Montmorency. Bullant's work consisted mainly of the addition of about four vaguely classical focal-points for entrances. One of them (not shown here) seems to have been based on Delorme's entrance at Anet; this entrance was destroyed in 1787. The most famous of the entrances (on the south side of the courtyard) is framed by four giant fluted Corinthian columns for the purpose of displaying two statues of slaves by Michelangelo donated by Henri II, but the system is weakened by the actual entrance, which consists of a pair of relatively small arches derived from Delorme's project for a house that contains both the twin arches and the giant portico.

The outside entrance to the north wing is much taller than the others and also appears to be the best design of them all. It consists of an arcaded basement under a two-storey, three-bay portico articulated with Tuscan and Ionic pilasters, and containing large arches (now filled with glass, but once open). The upper central arch projects above the cornice into the pediment. The final entrance (on the north side of the courtyard) is a weak mannerist structure with Doric columns at its lower level and Corinthian columns on the upper level, crowned by an arrangement of linked dormers. Écouen now serves as the Museum of the Renaissance.

Pavilion, Tuileries Palace, Paris PLATE 45

Bullant's other building shown in this book was a pavilion in the Tuileries Palace substituted for a design by Delorme that for some reason remained unbuilt when much of the rest of Delorme's scheme was complete. The front was divided into two storeys of seven bays by Ionic and Corinthian half-columns, the even-numbered bays containing windows and the odd-numbered bays containing niches with statues. The same rhythm was repeated with genuine dormer windows and pedimented panels in front of the high roof; the addition of these panels spoiled the design by making it look unnecessarily busy, although a similar motif by Delorme succeeded due to its better proportions.

Valois Mausoleum, Saint-Denis PLATE 46

Francesco Primaticcio of Bologna is one of the better-known Italian workmen employed in France. He had initially been hired to execute parts of the interior decorations at Fontainebleau, having received his training in that field under Giulio Romano. In the last decade of his life he ventured into the field of architecture where he achieved some success. About 1559 he was hired to design a proper mausoleum for the Valois dynasty at Saint-Denis just outside Paris. A decade later, Lescot and Bullant were put in charge of its completion but without changing the design. Unfortunately, the building no longer stands, but it was once one of the most impressive buildings in France. The ground-floor was a circular drum trimmed with Doric columns surmounted by a slightly smaller drum of the Ionic order. The top storey was a much smaller drum decorated only by panels and crowned by a large dome with cupola atop. In some ways it was a larger and more complicated variation of the theme first expressed by Bramante at his Tempietto in Rome. It must have served as inspiration

Courtyard, Château Suze-la-Rousse (Drôme)

Pavilion, Tuileries Palace, Paris

PLATE 45

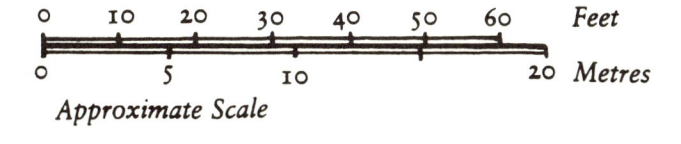

Part of courtyard,    *Part of courtyard,*

Hôtel d'Assézat, Toulouse

Approximate Scale

Courtyard entrance, South wing,   *Courtyard entrance, North wing,*   *Entrance, North wing,*

Château Écouen (Seine et Oise)

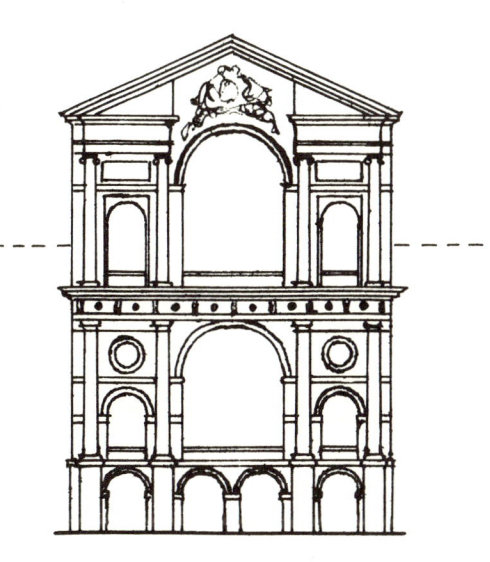

Plan, Valois Mausoleum, Saint-Denis

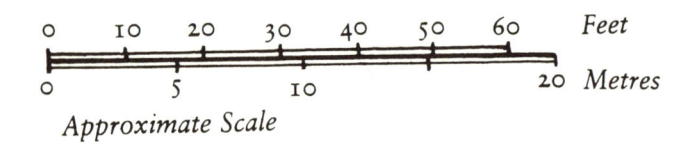

Valois Mausoleum, Saint-Denis

PLATE 46

Aile de la Belle Cheminée, Fontainebleau

for some of the seventeenth-century domes by Lemercier, Mansart and others. Its interior space was divided into a series of six side-chapels and the central rotunda.

Aile de la Belle Cheminée, Fontainebleau
PLATE 46

Primaticcio's last project was the so-called Aile de la Belle Cheminée (wing of the beautiful fireplace—the fireplace in question was actually a much later addition) at Fontainebleau, a successful marriage of classical forms with French spirit. The central feature of its rusticated ground floor is a screen formed by a pair of staircases ascending opposite each other. The piano nobile with its large windows is punctuated by a series of Tuscan pilasters. The high, hipped roof, which was once destroyed but now fortunately restored, is pierced by a handful of larger dormers with segmental pediments, but the central dormer is developed into a buttressed frontispiece to give the building focus.

Château Montceaux-en-Brie, near Meaux
PLATE 47

Primaticcio is normally credited with the Château of Montceaux-en-Brie near Meaux, built about 1565 for Queen Catherine de Medici. Delorme also worked briefly here, but his plans were not used. The central part of the large, complicated plan was a U-shaped courtyard of two storeys decorated with giant Tuscan pilasters. The windows of the lower floor were pedimented while the upper windows were plain. At the edge of the high roof stood dormers interspersed with pedimented panels, patterned after Delorme's work at the Tuileries. The central pavilion was crowned with a rectangular dome and cupola. Entry through the screen into the courtyard was gained through an enormous domed portal decorated with Corinthian engaged columns. Outside the central area, a series of four square, one-storey pavilions with ogival roofs stood near the angles of the rectangular moat. Montceaux was greatly expanded and modified beginning in 1609. After various periods of neglect, it was almost totally demolished in 1798 for its building materials, with only a few crumbling pieces still standing today.

Château Bournazel (Aveyron) PLATE 47

Guillaume Philandrier worked under Serlio for many years before settling to work on his own in Aveyron, southwestern France. There, he was hired about 1559 to add a two-storey loggia to the courtyard at the Château of Bournazel—a château that was already decorated in a crudely classical way by an earlier hand. Philandrier placed himself on secure ground by adapting Serlio's eventual design for the courtyard at Ancy in an original way. The loggia now lacks its roof and glazing, and stands open to the weather—which is, after all, the function of a loggia in warm climates.

Gable End, Cathedral, Rodez (Aveyron)
PLATE 47

About 1562, Philandrier was hired to do a most extraordinary piece of work: the gothic cathedral at Rodez lacked a gable-end above its rose window. Instead of completing the gable in the expected gothic, Philandrier perched a classical confection high atop the sheer walls so that it can scarcely be appreciated from the ground. His design, probably based on one of Serlio's drawings, foreshadows the famous Church of the Gesù in Rome, not built for another six years. It is of two storeys, the lower being wide and decorated with engaged Tuscan columns, and the upper narrow with pairs of Ionic columns; the two storeys are held together visually by a pair of volutes.

One of the most important figures in French architecture of the sixteenth century is Jacques Androuet Ducerceau I, the first of a large family of builders and architects. While he designed a great many buildings, some of which were built, his greatest contribution lay in drawing and recording in published books many of the buildings designed by his contemporaries that are otherwise lost to us; these are contained in the various volumes of *Les Plus Excellents Bastiments de France*, 1576–1579. He published many of his own (for the most part unexecuted) designs in his *Livre d'Architecture*; one of his projects in this book (volume II, 1582, plate xx) called for an elaborate cruciform château with an impressive two-storey circular courtyard. Another of his designs was for a small square château with circular towers at each corner, very similar to a design proposed a few years earlier by Alain Maynard to be built in England; were they so similar by coincidence, or was there some sort of close connection between Ducerceau and Maynard?

House project PLATE 48

A project in volume I, plate vii, is for a handsome U-shaped house that looks deceptively small. The central block was three bays wide, and the middle bay projected forward under a pediment. The piano nobile was considerably taller than the ground floor, almost to the point of exaggeration. The design would not have been out of place a century later.

Town-house project PLATE 48

Ducerceau produced a design for an enormous town-house in 1559, published as plate xxxviii in his first book. In the elevation shown in the present book, the street façade has been stripped away in order to reveal the more interesting courtyard view, whose five-part massing and separated high roofs is reminiscent of the earlier Cour du Cheval Blanc at Fontainebleau. The two-storey hyphens were substantially recessed behind the planes of the three-storey blocks.

Château Charleval PLATE 48

Like so many of the leading architects in France before him—and some of the not-so-leading architects—Ducerceau received a royal commission. In 1570, he began work on the Château of Charleval for François II. This was to have been immense, but the king died in 1574 before much of the work could be accomplished, and the project languished thereafter. The portion

One of 4 matching pavilions
Château Montceaux-en-Brie

Entrance, Château Montceaux-en-Brie, near Meaux

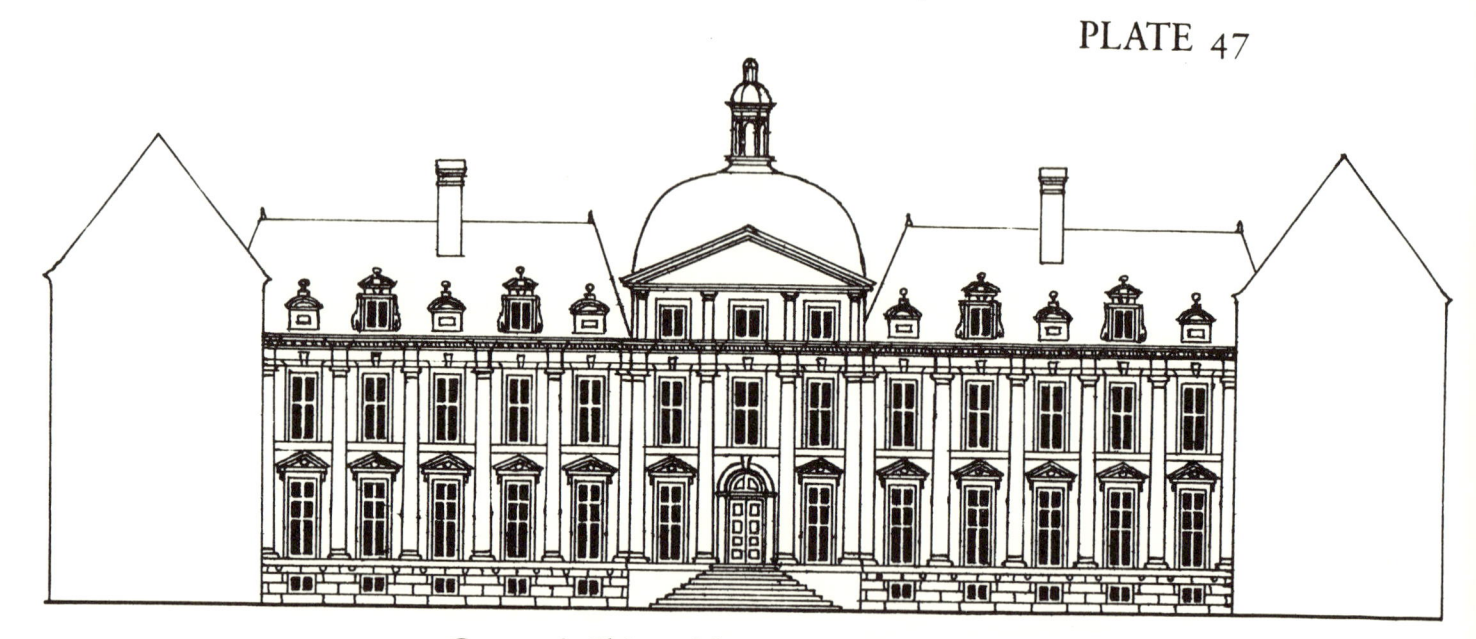

PLATE 47

Courtyard, Château Montceaux-en-Brie, near Meaux

Approximate Scale

East wing, Château Bournazel (Aveyron)

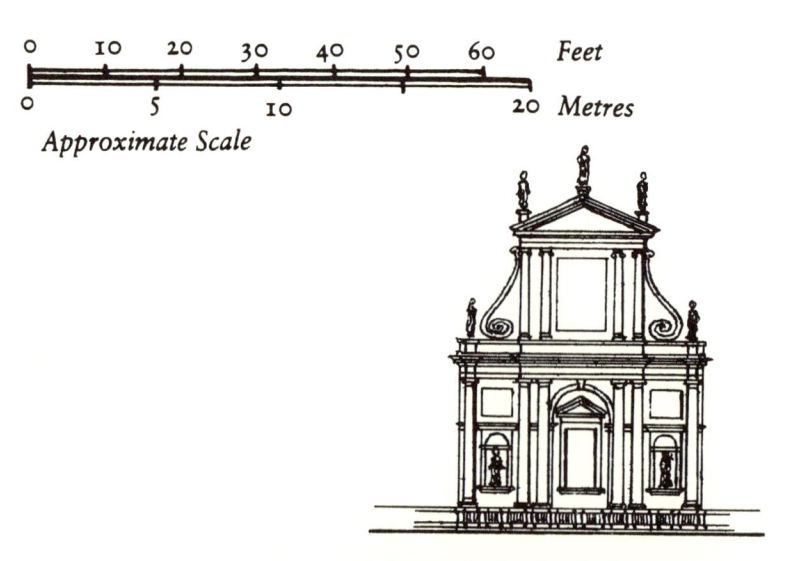

Gable End, Cathedral, Rodez (Aveyron)

House project

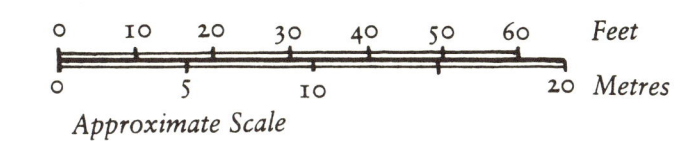

0 10 20 30 40 50 60 Feet
0 5 10 20 Metres
Approximate Scale

PLATE 48

Courtyard, Town-house project

Courtyard, Château Charleval

shown in this book was a two-and-a-half-storey wing decorated with fluted giant Doric pilasters. The ground floor was an arcaded loggia, and the piano nobile was probably intended to serve as a picture gallery or a ballroom. The central focus under a segmental pediment was composed of two bays, which produced a weaker result than could have been achieved with the more classical three bays. The general arrangement of this wing, perhaps by coincidence, closely resembles what was built at exactly the same time at Kirby in England.

Hôtel d'Angoulême/Lamoignon, Paris PLATE 50

Baptiste Androuet Ducerceau, one of Jacques' sons, worked with his father on various projects. One building he designed alone was the Hôtel d'Angoulême, or, as it later became, the Hôtel Lamoignon in Paris, 1584, for Henri II's daughter Diane. Early in the seventeenth century it was enlarged by the addition of wings and a row of ungainly dormers that preposterously cut large chunks out of the entablature. This house was one of the first in Paris to make use of giant order pilasters, and was thus influential.

Château Verneil (Oise) PLATE 49

Another founder of a family of architects was Jean Brosse, father of the more famous Salomon de Brosse, and husband of Jacques Ducerceau's daughter. His most celebrated building was the large Château of Verneuil (Oise), begun for Philippe de Boulainvilliers about 1565 by Ducerceau. Before much work could be done, the owner died, and the new owner, the Duc de Nemours, found that Jean Brosse had taken his father-in-law's place. Brosse's first design, which no doubt owed something to Ducerceau, called for a courtyard 35 metres square with staggered double pavilions at each corner, each two and a half storeys high, and a single-storey entrance screen decorated with pairs of engaged Corinthian columns. The duke requested major revisions. The resulting design had single, three-storey pavilions at the corners under square domes, and the entrance screen lost its columns (replaced with rusticated pilasters) and gained an unusually high domed portal decorated with giant fluted Corinthian pilasters. Verneuil, which was demolished in 1734, was not regarded as in the first rank itself, but it was a great influence on architecture of the next century.

Inside its courtyard was a two-storey wing whose lower storey was an arcaded loggia decorated with pairs of Tuscan pilasters, while the upper storey was probably a picture gallery with a flat, balustraded roof. Between the windows were piers, each containing a niche with a statue inside.

Château Uzès (Gard)

The same family that apparently had Serlio design the Château of Maulnes just before his death, commissioned an anonymous lesser architect to design a courtyard façade for the Ducal Palace or Château of Uzès (Gard) in the south of France, about 1570. Some writers have suggested Delorme as the architect, but the design is much too mechanical and lifeless for his style. Each of the three storeys is decorated with the orders, Doric, Ionic and Corinthian respectively. The ground floor has some rustication, and the windows and panels of the upper floors are crowned with triangular and segmental pediments in a crowded arrangement.

House at Saint Valentine's Day Massacre, Paris PLATE 50

In an engraving of Paris during the infamous Saint Bartholomew's Day Massacre (1572), an unusual square building is shown only one bay on a side but three and a half storeys in height (with a victim draped over a window-sill). The building has not been identified, but since it is decorated with pairs of Ionic pilasters on each storey it is shown in this book as an example of how even a small building could display classical forms in renaissance France. None of the other buildings in the picture is in the least bit classical.

Tour de Cordouan (Lighthouse), near Bordeaux PLATE

Finally, one of the most extraordinary classical buildings of renaissance France: the Cordouan Lighthouse, near Bordeaux. This was designed by Louis de Foix in 1583 to mark the mouth of the River Gironde. Construction was not completed until 1610, some four years after the architect's death, but since de Foix had presented a wooden model of the lighthouse to his patrons in 1584 it is reasonable to assume that the building was finished largely in accord with his plans. The lighthouse was built on a tiny island that was under water many hours each day, and it replaced an earlier, smaller tower built by the English Black Prince in the fourteenth century. The lower half of the new tower consisted of a tall drum decorated with Corinthian pilasters on top of a wider but shorter drum decorated with Doric pilasters and columns—decoration not really needed, since the island was far from land and yet could not readily be approached by ships because of treacherous sandbars in all directions. Above the upper drum was a conical roof with eight dormers. The upper half of the structure was a steeple formed out of two levels of octagonal cupolas and a spire with a royal crown on top. Except for a projecting balustrade at the cornice level of the lower cupola, this steeple design would have been entirely acceptable at any date during the next two centuries or so; the steeple of the London church of Saint Leonard's Shoreditch (by George Dance, 1736–1740), for example, is similar. In 1788, in spite of the prodigious height of the lighthouse, mariners insisted that it be made higher, so it was radically rebuilt at that time, and the original work was obliterated.[11] Louis de Foix must have been highly regarded, for he was invited in 1561 to submit plans for building the Raadhuis at Antwerp.

11. M. Saint-Jours, *Cordouan*, Bordeaux, ca. 1900.

Also useful are Anthony Blunt, *Art and Architecture in France 1500–1700*, Harmondsworth, Penguin Books, 1953 (rev. 1970), and Ernest de Ganay, *Châteaux de France*, Paris, Éditions Tel, many volumes, 1948ff; Louis Dimier, *Le Primatice*, Paris, 1928; Reginald Blomfield, *A History of French Architecture from the reign of Charles VIII till the death of Mazarin, 1494–1661*, 2 vols., London, 1911.

Project for Entrance

Entrance, Château Verneil (Oise)

Approximate Scale

PLATE 49

Courtyard, Château Verneil (Oise)

85

Courtyard, Château Uzès (Gard)

House at Saint Valentine's Day Massacre, Paris

PLATE 50

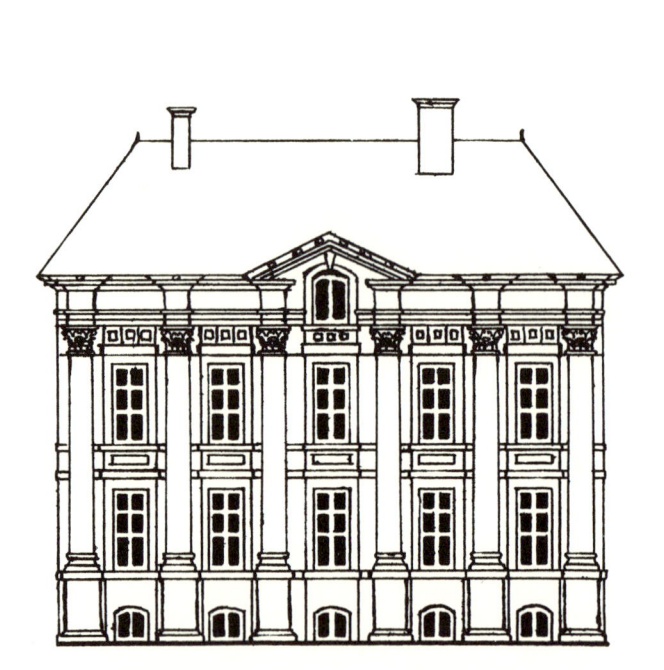

Hôtel d'Angoulême/Lamoignon, Paris

Tour de Cordouan (Lighthouse), near Bordeaux

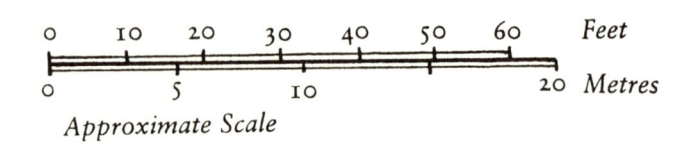

Approximate Scale

THE GERMANIC COUNTRIES

For reasons of convenience, the designs of Austria, Switzerland, the Federal Republic of Germany, the Democratic Republic of Germany, the Netherlands, Belgium and Denmark are treated together here in this chapter, even though the architecture of the more southern areas often has little connection with that of the northern areas. In fact, it could be argued that the buildings in Austria are more closely related to those of Czechoslovakia than to designs found in any other Germanic country.

The Italian word for Germans is Tedeschi, a cognate word of Deutsche and Dutch. The first known Germanic connection with classical architecture occurred in Venice in 1505, where a German architect named Hieronymus (or Gerolamo in Italian) designed a palace for the German merchants trading there, known as the Fondaco dei Tedeschi. It looks no different than if a local Venetian architect had been responsible for it (see Plate 18).

The Fuggerkapelle, Saint Anna's Church, Augsburg PLATE 51

Four years later, the classical influence trickled over the Alps to Augsburg along with the flow of money and trade in the hands of the wealthy Fuggers. A Fugger Chapel was built in 1509 onto the side of the church of Saint Anna. The severe exterior belies the rich interior. The high gable is trimmed in about 50 small crow-steps and sits above a large round window. The principal interior space is square, not unlike some contemporary Italian chapels but with a pair of irregular aisles on the sides that are treated as if they are irrelevant; their main function, it would seem, is to display the large arches connecting them, designed in an early Florentine renaissance style. A gallery is supported on a series of four small arches, and in 1518 most of the space above the gallery was filled, as now, with the case and painted wings of an organ. The architect of this building is said to be Sebastian Loscher, who seems also to have been at home with gothic architecture, for the shallow dome of the ceiling is decorated with gothic tracery, a poor match for the classical splendor below.

Damenhof, Maximilianstrasse 36, Augsburg PLATE 51

Loscher, who may have been retained by the Fuggers to build many new buildings for them in the Italian style, is believed to have been responsible for the courtyard of the Damenhof at 36 Maximilianstrasse, Augsburg, 1509. As originally built, the courtyard, which had to fit into a pre-existing irregular space, had a simple, Florentine-style arcaded loggia on the ground floor with a series of rectangular windows on the floor above, surrounded with a sea of *sgraffito* work that has since disappeared. Above the cornice was a balustrade. Many of this house's neighbors may well have had such courtyards, but little trace remains of them today.[1]

Saint Katherine's Church, Augsburg
PLATE 51

A third building attributed to Loscher was Saint Katherine's Church, Augsburg, built in 1516, but now somewhat altered. The nave of the church is unusual in that it is divided longitudinally into two by a row of attenuated Corinthian columns supporting the semicircular longitudinal and transverse arches of the ceiling; these arches have ribs on the diagonals of the vaults that are reminiscent of gothic vaults. The building looks less gothic now than it did originally, because the floor has been raised so as to hide the high bases on which the columns and half-columns stand, and so that the proportions of the room are less perpendicular. The building is now a museum.

Project for Saint Sebald's Shrine, Nürnberg PLATE 51

Loscher is known to have worked also in Nürnberg, where he designed and perhaps executed a Florentine side-altar at Saint Rochus' Church. This may have brought him in contact with another early German classical architect, Hermann Visscher II (also sometimes spelled with only one s). At least two of Visscher's designs survive, but neither was executed. One is for the Shrine of Saint Sebald proposed to be built in Nürnberg in 1516. The design, part of which resembles a Roman tetrastyle temple-front without a pediment (using giant fluted Corinthian columns), gives little indication of the intended scale. The shrine could have been intended to be the size of a small altar with reredos, until one notices the pairs of round-headed windows hidden in the base. If the windows are made to be any normal size, the shrine assumes heroic proportions, and would have been one of the first uses of the giant order outside Italy. In the event, the design was rejected in favor of a gothic plan by Visscher's father.

Palace Project PLATE 51

In the same year, Visscher sketched a project for a courtyard façade of a palace. The lower storey consisted of a Corinthian colonnade, behind which stood two large doorways. The upper floor repeated the Corinthian motif at a smaller scale with pilasters framing arched windows grouped in threes. Serlio could easily have produced such a design three decades later in Paris. At the time that he produced these two designs, Visscher had just returned from a visit to Italy, where he had drawn detailed sketches of ancient Roman buildings and recent works by Bramante and Raffaello (now at the Louvre). Visscher showed great promise, but unfortunately died only a year after drawing the two designs shown here.

Savoie Palace, Mechelin/Malines, Belgium PLATE 51

The earliest moment that any elements of the classical style appeared in northern Germanic countries was in the early 1520s, when Rombout Keldermans II and

1. Norbert Lieb, *Die Fugger und die Kunst,* Munich, Verlag Schnell & Steiner, 1952.

Ceiling plan,
The Fuggerkapelle,
Saint Anna's Church, Augsburg

Courtyard, looking north,
Damenhof, Maximilianstrasse 36, Augsburg

Project for Saint Sebald's Shrine, Nürnberg

Section looking west,
The Fuggerkapelle,
Saint Anna's Church, Augsburg

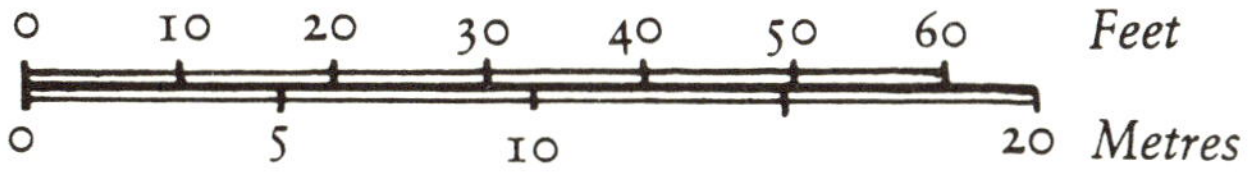

Courtyard, Palace Project

PLATE 51

Section of the Nave,
Saint Katherine's Church, Augsburg

Part of Savoie Palace,
Mechelin/Malines, Belgium

Section looking west,
Chapel, Schloss
Neuburg-on-the-Danube

Guyot de Beaugrant built parts of the Savoie Palace at Mechelin/Malines, Belgium. Work began in 1517 on what was a typical building of its day with such classical details as pediments added over windows, some of which were arranged symmetrically. An end elevation, shown here, offers considerable promise, not delivered by the rest of the building. The elevation, like so many Flemish buildings, is tall and narrow, but it is symmetrical. Two of the central windows are capped with pediments, and the upper of the two, with a balcony at its base, is an arched window flanked by a pair of narrow, rectangular windows, strongly suggesting a Venetian arch.

Chapel, Schloss Neuburg-on-the-Danube PLATE 51

Not far from Augsburg is Schloss Neuburg on the Danube, a castle built largely by Hans Knotz from Nürnberg. The castle has some interesting gables trimmed with scrolls and volutes, a poorly-executed two-storey entrance, and a courtyard with multi-storey arcaded loggia; the latter lacks symmetry and its arches are some semicircular, some elliptical and others merely flattened. Work began about 1530 and continued after Knotz left in 1538. The patron, Prince Ottheinrich, was a Lutheran, and he had Knotz incorporate a Lutheran chapel into the castle. The chapel was squeezed into an irregularly-shaped space, but Knotz cleverly gave it a shallow vaulted ceiling with intersecting side vaults that helps to make the room look symmetrical. A gallery around the sides is supported on heavy brackets, but across the end the gallery stands on three arches with Corinthian columns. The chapel was designed in 1538.[2]

Salmon House, Mechelin/Malines, Belgium PLATE 52

Because of patterns of urban land-ownership, buildings in Belgium and the Netherlands tended to be tall and narrow as they huddled close together. Because they had no windows or light from the sides they had to have larger window areas in the front, a tradition that was later transferred to such large English country houses as Longleat and Hardwick. No such tradition existed in Italy, so Italian architects working in Belgium had to invent ways of reconciling the classical language to the local requirements. The first example of this is a house called De Zalm (the Salmon) at Zontwerf 5 on the bank of the Dijle River at Mechelin/Malines, Belgium. It is thought to have been built by Tommaso Vincidor from Bologna about 1533, but the gable as shown here is a much later alteration. The three principal storeys of the four-bay house are articulated with half-columns of Tuscan, Ionic and Corinthian orders, the lower two storeys also having blind arches above the windows.

Kasteel, Breda, the Netherlands PLATE 52

Vincidor's major work in the north is the Kasteel at Breda, the Netherlands, from 1536 onwards, and now altered. Notable features of the exterior were the triumphal entry arch with its over-high pediment, and the southwest end with its elaborate gable, both by Vincidor's associate, Pasqualini. Inside the courtyard a 14-bay arcaded loggia supports two storeys of windows with pilasters between them; the Ionic half-columns of the lower floor stand under flying entablatures, to which are attached, rather incongruously, a pair of volutes each. Above the upper windows, which were arched, there once stood a row of curious scrolled gables. The windows of the lower storey were once pedimented. It is typical of designers from Bologna that the elevation should be so cluttered with extraneous details, rather than relying on pure classical forms. The castle is now part of the Koniglijk Military Academy.

Griffie, Brugge/Bruges, Belgium PLATE 52

Italians had no monopoly on the new forms in the north. Jan Wallot designed the three-part, five-bay front of the Griffie or Hall of Records at Brugge/Bruges, Belgium about 1534, which was executed by Christian Sixdeniers by 1537. The two main storeys are well lit by large windows, between which stand Tuscan half-columns. At the roof level, a pair of low scrolled gables flank the central high gable, which is trimmed with volutes and a pair of twisted columns framing a window. Minus the gables, the influence of this building on later English architecture seems to be pronounced.

Church Tower, Ijsselstein, the Netherlands PLATE 52

Alessandro Pasqualini of Bologna worked briefly with Vincidor at Breda.[3] He also designed the church bell-tower at Ijsselstein, the Netherlands about 1535. This is a three-story, three-bay structure in brick, decorated with white stone pilasters in the Doric, Ionic and Corinthian orders respectively, with niches in each of the upper bays. The contrast between the white trim and the red brick is a felicitous device frequently seen in the Netherlands, Britain and America in the seventeenth and eighteenth centuries, but this tower must be one of the earliest examples of the technique. Perhaps by sheer coincidence, this tower bears a remarkable resemblance to the bell-tower of the convent church of Santa Maria della Quercia at Viterbo by Ambrogio Barocci di Marco da Milano, 1481–3. Atop the Dutch tower is an octagonal belfry flanked by four pinnacles and capped with a spire, but now altered.

Kasteel, Buren, the Netherlands PLATE 52

About 1540, Pasqualini was employed by Floris van Egmond to do work on his Kasteel at Buren in Gelderland, the Netherlands in the late 1530s to 1545. The castle has long since disappeared, but an eighteenth-century painting of it shows a pedimented gable of the type that Serlio designed for churches, with a volute on each side. Henry-Russell Hitchcock has noticed that the octagonal lantern of the church at Buren appears to be related to the design of the Ijsselstein steeple, so Pasqualini may have worked at pieces of many buildings in the Buren area.

2. Henry-Russell Hitchcock, *German Renaissance Architecture,* Princeton, Princeton University Press, 1981, pp. 66–71.

3. Henry-Russell Hitchcock, *Netherlandish Scrolled Gables of the Sixteenth and Early Seventeenth Centuries,* New York, New York University Press, 1978, pp. 29–31.

Salmon House, Mechelin/Malines, Belgium

Courtyard, Kasteel, Breda, the Netherlands

Part of Kasteel, Breda, the Netherlands

Griffie, Brugge/Bruges, Belgium

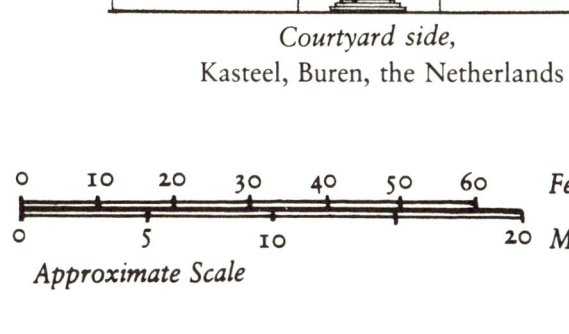

Courtyard side, Kasteel, Buren, the Netherlands

PLATE 52

Courtyard, Schloss Bedburg, Rhineland

Church Tower, Ijsselstein, the Netherlands

Approximate Scale

North entrance, Zitadelle, Jülich

East elevation, Chapel, Zitadelle, Jülich

91

Zitadelle, Jülich PLATE 52

Pasqualini's major work was across the border in Germany, the Zitadelle at Jülich in 1552 for Duke Wilhelm V of Cleve & Gelderland. What little that remains of this impressive structure is in ruins. It was built around a square courtyard that contained a loggia whose design is now lost. The exterior was heavily rusticated, presumably in an attempt to convey the idea of great strength to any potential adversary, and is reminiscent of early work by Delorme in France. Particularly notable was the Lutheran chapel, whose east end projects through the castle wall and has a two-storey apse trimmed with Ionic pilasters above and rusticated Tuscan pilasters below. The present pediment (shown here) is an eighteenth-century replacement for a wider original.

Schloss Bedburg, Rhineland PLATE 52

Henry-Russell Hitchcock, who has made a study of Pasqualini, believes that Pasqualini may have worked at another German castle, Schloss Bedburg in the Rhineland, built at about the same time as the castle at Jülich. There, the castle itself is probably the work of others, but a three-bay, two-storey arcaded loggia between two wings—in spite of ugly modern alterations to it—looks more like Pasqualini's style.

Stadtresidenz, Landshut PLATE 53

Pasqualini's equivalents in southern Germany were a family of builders from Mantua, known as Sigismondo, Antonio and Bernardo Mantovani. They were hired to build the Residenz at Landshut from 1536 onwards for the dukes of Wittelsbach. If Pasqualini and Vincidor were forced to compromise their designs with the traditions and needs of northern Germany, the Stadtresidenz was a purely Italian design in the mould of Giulio Romano, even to the characteristic Italian chimneys. The west or rear façade has heavy rustication on the ground floor, including large keystones over the door and six windows. The windows of the next storey are alternately covered with triangular and segmental pediments, and the storey above that has blank panels, corresponding to a vaulted ceiling inside; giant Tuscan pilasters stand between the bays, some of them in pairs. Windows of an attic storey peer out from the frieze of the entablature.

At the west end of the courtyard stands a five-bay arcaded loggia with rusticated voussoirs, the central arch being slightly larger than the others. Above them is a row of pedimented windows with another storey of low, rectangular windows above, giving light to a passage in front of the great room with the vaulted ceiling; the cornice line is lower on the courtyard side than on the exterior. The loggia and similar window treatment extend around other sides of the courtyard. The building is built largely out of brick covered in stucco, probably the first use of this combination on a large scale in Germany. The interior is lavishly decorated in the Giulio Romano taste with frescos and panelled ceilings, especially the vaulted "Italian" room and the "Venus" room.

Schloss Salamanca/Porcia, Spittal-an-der-Drau, Austria PLATE 53

Archduke Ferdinand of Austria had a Spanish chancellor, Gabriel de Salamanca, also called von Ortenberg, who married an Austrian in 1533. Salamanca then hired an anonymous Italian from the Lake Como region to design him a castle at Spittal. The exterior of Schloss Salamanca contains a few classical details, but the elevation can not be called classical by any means. However, the central courtyard has a three-storey arcaded loggia on all four sides, three bays on the short sides and five on the long sides. Its columns are stunted, but otherwise the design is Lombardian classical. On one side, the loggias are bent downwards in a grand staircase, somewhat reminiscent of the stairs at Breda that were destroyed in the nineteenth century. It is likely that the courtyard is the work of a different architect from the exterior, especially since it was still being built in 1551, twelve years after the death of Salamanca. The castle is also known by the name of a later owner, Porcia.

Raadhuis, Utrecht, the Netherlands PLATE 53

It has been fashionable to criticize the proportions of Willem van Noort's design for the Town Hall or Raadhuis at Utrecht, the Netherlands, begun 1546, but he made a valiant attempt to impose the classical orders to the outside of three existing buildings that were being combined into the Raadhuis, and he was therefore obliged to stay within the bounds of the existing heights between floors. In the event, although he coped well with the design problems, only the right-hand end was allowed to be completed, and even that was swept away in 1828 when all three buildings were covered by a new face. The drawing shown here presents the left-hand end as a mirror-image of the right end, but leaves the center almost blank, as Van Noort's plan for that has been lost. The ground floor had an arcaded loggia with Doric pilasters standing in front of the arches. On the floors above, Ionic and Corinthian pilasters were used to frame pedimented windows. A single elaborate dormer stood on the roof in front of a steeple. Van Noort's design for a handsome arched doorway was used for the middle part, but no further work was done after that. Van Noort's design was entirely for stone with no brickwork.

Reviewing Stand, Antwerp, Belgium
Triumphal Arch, Antwerp, Belgium PLATE 53

The Emperor Charles V, who was also King of Spain, made a triumphal visit to his Netherlands dominions in 1549 with his son, later Philip II. At this point, in spite of the prodigious growth of Calvinism in the Low Countries, relations between the emperor and his northern subjects were for the most part cordial, so great

West elevation, Stadtresidenz, Landshut

Courtyard side, Stadtresidenz, Landshut

Triumphal Arch, Antwerp, Belgium

PLATE 53

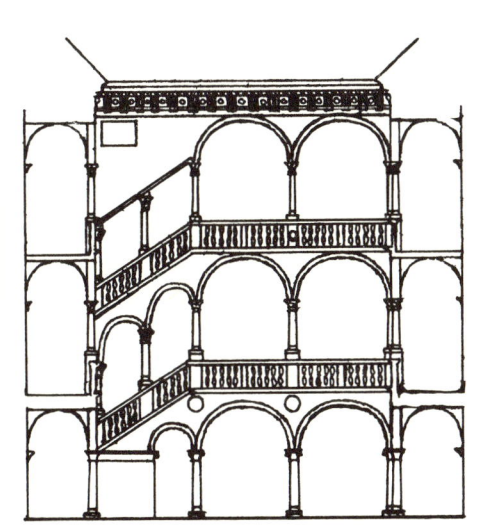

North elevation *East elevation*
Courtyard, Schloss Salamanca/Porcia, Spittal-an-der-Drau, Austria

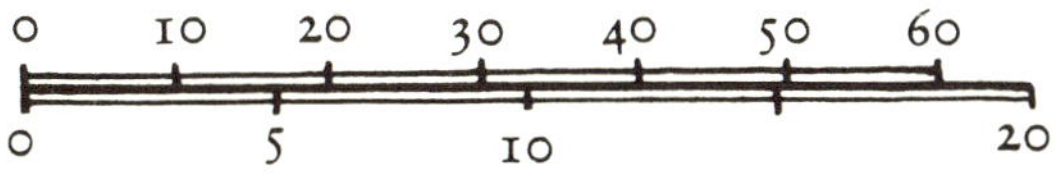

Approximate Scale

Reviewing Stand, Antwerp, Belgium

Raadhuis, Utrecht, the Netherlands

efforts were made to welcome the emperor at the cities he visited. Antwerp put on the greatest show, with a number of triumphal arches and a reviewing stand. Thanks to Pieter Coecke, who published the designs for these structures, we know how they looked, but no record exists of who designed them; perhaps they were the result of a committee including Coecke, the sculptor Cornelis Floris de Vriendt II, Sebastian van Noyen, Hans Hendrik van Paesschen and Hans Vredeman de Fries and others. Some of the designs were distinctly mannerist, but the two shown here demonstrated sophistication. One was a simple rusticated structure with two arches, presumably one for entering and the other for leaving the city. The other was a covered stand for reviewing a parade, which looked like a Roman portal with Corinthian half-columns and pilasters and three blind arches. Shown only in outline here is the mannerist collection of sculpture that perched awkwardly on top of the structure.

Cornelis Floris had spent time studying in Italy, as had many other northern artists at one time or another. He was also highly regarded in Antwerp as an advisor on the arts. Probably as a result of this, recent commentators have tended to attribute the designs of many buildings to Floris (such as the Antwerp Raadhuis and the Hanseatenhuis) that were quite beyond his capabilities. As a sculptor, Floris was as good as anyone in northern Europe, and as a result he was given commissions for sculpture in many parts of the North Sea and Baltic regions, but his few documented architectural designs are decidedly inferior. Two such buildings are shown here.[4]

Doxal, Rathaus, Cologne PLATE 54

Copies of Floris' own drawings for the Doxal or loggia/porch for the Rathaus or City Hall in Cologne, Germany show the evolution of his thought. The first was relatively simple, a two-storey, five-bay structure with Doric columns below and Ionic above, with urns around the cornice and a giant escutcheon of the city's seal in front of a high hipped roof. The second design replaces all the columns with the Corinthian order, inserts slightly pointed arches on the ground floor, adds large brackets to the upper entablature, and projects forward slightly the central bay; the lower columns are also given high bases on which to stand. The final design, as built, replaces the escutcheon with an aedicule and a statue, adds a row of dormers, pulls forward three bays in projections, groups the central columns into clusters and inserts arches (slightly pointed rather than semi-circular) on both storeys. The earliest design dates from 1557, and the structure was not built until 1573. How much, if any, of the final design is attributable to its builder, Wilhelm Vernukken, is debatable.

Frans Floris House, Antwerp, Belgium
PLATE 54

Floris presumably allowed his imagination free rein when he designed a house for his brother Frans in Antwerp, 1563 (long since destroyed). The two-storey house had stepped gables on the ends and was almost symmetrical. The ground floor, which was decorated by carved swags and a Doric doorway was unexceptionable, but the upper floor invented some new forms that, fortunately, hardly any subsequent architect has copied. Ionic pilasters at each end of the façade established its order, which was echoed by distorted Ionic capitals attached to the tops of all the windows, both wide and narrow. Between the windows were no fewer than seven niches containing classical statues. The space over the front door was reserved for a large rectangular panel, on which Frans painted a fresco. Frans needed a new house, it is said, because the kitchen chimney of his old mansion filled the house with smoke and ruined his paintings.

Floris published some of his designs, many of which were exercises in strapwork and mannerism. He designed and built many funerary monuments, of which the finest is that of Count Albrecht at Kaliningrad, USSR (formerly Königsberg; we have been able to obtain no confirmation from Soviet authorities that this monument still survives), erected 1570. He also built fittings for churches, of which the most impressive is the 1572 jubé or rood-screen at Tournai/Doornik, Belgium, based on a series of three imperfectly-designed Venetian arches. A second similar jubé he designed for the cathedral at Antwerp, but it was not executed until 1592, long after Floris' death.

Project for Raadhuis, Antwerp, Belgium
PLATE 54

It is documented that the City of Antwerp put Floris in charge of the construction of the Raadhuis there in 1561, and also that Floris subsequently placed Hendrik van Paesschen in control of the building, but not until after many architects from all over submitted proposals. These include a certain Niccolo Scarini of Florence, the Frenchman Louis de Foix and the Lombardy-trained Belgian, Lamberto Sustris. A wooden model was constructed, which still survives, of a synthesis of these designs, possibly under the direction of Floris. The model has nine bays across the front, the central three projecting slightly forwards. The ground floor is an arcaded loggia, while the next floor has six rectangular and three compass-headed windows, and the top floor has an open gallery under the eaves. A prominent steeple made of two storeys of arches stands over the center in front of the high hipped roof. The model is only vaguely like the eventual building, and it may have been merely intended as a concept from which Hendrik was to develop his own design. The design of the actual Raadhuis will be discussed further in the section about Hendrik.

Church of Saint-Jacques, Liège, Belgium
PLATE 55

Lamberto Sustris, father of the Munich architect Friedrich Sustris, was a member of an Italian family

4. Robert Hedicke, *Cornelis Floris*, Berlin, 1913.

Project I for Doxal, Rathaus, Cologne

Project II for Doxal, Rathaus, Cologne

Approximate Scale

Frans Floris House, Antwerp, Belgium

PLATE 54

Doxal, Rathaus, Cologne

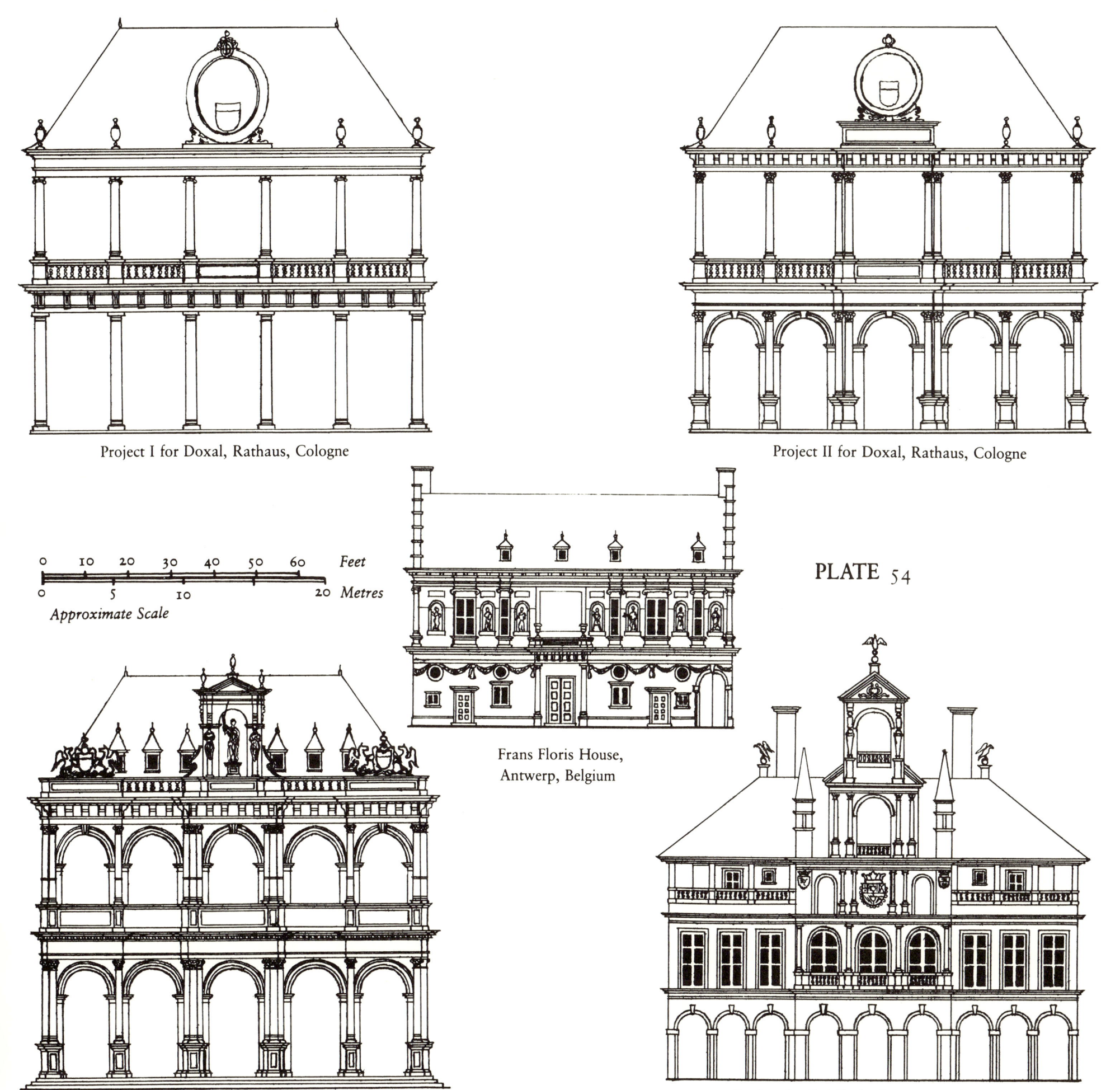

Project for Raadhuis, Antwerp, Belgium

95

living in the Low Countries. He spent years in Lombardy studying art, and was one of those submitting projects for the Antwerp Raadhuis. His most important work is the north portal of the church of Saint-Jacques at Liège, Belgium, built 1558–1560. This is a three-storey confection using the Corinthian order throughout. The ground floor is reminiscent of a Roman arch, while the next floor repeats the same motifs with a rose window replacing the doorway. The top looks as if Sustris was not sure how to finish what he had begun, and elements flanking the central aedicule are closely related to strapwork designs; the whole top floor lacks any sense of unity either within itself or with the rest of the building.

Cardinal Granvelle's Palace, Brussels, Belgium PLATE 55

Sebastian van Noyen, who worked with others on the designs for the gates at Antwerp in 1549, is believed to have studied in Italy under Antonio da San Gallo II in 1523 while the Dutchman Adrian reigned as Pope. While there he impressed Antoine Perrenot, Bishop of Arras, who later became Cardinal Granvelle. About 1550, the cardinal commissioned his friend to design him a palace in Brussels, unfortunately destroyed years ago. The palace had an irregular ground plan, according to Goetghebuer's *Choix des Monuments ... etc. du Royaume des Pays Bas,* but it also had two surprisingly Italian elevations—almost as if San Gallo had come to Brussels himself (he had already been dead four years by then). The garden front was seven bays wide and two storeys tall. The ground floor had an arcaded loggia with Tuscan pilasters between the arches, while the upper floor repeated the motif using Doric pilasters and blind arches, in which were set windows with triangular and segmental pediments. The pilasters were doubled at the ends. The courtyard elevation had a similar Doric arcaded loggia on its ground floor, and an Ionic loggia upstairs, in which were set Venetian arches. All these loggias would have been ideal in Italy, but one wonders how much use they found in cold, damp Brussels. At the right-hand end, a two-bay block projected up under a pediment to form a third storey. Granvelle's palace was the first northern building with as much sophistication as the Residenz at Landshut.

Entrance to Schweizertor
Stallburg Courtyard
Amalienburg
Old Hofburg Palace, Vienna, Austria
PLATE 56

Classical architecture first appeared in Vienna as early as 1515 in the form of the doorway added to the Salvatorkapelle, but many more years passed before entire buildings were built in the new style. Three portions of the old Hofburg Palace are attributed to Pietro Ferrabosco from near Lake Como, Italy: the Schweizertor (1552), the Stallburg courtyard, begun in 1559, and the Amalienburg begun in 1575. Because of later alterations to much of the building, only the bold Doric entrance to the Schweizertor is shown here. The Stallburg courtyard has three floors of an enormous Tuscan arcaded loggia with elliptical arches and a veritable forest of chimneys poking through the high roof. The north side of the Amalienburg is four storeys tall with one kind of rustication on the ground floor and the other three floors articulated in a specialized rustication limited to the piers between the windows. Rustication is often used to convey a feeling of power and strength, so it is entirely appropriate in a part of the royal palace.

Pigeon House, Grand-Place, Brussels, Belgium PLATE 55

By contrast, in Brussels (according to a 1627 engraving) the so-called Pigeon House was built in the Grand' Place in 1553. It was one of those typical high and narrow houses with large areas of glass. The lower three floors were articulated with Tuscan, Ionic and Corinthian pilasters respectively, while the next floor broke the rhythm but still employed Composite pilasters on either side of a truncated Venetian window with a balcony. The ground floor in the drawing shown here is left blank because the original engraving was cut off at that level.

Raadhuis, Nijmegen, the Netherlands
PLATE 55

Herman van Herengrave of Nijmegen, the Netherlands, was a traditional architect-builder of the gothic style, as witnesses his Apostolic School there, built in 1544. However, he felt a pull by the coming classical fashion, so he attempted to blend classical details into the forms he had always known. He built the Raadhuis 1554–1569 with stepped gables at each end and rudimentary pediments over each of the large rectangular windows that were arranged in two storeys of seven bays. A high parapet around the roof is decorated with carved white stone roundels against the red brick, and partially hides the three dormers. Classical, this was not, but it was a conscious effort to cross the gulf to the new style.

Chapel Entrance, Residenzschloss, Dresden, DDR PLATE 56

At this date in the Germanic countries, it was still necessary for an architect to have studied in Italy in order to be sure of the classicism of the design, which may explain van Herengrave's having fallen short. An alternative solution was to hire an Italian to design and supervise, which was the course followed for the chapel at the Residenzschloss at Dresden, East Germany. Giovanni Maria Mosca from Padua, who also worked in Venice, Poland and Prague, was hired to oversee the work of Johann Kramer, the builder, and Hans Walther II, the carver. The Residenz itself was no stranger to innovative architecture, in the form of exotic gables and loggias, but the chapel entrance was designed in a more

PLATE 55

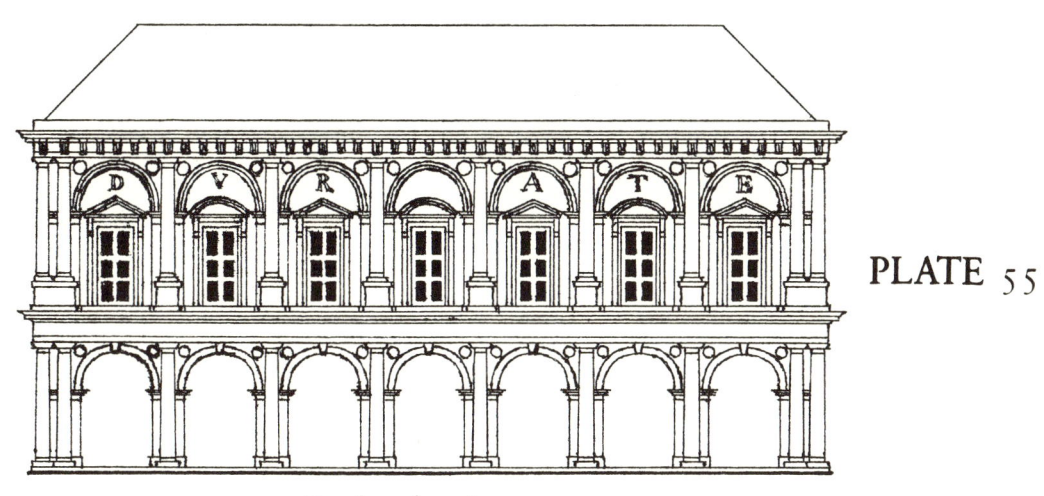

Garden elevation,
Cardinal Granvelle's Palace, Brussels, Belgium

North entrance,
Church of Saint-Jacques, Liège, Belgium

Courtyard side,
Cardinal Granvelle's Palace, Brussels, Belgium

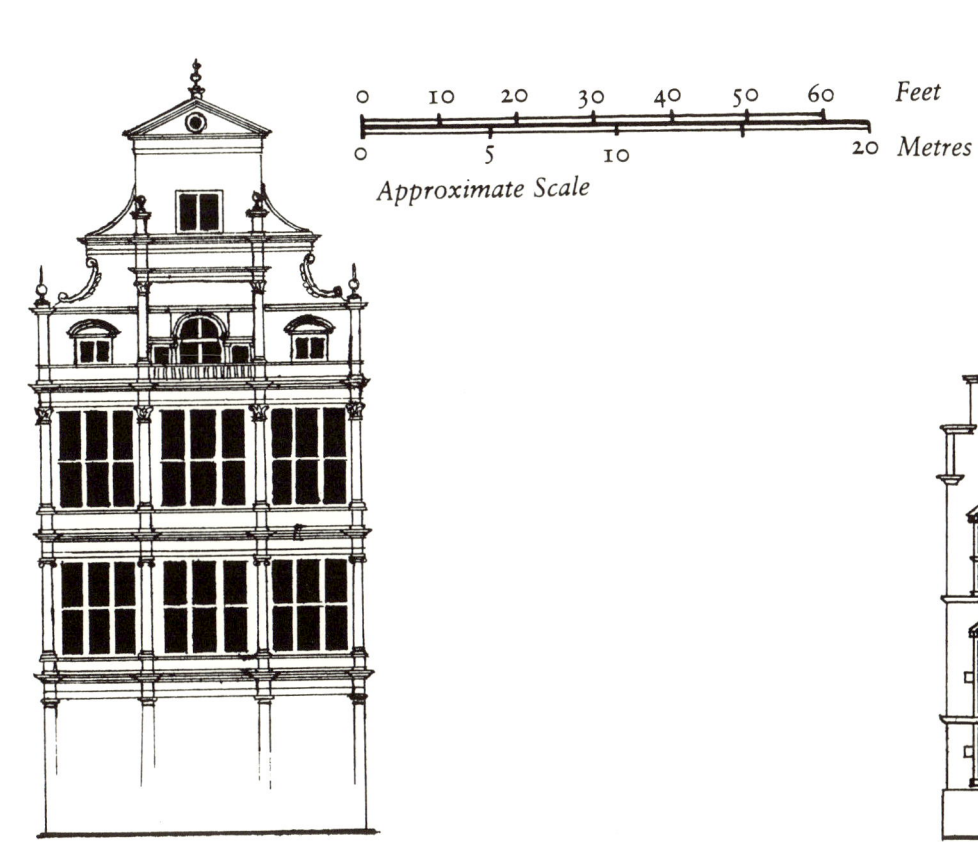

Pigeon House, Grand-Place,
Brussels, Belgium

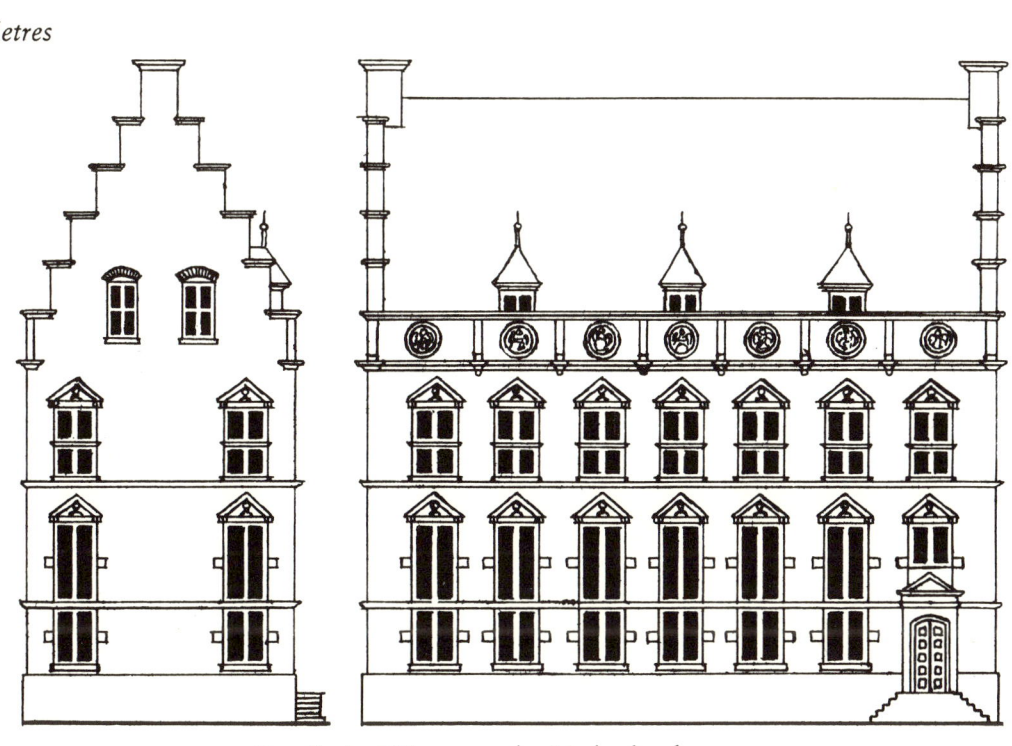

Raadhuis, Nijmegen, the Netherlands

97

Court Chapel, Dresden, DDR, with Heinrich Schütz leading a concert
Courtesy of the British Museum

Engraving from Christoph Bernhard's *Geistliches Gesang-Buch*

restrained manner in the form of a Roman triumphal arch with Corinthian pilasters. When the chapel was destroyed the entrance was allowed to remain standing for a time. The design of the inside of the chapel, which is known to us from an engraving in Christoph Bernhard, *Geistliches Gesang-Buch*, 1676, was a trifle less sophisticated than that of the entrance. The nave had four bays with compass-headed windows on the ground floor and rectangular windows in the gallery. Panelled piers and longitudinal arches supported the galleries, and squat Tuscan columns supported the elliptically-vaulted ceiling that was intersected by transverse vaults in each bay; the ceiling was nevertheless covered in heavy gothic tracery. A wall with a small arch cut in it connected each column to the side walls, this forming a buttress against the side thrust of the main vault. The organ was located in a gallery above and behind the altar in a recess that projected into the next wing of the schloss, and a second, lower gallery was fitted in front of the organ gallery in order to accommodate two additional chamber organs plus other musicians, but this gallery may have dated only from the tenure of Heinrich Schütz as music-master in the mid-seventeenth century.

Ottheinrichsbau, the Castle, Heidelberg
PLATE 57

Prince Ottheinrich of Bavaria commissioned the construction of the so-called Ottheinrichsbau at Heidelberg Castle in Germany in 1556. For this, he is said to have hired Alexander Colin of Mechelin/Malines, Belgium, although Henry-Russell Hitchcock claims that Colin arrived too late to have been the actual designer, for part of the ground floor had already been erected by then. The building is a three-storey block of red-brown sandstone on a high basement, divided by crude pilasters into five bays, each of two windows and a niche. The building stands gutted and roofless today, but it once had a pair of two-storey gables in front of its high hipped roof, in which were no fewer than four rows of dormers. The façade is covered all over with the kind of carved "busy" work typical of many Flemish craftsmen of the period; they in turn seem to have been trying to imitate earlier Florentine carvings, but the profound difference between them is that the Florentine carvings were usually subordinated to the overall design and its components, while some of the Flemish work over-

Entrance to Schweizertor,
Hofburg Palace, Vienna, Austria
(not drawn to regular scale)

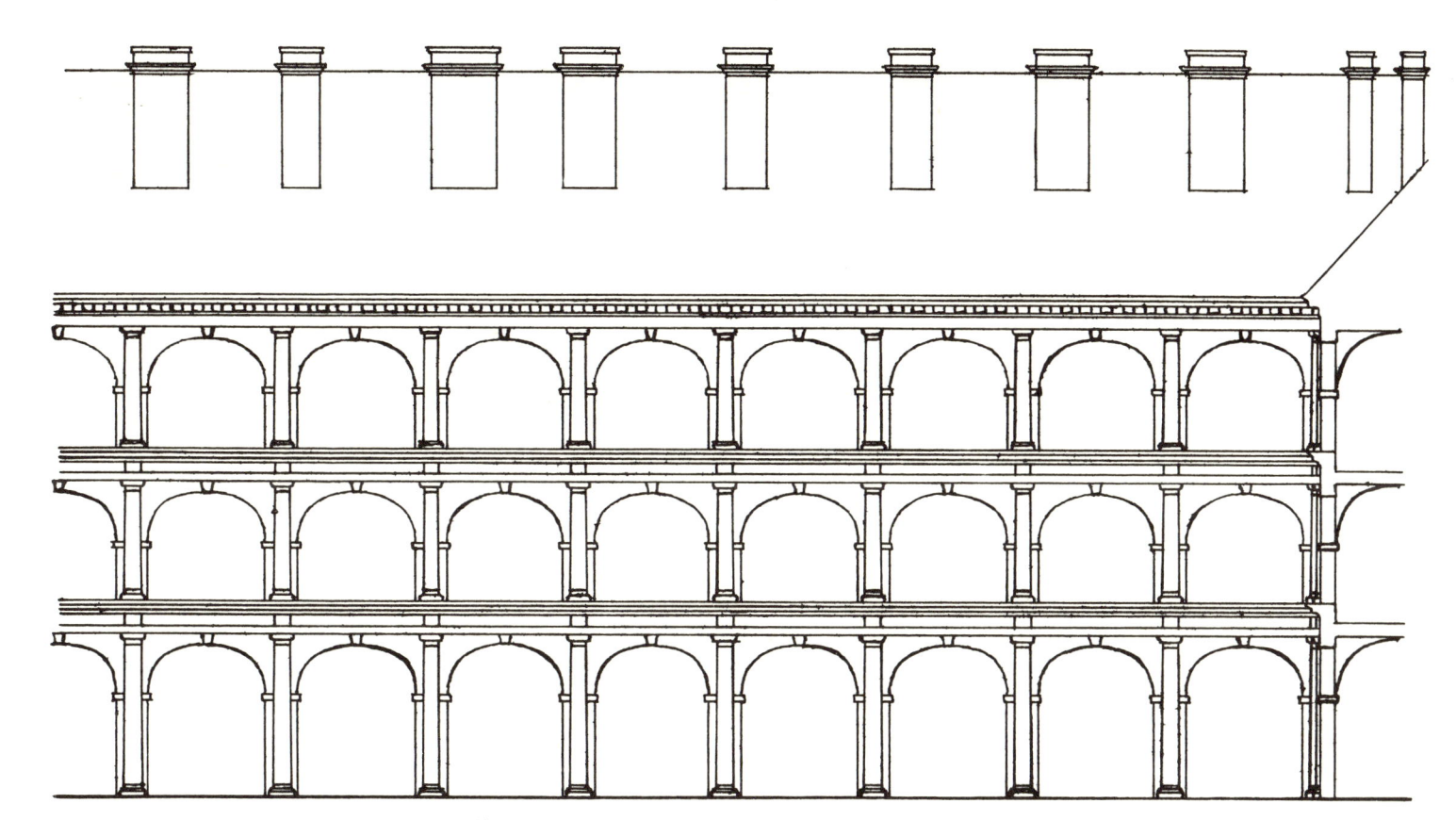

Part of courtyard, Stallburg Courtyard, Old Hofburg Palace, Vienna, Austria

PLATE 56

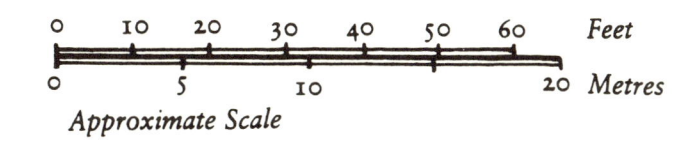

Approximate Scale

Part of North elevation, courtyard, Amalienburg, Hofburg Palace, Vienna, Austria

Court Chapel Entrance,
Residenzschloss, Dresden, DDR
(not drawn to regular scale)

whelmed the viewer with the carving in an effort to distract attention from the fact that the overall design was poorly conceived. Much the same can be said about the use of strapwork, which Colin employed here.

Landhaus, Graz, Austria PLATE 57

By contrast, the Swiss-Italian architect Domenico dell'Allio from Lugano was hired in 1557 to design the courtyard of the Landhaus at Graz, Austria, the administrative building for the province of Styria, and he produced a monument the equal of any of its type. He built a three-storey loggia around the courtyard. The long side is nine bays wide, with numbers three and seven being wider than the others, with elliptical arches. Between the arches are Tuscan pilasters which are clustered above the impost lines. Occasional dormers on the high roof repeat the motif of the arches below. The Landhaus courtyard should be compared to its close contemporary, the Stallburg at Vienna.

Weeshuis, Edam, the Netherlands PLATE 57

The erratic chronological track of renaissance architecture next leads north to the Low Countries, where an anonymous builder designed the Weeshuis (Guildhall) at Edam, the Netherlands cheese center, in 1558. This simple brick building with stone trim had few classical details on it, but its arrangement prefigured the important Antwerp Raadhuis that would be begun two years later. All its windows were placed under relieving-arches; the central three bays were carried up into a central gable; and the top floor was an open gallery under the eaves. The building, which was seven bays wide, no longer stands, but is known through an eighteenth-century drawing.

Kardinalshuis, Groningen, the Netherlands PLATE 57

The following year, the so-called Kardinalshuis was built in Groningen, the Netherlands, also anonymously. This little confection has been moved and re-erected as an addition to the local Provincie Huis. Built of stone on a small scale, it makes bold use of the classical orders, with Doric, Ionic and Corinthian engaged columns framing the large windows of its three-storey front. As the gable narrows above the eaves, various mannerist and strapwork carvings are used to suggest volutes, probably influenced by an illustration by Floris.

Paalhuis, Amsterdam, the Netherlands PLATE 57

The Amsterdam Paalhuis, built in 1560, once stood next to the "New Bridge" over the Damrak, but is now known only from portraits from the seventeenth and eighteenth centuries. Its anonymous designer produced essentially a simple building with double ogee curves on its gables at the ends of the building, but he added an impressive frontispiece that seemed to follow ideas of Giulio Romano or Sansovino. The entrance was framed by pairs of giant rusticated Tuscan pilasters, and above the cornice a window was framed by single Doric pilasters and volutes in a smaller system. A chimney attached to this central gable may have been a later addition, as was a cupola on the middle of the roof. This sophisticated gable was reminiscent of Pasqualini's design at the Kasteel at Buren.

This would be a good place to say a few words about the unusual Hans Vredeman de Fries (the last part of the name merely means that he was from Dutch Friesland, a Coastal region that stretches on both sides of the Dutch-German border). Although he was occasionally capable of producing an acceptable classical design, he was chiefly instrumental in spreading strapwork and mannerist designs through his various publications. Few extant buildings can be attributed to him, but one charming survivor is the Boterhal of Sint-Jansgasthuis (Saint John's Hospice) in the Kerkplein at Hoorn, the Netherlands, dated 1563 (not shown in this book). Its front is surprisingly not symmetrical, while at the same time expressing an intent at symmetry. On its four upper floors anywhere from two to four windows are grouped under a single pediment. The angles between the steps of the brick gable are filled with elaborate white stone carvings.

Capriccio Gate PLATE 58

Just to prove that Vredeman occasionally handled classical forms, this book has included a drawing based on a capriccio of a rather rangy two-storey triumphal arch that he drew for his *Scenographiae sive Perspectivae*, 1560. The lower storey is decorated with panelled Tuscan pilasters, and the upper floor, with its three blind arches, has Ionic columns and pilasters. Behind the pediment is a balustrade with pinnacles flanking a square cupola. Vredeman, like so many of his northern colleagues, seemed incapable of knowing when to leave well enough alone, for the cupola and perhaps the pinnacles would have been better omitted.

The one northern architect with a reliable sense of classical design was Hans Hendrik van Paesschen, to give him his correct name, as his own wife spelled it. Since Hendrik is undoubtedly the most important "discovery" of this book, it will be worth spending a little more space than usual on him. In the first place, the most likely reason that he has been overlooked heretofore is that his name is spelled in over a dozen ways. The most typical ways are: Henri de Pas, van de Passe, Henryke, (possibly) Hans the Fleming, Hans Pascha, Paska, Paschen, Passe and von Paaschen. Paesschen derives from the fact that his family originally came from the area of northeastern France and western Belgium known as the Pas de Calais, where the World War I Battle of Paeschendaele was fought (pronounced, incidentally, *Pahskendahl*, not *Passiondale*; Hendrik's last name is pronounced *Pahsken*). His probable son Crispin I (1540–1629), grandson Crispin II (1565/70–1637) and great-grandson Crispin III 1593/4–ca. 1663) and other descendants were prominent artists, mostly copper engravers.[5] Although Hendrik was the family name, it was gradually replaced by variations of Passe.

5. Daniel Franken, *L'Oeuvre Gravé des Van de Passe*, Amsterdam, 1881.

Kardinalshuis, Groningen, the Netherlands

Weeshuis, Edam, the Netherlands

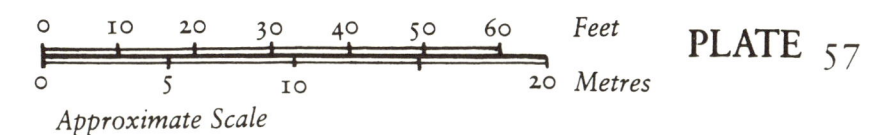

PLATE 57

Ottheinrichsbau, the Castle, Heidelberg

Paalhuis, Amsterdam, the Netherlands

Courtyard, Landhaus, Graz, Austria

Capriccio Gate

End elevation, Raadhuis, Antwerp, Belgium

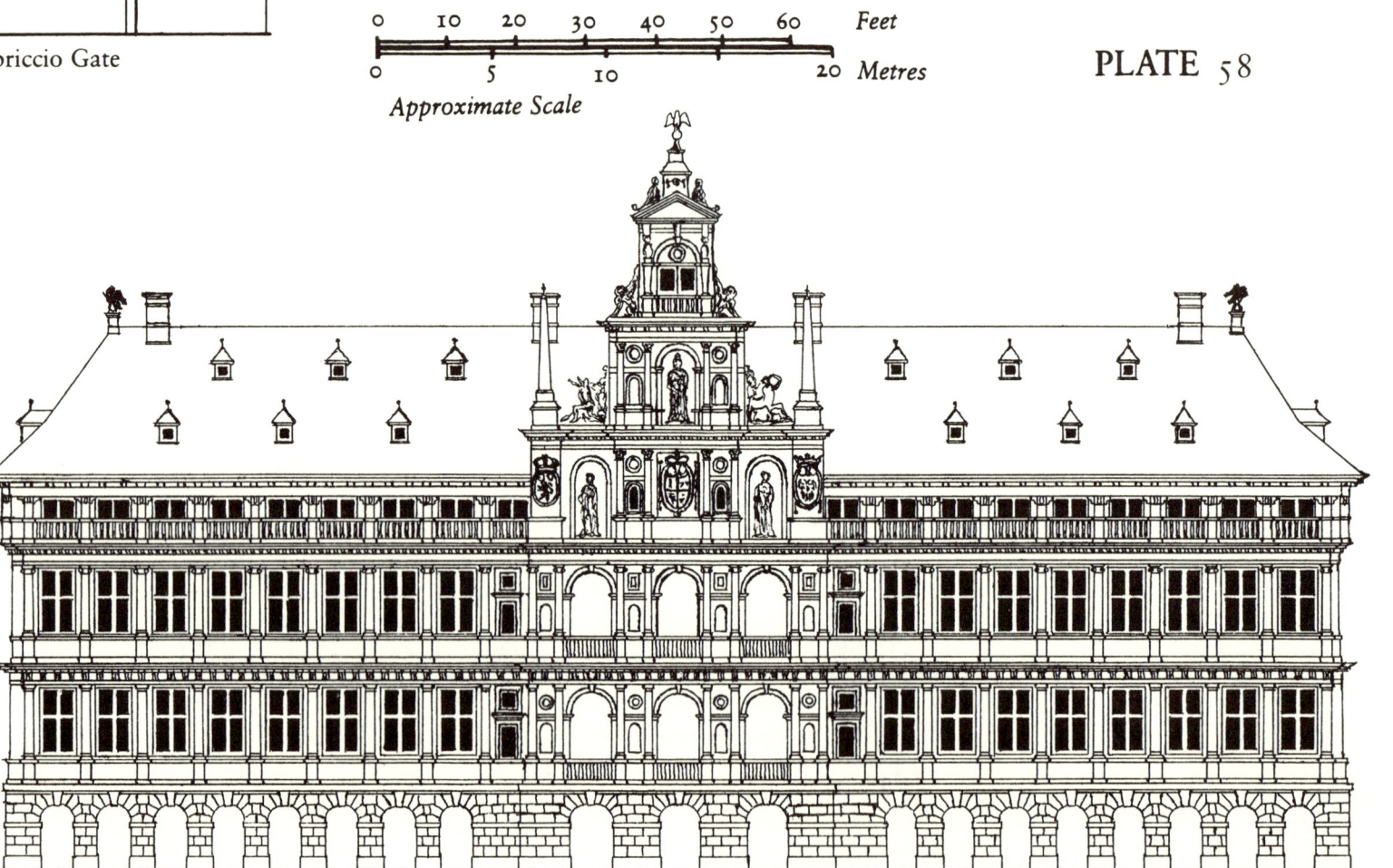

PLATE 58

Raadhuis, Antwerp, Belgium

Little is known about his early life, which presumably began just before 1520 in Antwerp. It appears that he spent time in Italy in order to study the latest theories about fortification design, and he spent much of his time after the trip to Italy designing and building fortifications in the Low Countries (as at Dendermonde and Antwerp) and Scandinavia. He was apparently a close friend of Floris; Floris, as the prominent (supposed) art expert, would be asked to undertake the construction of an important building that was more than he could handle, so he would award the contract to Hendrik. His work for Floris made him famous, with the result that he received commissions to design buildings in England, Wales, Germany and Denmark—one wonders how he managed it all before the advent of the Eurailpass! Towards the end of his life he was thrown in prison in Denmark when part of one of his buildings collapsed, but was released when it was realized that the collapse was not as serious as first believed. No further reference to him can be found after 1582, by which time his pure style of architecture was considered out of date while strapwork and other mannerist devices reigned supreme in Britain and the Low Countries. It was also a time of all-out war in the Low Countries as ruthless Spanish armies tried to crush the Protestant revolt there—not a good time for an architect, especially one who may have been a Protestant. His dates nearly coincide with Palladio's.

Raadhuis, Antwerp, Belgium PLATE 58

Hendrik's first known non-military building was the Antwerp Raadhuis or Town hall, 1561–1566, the most important building in Flanders in this period. Antwerp was the most prosperous city of northern Europe at this time, and thus needed an impressive building for its seat of government. The Raadhuis was still new when it was gutted by fire during the 1576 riot of the Spanish troops known as the Spanish Fury, but it was rebuilt exactly as before. At some later date, the central courtyard was roofed over to provide more offices, and plate glass has replaced the small-paned casement windows, but otherwise it remains today substantially as built.

The Raadhuis is a large, four-storey building with its front divided into three sections. On either side of the central section, which dominates the rest, are eight bays. On the ground floor is a heavily-rusticated arcade of small arches, while the next two floors consist of large windows separated by Tuscan and Ionic pilasters respectively, and the top floor is largely hidden by a massive overhanging gallery and the heavy eaves of the roof. The central section is composed, above the arcade, of variations on a theme of loosely-paired columns arranged around arches and niches in four storeys, the rhythm being similar to Bramante's design that Serlio adapted a decade earlier for the courtyard at Ancy. Towards the top of this section, the structure narrows into a single bay with a pediment on top and a pinnacle on each side. On the four corners of the large hipped roof are small plinths, as later appeared on London's Royal Exchange, surmounted by the city's emblem of an eagle. Two rows of small dormers pierce the roof. The central courtyard is surrounded by an arcaded loggia, and a contemporary painting shows that the city government conducted some of its official business in the courtyard, when the often unfriendly Belgian weather permitted.

Until now, most historians writing about this building have attributed its design to Floris. The record shows that many leading artists submitted plans, including the otherwise unknown Niccolo Scarini of Florence, Louis de Foix and Lamberto Sustris, and Floris was awarded the contract to supervise construction, at which point a still-extant wooden model was made to show the desired concept (see Plate 54). Floris then turned construction over to Hendrik, but from what we know of Hendrik's other activities in Britain and Scandinavia he had no time to be physically present to watch all the stones being laid true, so his role was limited to providing the design, while Floris probably carved the statuary for the building.[6]

Hanseatenhuis, Antwerp, Belgium
PLATE 59

Antwerp's prosperity attracted the attention of merchants in England and Germany. German Baltic towns of the Hanseatic League suspected that one way to slow the ebb of commerce away from their league to Antwerp was to build their own trading center in Antwerp. This large building, known as the Hanseatenhuis, was built around 1564, and once more Floris was engaged as an intermediary to hire Hendrik. The huge building contained over 300 rooms, which were furnished so luxuriously that the merchants in the Hanseatic port of Gdansk/Danzig issued a complaint. In Napoleonic times, the building was altered by the removal of its lofty steeple, and many changes were made to its fenestration. It was falling into ruin when it was destroyed by fire in 1893.[7]

As a work of architecture, the Hanseatenhuis was even more successful than the Raadhuis, for it achieved a unified brick façade in classical style without the use of pilasters to divide the wall into bays. The building was arranged around a rectangular courtyard over an arcaded loggia. The front was thirty bays wide (an unclassical even number, but here scarcely noticeable because of the skillful treatment of the entrance). It was four storeys tall, divided into a ground floor, a mezzanine and two tall and well-lit upper floors. The ground floor had numerous large and small doorways for receiving shipped goods. The double-pile hipped roof was pierced by two rows of hipped dormers, and had a plinth at each corner surmounted by the symbol of the Hanseatic League, a two-headed eagle. The chimneys, with tall, thin arches on the sides, were similar to those on the Raadhuis. The roof's cornice was appropriately heavy for the mass of the building. Above the roof soared an impressive steeple with an overhanging balcony like the one on London's Royal Exchange but more richly decorated. The Corinthian columns of the overhanging

6. Hedicke, *Floris*, pp. 88, 136.
7. *Histoire de l'Architecture en Belgique* (no author, place or date given), pp. 496–497.

Hanseatenhuis, Antwerp, Belgium

PLATE 59

Courtyard, Hanseatenhuis, Antwerp, Belgium

stage linked the steeple visually with the two-storey Roman triumphal arch that surrounded the principal entrance on the ground floor. The Hanseatenhuis was a fitting symbol of the commercial power of the Hanseatic League, which although waning was still great.[8]

Further research will be necessary to establish any connection between Hendrik and a large new house that Sir Thomas Gresham built in the Long New Street, Antwerp in the early 1560s; Gresham was Hendrik's principal patron in Britain, and any such establishment for the English merchants in Antwerp may have given the Hanseatic merchants the original idea for building their palace.[9]

Unidentified Raadhuis PLATE 60

Tracing the career of Hendrik has much in common with trying to catch a criminal who is careful to leave few clues, but nowhere is this more true than with an impressive building that is the central focus of a contemporary oil painting. The painting, whose present location is unknown, was published in *Country Life* in 1963, and was there attributed to Frans Francken II on stylistic grounds. The building, which is obviously either a provincial raadhuis or possibly a bourse, is too well composed to have been a figment of the artist's imagination, and it combines important elements from many other buildings attributed to Hendrik, both in Flanders and in Britain. Experts in England, Belgium and the Netherlands have so far been unable to identify the building.[10]

The building appears to have been arranged around a rectangular, perhaps arcaded, courtyard. The principal exterior front, facing the artist, was on one of the short sides, and the long sides each had a tower with cupola atop. The front was nine bays wide, the central three bays being included in a projection that rose above the roof with a pair of volutes and closely resembled the similar device on the Antwerp Raadhuis. The hipped roof was pierced by two rows of hipped dormers and had a plinth at each corner bearing a finial. The ground floor was fronted by a Tuscan arcaded loggia, while the next floor had pedimented windows separated by Ionic pilasters (minus the bases that slightly detracted from the pilasters on the Antwerp Raadhuis). The top floor had square windows under its full entablature which was supported by simple pilaster strips. Other notable features were the pinnacles on either side of the top of the central projection, and the overhanging gallery on the left-hand tower. While the building had so much in common with Hendrik's other buildings, it also lacked any sign of strapwork, a device that Hendrik almost always eschewed, while nearly all other architects and artists of the area in the late sixteenth and early seventeenth centuries made extensive use of strapwork.

Palace of the Duc de Brabant, Brussels, Belgium PLATE 60

Another oil painting possibly provides a further hint of Hendrik's work in Belgium. This is a view of the Palace of the Dukes of Brabant in the Coudenburg district, Brussels, as seen from the park about 1560. Prominent in the painting is a seventeen-bay recent addition to the otherwise-gothic palace. It had a Tuscan arcaded loggia on the ground floor and a regular row of windows on the single floor above, which may have housed a picture-gallery. The roof, which ended in a crow-stepped gable (found on other buildings attributed to Hendrik), had two rows of hipped dormers. The building was compatible with Hendrik's style and period more than with any other known architect, but it would be injudicious to claim more than that.

Laube, Rathaus, Lübeck PLATE 60

Hendrik was also possibly involved in the design of a mannerist building in Lübeck, Germany, the Laube or Gallery attached to the old gothic Rathaus or City Hall. The Laube was built in 1570-1, by Herkules Midow, the mason who did the work, and someone called Hans the Fleming, who provided the plans. Only one Flemish architect called Hans was widely enough known to be called by that name, Hans Hendrik van Paesschen, who was working in Denmark at the time; Hans van Steenwinckel would not become well-known for two decades. Moreover, some of the details of the design, such as the execution of the pedimented windows, are similar to the work Hendrik was doing in Scandinavia at the same time, and where the building falls short of Hendrik's usual standards it is tempting to ascribe that to alterations by Midow; by contrast, no one with less training than Hendrik could have been expected to have conceived such classical details as the Venetian arch motifs in all three gables.

The ground floor is a series of six large arches on thick chamfered piers, supporting a band of four courses of severe rusticated stonework. Above the band is a row of twelve pedimented windows, separated by Ionic pilasters, the shafts of half of which are formed by caryatids (female figures). Above the entablature are three gables, the center one being two storeys high. Each contains a form of modified Venetian arch. The top of the central gable is flanked by correct volutes, but in the place of volutes at the lower level on all three gables are clumsy strapwork concoctions that surely must have replaced volutes in the original design. The interstices of these strapwork shapes look as if they once had pinnacles, which have been drawn in dotted outline in this book.

For the rest of the surviving details of Hendrik's continental career it is necessary to turn to Scandinavia. From 1559 to 1563, while the Raadhuis was being built in Antwerp, Hendrik was employed part-time by King Eric XIV of Sweden to design and supervise construction of fortifications at Älvsborg (demolished 1660-1673), and to lay out the town across the river, but for some reason he lost favor with the king and felt obliged to flee from Sweden.[12]

The same year that Hendrik left Sweden, Sweden and Denmark went to war in what is known there as the

8. Lodovico Guicciardini, *Descrittione di Tutti i Paesi Bassi*, 1588, states that Hendrik van Paschen of Antwerp was responsible for the design of the "Palazzo e fondaco de gli Ostarline." According to a 1566 letter from Richard Clough to Sir Thomas Gresham about work for Sir William Cecil at Burghley House (quoted in Robin G. Jones, "Sir Richard Clough of Denbigh c. 1530–1570," *Denbighshire Historical Society Transactions*, vol. 19, p. 64), Hendrik and Floris were apparently associated in some way: "I can nott wrytt you answere by thys my letter for both Henryke and Florys ar both hout of ye towne."

9. *Dictionary of National Biography*, "Gresham," p. 145.

10. "Collectors' Queries," *Country Life*, vol. 133, p. 156, and letters from E. H. ter Kuile and Luc Devliegher to the author written in 1980.

11. In the National Collection, Brussels.

12. *Weilbachs Kunstnerleksikon*, Copenhagen, 1949, vol. 2, p. 520, and letters from Sten Karling to the author in 1980.

Wing, Palace of the Duc de Brabant, Brussels, Belgium

Entrance, Vallø Castle, Sjaelland, Denmark
(conjectural reconstruction)

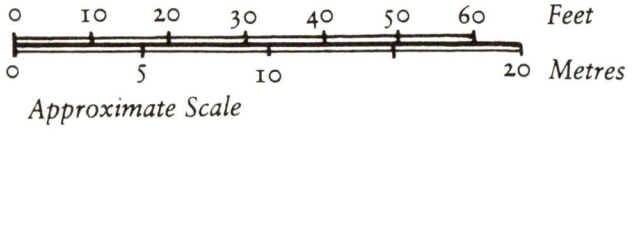

Laube, Rathaus, Lübeck

Unidentified Raadhuis

PLATE 60

Seven Years' War of the North—allegedly fought over which of the two kings should be entitled to use a coat-of-arms of three crowns that dated from the time that Sweden, Norway and Denmark were all united. King Frederik II of Denmark (reigned 1559–1588) stood to lose more than Eric in such a war, so he quickly hired Hendrik on 25 June 1564 to design fortresses for him. Although he did not trust Hendrik because of his previous service to Eric, Frederik paid him well—200 Crowns a year plus a free house and other allowances. In 1566 Hendrik was sent to Bohus, which is a medieval fortress now part of Sweden, but then under the control of Denmark. There he made unspecified improvements to the fortifications.

The following year, he was sent to Akershus, now part of Norway but then under the control of Denmark, to improve the fortifications around the old castle, and he built the King's Battery and the Queen's Battery there in 1568. Tradition says that Hendrik also laid out the town of Frederikstad (about 100 kilometres southeast of Oslo), which was rebuilt on a new site at that time, but no documentary evidence supports this.[13]

Kronborg Castle, Helsingør, Denmark
PLATE 61

No further record of Hendrik in Scandinavia has been found until 1574. The Dano-Swedish war being over, Frederik was interested in rebuilding the medieval castle of Krogen at Helsingør (Elsinore in Shakespeare's *Hamlet*). The renewed structure, which was to be both fortress controlling the entrance to the Baltic and royal palace, was renamed Kronborg. Hendrik was forced to incorporate much of the earlier fabric into his plan, which may explain many of the irregularities in the design. Hendrik worked there until 1577, when he returned to Dendermonde, Flanders, and his place was taken by Antonius van Opbergen from Mechelin, but he is thought to have followed Hendrik's plans. The castle as it exists today has been somewhat altered by rebuilding after a disastrous fire in 1629 and subsequent neglect, but it is now being slowly restored.[14]

Kronborg, which is built of stone, has a nearly-square plan around a large courtyard. The outside corners are formed into towers each of a different design and character, the tallest of which would have been useful for spotting fleets of warships approaching the entrance to the Baltic. The inside of the courtyard contains five polygonal staircase towers spaced irregularly; these recall similar towers in other buildings by Hendrik both in Denmark and Britain. The east side of the courtyard has no towers and was built as a long gallery over an open loggia; the loggia was soon closed in because of the Danish weather. Most of the windows on the two lower floors around the courtyard are pedimented. The chief glory of Kronborg is the enormous east gable facing the sea, rising through five storeys above the gothic windows of the chapel. The pedimented windows of the gable are balanced by engaged columns of five orders and a niche at each level containing a statue. The main entrance on the north is a handsome Roman triumphal arch with four engaged Corinthian columns. Kronborg is a marriage of the medieval with the Renaissance; the two co-exist in tension, neither entirely happy.

76 Stengade, Helsingør, Denmark PLATE 61

While he was living at Helsingør, Hendrik is believed to have designed the house at 76 Stengade, 1579. The house has the end with its crow-stepped gable facing the street. The five-bay front has pediments over all the windows on the lower two floors, and can be related to details at Kronborg and at the Bath-house at Hillerød.

Bath-house, Hillerød, Denmark PLATE 62

In spite of a seemingly perennial shortage of money, Frederik embarked on extensive building schemes, including at Hillerød, between Helsingør and Copenhagen, where he intended to escape from the cares of the other two places. He constructed a village of buildings on a network of islands there in the late 1570s. The most important building he built there was known as the Bath-house or Badstuen, which was used for bathing and other entertainment. This is a brick building with stone dressing, built on a slightly asymmetrical E-plan, and is two storeys high with five crow-stepped gables. The principal entrance is through the side of a polygonal staircase-tower placed in the middle of the long façade; the doorway closely resembles one of the tower doorways at Kronborg. The tower has since been augmented by the addition of a steeple, while the handsome domed cupola that originally stood on the middle of the roof (and appears in a 1680 sketch) has disappeared. The ground-floor windows on the front are pedimented. As the King's Architect, Hendrik was undoubtedly responsible for the design, although no documentation survives. Two young members of the Floris family were hired to work on the interior.[15]

Fadeburslangen, Hillerød, Denmark
PLATE 62

A second building constructed at Hillerød at this time was the Fadeburslaengen or Long Pantry next to the tiltyard. This is two storeys high, built of brick with stone dressings. Its crow-stepped gables on the ends are decorated with a ball finial on each step. The ground-floor openings are now irregularly spaced, but they have almost certainly been altered; the upper windows, small and square, are regular, sixteen in number along the side. Frederick apparently liked Hillerød so much that his son Christian IV decided to build a substantial palace there called Frederiksborg in 1603.

Vallø Castle, Sjaelland, Denmark PLATE 60

Francis Beckett has suggested a few other works by Hendrik in Scandinavia, such as the former altar-piece of the high altar at the cathedral at Lund, Sweden, and two Danish manor houses, Vallø and Lystrup. Lystrup turns out to be both too late and not in Hendrik's style (too much strapwork, among other things), but part of

13. *Weilbachs K.*, pp. 520–521, and letter from Christian Eldal to the author in 1980.

14. Joakim Skovgaard, *A King's Architecture*, London, Hugh Evelyn, 1973, pp. 17–25 and 75–77.

15. D. F. Slothouwer, *Bouwkunst der Nederlandsche Renaissance in Danemarken*, Amsterdam, 1924, plates 76, 80 and 84, and 1680 sketch at Kunstakademiets Bibliotek, Copenhagen.

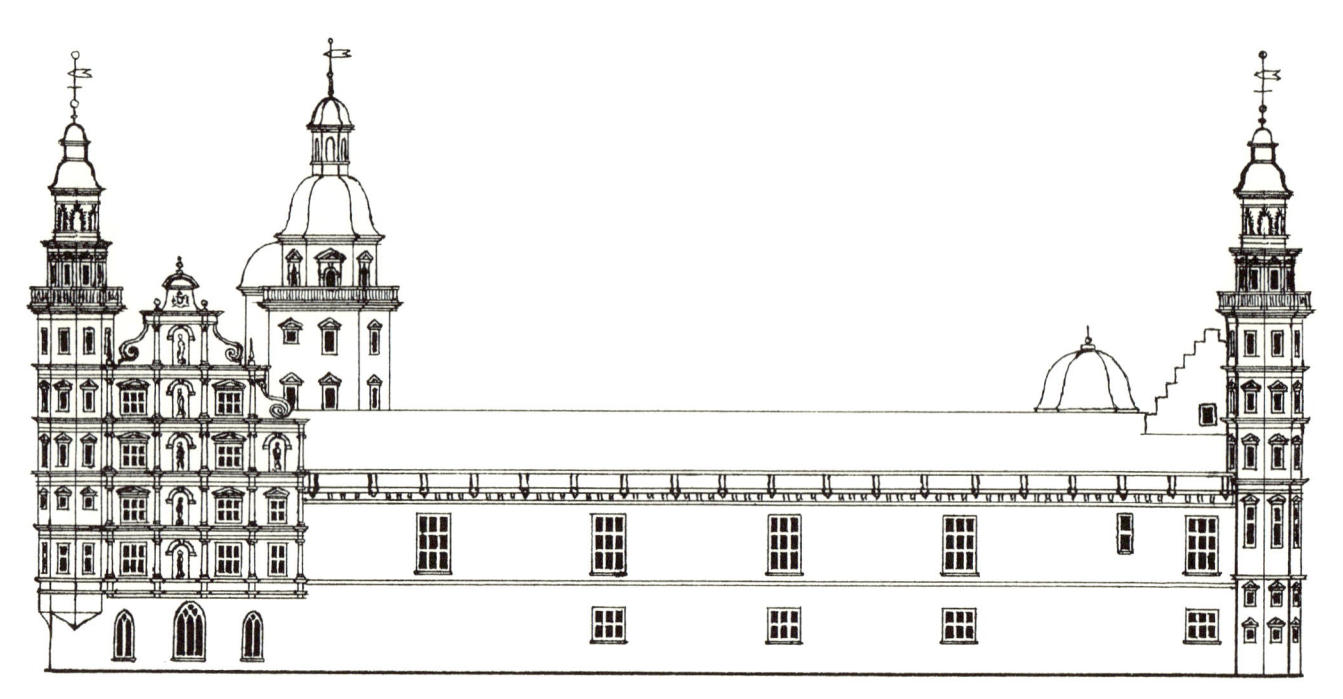

East elevation, Kronborg Castle, Helsingør, Denmark

76 Stengade, Helsingør, Denmark

Courtyard, looking east, Kronborg Castle, Helsingør, Denmark

PLATE 61

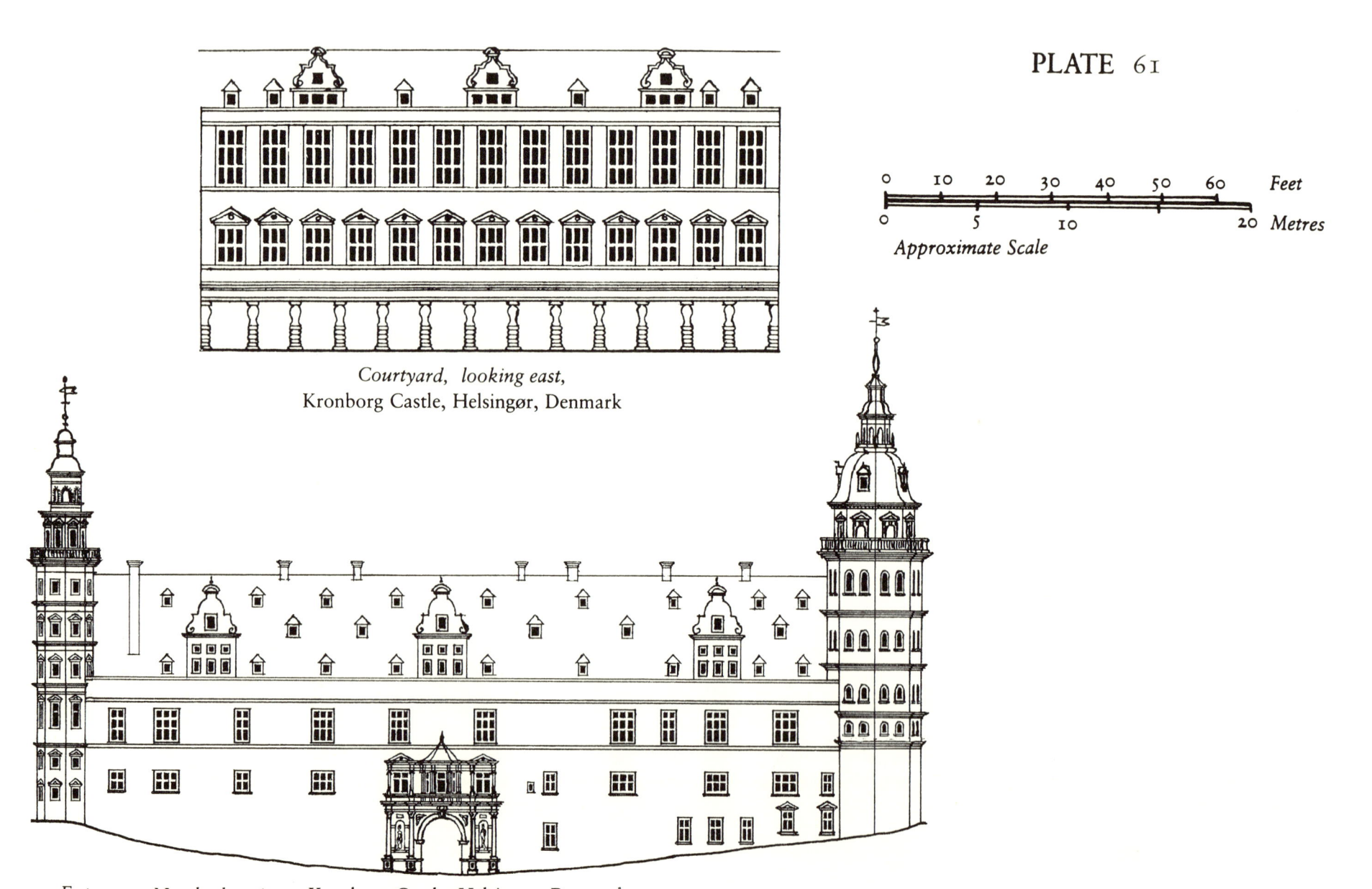

Entrance, North elevation, Kronborg Castle, Helsingør, Denmark

Fadeburslangen, Hillerød, Denmark

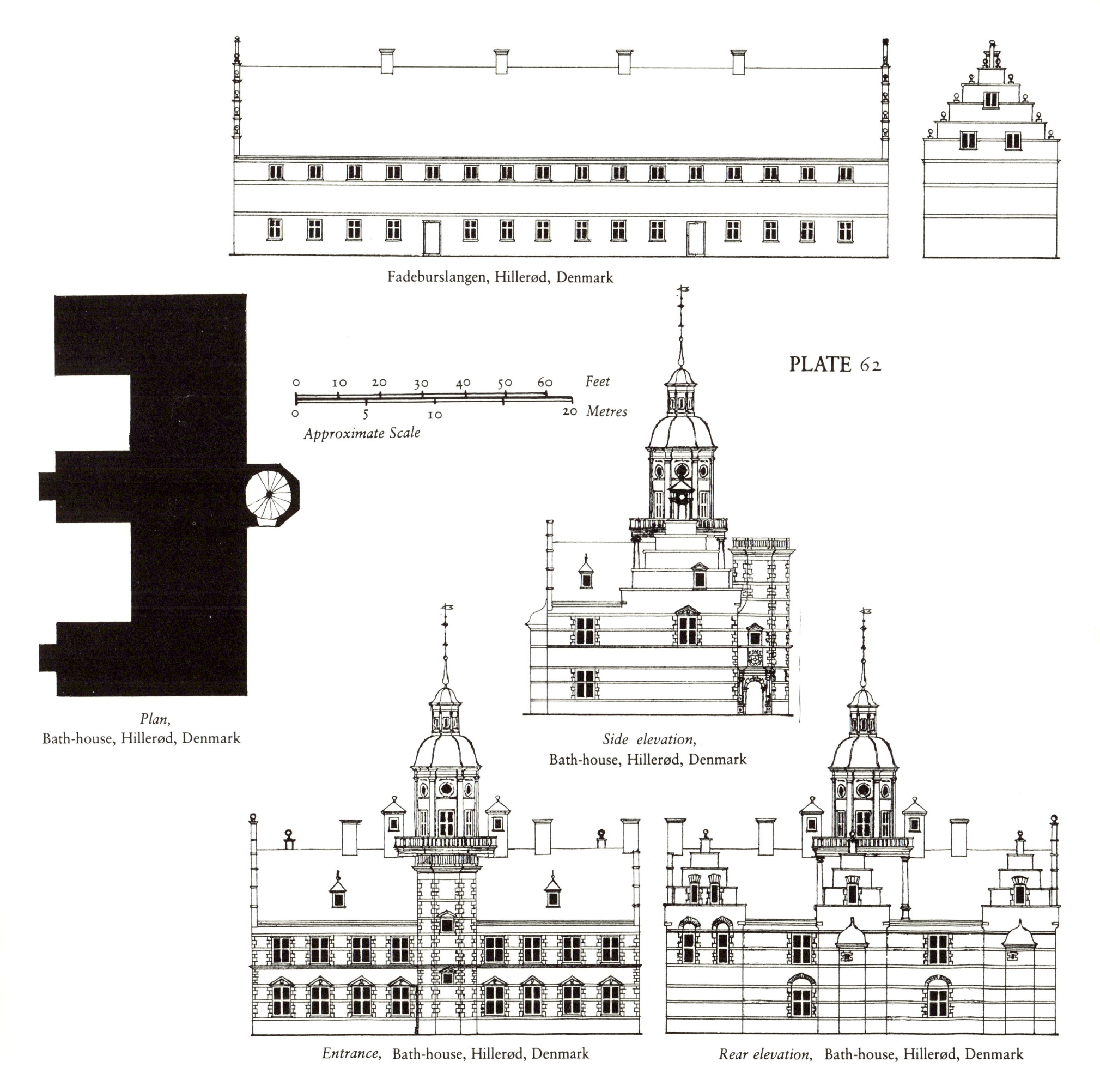

PLATE 62

Plan, Bath-house, Hillerød, Denmark

Side elevation, Bath-house, Hillerød, Denmark

Entrance, Bath-house, Hillerød, Denmark

Rear elevation, Bath-house, Hillerød, Denmark

Vallø, a brick, courtyarded tower-house later much enlarged, may be by Hendrik. Its entrance and its pedimented windows seem to be related to the Bathhouse and Kronborg.[16]

Uraniborg, Hven Island, Denmark PLATE 63

Many of the buildings here attributed to Hendrik were quite extraordinary for their period, but they pale beside Uraniborg on Hven Island off the Helsingør coast. Frederik was concerned lest the Danish astronomer Tycho Brahe should leave the kingdom, so to entice

16. Francis Beckett, *Uraniborg og Stjaerneborg*, Copenhagen, 1921, p. 37, and Francis Beckett, *Renaissancen og Kunstens Historie i Danmark*, Copenhagen, 1897, pp. 151–154.

him to stay he gave him the island and told him he would pay for a house and observatory to be built there to meet Tycho's requirements. Construction began in 1576 and was finished in 1581. The building consisted of a square block with curved gables, attached on each end to a two-storey drum with conical cap, and around the base of the drums were one-storey apartments for servants and visitors.

The principal windows of the square block were capped with elaborate scrolled pediments, and a few round windows high on the walls were to light rooms

Garden Plan,
Uraniborg, Hven Island, Denmark

Plan, Uraniborg, Hven Island, Denmark

Uraniborg, Hven Island, Denmark

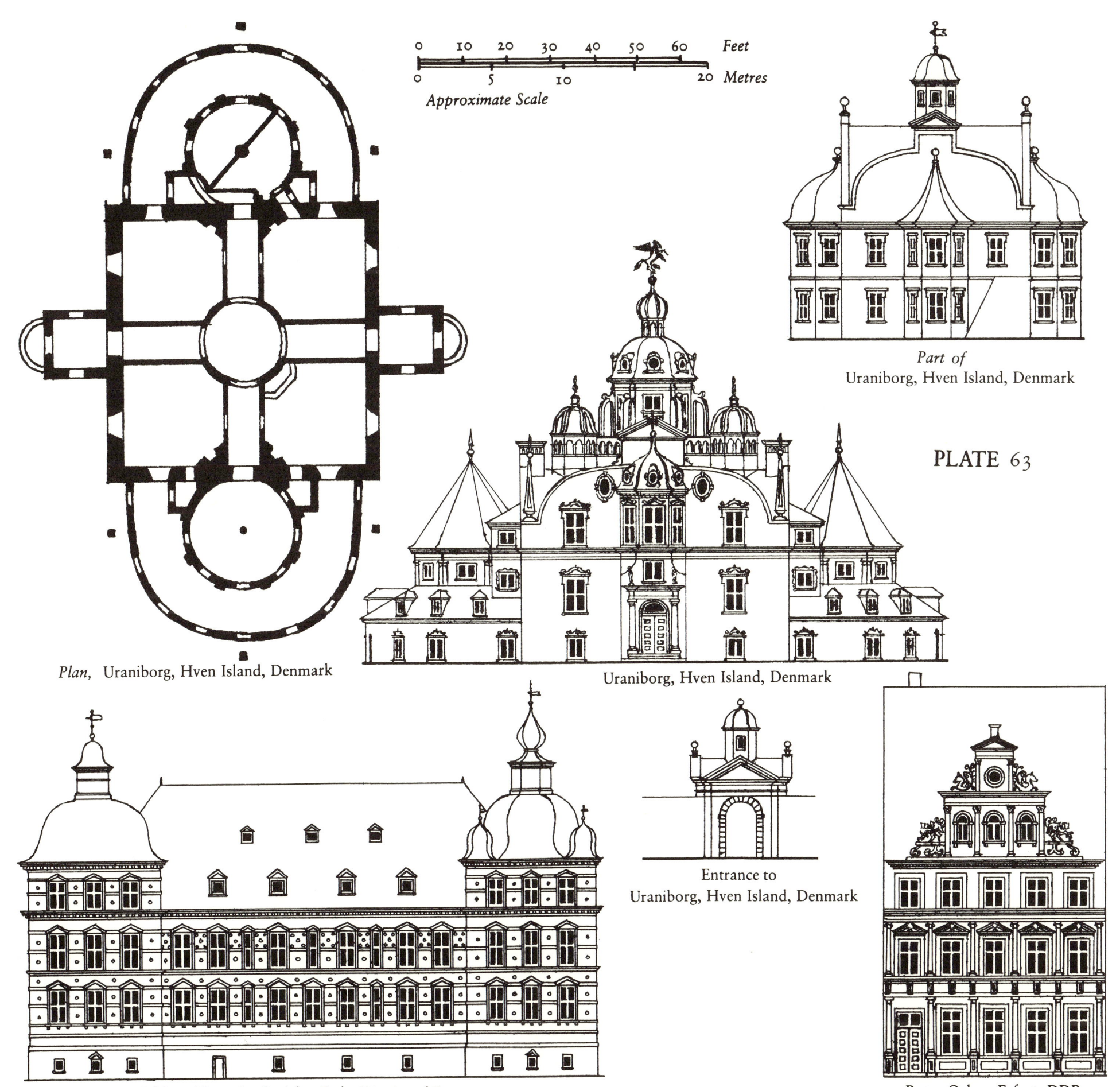

Part of Uraniborg, Hven Island, Denmark

PLATE 63

Schloss, Horst-im-Broiche, Ruhr District of Essen

Entrance to Uraniborg, Hven Island, Denmark

Roter Ochse, Erfurt, DDR

for students. On the roof were three domes, the largest being in the center; this was octagonal and of pure Renaissance design, one of the earliest in northern Europe, but the little cupola on top of it had an uncharacteristic onion-like open top, on which perched a giant statue of Pegasus. The chimneys were almost identical to the unusual chimneys of the Antwerp Raadhuis and Hanseatenhuis. All the domes and conical roofs were apparently to assist in making celestial observations. Tycho was evidently not satisfied with Uraniborg as an observatory, so he arranged for Steenwinckel to build him a new one a few feet away in 1584, called Stjerneborg, which was mostly underground, but eventually he left Denmark regardless and went to Prague to match wits with Kepler. As the King's architect, Hendrik was undoubtedly responsible for Uraniborg, which should be compared with the very different Villa Rotonda by Palladio.[17]

Hendrik is known to have been the architect of one further Danish building, the so-called Kommunitetsbygningen or Community Building for the University of Copenhagen, on the western side of University Square. The contract was signed on 3 April 1574, but construction was delayed for a year or more. No picture exists of this building, which burned down in 1728, although pieces of its walls were re-used in subsequent buildings.[18] Hendrik left Denmark in 1582 after a brief imprisonment, and is presumed to have died shortly afterwards.

Schloss, Horst-im-Broiche, Ruhr District of Essen PLATE 63

The German castle of Horst near Essen was built about 1560 around a quadrangle. Many names have been associated with the design, including Joist de la Cour, Arndt Johanssen and Laurentz von Brachum, and each may have contributed a share. The main block and its heavy corner-towers had simple pedimented windows, most of them two lights wide, but a few a single light wide. The massing was faintly reminiscent of Ancy, but many other castles had such a general configuration. The courtyard side had fussy loggias with narrow double arches for each bay, and a gable dripping with strapwork. Much of the castle has been destroyed.

Roter Ochse, Erfurt, DDR PLATE 63

At Erfurt, East Germany, the Roter Ochse (Red Ox) was built by an anonymous designer in 1562. The two lower floors were trimmed with Doric half-columns and Ionic pilasters, and pediments on the upper windows, but the lower floor has subsequently been altered. The next storey is plain with five windows, but above it stands a handsome gable with elaborate carvings in the place of volutes.

Chapel, Schloss Augustusburg, near Karl Marx Stadt, DDR PLATE 64

Also in East Germany is Schloss Augustusburg, near Karl Marx Stadt. The chapel in that castle was built 1569–1573, by Erhard van der Meer. The exterior is devoid of decoration, with large compass-headed windows in two storeys. The interior is chaste but handsome. The nave is covered by a barrelvault decorated with a form of strapwork that rests on an entablature. Below the entablature are two rows of transverse barrelvaults, both above and below the galleries; Doric and Ionic half-columns are attached to the front of these arches. This interior seems to be influenced somewhat by the chapel of the Residenz at Dresden, even to the point of having a recessed gallery over the altar.

Schloss, Rheydt PLATE 64

Two parts of the Schloss at Rheydt, West Germany, have some classical details. The left wing, dated 1567–1569, is sometimes attributed to Joist de la Cour. Its ground floor is boldly articulated with sculptured Doric half-columns on panelled bases, and the windows are capped with pediments. The upper windows also have pediments, but the upper wall looks bare with no other decoration. The other side of the right wing is actually later than the left wing, but looks more like a product of the early Renaissance. It was built by an anonymous architect in 1580. The lower storey is a Tuscan arcaded loggia of seven regular arches and one wider arch at the left end. Above an entablature are Ionic pilasters with unexpected bases, and between every other pair of them is a window. The roof over this section is a series of small hips, each with a dormer window.

Antiquarium, Residenz, Munich PLATE 64

The Mantuan architect Jacopo Strada, who may have studied under Serlio, was hired about 1569 to design a special building for the Residenz at Munich, the so-called Antiquarium. This was erected with a few changes to the design by Wilhelm Egckl in 1571. It had a crypt-like gallery on the ground floor for displaying art, and a library for Albrecht V, Duke of Bavaria. A few years later, it was rebuilt to a different design by Friedrich Sustris and others. As first built, the ground floor with no windows was composed of heavily rusticated stonework with delicate Ionic pilasters superimposed. The upper floor had seventeen segmentally-pedimented windows divided by clusters of Corinthian pilasters sitting on a deep base. The hipped roof, no doubt Egckl's contribution for it looked extremely Flemish, had two rows of small hipped dormers with one larger dormer in the center decorated with volutes and Composite pilasters. Further work done at the Residenz by Sustris will be covered presently.

14 Lunertorstrasse, Lüneburg PLATE 64

At Lüneburg in the north of Germany, a modest house on a street corner at 14 Lünertorstrasse somewhat awkwardly combines three storeys with only two levels of orders under a high hipped roof. This was accomplished by the anonymous architect by adding giant-order Doric half-columns (with curious ribs on them) on high bases and with flying entablatures to the lower two floors, while the top floor alone has a diminished size of Ionic half-column. The design's weakest point is where

17. Skovgaard, Architecture, pp. 41 and 44, and Beckett, *Uraniborg*, passim.
18. Letters to the author from Ejvind Slottved and Hakon Lund, 1982.

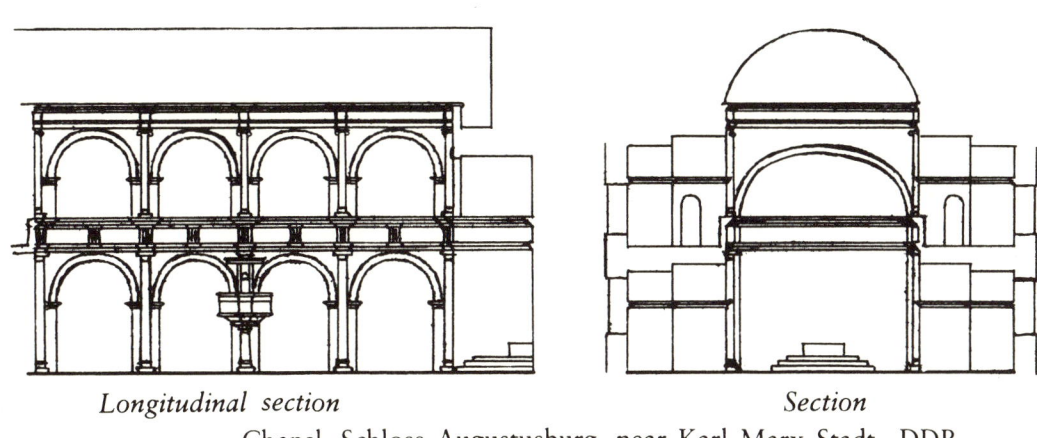

Longitudinal section *Section*
Chapel, Schloss Augustusburg, near Karl Marx Stadt, DDR

Courtyard side, Schloss Rheydt

PLATE 64

14 Lunertorstrasse, Lüneburg

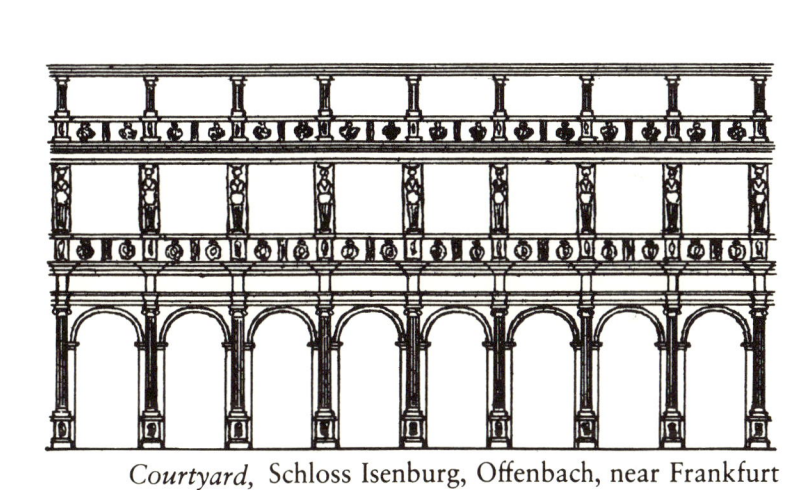

Courtyard, Schloss Isenburg, Offenbach, near Frankfurt

Wing, Schloss Rheydt

Antiquarium, Residenz, Munich

113

the windows of the middle storey intrude above the capitals of the Doric columns and oblige them to carry only flying entablatures rather than a full entablature.

Schloss Isenburg, Offenbach, near Frankfurt PLATE 64

Near Frankfurt in central Germany is the Schloss Isenburg at Offenbach. There an eight-bay, three-storey loggia was built, possibly by Conrad Büttner, on the courtyard façade from 1570 to 1578. The loggia has a rather French look about it. The ground floor consists of arches with carving in the spandrels and fluted Ionic pilasters standing in front of the piers on top of carved bases. The middle storey has no arches but a set of short herms or caryatids holding up an entablature. The top floor is even lower; it has short fluted Tuscan pillars supporting the roof. Apparently, this design was intended to be carried around many sides of a court, but only one side was built.

Börse, Hamburg PLATE 65

Hamburg, as the most important North Sea port for Germany, could have been expected to have a Bourse or Merchants' Exchange as important as London's Royal Exchange or Antwerp's Hanseatenhuis. One was founded in 1558, and eventually the money was raised to construct an appropriate building on wooden pilings over the harbor. It was built 1577–1583 by Jan Andressen from Amsterdam. Although it was built of wood it survived with no marked deterioration until it was swept away by a large city-wide fire in 1842, but its appearance is known through a variety of paintings and engravings. The front of the ground floor had six open bays marked by pairs of Tuscan columns tied together at their mid-points by wooden blocks. In place of the expected cornice was a large swelling, on top of which sat the upper storey. Andressen may have intended for the upper storey to be open behind a balustrade and Ionic columns arranged in a rhythm of a single column standing between two pairs of columns with a light lattice covering all, but the North Sea weather soon required the spaces to be glazed. Above the entablature, the ogival roof had a few hipped dormers in two rows; three cupolas stood on top, those on the ends being square in section, and the taller one in the middle being a handsome double-decked octagon. While the overall design was quite far from anything likely to have been found in Italy many of its individual components were bold and clever.

Burg Trausnitz, Landshut PLATE 65

Lamberto Suavius Sustris, who designed part of the church at Liège and took part in the design competition for the Antwerp Raadhuis, trained his son Friedrich in architecture and may have apprenticed him to an architect in Italy. The young Sustris did most of his work in the Munich area. His earliest major project was at the castle of Burg Trausnitz at Landshut in 1578. Some of his work consisted of adding a rich interior to the castle, but he also added an impressive loggia in the irregular courtyard. The ground floor is a simple wall of channelled masonry pierced by a few small windows, but the two storeys above, identical to each other, have elliptical arches with rusticated Tuscan pilasters standing in front of the piers. In the middle is a wider bay containing a central arch the same size as the others, flanked by a pair of narrow arches sharing the same impost, with oval openings above them. A grand staircase at the left end bends a pair of elliptical arches to follow the line of the stairs.

Grottenhof, Residenz, Munich PLATE 65

Sustris was hired by the man who became Duke Wilhelm V of Bavaria in 1579 to work at Burg Trausnitz, so it was no surprise that Wilhelm had Sustris do work on the Residenz at Munich, starting in 1580. Here he built the courtyard known as the Grottenhof following a fire in the old building. The ground floor was a Tuscan arcaded loggia with seven bays on east and west and nine bays on the south. Unexpectedly high above the arcade was a belt of panels, on top of which were windows, each with a cornice moulding at its head, and between the windows were niches containing statues. In the center of the high roof was a large, formal dormer, flanked by a pair of small, informal dormers. The three sides of the courtyard have been altered over the years, two of them being completely transformed.

Saint Michael's Church, Munich
PLATES 65 & 66

While he was in Munich, Sustris worked on other buildings, the best-known of which is Saint Michael's Church, the finest Renaissance church in Germany. Work began in 1583, and at various points other people had a say in the design, notably Hans Krumpper (Sustris' son-in-law) and master-mason Wolfgang Miller, who made no secret of his dislike for Sustris; in fact, he blamed Sustris when part of the building collapsed during the construction. The collapse caused Sustris to re-think his plans and he added transepts and a large choir beginning in 1593, but the drawings shown here reflect the earlier plans.

The interior, influenced by the Church of the Gesù in Rome and by some of Serlio's designs, was built for the Jesuits in a period when they felt they had turned back the tide of the Reformation, so it is an elaborate attempt to reflect the Church Triumphant. The entrance façade on the exterior is a disappointment because Sustris' plans were altered. The nave consists of three large bays on each side, delineated by pairs of fluted Corinthian pilasters on the front of piers. Between the piers are semicircular side-chapels with half-dome ceilings. As the piers are extended upwards, they provide the impost for clerestory arches in which are tall compass-headed windows. The main ceiling is a high barrel-vault moulded in panels. The liturgical "west" end (not actually facing west) is not as originally designed, having more windows now than intended. In Plate 66, the present

Börse, Hamburg

Longitudinal section of the Nave, Saint Michael's Church, Munich

PLATE 65

0　10　20　30　40　50　60　Feet
0　　　5　　　10　　　　20　Metres
Approximate Scale

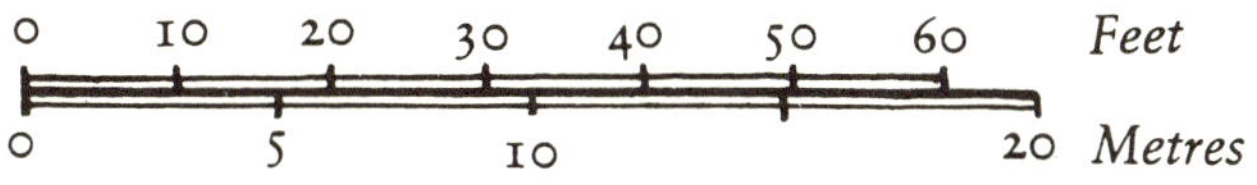

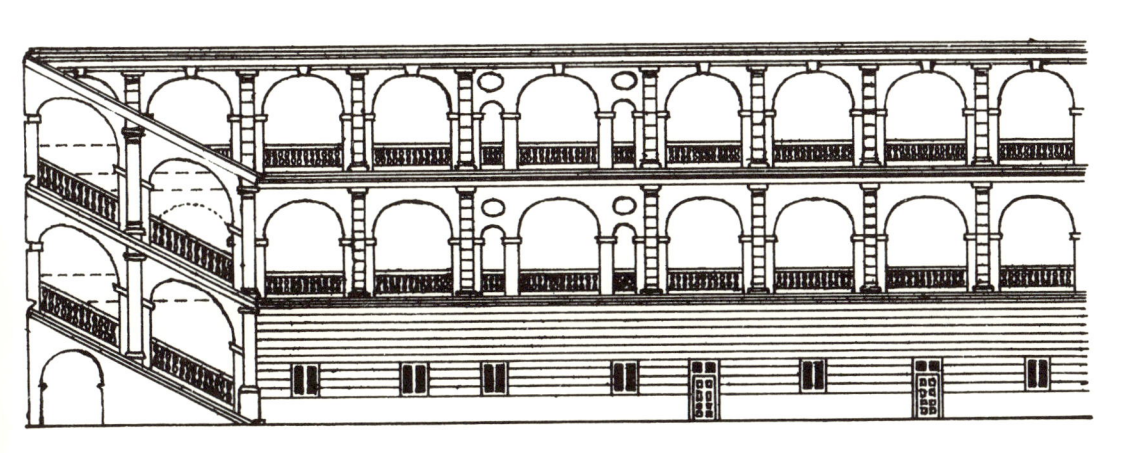

Part of courtyard, Burg Trausnitz, Landshut

East wing, courtyard, Grottenhof, Residenz, Munich

Original Plan

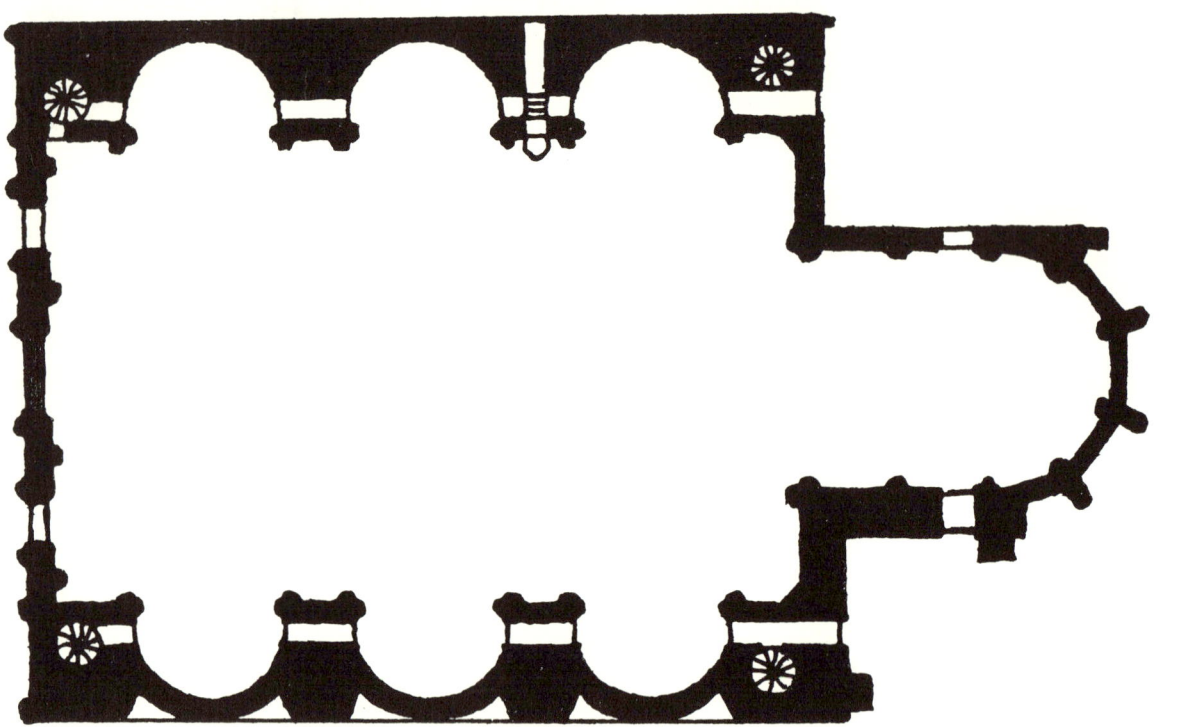

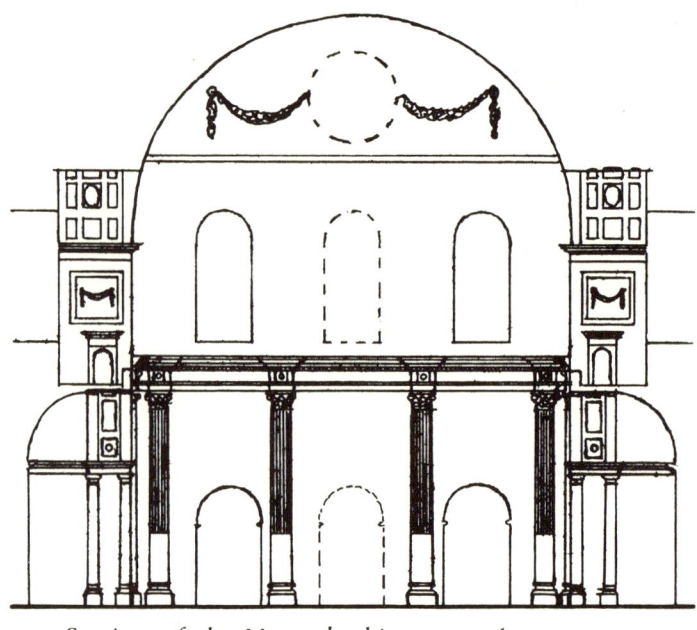

Section of the Nave, looking towards entrance, Saint Michael's Church, Munich

Approximate Scale

PLATE 66

Entrance

Original entrance (conjectural reconstruction)

façade is shown on the left and an attempt has been made to reconstruct in part Sustris' elevation on the right, based on a few written descriptions. Apart from the number of windows, the principal difference is in the shape of the gable, the area in which the present design is weakest.

Jesuit College, Munich PLATE 67

In 1585, the Jesuits hired Sustris to design them the Jesuit College in Munich, part of which is shown here. It is a rather dry, academic building of four storeys under a high roof with dormers. The ground floor has rusticated stonework, while the face of the other floors is smooth. The windows of the next storey are pedimented, but the windows of the floor above have only individual cornice mouldings. The top-floor windows are oval in rectangular panels under split pediments.

Bollaertskamer, Gent/Gand, Belgium PLATE 67

In Belgium, enough time had elapsed since the construction of the Antwerp Raadhuis for the Flemish part of the rebellion against Spain to collapse and for construction to begin on buildings that imitated various aspects of the Raadhuis. The most obvious of the early imitations is the Bollaertskamer, a four-bay wing added to the old Gent Raadhuis in 1580 by Joos Rooman. Each bay is articulated with columns, as in the central part of the Antwerp building, but the Gent building arranges its columns in pairs rather than singly. The columns of the ground floor are rusticated Doric, those of the floor above are Ionic, and the top floor's are Corinthian. A variety of dormers, large and small, pierce the roof. The design fails to be an improvement on the Antwerp Raadhuis because it is too busy.

Cathedral of Saints Peter & Paul, Klagenfurt, Austria PLATE 67

The Münster Church of Saints Peter & Paul, Klagenfurt, Austria, was built for the Lutherans in 1580. By 1604, it was taken over by the Jesuits, who later enlarged it and filled it with rococo decoration. Since 1787, it has been the local cathedral. The nave was relatively short with four bays marked by giant-order Corinthian pillars. Part of the way up the pillars are elliptical arches supporting a tribune or gallery, over which are more transverse arches. The pillars support the main cornice through flying entablatures, above which are further arches in which are set the clerestory windows. This is the first appearance of the giant order in a church in any of the Germanic countries.

Spieshof, Basel, Switzerland PLATE 67

Another building by an anonymous architect is the Spieshof in Basel, Switzerland, built about 1580. The ground floor is composed of three wide elliptical arches with Tuscan half-columns standing in front of the piers. The next storey consists of six Venetian arches with Tuscan columns in the form of a loggia and Ionic half-columns standing in front of the arches; the floor above duplicates that exactly, but with Corinthian columns replacing the Ionic of the floor below. The top floor is twelve windows separated by large volutes that support the overhang of the roof. Three heavy dormers stand on the roof. Naturally, with the cold climate of Basel, the loggias have long since been filled by windows.

Juliusuniversität, Würzburg PLATE 68

The Robin brothers, Jan II and George, from Ypres, Belgium, worked at Würzburg in south-central Germany in the 1580s, where they were hired by the Roman Catholic Bishop Julius Echter to build the Julius University building attached to the new gothic-style church that Echter was also having built at the same time. The Robins designed the courtyard to have a rusticated loggia form the ground floor (many of the arches have now been filled in with windows and doors), above which are three storeys of plain double windows. The roof, which dates from about 1590, has a few small hipped dormers in two rows, and an ugly mannerist gable in the middle of the west side of the courtyard. With the exception of the ground-floor loggia, the bulk of the building might as well be a product of the 1950s.

Capriccio Gate PLATE

No account of the Renaissance in Germany would be complete without a mention of Wendel Dietterlin of Strasbourg (which is now part of France). His book *Architectura* came out in many volumes, beginning in 1593, although he probably actually wrote it and drew the preliminary illustrations in the 1580s. He is not known to have designed any extant buildings, but his books were widely influential. They followed in the footsteps of Floris and Vredeman in being devoted primarily to mannerist ideas and strapwork, but occasional classical forms can be found in them, such as the Corinthian triumphal arch shown here, shorn of the strapwork decoration in which he clad it.

Also useful are Eberhard Hempel, *Baroque Art and Architecture in Central Europe*, Harmondsworth, Penguin Books, 1965; H. Gerson and E. H. ter Kuile, *Art and Architecture in Belgium 1600–1800*, Penguin Books, 1960; and Jakob Rosenberg, Seymour Slive and E. H. ter Kuile, *Dutch Art and Architecture 1600–1800*, Penguin Books, 1966 (rev. 1977). In spite of their titles stating to the contrary, they each contain information on the sixteenth century. Also Anthony Blunt, *Baroque and Rococo*, New York, Harper & Rowe, 1978.

Part of Jesuit College, Munich

Bollaertskamer, Gent/Gand, Belgium

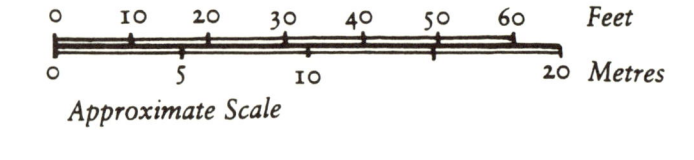

PLATE 67

0　10　20　30　40　50　60　Feet
0　　　5　　　10　　　　20　Metres
Approximate Scale

Longitudinal section of the Nave,
Cathedral of Saints Peter & Paul, Klagenfurt, Austria

Spieshof, Basel, Switzerland

Courtyard, looking west, Juliusuniversität, Würzburg

PLATE 68

Capriccio Gate

Approximate Scale

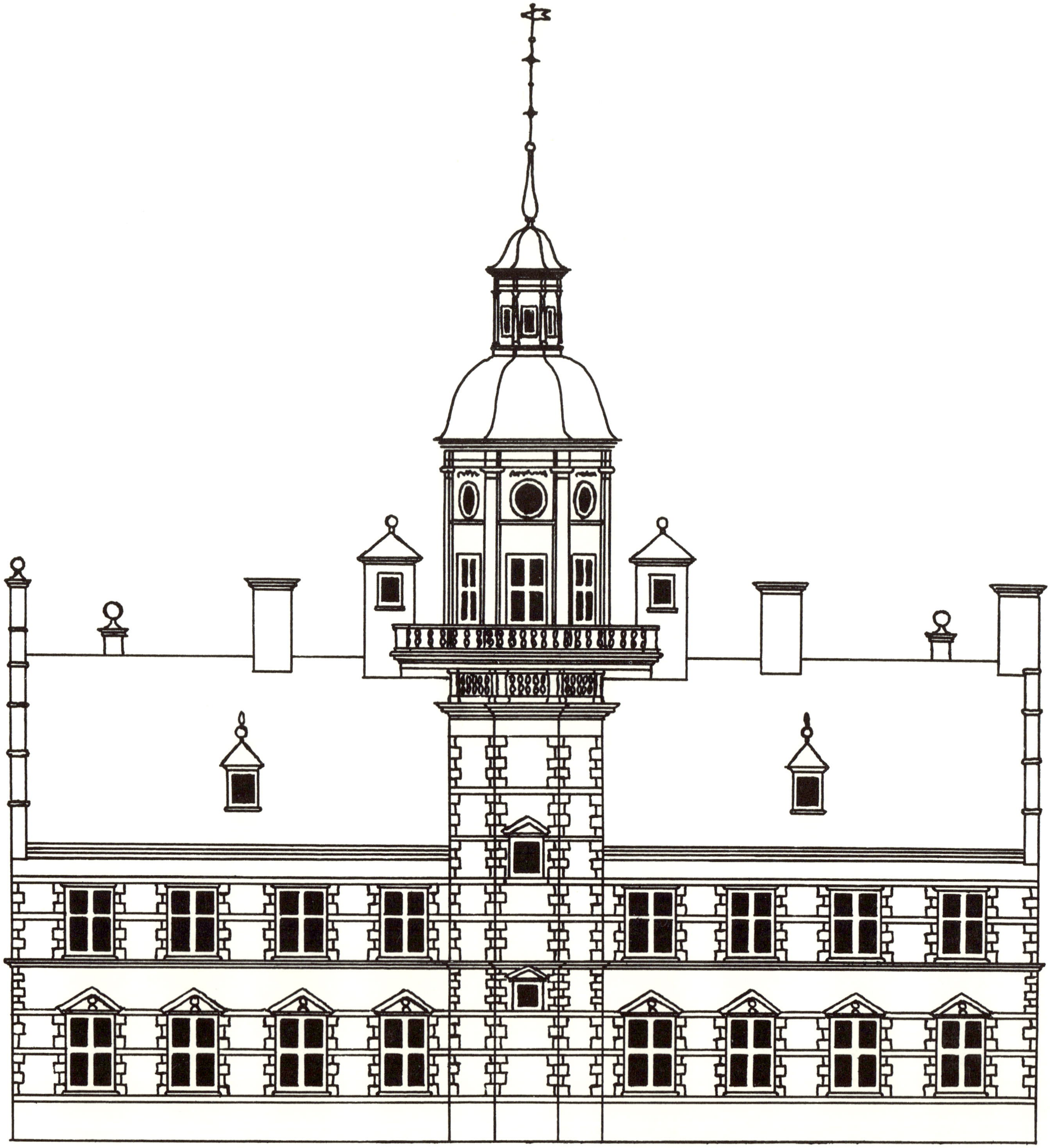

GREAT BRITAIN

Fife
Midlothian

Conwy
Ruthin
Clwyd

Shropshire

Nottinghamshire

Norfolk

Burghley

Warwickshire
Northamptonshire
Cambridge

Gloucestershire
Hertfordshire
Essex

Middlesex
Windsor London
Bath Wiltshire Berkshire
Surrey
Winchester
Sussex

Even though the English had pacified substantial portions of Ireland during the sixteenth century, no record of any classical architecture from that period has thus far been discovered in Ireland, which may come as no surprise to most readers. However, many will be surprised to learn of buildings in the classical style in both Scotland and Wales, in addition to the score or so of examples found in England. Although Scotland and England had as little as possible to do with each other in this period, this book will group their respective architecture together for the sake of convenience.

Late in the fifteenth century, England was preoccupied with the dynastic wars between the house of York and the house of Lancaster. When Henry VII came to the throne in 1485 following the Battle of Bosworth Field, he did everything he could to promote stability to prolong the peace achieved by that battle. He tried to make all aspects of culture reflect a sense of continuity with the past two centuries, and so he was not receptive to any new style of architecture that looked back so far into the past that it failed to demonstrate any connection with the more recent past. Henry's concern centered around the eating arrangements of his palaces and of the great houses of the nobility, which he felt were crucial to maintaining order, stability and continuity; since the new Italian forms of architecture were accompanied by radical floor-plans that implied the abandoning of the traditional eating arrangements the new forms had to be discouraged. Instead, the old gothic forms were developed to a new stage, characterized by slimmer masonry piers, increased areas of glass, the four-centered arch and occasionally the fan-vaulted ceiling, all described under the heading of perpendicular gothic.

After Henry VII's fastidious rejection of the new forms, his son Henry VIII commissioned Italian workmen under Pietro Torrigiano (sometimes spelled Torrigiani) of Florence to create a sumptuous Florentine monument for Henry VII and an elaborate classical altar for the perpendicular-gothic Henry VII Chapel at Westminster, 1512–1518 (destroyed 1644). Henry also made heavy use of Italian designers for the new fortifications required to counter the recent invention of artillery, but apart from a few church monuments the Italians were kept at military, not civil tasks. Even Cardinal Wolsey's new palace at Hampton Court added no more than a few sculpted roundels of Italian work to the otherwise English gothic building. The finest classical achievement of the day in England was the lower half of the wooden choir-screen at King's College Chapel, Cambridge, designed possibly by a man from Genoa in 1533. Italian and French workmen like Nicolas Belin or Belini were employed at Nonsuch Palace, Surrey, but only to equip the interior with quantities of strapwork decoration and grotesque sculpture in imitation of similar work recently done at Fontainebleau. Henry's break with the Church of Rome tended to inhibit further Italian influence.

One of Henry's decrees had far-reaching effects in architecture: in an effort to increase the internal security of the realm, he forbade any of his nobles from building any new fortified castles, secure in the knowledge that any existing fortifications could be easily reduced by artillery. From Henry's point of view, this meant that he would be less likely to be faced with a serious rebellion, since the rebels would have no secure place to hide. From an architectural point of view, it meant that all new major houses would henceforth be facing outwards rather than inwards, and many houses would thus be equipped with large glass areas on their outside walls.

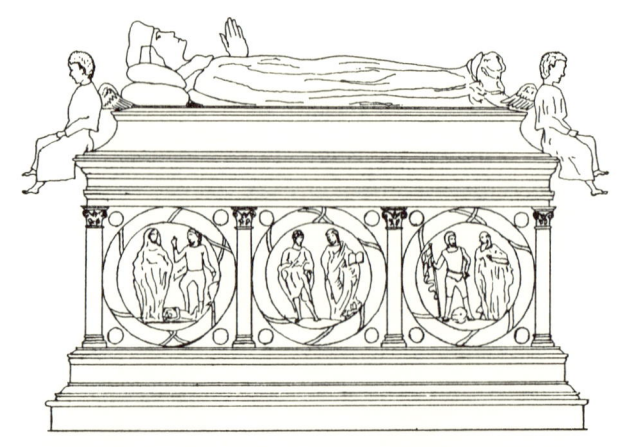

Tomb of Henry VII, Westminster

Altar, Chapel of Henry VII, Westminster

Technologically, this followed the lead of perpendicular-gothic churches, and most of the houses so built thus tended to be in the gothic style, since neither the defense-conscious Italians nor the ancient Romans had even dreamed of marrying the classical style to large areas of glass. However, the Dutch and Belgians had already done so with their narrow city houses, and it was to the Low Countries that the architects of such otherwise French-inspired houses as Longleat turned for inspiration about windows. Glazing in country houses probably reached its apogee in the gothic Hardwick Hall, which a doggerel poet has described as "more glass than wall."

Whitehall Palace, London PLATE 69

With the fall of Cardinal Wolsey in 1529, Henry VIII confiscated Wolsey's far-flung property. Hampton Court was the most famous of these, but York Place in Westminster was more useful, as it was close to Westminster Hall. Henry quickly set about converting the many buildings of York Place into a single large palace, which he called Whitehall. Nearly all of Whitehall Palace, which was ready by late 1533 to receive Queen Anne Boleyn, was built in the prevailing gothic style, but two parts of it, the King Street Gate and the Orchard Garden Loggia, combined classical elements. The lower floor of the Gate consisted of a large rectangular opening for carriages flanked by a pair of compass-headed arches for pedestrians, and all three trimmed with Tuscan pilasters. The façade over the pedestrian ways was moulded in the form of round towers, and the whole upper storey was decorated with Ionic pilasters, along with some large gothic windows. The Gate was demolished in 1723. Wolsey's Orchard Garden was eventually made into Henry's Great Garden in the 1540s, but the loggia was probably built in the early 1530s. Its appearance is known from a portrait of Henry and his family in the Royal Collection. The loggia was formed out of a colonnade of (probably wooden) Ionic columns, the bottom third of whose shafts was fluted with some reeding, and the upper two-thirds carved all over with mannerist vines. The portions of the entablature over the columns projected forward. The painting does not reveal whether any other storeys were built on top of the loggia, but written descriptions of the palace seem to suggest that the so-called Stone Gallery was built over the loggia.

Falkland Palace, Fife, Scotland PLATE 69

Classical details first reached Scotland in the 1530s in the form of some wings at Falkland Palace, Fife and also some alterations to Stirling Castle, the latter not being of sufficient quality to include in this book. James V came to the Scottish throne in 1523 at age 11. He married the daughter of the French King François I in 1537, and when she died, he married a second Frenchwoman, Marie de Guise, in 1539. With such a strong French orientation, James imported some anonymous French masons to enlarge Falkland Palace in the late 1530s. What they built is hardly classical, but the two court-yard wings are symmetrical and regular. The east wing, containing the chapel, stretches for six bays, each delineated by a Corinthian column on an exceptionally high base. The ground floor is low, but the next storey has the appearance of a piano nobile. The roof is edged with a high parapet, some statuary and dormers of French character. The south wing, now in ruins, contained the king's apartments on the ground floor, with its low but wide windows, and the queen's apartments on the piano nobile. The system of Corinthian columns is similar to that of the east wing but with flying entablatures. Both elevations have two square panels containing roundels in each bay.

Old Somerset House, London PLATE 70

French influence on English architecture was first noticeable at Old Somerset House in London, the residence of the Lord Protector Edward Seymour, Duke of Somerset, who served as regent during the first part of the reign of the boy-king, Edward VI. Somerset's steward, John Thynne, was in charge of the construction of Somerset House from 1547 to 1552; Somerset's execution caused work to stop before the house was completed. The front on the Strand was arranged symmetrically in five sections; the central part had a Roman Doric triumphal arch for the entrance, and above that was a balcony with Ionic columns; a third level had a partial loggia of Corinthian columns projecting above the roof balustrade. The middle sections on each side of the entrance each had two bays with two storeys of pedimented windows. The outside portions of the façade had pairs of windows wrapped in Doric and Ionic orders, and some abstract mannerist designs projecting above the roof balustrade. The courtyard side of the main entrance had a handsome arch with four Tuscan columns on the ground floor, a pair of windows with split segmental pediments above, and a single large window with broad triangular pediment on the top level. Across the courtyard from the entrance was a nine-bay Tuscan arcaded loggia with an open top, in front of a two-storey block with seven windows. On top of the roof was an octagonal cupola standing on a square base containing a clock. The entire building was demolished by 1776 when Sir William Chambers built a new Somerset House, but a number of pictures of the early building survive from before Inigo Jones' seventeenth-century additions.

Bishop Gardiner Chapel, Cathedral, Winchester PLATE 70

Somerset and most of the rest of the court were staunch Protestants, but felt quite free to borrow French versions of the new Italian classical forms. Stephen Gardiner, Bishop of Winchester, was roughly treated by the Protestants, but when Edward's sister Mary came to the throne in 1553, Gardiner's fortunes were restored for the last two years of his life. Mary, who found Gardiner's advice invaluable, saw that a lovely classical memorial was erected to him in Winchester Cathedral in

PLATE 69

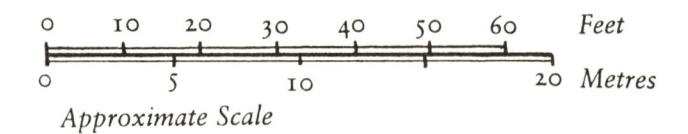

King Street Gate, Whitehall Palace, London

Orchard Loggia, Whitehall Palace, London

Courtyard, looking east, Falkland Palace, Fife, Scotland

Courtyard, looking south, Falkland Palace, Fife, Scotland

124

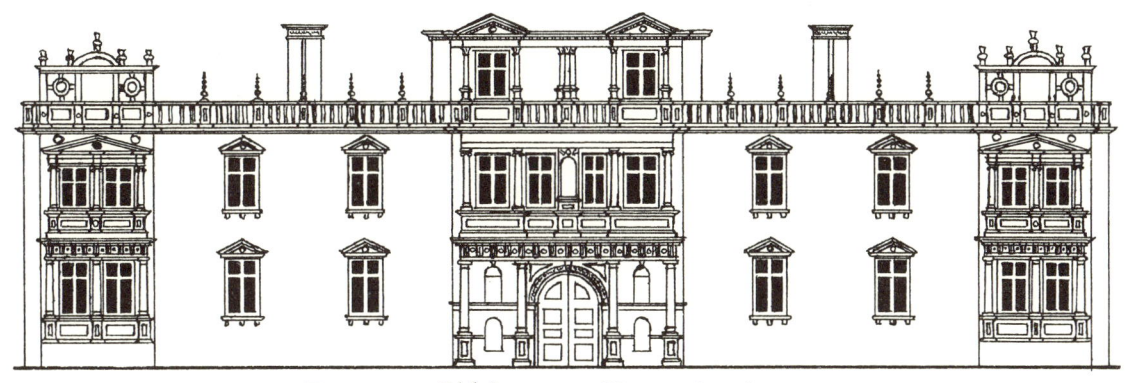

Entrance, Old Somerset House, London

Bishop Gardiner Chapel, Cathedral, Winchester
(not drawn to regular scale)

PLATE 70

Courtyard side, Old Somerset House, London

Entrance, Courtyard side, Old Somerset House, London

Villa, Moorfields, London

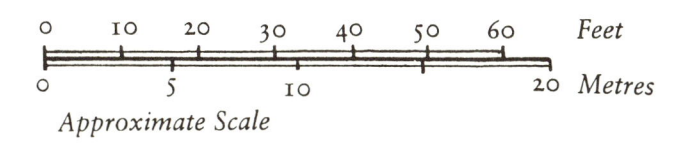

0 10 20 30 40 50 60 Feet
0   5   10   20 Metres
Approximate Scale

Queen's Loggia, near Windsor

Room at Victoria & Albert Museum, London
(not drawn to regular scale)

Window, Newark Park House, Gloucestershire

125

a Florentine style. Beyond that, Mary's five years on the throne produced little or nothing in the way of classical architecture.

Villa, Moorfields, London PLATE 70

The Duke of Somerset had performed another service for English architecture that was not to bear fruit until after his death: he sent the young John Shute to study architecture in Italy in 1550. Shute tardily published a slim book in 1563, *The First & Chief Groundes of Architecture,* and the book enjoyed many reprints. No record exists of Shute having actually designed any buildings, but, if he did, any of the next three designs would be likely candidates. The so-called Copperplate map/view of London is dated about 1559, and it shows a house in Moorfields with an elliptical dome, two storeys high and five bays wide; a different view shows that the angles of the building were dressed by giant Tuscan pilasters standing on bases and supporting a complete entablature. In John Stow's *Survey of London* (1598), this house is described as one of many "fayre summer houses . . . ., not so much for vse or profite, as for shewe and pleasure, bewraying the vanity of mens mindes, much vnlike to the disposition of the ancient Cittizens, who delighted in the building of Hospitals, and Almes houses for the poore, and therein both imployed their wits and spent their wealthes in preferment of the common commoditie of this our Citie." The identity of the owner and the architect and the date of destruction of the house are unknown, but it must have been constructed about 1558.

Room at Victoria & Albert Museum, London PLATE 70

The Victoria & Albert Museum in London has a remarkable panelled room, on display for over 50 years until recently, once installed at Haynes Grange, Ampthill. Dr. Mark Girouard, at a public lecture, has stated that he is convinced that the room is Elizabethan, in spite of a previous attribution (unsupported) to Inigo Jones. Girouard suggests that the room may have been built for Chicksands Priory about 1575, but it may well be earlier, such as about 1560. Could this be a work by Shute? The unpainted pine room has most of its available wall space filled with fluted Corinthian pilasters. The windows and the overmantel, both with pediments, are also of the Corinthian order, while the doorway is of the Doric order with fluted pilasters.

Window, Newark Park House, Gloucestershire PLATE 70

Newark Park, Ozleworth, Gloucestershire, was built in 1560 by Sir Nicholas Poyntz as a hunting lodge, but it has been enlarged and altered in each of the succeeding centuries, so the original form has been lost. One pedimented window (now a door, and perhaps also originally a door) remains from the external trim, with Tuscan fluted columns on high bases. While the room at the Victoria & Albert could never have come from Newark, they may have been designed by the same man. Newark now belongs to the National Trust.

Queen's Loggia, near Windsor PLATE 70

An engraving by Marcus Gheeraerts I, dated 1576, shows Elizabeth I in her Garter robes in a procession in a loggia with Windsor Castle in the background. Marble Ionic pilasters stand between the arches. Howard Colvin writes that the loggia never existed, but is "one of those pictorial fictions that were often used" in this period. Nevertheless, although no record or trace of it survives today, there is no reason why Elizabeth or one of her court may not have had such a loggia near Windsor with such an excellent view of the Castle. If so, it would have been built about 1560. Because of the marble, it may have been the work of the Flemish architect, Hans Hendrik van Paesschen, who was doing stonework for Sir William Cecil and Sir Thomas Gresham as early as 1559, and who was noted for his marble columns and pilasters.[1]

Gresham House, London PLATE 71

Gresham and Cecil worked together as a team in many of their endeavors, the former serving the queen as her chief financial advisor and the latter as her prime minister. Gresham was frequently in Antwerp on business, both for the queen and for himself, and there he made the acquaintance of both Floris and Hendrik (see the previous chapter for both of these Flemish architects). Both Cecil and Gresham apparently employed both men for a variety of purposes. Cecil, who was his own architect for much of Burghley House, initially had Hendrik procure the right kind of paving stones for him, and may have had Floris do some sculpture work. Gresham recognised Hendrik's architectural talents, and hired him to design him an impressive house in London's financial district, beginning about 1561. Gresham House, later Gresham College, was a brick structure with white stone trim and an arcaded courtyard loggia of marble Tuscan columns, the first Italianate palace in London (Somerset House was not in the Italian style). The house was completed by 1566.[2]

Apart from the loggia, that extended completely around the courtyard, Gresham House was innovative in another way: the courtyard elevation had only one storey above the single-storey loggia below the hipped roof with its hipped dormers, but the exterior elevation had three storeys and a low roof. Thus, the ridge of the roof was moved outwards from its normal central position. The design of the house was flexible enough that Gresham was able to devote one wing of it (with a series of five little porches) as an almshouse for indigents. The rest of the house he willed to Gresham College, which he had founded a few years before his death in defiance of the authorities of his *alma mater,* Cambridge University, and the college quickly took over the house as its headquarters. The college hired many distinguished London scholars for its faculty, including John Bull as the first Professor of Music, and Christo-

1. Letter to the author from Howard Colvin, July 1986.
2. John Ward, *Lives of the Professors of Gresham College,* London, 1740, pp. 19–20.

North elevation, Gresham House, London

West elevation

Courtyard side, looking east

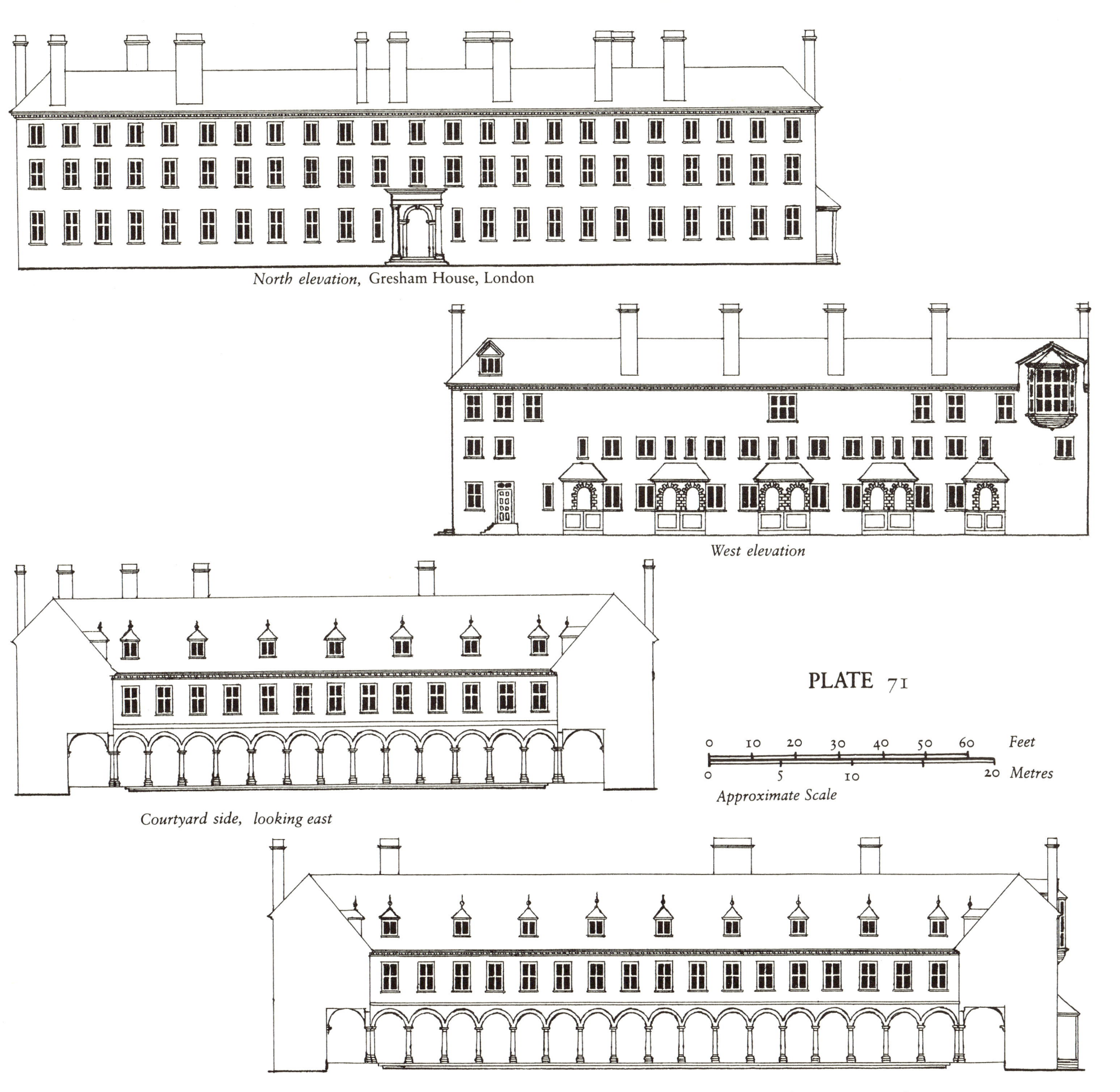

PLATE 71

Approximate Scale

Courtyard side, looking south, Gresham House, London

127

pher Wren, who was Professor of Astronomy resident in the college from 1657 to 1661. The classical lines of this building and the crisp contrast between its salmon bricks and white trim undoubtedly had a profound influence on the young Wren and encouraged him to design many buildings that reflected its best features. The college building was fortunately spared by the Great Fire of London in 1666; in fact, some of the business of the Royal Exchange was transferred to the college until a new Exchange could be built. The college, however, was not well maintained, and by the middle of the eighteenth century the great house where Gresham had entertained Elizabeth at a state dinner was abandoned and sold; it was demolished by its new owners, and the land was developed. Its appearance is known from three engravings made in the seventeenth and eighteenth centuries.

Gresham House represents a significant departure from English tradition also in the arrangement of its rooms, which were in only a single row deep around the courtyard, and allowed no room for a Great Hall, Great Chamber, Withdrawing Chamber and Privy Chamber, which formed the kernel of every other large house of the English nobility. Instead, the house can only have been divided into apartments, and thus followed up-to-date Italian and French practices.

Burghley House, near Stamford PLATE 72

Gresham had first travelled to Antwerp as early as 1543 and soon became a frequent visitor there. Consequently, he was in a good position to collaborate closely with his friend Cecil regarding business with Flanders, including a successful conspiracy to acquire stolen Spanish weapons. Gresham represented Cecil in Antwerp to purchase building materials, and to hire Hendrik to design parts of Burghley House, near Stamford. Burghley House, sometimes spelled Burleigh in the sixteenth century, was built in stone from about 1553 to about 1587. It is usually described as an Elizabethan prodigy-house, meaning that it is very large, somewhat whimsical in design, and intended as a place for Elizabeth to stay comfortably on one of her progresses around the country. Cecil acted as his own architect most of the time, but is known to have used the services of Hendrik on various occasions. It is arranged almost haphazardly around a courtyard, and has been only slightly altered since Cecil's death. Burghley is open to the public.[3]

Of the exterior elevations, only the south or garden face, begun about 1564, can have any connection with Hendrik on stylistic grounds. The center once contained an eight-bay arcaded loggia, whose central two bays projected slightly as a focal-point (thus disobeying the same rules of classical design that Hendrik was later to disregard at the Royal Exchange and at Bachegraig); this was altered in the eighteenth century by the insertion of more arches to give an odd number of bays, and the parapet around the roof was raised.

Hendrik's work is more evident in the courtyard. According to Sir John Summerson and Christopher Hussey, the attractive loggia at the east end was built about 1563–1570 in Antwerp and shipped in pieces by Gresham; upon the strong recommendation of the "Dutch mason," the columns were made of single pieces of stone. The original correspondence about this is at Hatfield, and included with some of Cecil's papers was a drawing (now lost) endorsed by Cecil, "Henryck's platt of my bay window." This is clear evidence that Hendrik was employed by Cecil as architect.[4]

The Tuscan arcaded loggia in the courtyard originally consisted of three bays on each side of a central structure of two storeys of superimposed Roman triumphal arches, the lower having engaged Tuscan columns and the upper Ionic. Cecil himself later added a third storey (perhaps the location of the bay window that Hendrik drew) and crowned it with a huge obelisk. About 1835, copies of the loggia were extended around the north and south sides of the courtyard, and all the loggias were later enclosed to make corridors.

In the middle of the north side of the courtyard a large projection was erected about 1564. The upper storey contains a massive arch with windows on either side in the form of a Venetian arch. This was the first example of this device in Britain, and the scale and proportions of this example suggest that it may have derived from the Pazzi Chapel in Florence. The south side of the courtyard is a mirror image of the north. Both arches have now been glazed.

Other features of Burghley that may be associated with Hendrik are the many collections of chimneys in the shape of Tuscan columns supporting entablatures, and two interior features: the so-called Roman staircase with its elegant ceiling and the Serlian chimney breast in the Great hall, both from the 1560s.

Copthall, Essex PLATE 72

One of Cecil's closest friends was Sir Thomas Heneage. They were keenly interested in each other's building projects and maintained a friendly rivalry as to whose house would best satisfy Elizabeth when she came to visit. Heneage's house was Copthall (also spelled Copped Hall) in Essex, built 1564 to 1567, and demolished in the eighteenth century. The house was a typical late gothic design with a U-shaped plan. An eighteenth-century picture shows that a handsome, nine-bay classical arcaded loggia, probably of marble, with Doric half-columns, was erected across the open ends of the courtyard, and John Newman has proved that this loggia was contemporary with the house. The style is entirely compatible with Hendrik's work, and Cecil could easily have suggested to his friend that an arcade by Hendrik would enhance his new house.[5]

Steelyard Project, London PLATE 72

Antwerp was northern Europe's most important port in the 1560s, which is why the Hanseatic merchants commissioned such an impressive palace to be built there for them. London was also becoming more important, so the Hanseatic merchants, who had been trading

3. *Country Life,* vol. 114, pp. 1828–1832 and 1962–1965 (by Christopher Hussey), and vol. 158, pp. 982–985 (by Eric Till).
4. J. S. Gotch, *Early Renaissance Architecture in England,* London, 1914 (second edition).
5. John Newman, "Copthall," in Colvin & Harris (ed.), *The Country Seat,* London, 1970, pp. 18–29.

Part of south front, Burghley House, near Stamford

Courtyard, looking north, Burghley House, near Stamford

Intwood House, Norfolk

Courtyard, looking east, Burghley

External loggia, Copthall, Essex

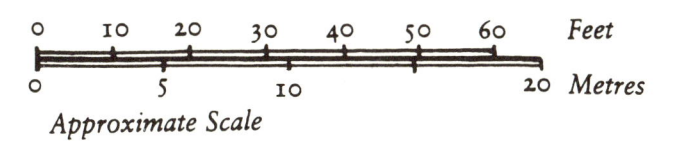

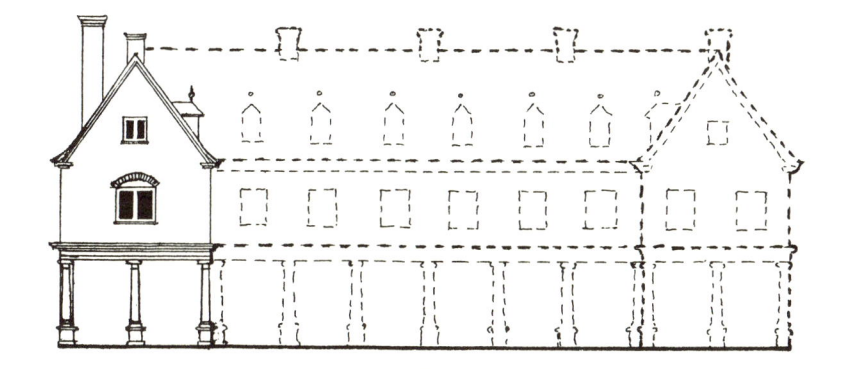

PLATE 72

Approximate Scale

River elevation, Steelyard, London

Side elevation, Steelyard, London

in London through a property known as the Steelyard or Stiliard along the Thames since 1259, apparently decided to enlarge their buildings there about 1559. The enlargement can be clearly seen on various views of London, but it looks as if the structure had been intended to be substantially larger than actually was built, and that the contract was cancelled after about a quarter of the work had been done. The unbuilt portion is shown in dotted lines in this book. The quarter that was built was two storeys tall with a gable roof. The lower storey was an open loggia of stone Tuscan columns, and the upper storey was brick, and the roof had dormers on the east side. Goods would have been stored in the shelter of the loggia after having been unloaded by the large crane that in the early views can be clearly seen standing in the space where the courtyard of the completed building would have been. Since Gresham was a part-owner of the Steelyard and since the Hanseatic merchants would later have Hendrik design their Antwerp palace, it seems logical that Hendrik would have been the designer of the Steelyard addition, especially in view of the use of the stone Tuscan columns.[6] Blackfriars Railway Station stands over the original site today.

Intwood House, Norfolk PLATE 72

Gresham was wealthy enough to own estates in many parts of England, especially in East Anglia. Intwood Hall, Intwood, Norfolk was originally built by Gresham's father, and enlarged by Gresham about 1565. The house was altered again about 1807 by Arthur Browne and again about 1835. The only surviving picture of it is an engraving made a few years after the Browne work, and it shows no fewer than six Flemish-type crow-step gables across the façade, the inner pair being recessed some distance behind the plane of the outer four. Each gable sat above a three-storey column of pedimented windows. It is tempting to recognise the windows and gables as Hendrik's method of dressing up the earlier gothic house. Elizabeth stayed at Intwood in 1578, but her opinion of it is not recorded.[7]

Royal Exchange, London PLATES 73 & 74

Much of Hendrik's work in Britain is difficult or impossible to document, and must be attributed through circumstantial evidence, but Hendrik's part in the design of the Royal Exchange in London, built 1566–1568, is clear. Britain's commercial relations with the Continent were once strengthened by the possession of Calais, but the French captured Calais during Mary's reign; in retaliation, the English took Le Havre, but when the English were weakened by a serious outbreak of the plague the French recaptured it, leaving England with no potential *entrepôt* on the Continent. The lack of such an English base, coupled with growing conflict between the Low Countries and their Spanish overlords, convinced Gresham and others that a merchants' exchange in London like the Antwerp Bourse would be profitable for England. The death of Gresham's only son Richard in 1564 convinced Gresham to put up the money for the building if the citizens of London would donate suitable land. On 23 January 1570, Elizabeth visited the Bourse after dining with Gresham; she announced that she was pleased with it, although she disliked its foreign name, so she issued a proclamation that thenceforth it should be called the Royal Exchange. The Royal Exchange prospered until it was destroyed in the Great Fire of London in 1666. Its replacement, designed by Edward Jerman, and the third or present Royal Exchange, which replaced it in 1838, were given a courtyard with arcaded loggias, following the lead of Hendrik's building.

The contemporary Italian writer Lodovico Guicciardini in the 1588 edition of his *Descrittione di tutti i Paesi Bassi* (Description of all the Low Countries) claims that the designer of the London Bourse was "Henrico van Paschen d'Anversa, architettore eccellente," and subsequent writers, with some exceptions, have tended to agree. The last word, however, must be from Hendrik's wife, who testified in a court document in Antwerp on 19 October 1568 that her husband was then "designing and building the Bourse" in London.[8]

The Exchange was a splendid building, built of brick with white stone dressing around a rectangular courtyard. The ground floor of the courtyard was an arcaded loggia supported on marble Tuscan columns (see the cover of this book). Above the arcade was a storey containing businesses that had a total of only four windows looking on the courtyard; where other windows normally would have been placed were compass-headed niches housing Floris' statues of the kings and queens of England, the niches being separated by Ionic pilasters. It had a hipped roof in a double-pile on all four sides, like the Hanseatenhuis. A handsome tower and cupola with overhanging balconies stood beside the main entrance on the south side; on the north side, the tower was balanced by an enormous Corinthian column. The cupola, the column and plinths on all four corners of the roof were surmounted with Gresham's personal emblem, the grasshopper. The only feature that tended to mar the high level of classical design was the use of an even number of bays on the north and south sides of the courtyard rather than the more correct odd number. All the carved stone-work was imported from Antwerp, but the bricks were English, and the timber came from Gresham's estate at Ringshall, Suffolk. The design of the Exchange shows that Hendrik was the first person in northern Europe to solve the problem of how to make a classical arcade continue gracefully around a corner by clustering three columns in the corners, something that Brunelleschi, for example, never managed to achieve. The Royal Exchange was closely imitated in 1608 for the Amsterdam Exchange by deKeyser.

Osterley Park, Middlesex PLATES 74 & 75

Gresham, who by this point had been involved with Hendrik on the Steelyard, Gresham House, Intwood and the Royal Exchange, as well as acting as go-between for Cecil at Burghley and presumably for Heneage at

6. The Wyngaerde Panorama (ca. 1550) shows no new building with loggia, but the "Copperplate Map" (ca. 1559) includes it. The building is shown most clearly in the Visscher Panorama (1616), but is already absent in the Hollar Long View (ca. 1647). Maps are courtesy of the Guildhall Library, London.

7. *Norfolk Archaeology*, vol. 32, p. 188 and illustration supplied by Norfolk County Library, Norwich.

8. *Certificatieboek* 28, fo 34 ro, 19 October 1568, Stadsarchief, Antwerp. See also Henri Hyman, "L'Architecte Henri van Paesschen et l'ancienne Bourse de Londres," *Bulletin de l'Académie Royale d'Archéologie de Belgique*, Antwerp, 1908/9, vol. 5, pp. 343–354.

Courtyard looking east, Royal Exchange, London

PLATE 73

South elevation, Royal Exchange

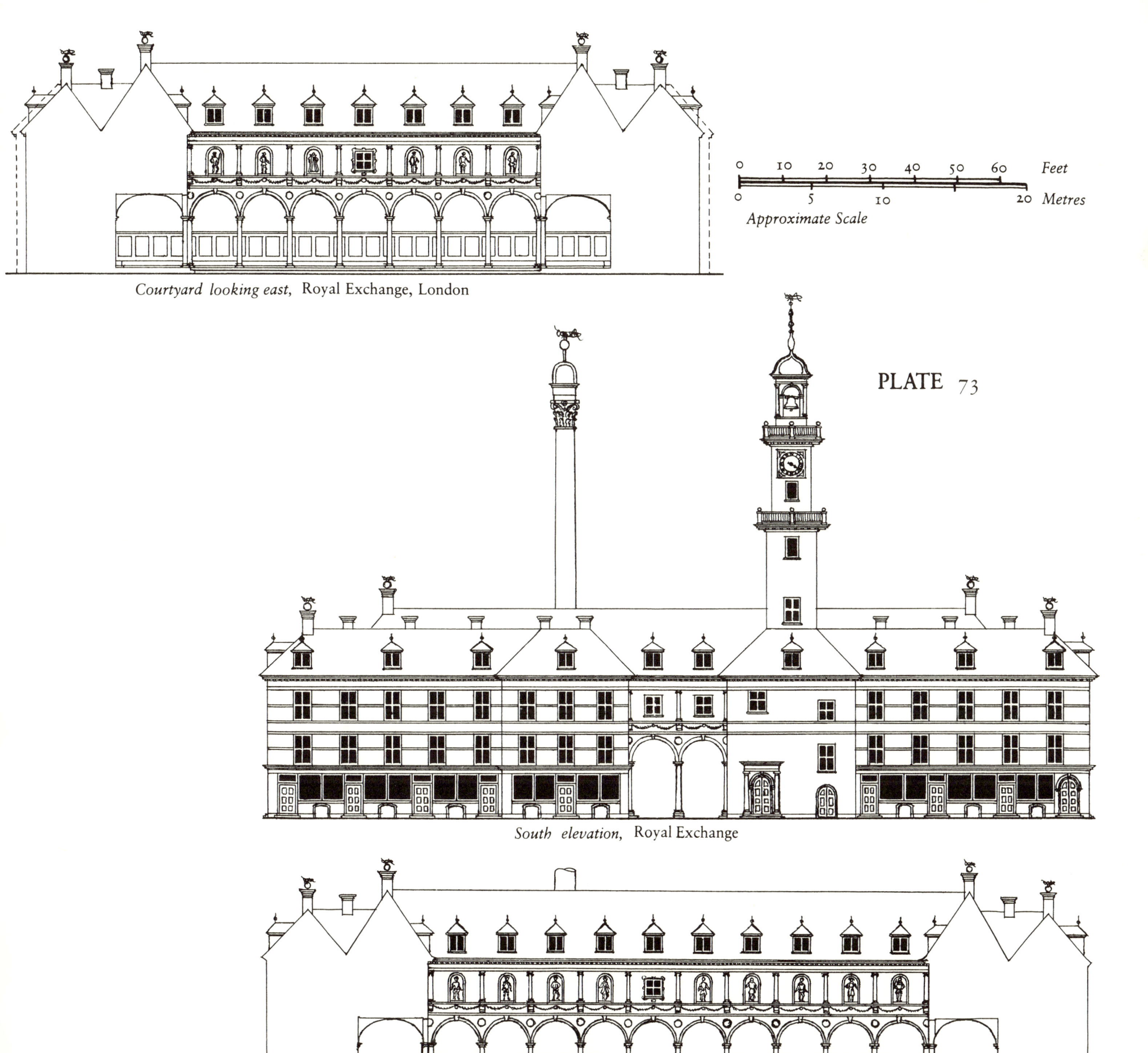

Courtyard, looking north, Royal Exchange

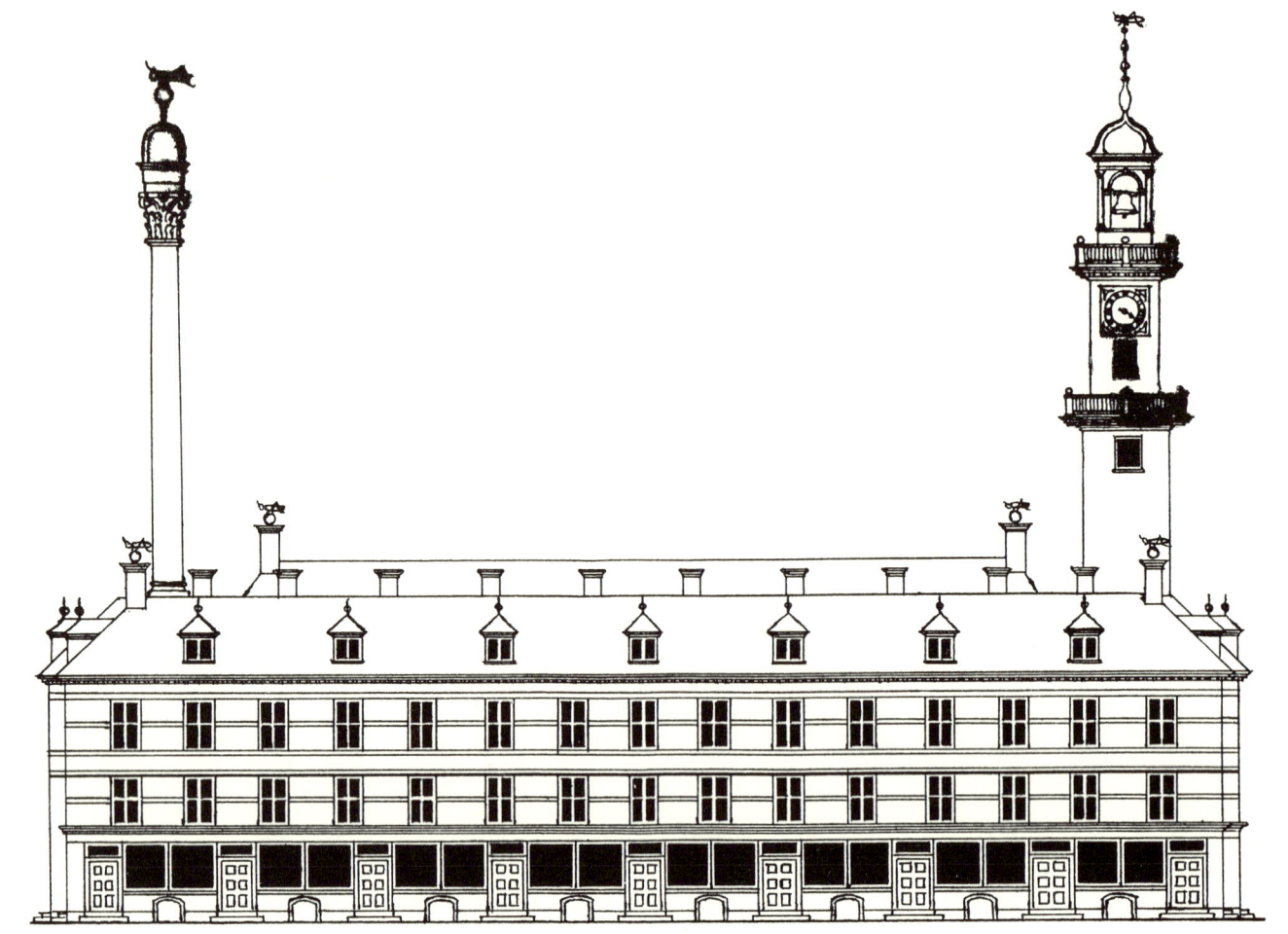

West elevation,   Royal Exchange, London

PLATE 74

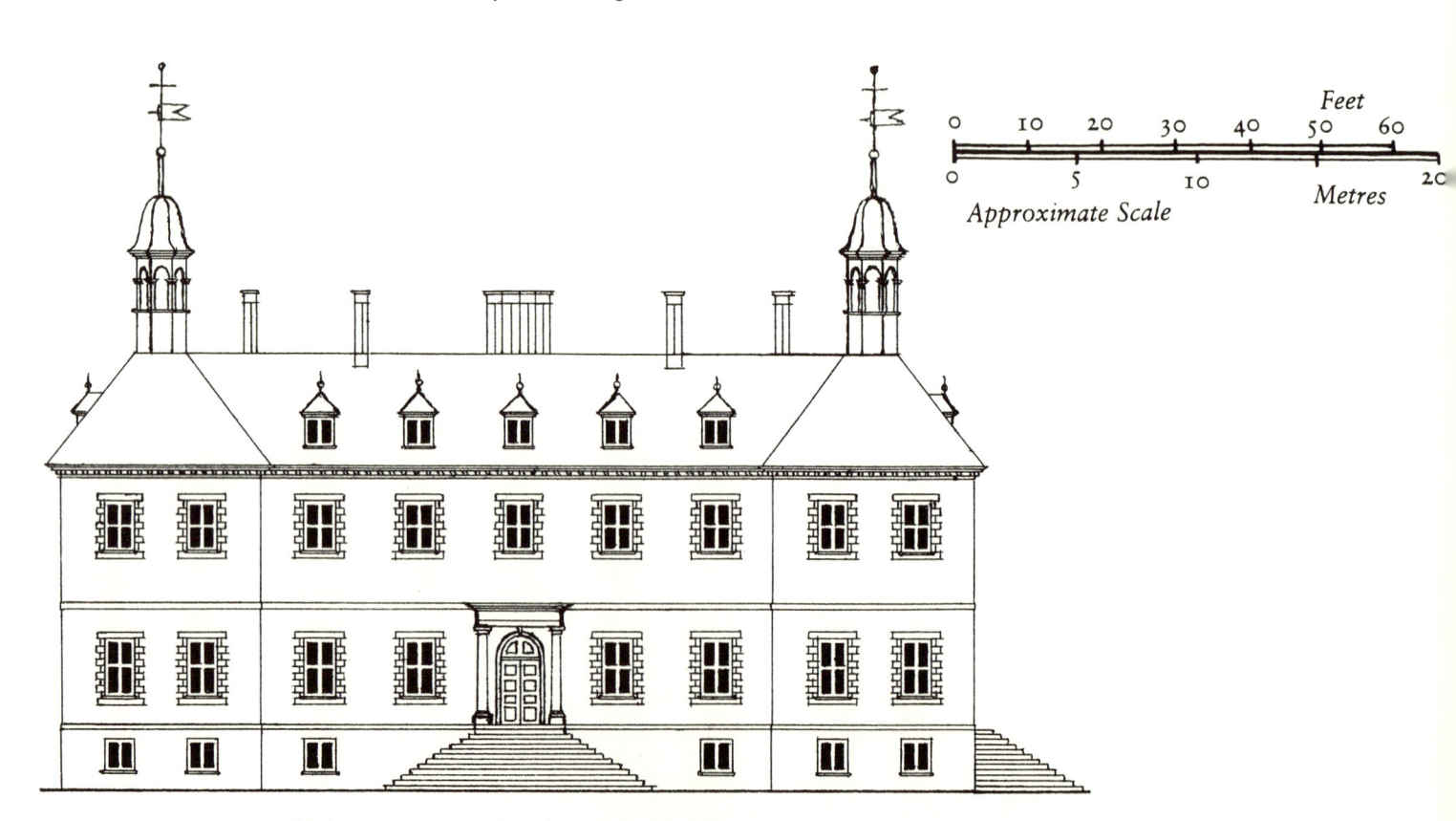

Main entrance,   Osterley Park, Middlesex

Copthall, decided to engage him to build a country house just west of London about 1567. He called the house Osterley Park, probably in honor of the Hanseatic merchants who were called Osterlings (the same source that gave us the word "sterling" to describe silver or money). It is possible that Gresham built around part of an existing house, because archaeologists have found some features on the site that are difficult to explain otherwise. Both Gresham's house and stables still stand, although in greatly altered form. At some point, the stables were reduced in size by more than half, and the house was enlarged early in the eighteenth century for the Child family; some alterations had already been made in the seventeenth century for Nicholas Barbon. Further alterations were made in the middle of the eighteenth century by Sir William Chambers, who was then replaced by his arch-rivals, the brothers Adam. They contributed some interior decoration and pierced the east wall with a giant hexastyle portico. The house is now owned by the National Trust and open to the public by the Victoria & Albert Museum.

The original house was very different, according to the few surviving pictures of it. The earliest of these is a 1635 estate map containing a small aerial sketch of the house and stables by Moses Glover. The house appears as a high, rectangular building with a cupola at each corner, not unlike Serlio's Ancy. Each corner of the house projected slightly so as to give the impression of a bastion, but the amount of each projection was smaller than on the present house, while the bastions themselves were, like Ancy, much larger than on the present Osterley. A floor-plan for Osterley, presumably from the late seventeenth century, agrees closely with the Glover picture. It shows that the house had a courtyard surrounded on at least three sides by an arcaded loggia. The plan shows clearly that the house was much smaller than the present house. An elevation drawing of a later date shows a stone doorway in Hendrik's style, similar to one that survives still on the stables.[9]

The Glover sketch shows that the stables consisted of two U-shaped buildings plus a small rectangular house, together forming a courtyard. Only the northerly block remains, and that has been altered by moving the original doorway off-center, by replacing the two cupolas in the corners with a single central one to a similar design, and by raising the two wings from their original one storey to the two-storey height of the central section. The windows are trimmed with stone quoins, one of the earliest uses of this device.

Bachegraig House, Clwyd, Wales

PLATES 75 & 76

Gresham's chief factor or assistant at Antwerp was Sir Richard Clough (pronounced Cluff), who came from north Wales. Clough made many of the arrangements for the Royal Exchange, and Hendrik's name appears frequently in Clough's correspondence—"glad yt you do so well lyke Henryke and yt yor workes go so well forwardes . . ." and ". . . Henryke and his men are arrived here [Antwerp] . . ."[10] Gresham and Clough together were able to raise the value of English currency by astute manipulation of the Antwerp money exchange; they also conspired with Cecil to corrupt Spanish officials in the Low Countries and thereby procured quantities of arms and gunpowder purloined from Spanish arsenals, this at a time of rebellions there, the anguish of which is evident in Clough's letters.

Perhaps because of the unrest at Antwerp, Clough came back to Wales, got married, and embarked on a frenzy of construction. His most impressive building was Bachegraig House, near Tremerchion, Clwyd, which should be compared with some of Palladio's villas. Apparently, Clough hoped to "canalize" the nearby River Clwyd in order for larger ships to reach the house, and he then intended to make the place into a large trading center. The three sides of the courtyard in front of the house, with their colonnaded loggias of marble Tuscan columns were intended to serve as temporary warehouses.[11]

The house, which displayed its date of 1567 in wrought-iron figures on the front, was built of brick with white stone dressings. It had a high basement and a six-bay main floor or piano nobile, the only jarring note being the fact that the handsome Tuscan entrance porch was off-center to the left because of the even number of bays—reminiscent of the Royal Exchange. The high hipped roof was set off by a collection of end-chimneys and pierced by two rows of hipped dormers. Atop the roof stood an enormous, two-storey cupola, the lower floor of which apparently contained a room for eating with a view out over the countryside. The rear of the house had three windows on each side of a central, semi-octagonal projection that rose the full height of the walls and was crowned with a balustraded balcony. The dormers in the rear were arranged in three tiers. The main house, which is known through many eighteenth-century paintings and sketches, was already becoming ruinous when Dr. Johnson visited it in 1774, and has long since been demolished, but the forecourt buildings still stand in altered form. Only two sides of the forecourt buildings were completed, for Clough's untimely death halted construction before the third side could be built. In the middle of the side opposite the main house was a gatehouse with a high hipped roof and iron numerals showing the date 1569.

Clough Town House, Ruthin, Wales

PLATE 75

At the same time, Clough rebuilt, presumably with Hendrik's plans, a medieval town house in Ruthin. The building still stands, somewhat altered, and is known as the Myddelton Arms, an adjunct to the Castle Hotel. The walls of the house are only one storey in height, but its high, hipped roof, set off by three massive chimneys, is pierced by no fewer than three rows of dormer windows, echoing the similar arrangement at the rear of Bachegraig.

9. The Glover sketch is in a private collection, but a photograph of it may be seen at the Victoria & Albert Museum, London, which also owns the plan and elevation drawings mentioned.
10. Robin G. Jomnes, "Sir Richard Clough of Denbigh c. 1530–1570," *Denbighshire Historical Society Transactions*, vol. 19, p. 64, quoting letter at PRO, S.P.For.70/85.
11. Mark Girouard, "Bachegraig," Colvin & Harris (ed.), *The Country Seat*, London, 1970, pp. 30–32.

Courtyard, Osterley Park, Middlesex

Market/Town Hall, Faringdon, Berkshire

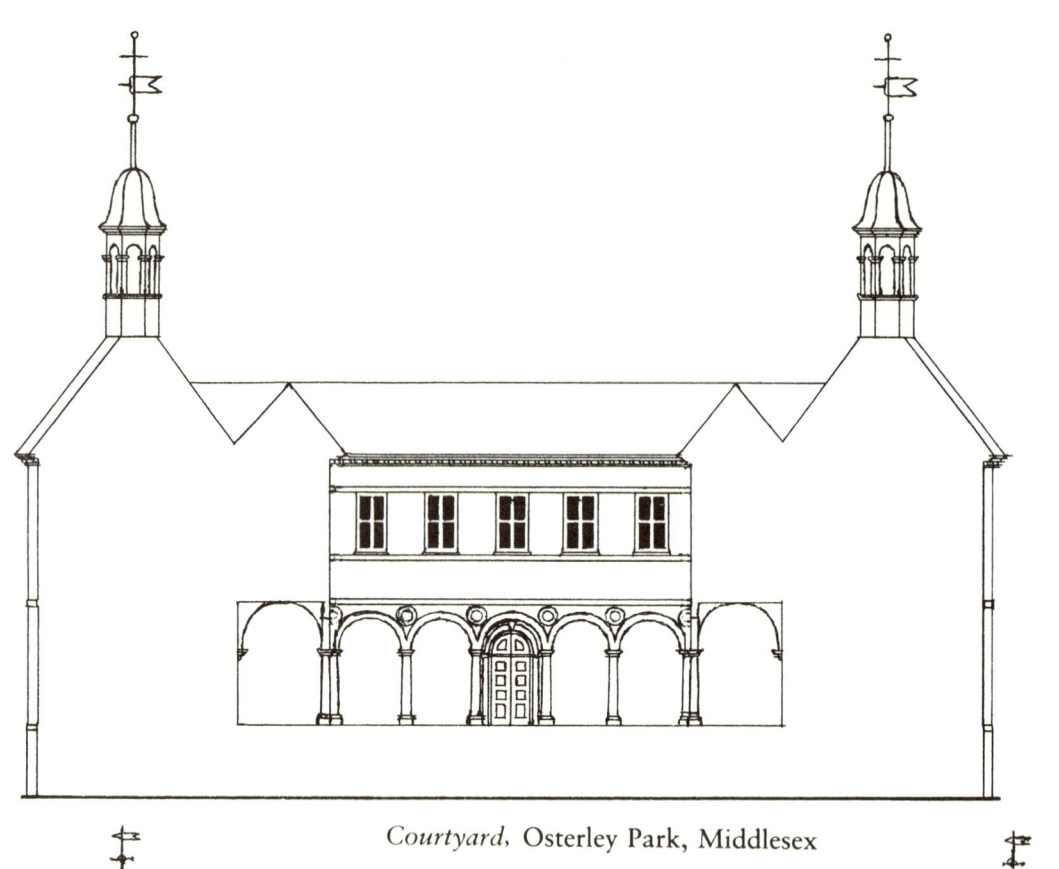

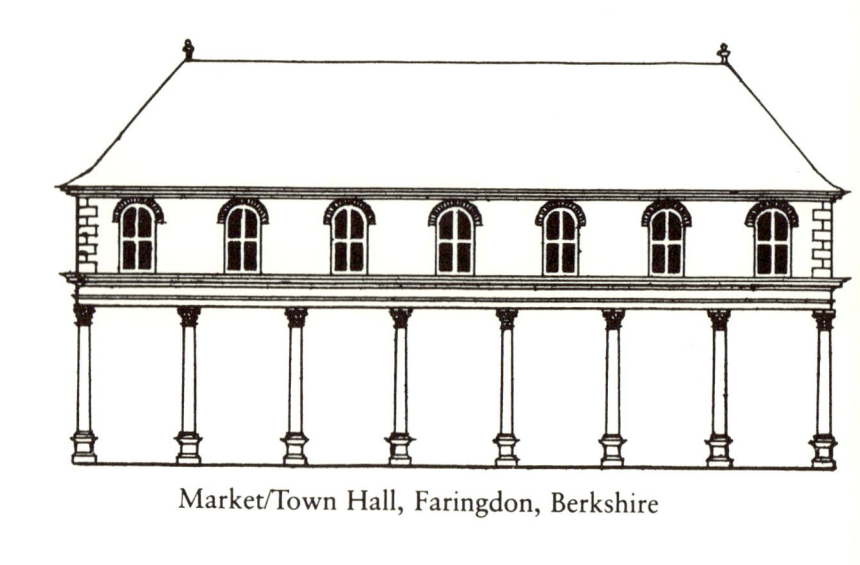

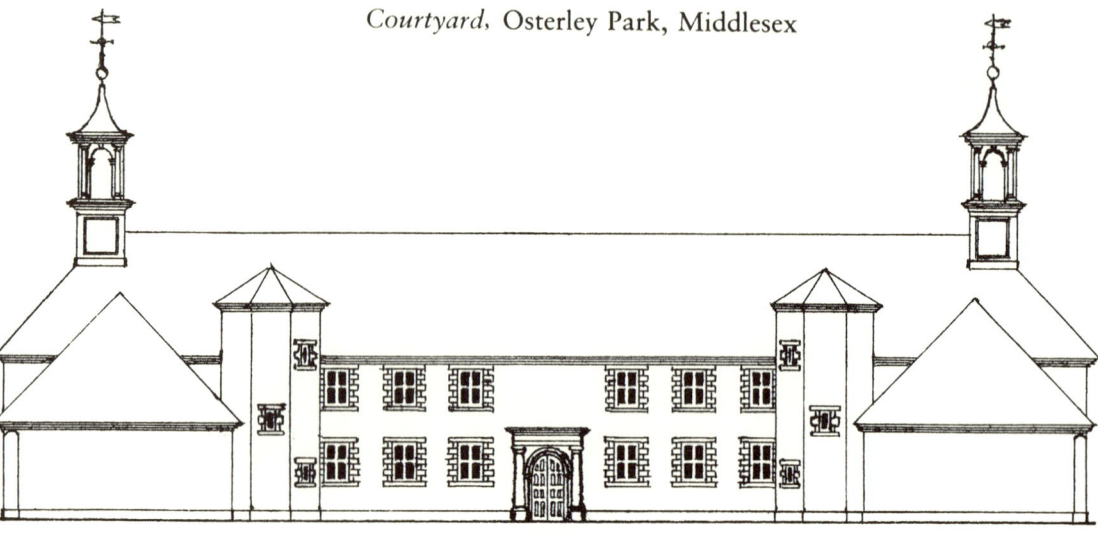

PLATE 75

Clough Town House, Ruthin, Wales

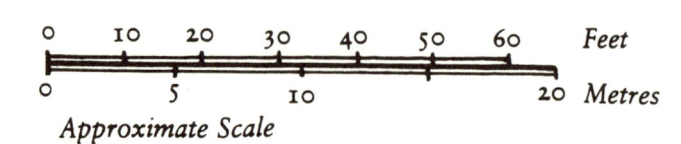

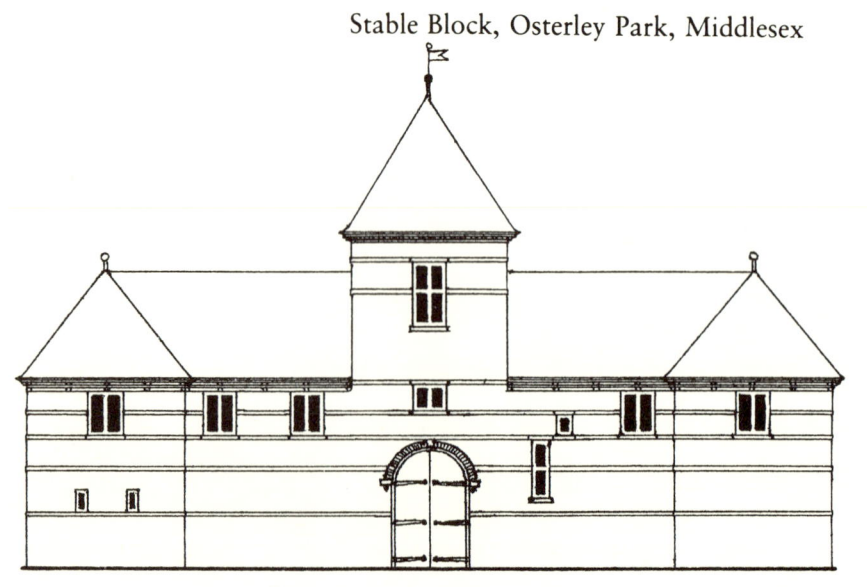

Stable Block, Osterley Park, Middlesex

Approximate Scale

Entrance, Bachegraig House, Clwyd, Wales

Entrance, Courtyard side, Bachegraig House, Clwyd, Wales

West wing, Gorhambury Park, Hertfordshire

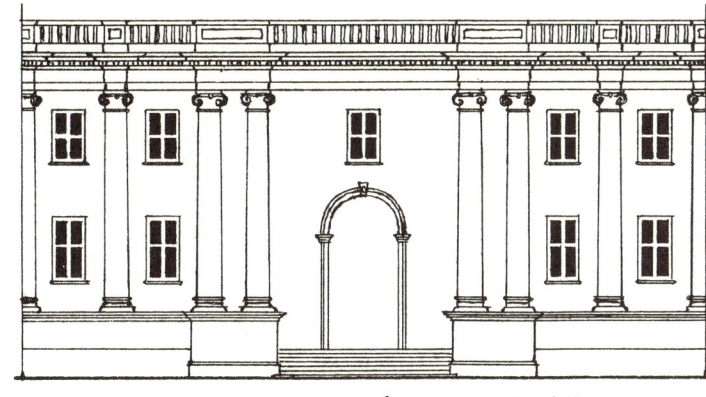

Project for screen, Middle Court,
Theobalds Park, Hertfordshire

Middle Court, Theobalds Park, Hertfordshire

PLATE 76

Rear elevation, Bachegraig House, Clwyd, Wales

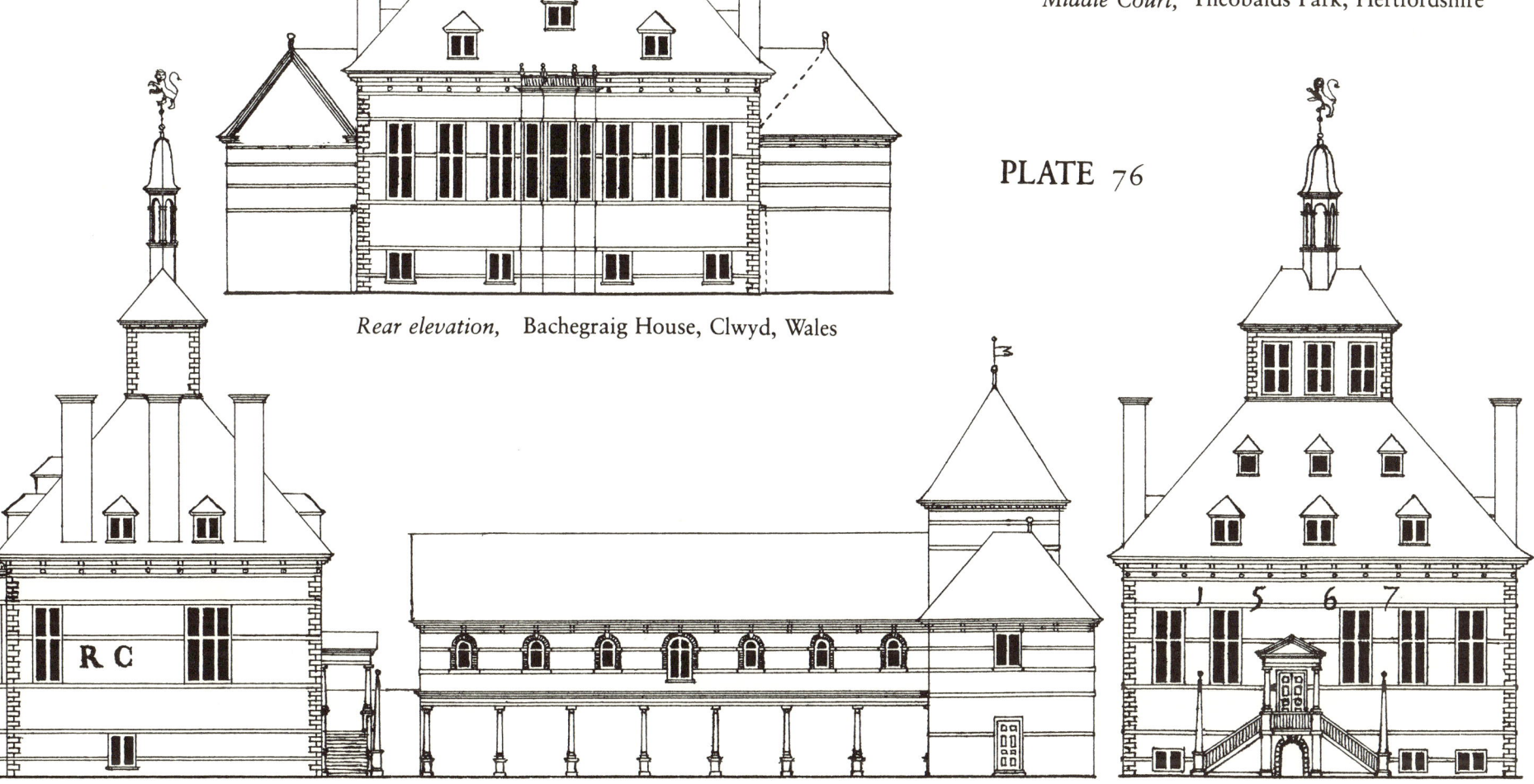

Side elevation,   Bachegraig House, Clwyd, Wales   *front elevation,*

135

Clough's third house was Plas Clough, built in the country near Denbigh in a rather more vernacular style (not shown in this book). It may be the work of one of Hendrik's masons. The three projections of its E-plan are crowned with crow-step gables, and the central projection consists of a room over an entrance porch, supported by a pair of marble Tuscan columns. What connection, if any, this house has to certain similar buildings of the period, such as Plas Mawr in Conwy (1576), Eastbury Manor, Barking (London, 1572) and the Gresham School, Holt, Norfolk (1555), remains to be explored.

Market/Town Hall, Faringdon, Berkshire
PLATE 75

The National Portrait Gallery has an anonymous allegorical painting of Sir Henry Unton painted at his death in 1596. On the left is a seven-bay stone building raised above a colonnade of Corinthian columns. Unton's father, Sir Edward, was made Sheriff of Berkshire in 1567, probably in part a result of his having given the money to build a new market/town hall at Faringdon, Berkshire. The Untons were connected to Gresham and Cecil through their friend and associate, Sir Christopher Hatton, the Lord Chancellor, so it is not inconceivable that the new market was built from designs by Hendrik procured through Gresham in 1567. The building, with its high Flemish hipped roof, was demolished long ago.

Theobalds Park, Hertfordshire PLATES 76 & 77

Sir William Cecil lost interest in Burghley House for many years in the middle of its construction, for he was engrossed in building an even grander house at Theobalds Park (pronounced Tibb'lds) in Hertfordshire. Theobalds was destroyed before 1660 by Cromwell's supporters, so very little information survives about it beyond Cecil's correspondence and drawings. Nevertheless, Sir John Summerson has managed to piece together a reasonable account of the house's construction.[12]

When Cecil first acquired it, Theobalds was an unpretentious house, but Elizabeth visited it and Cecil decided to enlarge it to make her more comfortable should she decide to return. When the house was finally completed, it had two closed courtyards and one open courtyard plus an extra wing projecting to the side. It had many loggias, some of them formal and others obviously by the hand of a local builder unschooled in classical design. The most significant loggia was in front of the Great Hall at the western end of the Middle Court, and was probably very similar to the one Hendrik built at Burghley, except that it had but two arches on each side of the two superimposed arches in the middle. This can be dated close to 1567, for one of Cecil's letters of that year in the Hatfield collection refers to delays caused by Hendrik having lost the plans—meaning that Hendrik had lost the plan of the space into which he was supposed to fit the loggia he was making in Antwerp. A drawing at Hatfield shows a plan of Theobalds with an earlier, alternative design for the block containing the loggia: it shows a colonnade of eight giant-order Ionic columns rising through two full storeys, the middle four columns being grouped in pairs. No evidence links this design to Hendrik or anyone else, but, Kirby notwithstanding, it represents the kind of thinking about architecture that was never accepted—nor even offered—in Britain until the success of Inigo Jones half a century later, and Hendrik would have been the most likely source for such a design.

A loggia similar to the one on the garden side of Burghley formed part of the south or garden face of the "fountain" block, and the proportions suggest once more Hendrik's authorship.

Archaeological studies at Theobalds have so far not revealed any formal stable plan, nor does one appear in John Thorpe's record of plans of the estate. However, Robert Smythson recorded "the Platforme of ye King's Stabell at Tyballs," designed around a square courtyard with a pair of stair-towers in the corners nearest the entrance, rather like the Osterley stables. The possibilities are that Smythson designed the building for James I in 1609 or that Smythson, who like Thorpe was fond of copying down designs by other architects, recorded the plan that he had found on his way to London in 1609. The plan is compatible with Hendrik's style and displays considerable ingenuity. It offers stalls for up to 94 horses in six completely separate compartments, perhaps with the intention of helping prevent the spread of equine diseases.[13]

Gorhambury Park, Hertfordshire PLATE 76

Not far from Theobalds stood Gorhambury, also in Hertfordshire. The property belonged to Sir Nicholas Bacon from 1561 onwards. Bacon, father of the Jacobean statesman and scientist Francis Bacon, was related by marriage to both Gresham and Cecil, and was an intimate friend of both. Elizabeth appointed him Lord Keeper of the Great Seal.

Bacon completely replaced Gorhambury with a new house from 1563 to 1568. This was arranged around a square courtyard, but was architecturally undistinguished. Elizabeth visited Bacon at Gorhambury and pointedly remarked about its small size, to which Bacon is reported to have replied that the house was adequate, but "madam, you have made me too big for it." Eloquence aside, Bacon was troubled by the queen's observation and he asked Cecil for advice, after which he resolved to build a large addition to the west. He built one and a half sides of what may have been intended as a second complete courtyard. This L-shaped wing contained a great picture-gallery upstairs, supported on a loggia of marble Tuscan columns. The central bay of the south side of the loggia was larger than the others and contained an arch which framed a niche that contained a handsome statue of Henry VIII (perhaps carved by Floris; part of it still survives). The bay with the arch projected forwards slightly, and above it was a

12. Sir John Summerson, "The Building of Theobalds," *Archaeologia,* vol. 97, pp. 107–126.

13. Mark Girouard, "The Smythson Collection of the Royal Institute of British Architects," *Architectural History,* vol. 5, pp. 30 and 67.

Part of South elevation,
Theobalds Park, Hertfordshire

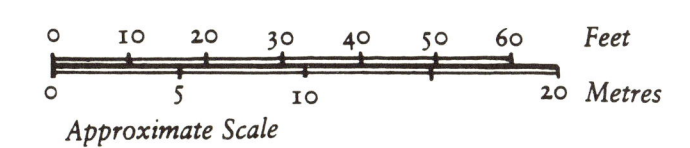

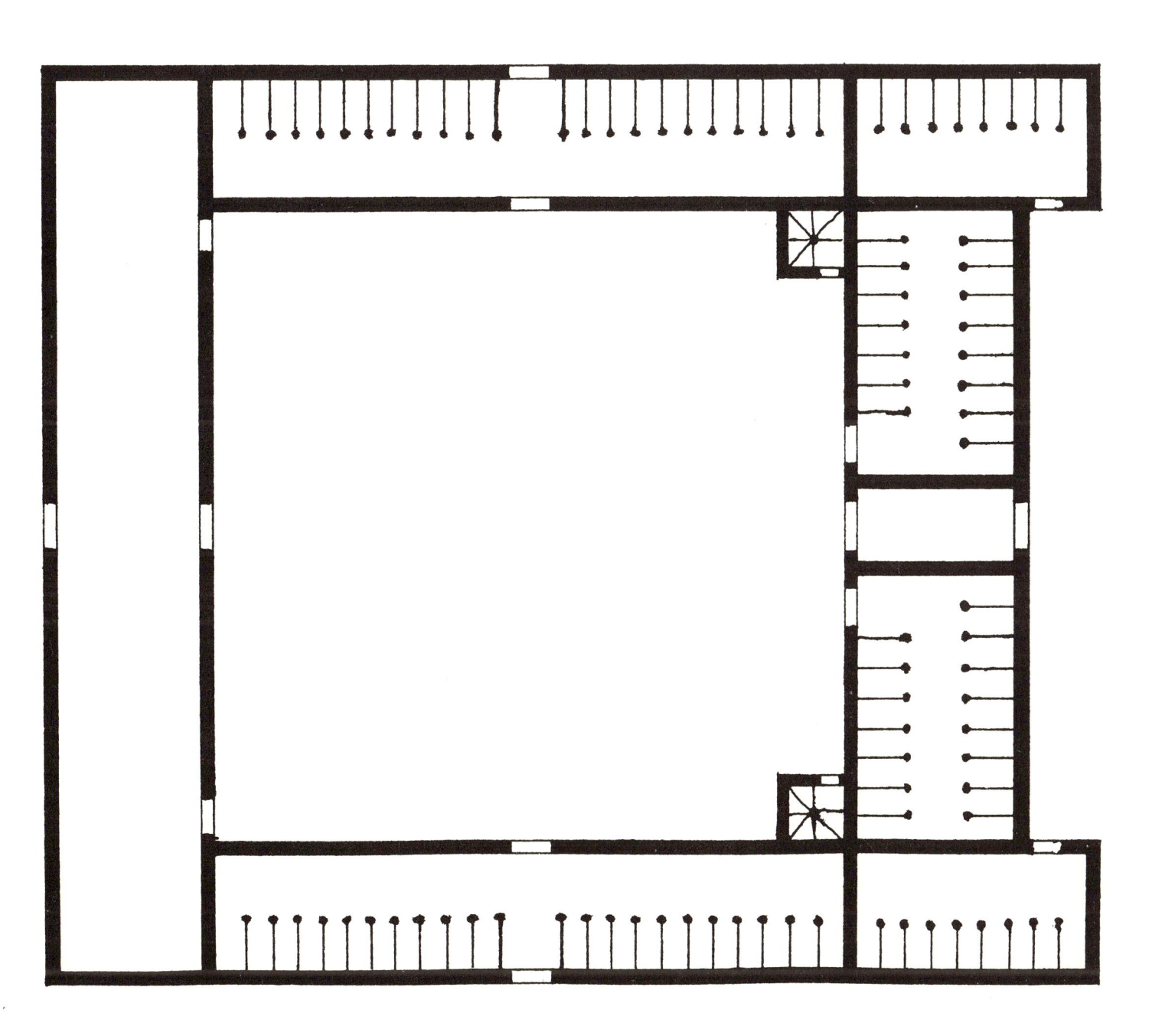

PLATE 77

Plan, Stable Block, Theobalds Park, Hertfordshire

Venetian window, still rare outside Italy at this date.

Bacon's efforts were not in vain. When Elizabeth made her next visit in 1577, she was apparently so pleased that she spent five days there, and his costs for entertaining her came to over £575, about a fifth of the original cost of the house! A new house was built in 1777 next to Bacon's house, and the old building was partially demolished by 1787, the rest being allowed gradually to fall into ruins. Bacon's house and the presumed Hendrik wing are known through an eighteenth-century watercolor and plan, as well as period writings and recent archaeological investigations.[14]

Gorhambury's addition is probably the last work Hendrik did in Britain. Hendrik, as can be seen in the previous chapter, worked in Denmark, Norway, Sweden and Germany, in addition to England, Wales and his native Flanders. Apart from the difficulty of juggling so many major building projects, he was presumably faced with the rigors of travel in the sixteenth century. However, travel by sea in Hendrik's day, at least over short distances, was fairly routine. The amount of travel Hendrik must have done, while well above average, was not more than an enterprising merchant might have done. Gresham, for example, reported that in the first two years of Elizabeth's reign he made no fewer than forty round trips between London and Antwerp. While Hendrik did actually travel to all or most of the building-sites in which he was involved, it is clear that he did much of his work by letter from his office in Antwerp, where loggias were made to order and shipped out to clients to be erected in another country.

House project PLATE 78

Roughly contemporary with Hendrik was Alain Maynard (also spelled Allen and Alenus), who came to England from France, possibly as early as 1555 (Mark Girouard has suggested that Maynard may have been one of the team that built the Gardiner monument at Winchester). He specialized in carving anything but human figures, but he also drew architectural drawings. From 1563 to 1566 he was at Longleat, where he was allotted his own private room as he carved chimney-pieces and other details, and in 1567 he was naturalized as a British subject, the same year in which Longleat was badly damaged by fire. Although repair work was begun immediately, Maynard's name does not appear in the account books again until 1570.[15]

In the library at Longleat is a drawing of an entrance façade that Girouard attributes to Maynard, and for good reason, for many of its details are reflected in overmantel carving at Longleat by Maynard. The design calls for a central block two storeys high and three bays wide, flanked by a pair of round towers. All the windows are enclosed in Corinthian aedicules, some with triangular pediments, some segmental and others split scrolled pediments. The overall design is not unlike one or more of Ducerceau's published drawings. The roof has been reconstructed for the drawing shown here.

Sherborne House, Gloucestershire PLATE 78

Maynard was apparently absent from Longleat for almost four years. It is possible that he was working at Sherborne House, Gloucestershire, which was being enlarged at that time, and whose architectural forms seem to be a more primitive version of what was done at Longleat after the fire. Whatever the plans were for Sherborne, work was halted before much of the building could be built, although Elizabeth visited Thomas Dutton there in 1574. Alterations were carried out in the seventeenth and nineteenth centuries. In 1829, Lewis Wyatt was hired to rebuild the house in the same style, so the present house, now rented as 35 flats, is almost entirely his work, but preserving the idea of the applied orders of Ionic, Corinthian and Composite engaged columns (not pilasters as found at Longleat). The original house had no parapet, but Wyatt added one.

Longleat House, Wiltshire PLATE 78

As Mark Girouard has pointed out, one of the difficulties in writing an architectural history of Longleat, Wiltshire, is that many of the people involved were perfectly capable of drawing the designs for it, from the owner, Sir John Thynne (who had previously been responsible for Somerset House), to the chief mason, Robert Smythson, to Maynard and others, and in fact the design may reflect the ideas of many or all of them; Smythson claimed that he and Maynard were both responsible. Little information survives about the pre-fire Longleat, but it is known to have had some relatively narrow pedimented windows. A drawing in Maynard's hand survives in the Longleat library, showing a portion of the elevation of the new house almost exactly as built, but with a forest of French-style, almost baroque, dormer windows with oval lights set into the parapet. A decision was reached not to have a high roof, and so the dormers were abandoned, but the drawing does show that Maynard must have played a crucial part in developing the elevation design. The house is one of the enormous Elizabethan "prodigy-houses," but with a regular plan. The elevation is three storeys tall with a parapet and high basement. Four two-bay projections are arranged on the entrance front, each projection being decorated with Doric, Ionic and Corinthian pilasters whose entablatures are continued completely around the building. The house is an interesting compromise between the traditional late gothic and the forms and regularity of the classical style.

14. J. C. Rogers, "The Manor & Houses of Gorhambury," *Transactions of the St. Albans & Hertfordshire Archaeological Society,* 1933, pp. 35–112.

15. Mark Girouard, "New Light on Longleat," *Country Life,* 20 September 1956, pp. 594–597.

Dormer Project at Longleat House, Wiltshire

House project

Part of Rodmister Lodge

Part of Sherborne House, Gloucestershire

PLATE 78

Longleat House, Wiltshire

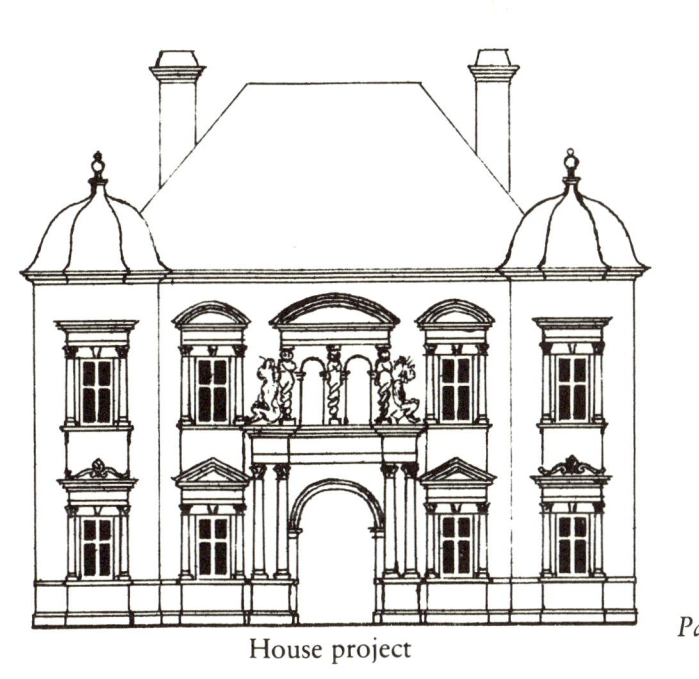

Feet
Metres
Approximate Scale

Chalcot House, near Westbury, Wiltshire

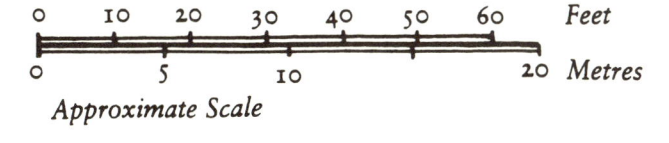

Corsham Court, near Bath

139

Chalcot House, near Westbury, Wiltshire
PLATE 78

Girouard thinks that Maynard may have been responsible for the classical front added to the medieval manor called Chalcot House, near Westbury, Wiltshire (although the house's brochure attributes the classical trim to a whole century later than Maynard). The Flemish-bond brickwork is trimmed with a golden stone in the form of quoins, entablatures and aedicules around the windows. The orders displayed on the three-storey, five-bay house are Ionic, Corinthian and Composite. Four places where windows probably once looked out are now filled in with sculptural details. The house was greatly enlarged in succeeding centuries; it is open to the public on a limited basis.

Rodmister Lodge PLATE 78

In the Longleat library is a drawing by Maynard dated 1585 for a two-storey circular tower with ogival roof and elaborate dormer. The dormer design is related to trim details at Longleat. The tower is known as Rodmister Lodge.

Corsham Court, near Bath PLATE 78

Robert Smythson, whose architectural career probably received its first major impetus at Longleat, also produced drawings for details of or studies for the Longleat design (see plate 14-B in Sir John Summerson, *Architecture in Britain, 1530–1830*). Girouard believes that Corsham Court, Wiltshire, near Bath, is also a Smythson design from the period 1575–1584. The house, which has been altered many times, was two storeys high and exceptionally wide for its height. Except for the doorway, no pilasters or columns were applied to the walls. Emphasis was provided instead by a series of pedimented projections that housed most of the windows, although each storey had a complete entablature running around the building. If Smythson was the architect, it shows that he was early in his career thinking of omitting classical orders.

Wollaton Hall, Nottinghamshire PLATE 79

Smythson's first great masterpiece for which he did not have to share credit was Wollaton Hall, Nottinghamshire, built 1580–1588 for Sir Francis Willoughby, Sheriff of Nottinghamshire. Once again, the inspiration for the construction was a visit from Elizabeth and the hope of further visits. Smythson apparently consulted Serlio's books for both plan and elevation details, as well as Vredeman's books and perhaps Floris'. In the center of the courtyard stands a gothic Great Hall that towers over the more classical exterior (the Great Hall has been omitted from the drawing in this book for the sake of clarity). Three-storey towers at each end of the front project forward from the plane of the next bays, which in turn project forward from the plane of the center. Each bay encloses an unusually large window with pairs of banded pilasters, Doric, Ionic and Corinthian. Occasional niches huddle awkwardly between some of the pilasters. Each tower is capped with a strapwork confection under a small pediment. The house derived great power from the fact that the decorations do not begin on the ground, as at Longleat, but stand on a massive basement. Wollaton was extensively imitated during the Elizabethan revival of the nineteenth century. Smythson later built the unclassical Hardwick Hall.[16]

Hill Hall, Theydon Mount, Essex PLATE 79

Sir Thomas Smith or Smyth, English Ambassador to Paris 1562–1566, built the brick, courtyarded house called Hill Hall at Theydon Mount, Essex, beginning about 1564. Smith, who owned at least one book on architecture (which he was asked to loan to Cecil), said that he designed the house himself, with the advice of the London carpenter, Richard Kirby. Smith, incidentally, was related to Cecil, Gresham and Thynne, but seems not to have used any of their architectural connections in designing the house. The house has been altered and enlarged many times, but some original features are still visible. On the south front, which is two storeys tall, a single bay projects at each end and is trimmed with a pair of giant Doric half-columns on high bases; because Smith used columns rather than pilasters, both here and in the courtyard, the poorly-proportioned entablatures are forced to stand out an uncomfortable distance from the walls. The windows, including the dormers (which are proportionately much too large), are all trimmed with quoins. Inside the courtyard, Doric half-columns are placed almost at random around the ground floor, and truncated Ionic half-columns stand on the upper floor under a heavy entablature. The house is an excellent example of how classical details can be incorrectly understood and applied. The house is now administered by the Prison Commissioners.

Gatehouse, Kenilworth Castle, Warwickshire PLATE 79

Between Coventry and Warwick stand the ruins of Kenilworth Castle, a medieval fortress now open to the public. In Elizabeth's reign it belonged to Robert Dudley, the famous Earl of Leicester, one of Elizabeth's favorite members of her Privy Council and an enemy of Cecil and his circle. Dudley made many improvements to make the castle more comfortable, and Elizabeth spent considerable time there—at more than considerable expense. Dudley built an arcaded loggia with little pretense at classicism, and a fine classical entrance to his lodgings that was removed by subsequent owners (ca. 1650) and attached as a porch to the gatehouse. It is like a Roman triumphal arch with four fluted Doric pilasters and a pair of niches. This high-style piece was built in 1571. The architect is anonymous, and were it not for Dudley's dislike for Cecil, Gresham and Bacon, it would be tempting to attribute it to Hendrik. Dudley began building a large church at nearby Denbigh, Clwyd in 1579, with the reported intention of supplanting the cathedral church of Saint Asaph, but it remained incom-

16. For more on Smythson, see Mark Girouard, *Robert Smythson & the Elizabethan Country House,* New Haven, Yale University Press, 1983.

Wollaton Hall, Nottinghamshire

Gatehouse, Kenilworth Castle, Warwickshire
(not drawn to regular scale)

PLATE 79

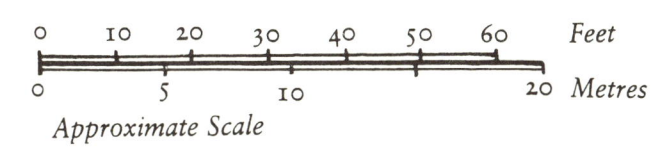

0 10 20 30 40 50 60 Feet
0 5 10 20 Metres
Approximate Scale

South elevation, Hill Hall, Theydon Mount, Essex

Courtyard
Hill Hall, Theydon Mount, Essex

Gate of Honour, Gonville & Caius College, Cambridge

Part of Kirby Hall, Northamptonshire

Part of Kirby Hall, Northamptonshire

141

plete at his death in 1588 and has since fallen into ruins. The church is mentioned merely because fewer than half a dozen churches of any size were built in England and Wales during all of Elizabeth's reign. The ruins of the church have not revealed any classical design.

Gate of Honour, Gonville & Caius College, Cambridge PLATE 79

Dr. John Caius (pronounced Kees) attended Gonville Hall at Cambridge along with Gresham. Years later, he returned to Cambridge and enlarged the hall so it could be renamed Gonville & Caius College. The most notable architectural improvement that he made was the so-called Gate of Honour in 1572, for which he hired from nearby King's Lynn an "artificer and architect" by the name of Theodore de Have from Cleves (whose name was Latinized for the occasion as Haveus). This is a three-storey structure, of which the base looks like a Roman Ionic triumphal arch—but with a pointed gothic arch in it!—and the next storey resembles a Roman tetra-style temple of the Corinthian order, flanked by pinnacles and containing three aedicules; the top storey is a hexagonal drum surmounted by a dome.

Kirby Hall, Northamptonshire PLATE 79

Kirby Hall was built about 1570 in Northamptonshire for Sir Christopher Hatton, a friend of Gresham and Cecil who later became Lord Chancellor. Most of the enormous house was built in regular Tudor-gothic style, but the ruins of two large screens in a French classical style are well preserved. One of these is the exterior of the Great Hall, decorated with fluted giant Ionic pilasters and with a central "tower of the orders." The other combines an upstairs gallery with pedimented windows over an arcaded loggia; once again, giant Ionic pilasters, some fluted and some covered all over with busy carving, give a vertical emphasis to the wall, but they terminate weakly in flying entablatures capped with finials. The central window with balcony, as shown here, was a seventeenth-century alteration. This wing is strongly reminiscent of the similar wing at the French Château of Charleval, built about the same time.

Rothwell Market House, Northamptonshire PLATE 80

Also in Northamptonshire is the unfinished Market House that Sir Thomas Tresham built for the town of Rothwell in 1577. Tresham was fined so frequently for failing to attend church (he was a Roman Catholic) that he ran short of money before the roof could be added. The plan is a rectangle superimposed in a cross, but with a round tower added at the back corner to contain stairs. The ground floor is an open arcade dressed with banded Tuscan pilasters on high bases, and the upper floor, intended for meetings of the local Council, has large windows and banded Ionic pilasters on high bases. All the pilasters and bases are covered in a pattern of ovals and rectangles. Tresham served as his own architect, with the assistance of the mason Robert Stickels.

Almost twenty years later, Tresham designed two lodges for himself in his own version of Elizabethan gothic, using no classical details.

Moreton Corbet Castle, Shropshire/Salop PLATE 80

Robert Corbett travelled in Flanders, France and Italy, where he was impressed by the classical architecture that he saw. Upon his return from Italy about 1578 he resolved to build to his own design a house that reflected what he had seen, or to quote the writer Camden, "carried away with the affectionate delight of Architecture, began to build in a barraine place a most gorgeous and stately house, after the Italians model." However, in 1583 he died of plague, and the unfinished house is now a stabilized ruin. Moreton Corbet Castle is a few miles northeast of Shrewsbury, Shropshire/Salop. Actually, the site was not entirely "barraine," for earlier Corbett family buildings stood all around. The house's south elevation followed somewhat the lead of Sherborne and Longleat in having large windows on two storeys interspersed with Doric and Ionic engaged columns and pilasters under a large parapet. During the seventeenth century, an attempt was made to finish the house to a different design that included tall, ogival gables. Beyond the addition of the classical orders, which looks almost like an afterthought, Moreton Corbet is a typical Elizabethan design; so much for the "Italians model"!

Slaugham Place, Sussex PLATE 80

Richard Covert, who died in 1579, is believed to have built Slaugham Place (pronounced Slaff'm) at Cuckfield, East Sussex shortly before he died. According to the ruins that remain and an inaccurate plan drawn by John Thorpe, it was a typical Elizabethan-gothic house arranged around a courtyard, to which two handsome classical loggias were added. Or perhaps it was designed as a classical house, but after the loggias were built the rest of the house was finished in the traditional style by Covert's heirs. The more impressive loggia, five bays long, was in the middle of the northwest outside wall facing the garden, and stood underneath the house's long gallery. The insides of the arches are coffered. Standing in front of the piers are fluted Doric pilasters on high bases. The central arch projects forward, and has enough depth inside it for a pair of niches. The courtyard loggia, not shown here, was five bays long, with rusticated masonry for its piers.

Entrance Lodge, Plas Mawr, Conwy, Wales PLATE 80

After Sir Richard Clough died, his widow married in 1580 a kinsman of Robert Wynn of Gwydir. Wynn built an impressive townhouse called Plas Mawr in Conwy from 1576 onwards. The main house, whose H plan seems to be related to Eastbury Manor in Essex and also to Plas Clough and the Gresham School, is built of rough stone trimmed with smooth stone quoins, and has pediments over its windows on the lower two floors, as well as crow-step gables and dormers. The entrance lodge, which is more symmetrical than the house, is shown here, because it is a small part of the story of the development of classical architecture in Britain, although it cannot really be called classical.

Crichton Castle, Midlothian, Scotland
PLATE 80

One other manifestation of classical forms in this period appeared in Scotland. This is the north quarter of Crichton Castle, Midlothian, built by an anonymous Italian builder for Francis Stewart, the notorious fifth Earl of Bothwell between 1581 and 1591. The work included the first staircase in Scotland to run in straight flights between landings. The courtyard façade is built on a seven-bay arcaded loggia with short Corinthian columns. Above that rise between two and three storeys of windows arranged assymetrically on a face of sharp, diamond-cut blocks that are not staggered. Bothwell may have seen the similar Palazzo Carnesali at Verona, which was under construction in 1580 while he was travelling in the area, and perhaps he brought back with him one of the masons from there. The castle has been in ruins for a long time, but is now stabilized and open to the public.

Longford Castle, Wiltshire PLATE 80

Longford Castle, near Salisbury, Wiltshire, is a remarkable triangular house with large round bastions at each corner. It was built in the early 1580s for Sir Thomas Gorges. Lady Helena Gorges, who came from Sweden, apparently requested that the house be made to resemble Hendrik's Uraniborg that had just been built on Hven Island, Denmark, but her wishes were not granted. Most of the castle was built in the prevailing Elizabethan-gothic style, but the front wing was a three-storey Flemish-style renaissance design. In the middle was a two-storey arcaded loggia, whose lower arches, according to a drawing by John Thorpe, were intended to be compass-headed but somehow got executed as four-centered arches (the drawing in this book shows the elevation split in the middle, with as-built on the left and as-designed on the right). After an intervening bay, the designer placed a typical three-bay Low Countries city house elevation with pedimented gable on either side of the loggia. Above some dormers on the roof were two prominent chimneys, made, as at Burghley, in the form of a pair of Tuscan columns under an entablature. Many years later, this elevation was disassembled and re-assembled in a different arrangement. The identity of the original architect is not known, but some have even suggested that Lady Gorges herself was responsible for it.

The house once had an impressive entrance lodge in the form of a Roman triumphal arch with four fluted Tuscan pilasters standing on bases of double the normal height. The upper part of it had four niches with statues and a single window over the arch. The roof was ogival.

Garden Ornaments, Nonsuch Palace, Surrey PLATE 80

Finally, the story of classical architecture in sixteenth-century Britain returns to a place where the Renaissance made one of its first, albeit imperfect, appearances in England: Nonsuch Castle, Surrey. John, Lord Lumley, who had visited Florence in the 1560s, inherited Nonsuch in 1579 (Mary had sold it out of royal ownership). Lumley was excluded from Elizabeth's court because he was a Roman Catholic, so he resolved to put all his efforts into the development of the gardens at Nonsuch and elsewhere. Among the work done at Nonsuch was the construction of a series of classical ornaments, such as fountains, a tall obelisk and several free-standing columns, each crowned with a popinjay (Elizabethan word for parrot) perched on a ball.[17]

The classical style was not the preferred style in Britain in the sixteenth century, otherwise such important civic projects as the London Guildhall would have been designed in that style. No doubt the style was associated with Rome, whose church was actively involved in trying to assassinate or dethrone Elizabeth, and hence it was generally rejected. In Scotland the dynastic situation was different: Mary Queen of Scots was brought up in the French court, where she observed the work of Serlio, Delorme and Lescot, but she was forced by her subjects to leave Scotland at such a young age that she had had no chance to sponsor any architecture even if she had wanted to do so.

17. For more on the Lumley garden ornaments, see Gervase Jackson-Stops, "Riches of a Renaissance Courtier," *Country Life*, 5 June 1986, pp. 1586–1588, and Roy Strong, *The Renaissance Garden in England*, New York, Thames & Hudson, 1979, pp. 63–69.

For further reading, see Sir John Summerson, *Architecture in Britain 1530–1830*, Harmondsworth, Penguin Books, 1953 (rev. 1963).

Gallery at Ely Place, Holborn, London

Information about this building was collected too late for it to be included in its proper place in this book, so it has been appended here. Ely Place, the medieval palace in London of the bishops of Ely, was forcibly borrowed by Elizabeth in order to loan it to Sir Christopher Hatton in 1576. Hatton modernized the place and appears to have erected a long gallery over an Ionic colonnade. Such a gallery would have been useful for displaying paintings and sculpture in the strong light provided by the numerous large windows, and for dancing the new longways sets of country dances. While the gallery could have been the work of Hendrik, who was by then hard at work in Scandinavia, it is more likely to have been designed by the anonymous architect of the two semi-classical elevations at Hatton's country mansion, Kirby Hall—perhaps even Hatton himself. Matthew Wren, a later bishop of Ely and uncle of Christopher Wren, lived at Ely Place on and off in the middle of the seventeenth century, and was no doubt visited there by his nephew. The only surviving picture of the gallery was engraved in 1805, after the building had been demolished. The fenestration had clearly been altered before the artist sketched the gallery, but the windows were probably originally closely-spaced, as at Gresham House (which had doubtless influenced Hatton to build such a gallery in the first place).

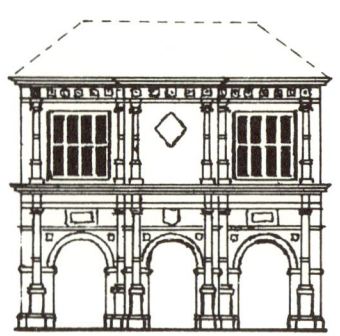

Part of
Rothwell Market House,
Northamptonshire

South elevation, Moreton Corbet Castle, Shropshire/Salop

PLATE 80

Part of Slaugham Place, Sussex
(conjectural reconstruction)

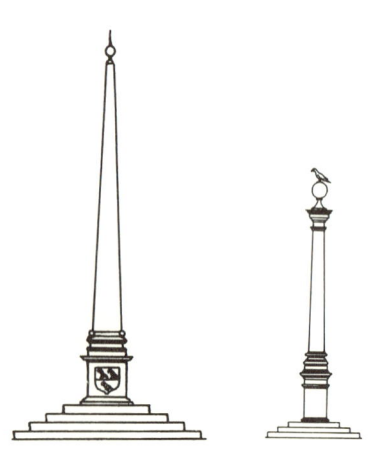

Garden Ornaments,
Nonsuch Palace, Surrey

Entrance Lodge, Plas Mawr, Conwy, Wales

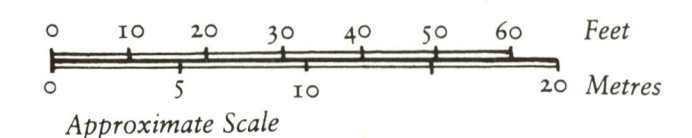

Approximate Scale

Courtyard
Crichton Castle, Midlothian, Scotland

Entrance Lodge,
Longford Castle, Wiltshire

Part of Longford Castle, Wiltshire

144

EASTERN EUROPE

For the sake of convenience, classical architecture in Eastern Europe is covered in a single chapter, in part because of linguistic similarities in most, but not all, the countries. In this chapter are buildings from Yugoslavia, the Soviet Union, Czechoslovakia, Hungary, Romania and Poland (but not the Democratic Republic of Germany, which is covered in the chapter on the Germanic countries). No classical architecture is known to have existed in Albania or Bulgaria from the Renaissance, probably because those areas were under occupation by the Turks. The same can be said for Greece, the original well-spring of the classical vocabulary; however, even if the Turks had not inhibited the importation of renaissance ideas about architecture to Greece, it is doubtful whether the Greeks would have been interested, for they were apparently satisfied with their version of the Romanesque/Byzantine style that had served them well for centuries.

Chapel of the Blessed John, Bishop Orsini, and the Baptistery, the Cathedral, Trogir, Yugoslavia PLATE 81

It should be no surprise that the first place that the new classicism of the Renaissance appeared outside Italy was in Yugoslavia, because the two are separated only by the narrow Adriatic Sea. The fact that Venice colonized parts of coastal Yugoslavia from 1420 to 1797 was also a major factor. The Florentine Michelozzo moved to Dubrovnik in 1461, where he built the Rector's Palace in a blend of gothic and romanesque. At the Cathedral of Trogir, two renaissance additions were built in the period 1468–1497 by another Florentine named Niccolo, and his associate, Paolo Romano. These are the Chapel of the Blessed John, Bishop Orsini, and the Baptistery. Both have coffered ceilings and a series of shell-headed niches separated by half-columns and pilasters. The chapel also has a clerestory with five small circular windows. The ceiling in the baptistery comes to a ridge-line like a gothic vault, whereas the chapel's ceiling is a barrel-vault.

The Cathedral, Šibenik, Yugoslavia
PLATE 81

The Cathedral at Šibenik, Yugoslavia, was built over many decades during the fifteenth and sixteenth centuries. The lower part of the building is in the gothic style while the upper part reflects Venetian renaissance ideas. The nave's western elevation and the transepts have curved half-gables over the aisles and a semi-circular gable over the rose-windowed clerestory, with huge stone slabs for roof covering following the curved outlines of the gables. Over the crossing is a square plinth under an octagonal drum and dome. The architect of the cathedral is not known for certain—indeed, doubtless many architects had a say in the design over nearly a century of work—but a local man, Giorgio Orsini de Sebenico (also called Juraj Dalmatinac), who worked at Urbino with Laurana in the 1450s and possibly in Venice with Coducci, is believed to have been involved; the outline of the west end is similar to some designs of Coducci. Another architect working in the area at the time was Paolo Romano.

If the penetration of renaissance architecture into Yugoslavia at such an early date should be no surprise, the arrival of renaissance forms in Moscow by the end of the fifteenth century is truly remarkable. In fact, the Bologna architect Ridolfo Fioravanti, nicknamed Aristotele, was brought to Moscow as early as 1475 by Prince Simyon Tolbuzin to build the Cathedral of the Dormition (Assumption) after indigenous architects had failed to prevent the new church from falling down. Fioravanti was told to complete the building in the Russian style, not the Italian, so he travelled around Russia to learn the style. As he was an engineer, he also spent time away from the job working on fortifications. His construction technology and his concept of interior space were different from Russian practice, but the exterior was indistinguishable from the other Russian churches in their local version of Byzantine/Romanesque.

Granovitaya Palace, Moscow, USSR
PLATE 81

Further Italian architects were imported for other purposes. Alevisio da Carcano did hydraulic engineering, while Pietro Antonio Solario and Marco Ruffo began in 1485 to build walls around the Kremlin, which were almost complete by 1516. Solario and Ruffo built the Granovitaya or Palace of Facets for the Czar, who used it in part as his audience chamber. The whole of the upper storey is a single room with the ceiling supported by a single heavy pillar in the middle. The outside surface of the hip-roofed building is composed of diamond-cut stone blocks. Tall, thin, twisted, engaged Tuscan columns form the corners of the building. The present windows were enclosed in rectangular aedicules, but an early picture of the building shows that the aedicules were added later. The windows of the top floor were large and compass-headed, and the windows of the floor below were double compass-headed.[1]

Castle Tovačov, Moravia, Czechoslovakia
PLATE 81

The first appearance of classical forms in Czechoslovakia was at the castle gateway at Tovačev in 1492, built by anonymous masons from Buda, perhaps including Benedikt Ried/Beneš Rejt. The wide arch is framed by fluted Corinthian half-columns and a full entablature.

Ludvík Wing, Hradshin Castle, Prague, Czechoslovakia PLATE 81

Ried also designed the so-called Ludvík Wing at Hradshin Castle in Prague, about 1500–1510. This is a three-storey, hip-roofed structure with individual cornices over the windows. Ried designed other classical details in Prague, such as the south doorway at Saint George's church, about 1520, but in spite of his mastery of classical forms he was better-known as a gothic architect.

1. Both Solario and Ruffo are occasionally given the last name of Friasin. Since Friasin is merely a Russian word for Italian, it should be disregarded. See Aida Nasibova, *The Faceted Chamber in the Moscow Kremlin,* Leningrad, Art Publishers, 1978.

Sections
Chapel of the Blessed John, Bishop Orsini, and the Baptistery, the Cathedral, Trogir, Yugoslavia

PLATE 81

Granovitaya Palace, Moscow, USSR

Entrance,
Castle Tovačov, Moravia, Czechoslovakia

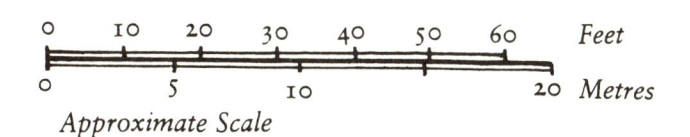

Approximate Scale

The Cathedral, Šibenik, Yugoslavia

Ludvík Wing, Hradshin Castle, Prague, Czechoslovakia

Castle, Piotrków, Poland

147

Castle, Piotrków, Poland PLATE 81

A nineteenth-century drawing, now in the Warsaw university Library Print Room, shows how Poland's first classical building appeared. This was part of the castle at Piotrków, built in 1511–1511 by "Master Benedikt," who may or may not have been Benedikt Ried. It was certainly in a similar style to Ried's Ludvík Wing. It was three storeys tall under a hipped roof, and the windows each had individual cornices. The corners of the building were dressed with quoins, which must be one of the earliest examples of that device.

Cathedral of Saint Michael Archangel, the Kremlin, Moscow, USSR PLATE 82

The next major construction in Moscow was the Cathedral of the Archangel Michael in the Kremlin, the burial-place for the royal family. For this, an architect was imported from Milan, traditionally known as Alevisio Novyi (meaning Aloisio the New, to distinguish him from the hydraulic engineer A. da Carcano who had arrived earlier); it is possible that the rest of his name was Lamberti da Montagnana. On his way to Moscow, he stopped in Bakhchisaray, Romania, where he designed the so-called Iron Gate in 1503 at the Demir Khapu Palace; this is a heavily-decorated doorway with a semicircular pediment (not shown in this book). The cathedral in Moscow, which was built 1505–1509, stuck closely to the traditional Russian plan and construction-technology, but is covered inside and out with renaissance details, such as panelled Corinthian pilasters, blind arches and a row of large shells to disguise a series of gables above the main cornice; the shells in detail are similar to those in the Chapel of Saint-Lazare in the Church de la Major at Marseille, France, carved by Francesco Laurana in 1475–1481, and the outline of the shells on the roof is perhaps related to two Venetian buildings, Coducci's Scuola di San Marco (1485–1495) and Pietro Lombardo's Santa Maria dei Miracoli, (1481–1489), but the shells were sufficiently like Kokoshnik gables of traditional Russian churches so as to cause no offence. It is likely that Alevisio left the design of the onion-domes to local builders. At a later date, heavy buttresses were added to the liturgical south side. With the exception of the Veliki Bell Tower, this cathedral was the last renaissance building built in Moscow, as the rulers commenced a period of more intense xenophobia.

Bishop Bakócz Chapel, Estergom Cathedral, Gran, Hungary PLATE 82

The oldest surviving building of the Renaissance in Hungary is a gem: the Bishop Bakócz Chapel at Estergom Cathedral, Gran, was built in 1506–1507 by Andrea Ferrucci, who was born in the Florence area. The memorial chapel, which is typical of many built in Italy in the fifteenth and sixteenth centuries, was attached to a medieval cathedral, and the cathedral fell into ruins by the eighteenth century. When a new cathedral was built, the little chapel was dismantled and re-erected slightly altered in a new position. It is essentially square with a high hipped roof, inside which is a dome standing on pendentives over the four main arches. The vaults of the arches are coffered, and flanked by fluted Corinthian pilasters; similar but larger pilasters once stood outside the chapel as well. The altarpiece (not shown here) includes a Venetian arch.

Castle, Simontornya, Hungary PLATE 83

In 1508, the first of the multi-storey arcaded loggias, of which there were many in Eastern Europe, appeared at Simontornya Castle, Hungary. It has been much altered over the years, so the reconstruction shown here is tentative. The ground-floor arches rested on square piers, which received additional strength from large brackets that projected from the wall behind. Above a balustrade, Ionic columns carried the next arches, and above the next balustrade Corinthian columns carried the top arches. The architect's name is unknown, but it could have been Ferrucci.

Royal Castle on Wawel Hill, Krakow, Poland PLATE 83

At almost the same time, a much larger courtyard was being decorated in Poland with triple-decked loggias, that of the Royal Castle of Wawel Hill, Krakow. This was built by Francesco Fiorentino and Bartolomeo Berecci, both from Florence, from 1507 to 1536. The Ionic order was used throughout the loggia, which extends on three and a quarter sides of the courtyard. The lower two storeys have arches on columns, the ground-floor columns being taller than the others, and the arches are interrupted periodically by a one-bay piece of blank wall. The top level of the loggia is a colonnade made of columns whose shafts are about twice as long as normal (with a band half-way up, as if to mark where two shafts were joined). When Francesco died in 1516, "Master Benedikt" (Ried?) took over a few years until Berecci's return.

Sigismund Chapel, Wawel Cathedral, Krakow, Poland PLATE

Berecci's part in the Wawel Castle can not easily be quantified along with the parts played by Francesco and Benedikt, but his ability can be gauged by referring to two chapels he built attached to the Wawel Cathedral at Krakow. The earlier and grander of the two is the funerary chapel of King Sigismund I (who had married Bona Sforza of Milan), built in 1517–1533; an almost identical copy was built next to it in the seventeenth century for members of the Vasa family. Like the Bakócz Chapel, the Sigismund Chapel is square, but its pendentives support an octagonal drum pierced by many round windows below the coffered dome, which is lit by a lantern on top. The exterior is trimmed with Tuscan pilasters, and the complicated arrangement of the lower part of the interior has Corinthian pilasters, heavily decorated by over-all carving; in fact, the same type of carving extends over most of the interior surface.

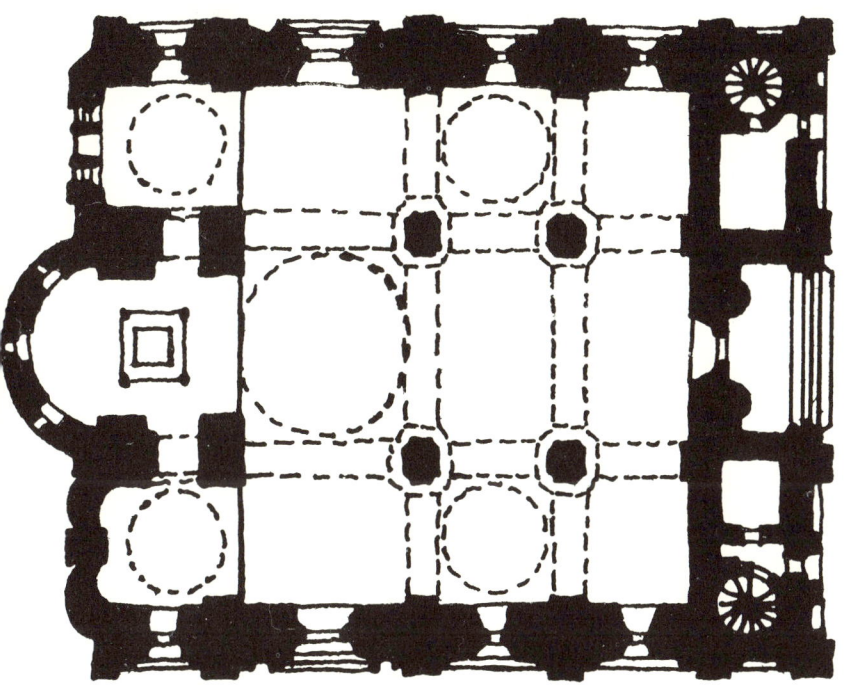

Plan, Cathedral of Saint Michael Archangel, the Kremlin, Moscow, USSR

Original entrance, Bishop Bakócz Chapel, Estergom Cathedral, Gran, Hungary

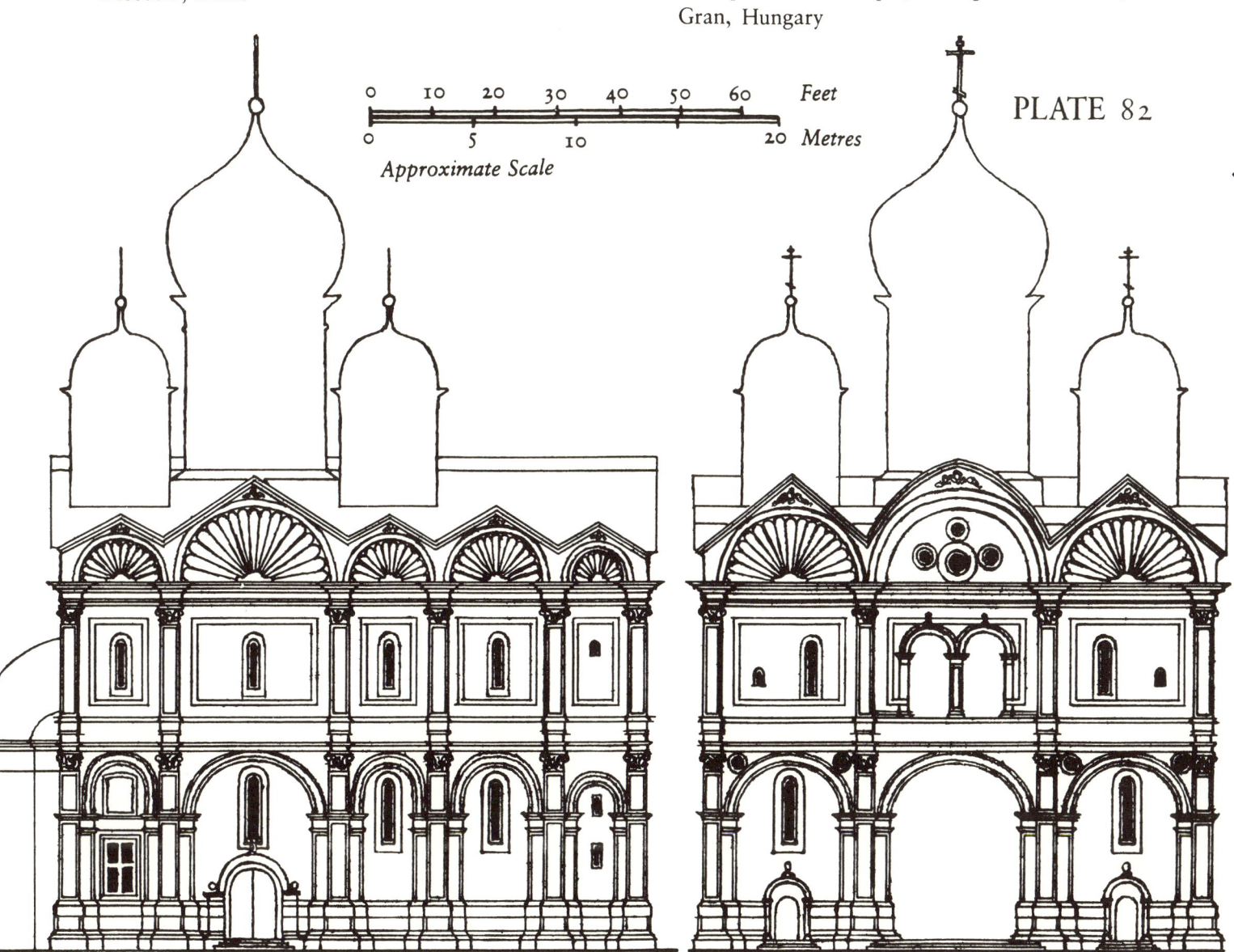

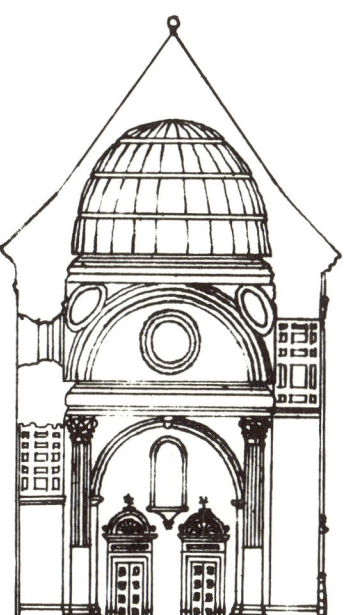

PLATE 82

Plan & two sections, Bishop Bakócz Chapel

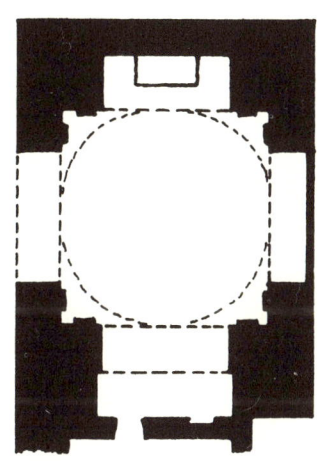

North elevation, Cathedral of Saint Michael Archangel, the Kremlin, Moscow, USSR *West elevation*,

149

Part of courtyard, Castle, Simontornya, Hungary (conjectural reconstruction)

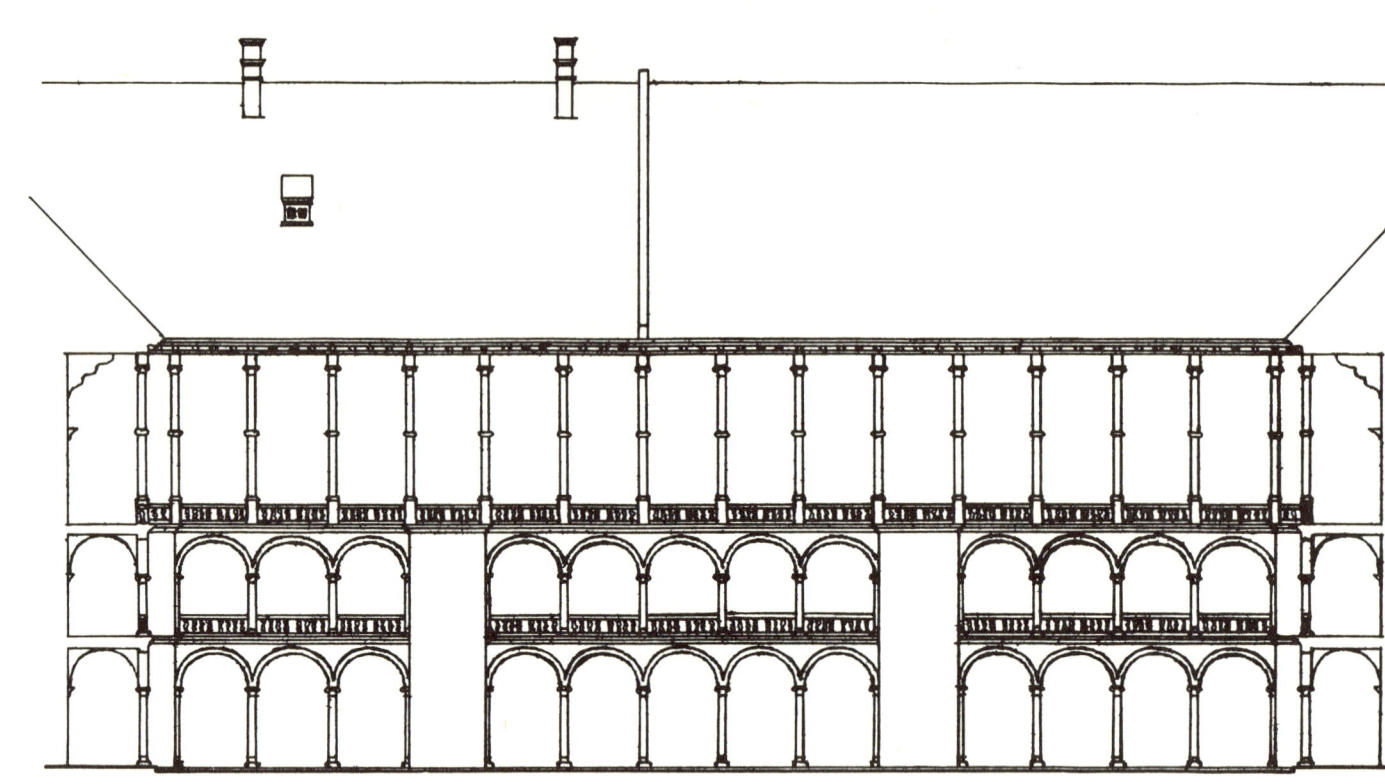

East wing, Courtyard, Royal Castle on Wawel Hill, Krakow, Poland

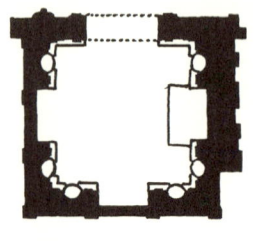

PLATE 83

Approximate Scale

Plan, elevation & section of Sigismund Chapel, Wawel Cathedral, Krakow, Poland

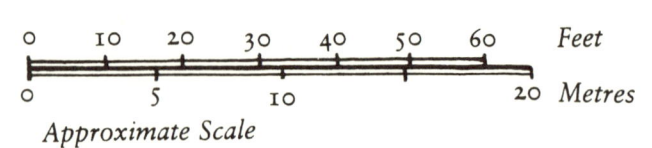

Tomicki Chapel, Wawel Cathedral, Krakow, Poland

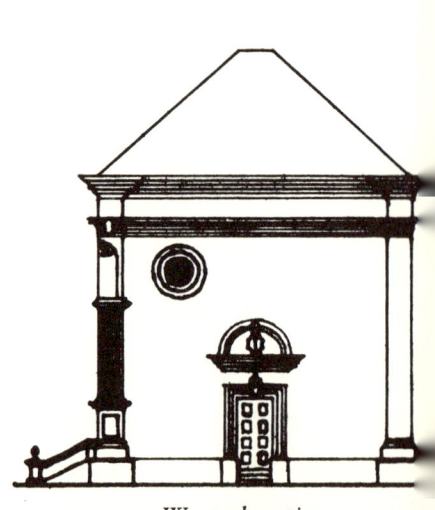

North elevation, Lázói Janos Chapel, Gyulafehérvár, Romania

West elevation,

150

Tomicki Chapel, Wawel Cathedral, Krakow, Poland PLATE 83

The Wawel Cathedral has many memorial chapels around its exterior, one of them being for Bishop Piotr Tomicki, built by Berecci about 1530. Its square, brick base is lit by a pair of compass-headed windows and a round window. Above the cornice, a simple dome (with no drum) stands under a lantern.

Lázói Janos Chapel, Gyulafehérvár, Romania PLATE 83

At about the same time, an attempt was made to build a similar chapel at Gyulafehérvár (Alba Julia), Romania. This is the Chapel of Lázói János, built 1512 by an anonymous architect. The building, which nestles alongside a large church, is a failed attempt to apply classical details without a thorough knowledge of classical design. It includes such items as partially-fluted pilasters, compass-headed arches, an entablature, niches with shells, and round windows, but all arranged with no understanding of how they ought to relate to each other. The interior has a vaulted ceiling with gothic tracery. Italian influence in Romania can also be seen in the Dealului Monastery near Targovishte at Bisritza, and the Episcopal buildings at Curtea de Argesh (not shown in this book).

Ivan Veliki Bell Tower, the Kremlin, Moscow, USSR PLATE 84

The last Italian building in Moscow (other than fortifications) was the Belltower of Ivan the Great or Ivan Veliki, designed by the Venetian architect Marco Bono. It was built in the Kremlin on the site of an old church, near the Cathedral of Saint Michael, in 1532–1542. Two additional storeys were built about 1600 on top of this octagonal tower that is so sparing of ornament. It contains 33 bells.[2]

Belvedere "Letohradek" Villa, Prague, Czechoslovakia PLATE 84

On the Hradshin Hill in Prague is the elegant Belvedere Villa or Letohrádek, a banqueting house begun 1535 for Emperor Ferdinand I. Ferdinand invited Italian masons to Prague, and under the direction of the Paduan sculptor Paolo della Stella they built the ground floor with its arcaded loggia thirteen bays long and five bays wide. The columns of the loggia are Ionic. When Paolo died in 1552, the upper part was still not finished, so Bonifaz Wohlmut from southern Germany took over. He apparently altered Paolo's design for the upper storey and roof without losing the appearance of organic unity. The upper floor has eleven bays, six of them having niches inside aedicules and the other five having windows, each under a bracketed cornice. The roof is ogival. The final result is reminiscent of Palladio's Basilica at Vicenza in a superficial way.

Florian Griespach Castle, Kačerov, Czechoslovakia PLATE 84

Wohlmut designed many other buildings in Czechoslovakia, and two that are attributed to him are castles built for Florian Griespach (from the Tyrol, Austria), the earlier at Kačerov, 1540–1558. An arcaded loggia extends completely around the small courtyard, four bays long and three bays wide. The lower arches stand on piers with engaged Tuscan columns standing in front of the arches, and the upper arches are supported on Tuscan columns that stand on the solid balustrade. After a period of neglect, the castle was burned in 1912 and is presently undergoing restoration.

Florian Griespach Castle, Nelahozeves, Czechoslovakia PLATE 84

The Griespach Castle at Nelahozeves was built 1553–1572. The plan of the exterior resembles a genuine fortress with sharp bastions, but in spite of the quoins and other rustication that give it an air of strength it was not intended to withstand military attack, having only three sides. The courtyard, larger than the Kacěrov courtyard, contains a loggia. The ground floor of the loggia has arches standing on heavy, rusticated piers. The bays of the floor above are marked by Ionic half-columns standing on the solid balustrade over the piers on the ground floor, and are divided into two arches each by small Ionic columns.

Organ Galleries, Saint Vitus' Cathedral, Prague, Czechoslovakia PLATE 84

Wohlmut was engaged to build an organ loft for Saint Vitus' Cathedral in Prague, and this took from 1556 to 1561 to build. Early in the twentieth century, it was moved to the left transept, but the stark contrast between the severe three-bay, two-storey classical loggia and the gothic ribbed vaulting of the old cathedral is still as strong as ever. The lower level has three tall arches with Tuscan pilasters standing in front of the piers. The upper level has shorter, wider arches with Ionic half-columns standing in front of the piers.

Royal Ball Court, Hradshin Hill, Prague, Czechoslovakia PLATE 85

Wohlmut's most famous work is the Royal Ball Court building on Hradshin Hill, Prague, built 1567–1569. Unusually, for a classical building, it is composed of an even number of bays in both directions, ten by two. The bold proportions of the building and its various component elements are somewhat similar to work by Giulio Romano. The six central bays are formed of large arches with giant Ionic half-columns standing between them. The other four bays also have the half-columns, but the spaces between have similar arches with wide niches above. Above the columns is a particularly heavy entablature with cushion frieze below a high hipped roof that has dormers. The walls are perhaps incongruously covered all over with sgraffito work.

2. For more information on the impact of the Renaissance on architecture in Russia, see George Heard Hamilton, *The Art and Architecture of Russia,* Harmondsworth, Penguin Books, 1954 (rev. 1975).

Ivan Veliki Bell Tower,
the Kremlin, Moscow, USSR

Belvedere "Letohradek" Villa, Prague, Czechoslovakia

PLATE 84

Side elevation,
Belvedere "Letohradek" Villa, Prague, Czechoslovakia

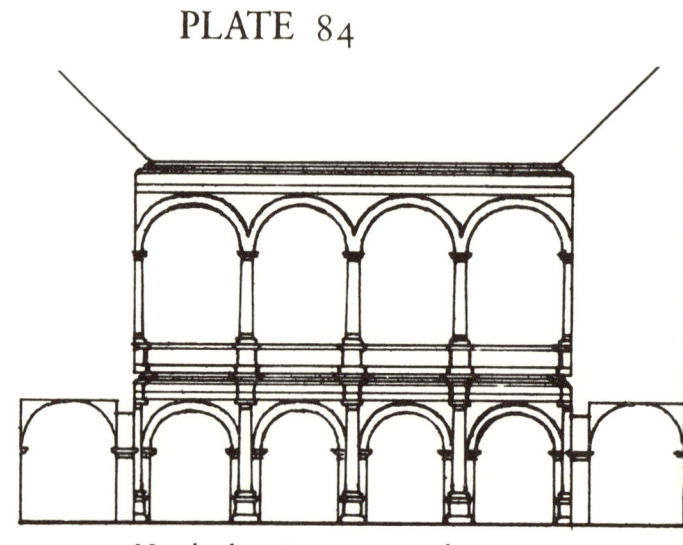

North elevation, courtyard,
Florian Griespach Castle, Kačerov, Czechoslovakia

Part of courtyard,
Florian Griespach Castle, Nelahozeves, Czechoslovakia

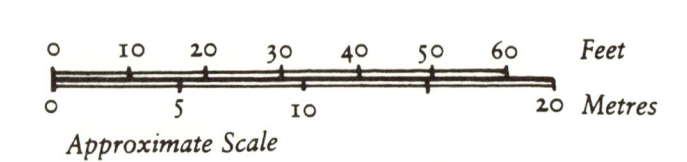

Approximate Scale

Organ Galleries, Saint Vitus' Cathedral, Prague, Czechoslovakia

Royal Ball Court, Hradshin Hill, Prague, Czechoslovakia

Decius Villa, Wola Justowska, near Krakow, Poland

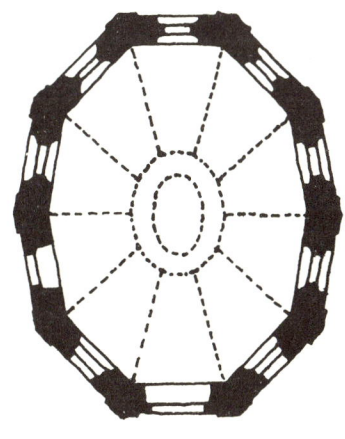

Plan,
Chapel of Saint Adalbert, Hradshin Castle, Prague, Czechoslovakia

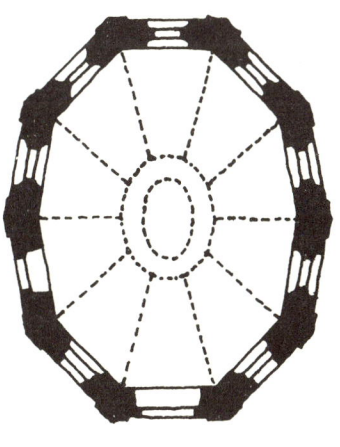

Church of Saints Peter & Paul, Kralovice, Czechoslovakia

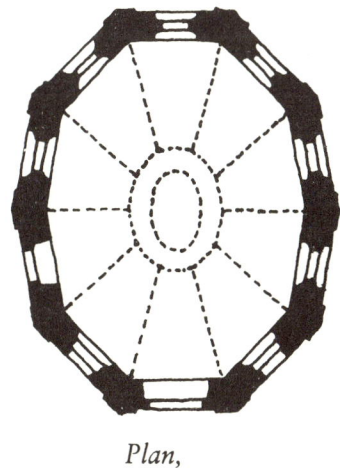

PLATE 85

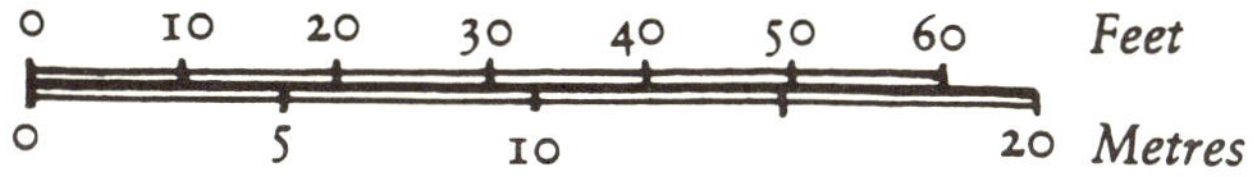

Approximate Scale

Courtyard
Castle, Kostelec nad Černými Lesy, Czechoslovakia

Part of Lobkovic-Švarcemberk Palace, Hradshin, Prague, Czechoslovakia

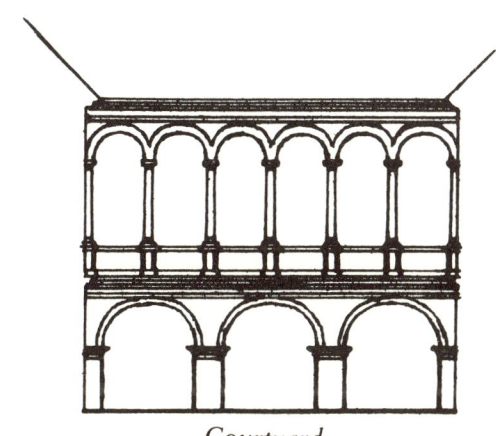

Courtyard
Castle, Brandýs nad Labem, Czechoslovakia

Chapel of Saint Adalbert, Hradshin Castle, Prague, Czechoslovakia
PLATE 85

Attributed to Wohlmut was the Chapel of Saint Adalbert that once stood in front of Saint Vitus's Cathedral in Prague. No pictures show its elevation, but its plan was an elongated decagon. It may well have been the most sophisticated building of its kind and period outside Italy. It was planned as early as 1563, but was not built until 1576. Also possibly by Wohlmut was Sr. Trojice Church (Holy Trinity), built in Prague in 1577. It is said to have been a fine, classical structure, but it is long since destroyed and very little is known about it.

Church of Saints Peter & Paul, Kralovice, Czechoslovakia PLATE 85

The Church of Saints Peter and Paul at Kralovice, Czechloslovakia, was given a new west end in 1575–1581. The brick façade is vigorously defined by a tetrastyle giant portico-motif of clustered Tuscan pilasters (executed in brick) with a cushion frieze in the heavy entablature. Above a high, panelled balustrade is the pedimented clerestory gable-end with curved buttresses on each side. Between the pilasters are several panels and three blind arches, inside one of which is the handsome doorway in an aedicule. Inside the nave, the gallery on three sides is supported on arches. Giant Tuscan pilasters on the front of the solid gallery piers support the elliptical ceiling, which echoes the gothic of the rest of the church by outlining the vaults in ribs. Wohlmut is believed to have been the architect.

Decius Villa, Wola Justowska, near Krakow, Poland PLATE 85

About 1540, a fine villa was built for Jost Ludwik Decius at the village of Wola Justowska near Krakow. The villa was remodelled early in the seventeenth century, so it is difficult to determine its original appearance. Across the front of the rectangular house was built a five-bay three-storey loggia between two one-bay towers. The towers are of rusticated stone on the ground floor and smooth stone with quoins above. The ground-floor loggia has Tuscan pilasters standing in front of the piers that hold the arches, and the upper two floors have arches resting on Tuscan columns. The architect is anonymous.

Lobkovic-Švarcemberk Palace, Hradshin, Prague, Czechoslovakia PLATE 85

The Lobkovic-Švarcenberk Palace on the Hradshin Hill, Prague, was built by Agostino Galli in 1545–1563. It was built on different levels around three sides of a courtyard. The gable ends facing the street are elaborately stepped, and on the sides is a heavy lunette or coved cornice. Below the gables the face of the wall is painted to look as if it were made of courses of diamond-cut stones in the manner of the Palazzo dei Diamanti at Ferrara. It suggests that this kind of busywork was more to the taste of the local people than the pure classical loggias that were being added to castles in various parts of Czechoslovakia.

Castle, Brandýs nad Labem, Czechoslovakia PLATE 85

The courtyard elevations of the old castle at Brandýs-nad-Labem, Czechoslovakia, have been altered substantially since the loggia was first installed by an anonymous architect in 1547–1552, so it is difficult to know exactly what they looked like. The ground floor has large arches on heavy piers, and the floor above has two arches for every one on the ground floor, each standing on Tuscan columns; these arches have now been filled in with windows, and another storey has been added above.

Castle, Kostelec nad Černými Lesy, Czechoslovakia PLATE 85

The otherwise mannerist castle of Kostelec nad Černými Lesy, Czechoslovakia has a fine three-storey arcaded loggia across the north side of its courtyard, built by Hans Tirol, Giovanni Battista Aostalli and Ulrico Aostalli in 1549–1560. The arches of the ground floor are rusticated. On the storey above, Tuscan half-columns stand in front of the arches (which have subsequently been filled in with windows). The top floor has twice as many arches as the floor below, each supported by small Tuscan columns.

Hvěsda Castle, near Prague, Czechoslovakia PLATE 86

Archduke Ferdinand of Tirol commissioned the construction of Hvězda Castle on the outskirts of Prague in 1555–1558, and Hans Tirol, Giovanni Maria del Pambio and Giovanni Lucchese saw to the execution and the details, but it is thought that the archduke himself drew the outline of the unusual plan: the building is in the form of a six-pointed star. The elevation is three storeys tall with a high hipped roof containing two levels of dormers. Bonifaz Wohlmut was hired to design the fortification walls outside the actual castle. Naturally, the rooms inside the points of the star are of unusual proportions with sharp angles, which must have caused some problems in furnishing them. Nevertheless, one of the components of architecture of the Renaissance was experimentation with geometric shapes.

Castle, Litomyšl, Czechoslovakia PLATE 86

Like the Lobkovic-Švarcenberk Palace, the castle at Litomyšl, Czechoslovakia is a mannerist structure whose outside below the roof is entirely covered by sgraffito work intended to look as if the surface was rusticated with diamond-cut stone blocks. However, its courtyard contains a three-storey arcaded loggia on three sides. The lower storey is of rusticated stone (genuine, not painted), and the arches of the two floors above stand on diminishing sizes of Tuscan columns. The most unusual feature about this loggia is that the

External loggia,
Castle, Litomyšl, Czechoslovakia

Courtyard,
Castle, Litomyšl, Czechoslovakia

PLATE 86

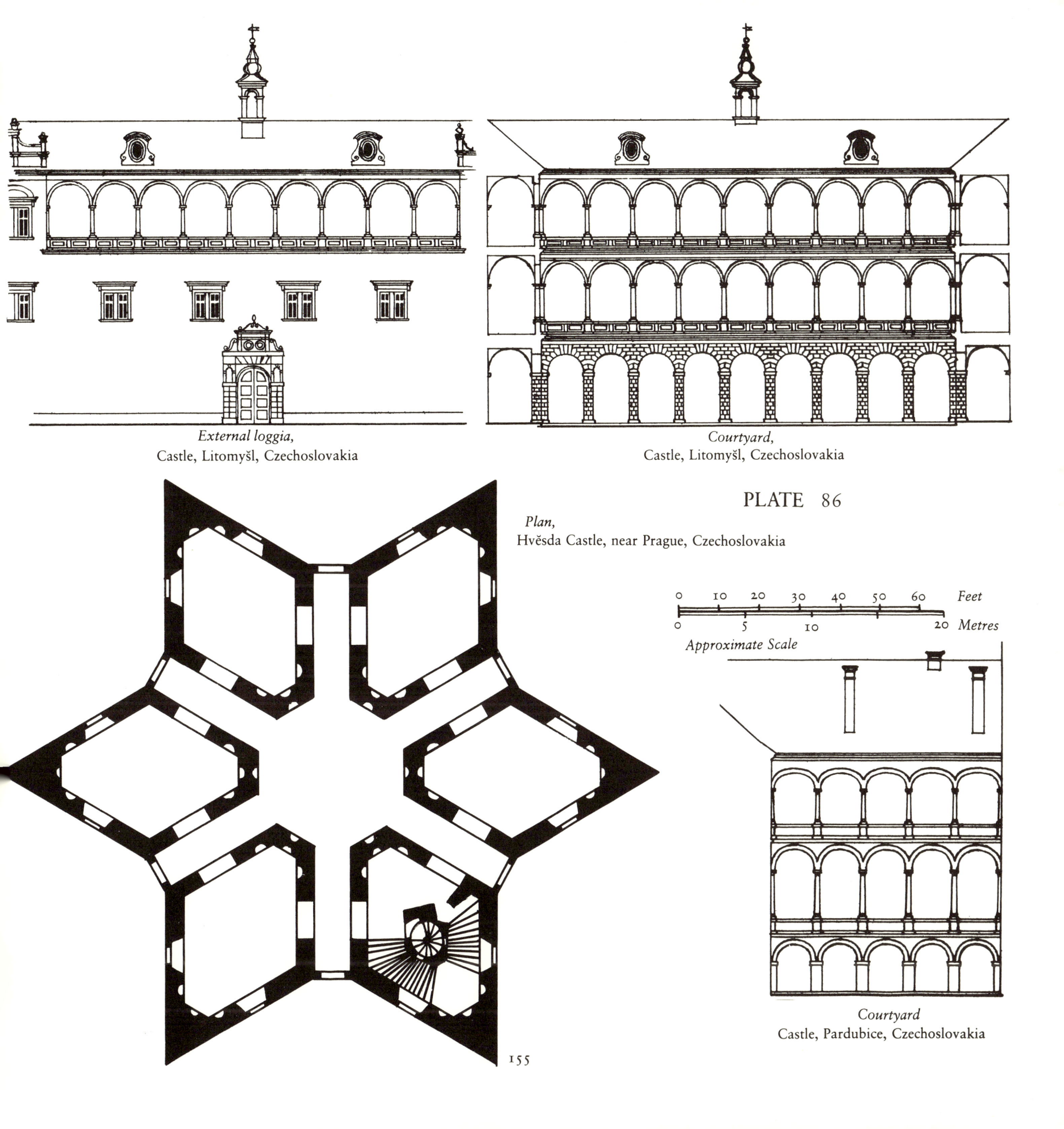

Plan,
Hvězda Castle, near Prague, Czechoslovakia

Courtyard
Castle, Pardubice, Czechoslovakia

top storey of it on the south side continues through to the outside of the castle. The roof over that south loggia has a cupola and two oval dormers a side. The architects of this castle were Giovanni Battista Aostalli and Ulrico Aostalli in 1568–1573.

Castle, Pardubice, Czechoslovakia
PLATE 86

Ulrico Aostalli by himself, some time after 1560, designed the three-storey arcaded loggia at the castle at Pardubice, Czechoslovakia, which has recently been restored. The ground-floor arches are relatively low, and stand on square piers. The two upper floors support the arches with diminishing sizes of Tuscan columns, but the upper arches are slightly elliptical, in order to reduce the height even further.

Castle, Brzég, Poland PLATE 87

The medieval castle at Brzeg, Poland received some alterations in 1551–1553 at the hands of Giovanni Battista Parr of Milan. The most noticeable parts are a three-bay loggia jammed into a corner of the courtyard (not shown here) and the main entrance to the castle. On the ground floor, this takes the form of a large arch on the right for carriages and a small arch on the left for pedestrians, all trimmed with clusters of Corinthian pilasters. On the two storeys above, the face is divided into three equal bays with further Corinthian pilasters of diminishing sizes, plus smaller Corinthian pilasters forming parts of the aedicules around the windows. The aedicules of the middle storey are capped with delicate carvings in the shape of a split scrolled pediment. Nearly the entire façade is covered with carving, which adds texture to a work that is generally conceived in low relief. Some of the detail, although in better proportion, is reminiscent of the Ottheinrichsbau at Heidelberg, which was built only a few years later.

Town Hall, Poznán, Poland PLATE 87

Giovanni Battista di Quadro came from Lugano in southern Switzerland and was made the state architect in Poznán, Poland. In 1553, he started work on the Town Hall there, which is a large building, much of which has no connection to classical design. However, some of the interior rooms are lavishly decorated in the style of Giulio Romano and Raffaello, and a three-storey arcaded loggia stands on the front of the building. The arches of all three storeys stand on piers with Tuscan half-columns in front of them. The arches of the top floor are half the width of most of the arches below them. The central five arches of the lower two floors are wide, but one arch on either end of the façade is almost half as wide as the others. Because of the unusual spacing of the floors inside the building, a row of panels had to be inserted above the arches of the middle floor, rather than make those arches taller than correct proportions would normally dictate.

Town Hall, Plzeň, Czechoslovakia PLATE 87

A Czechoslovakian Town Hall of about the same date is at Plzeň, and it is very different in character from the one at Poznán. This was built by Giovanni di Statio or Stazio (also called Hans Vlach, where Vlach is simply a Czech word for Italian) in 1554–1559. The ground floor is made of rusticated masonry, and its windows have shouldered architraves—a motif repeated two storeys above. The piano nobile has cornices on brackets over its five windows (which are not quite symmetrically arranged), and pediments are indicated in sgraffito work (sgraffito covers most of the building above the rusticated section). Stone blocks form pilaster-strips up each corner of the two storeys above the rustication to a main entablature, above which is a further storey trimmed with Tuscan pilasters and three scrolled gables with finials. In somewhat the same style is the Town Hall, Chelmno, Poland, built by an anonymous architect in 1555–1559 (not shown in the book).

Cloth Hall, Krakow, Poland PLATE 87

Another public building of the period is the enormous Cloth Hall at Krakow, Poland, built 1556–1560. Jan Białostocki thinks that Giovanni Maria Mosca from Padua was the architect of much of the building, including the entrance porch on the south end. The porch, with its two arches and its two-bay Ionic colonnade, is not a particularly exciting design, certainly not in the same class with Mosca's design for the entrance to the castle chapel at Dresden. However, the alteration of scrolled volutes and finials on top of plinths that forms both the gable end and the cornice trim of the roof is of interest, as it was widely copied in Poland, and, to a lesser extent, in Czechoslovakia and Hungary, and adopted as a regional characteristic.

Castle, Moravský Krumlov, Czechoslovakia PLATE 87
Castle, Rosice, Czechoslovakia PLATE 87
Castle, Náměšt' nad Oslavou, Czechoslovakia PLATE 88

Three castles in Czechoslovakia were fitted with three-storey arcaded loggias of very similar design, and all three are attributed to Leonardo Garda da Biseno (also called Garovi). The loggia at Moravský Krumlov (1557–1562) extends around three sides of the courtyard, eleven bays on the long side and four to five bays on the short sides. Like the other two castle loggias, the arches here rest on Tuscan, Ionic and Corinthian columns. The loggia at Rosice (built 1570–1597) is much smaller, as it covers only five bays on one side and three on the other. The loggia at Náměšt'nad Oslavou extends six bays on each side of two sides of the courtyard, and is dated 1573–1578.

Ungeltu Building, Praha-Staré Město, Czechoslovakia PLATE 88

The Czech three-storey loggias are breath-taking in appearance and impressive in numbers, but the loggia form was also used on a smaller scale on less formal buildings. One such is the Ungeltu building in a section of Prague known as Praha-Staré Město. The ground

Main entrance,
Castle, Brzég, Poland

External loggia,
Town Hall, Poznán, Poland

Town Hall, Plzeň, Czechoslovakia

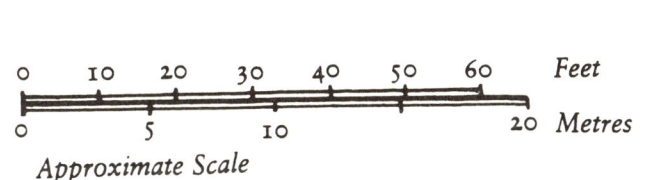

0 10 20 30 40 50 60 Feet
0 5 10 20 Metres
Approximate Scale

Courtyard,
Castle, Moravský Krumlov, Czechoslovakia

PLATE 87

South elevation, Cloth Hall, Krakow, Poland

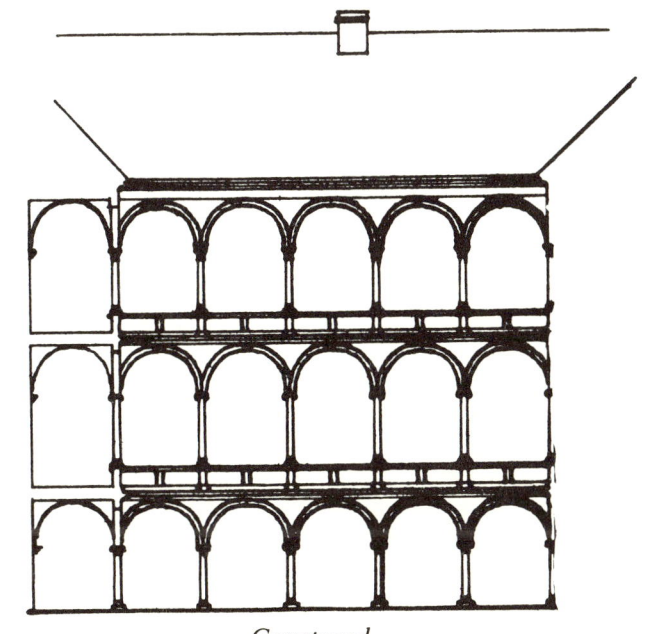

Courtyard
Castle, Rosice, Czechoslovakia

Courtyard,
Castle, Náměšť nad Oslavou,
Czechoslovakia

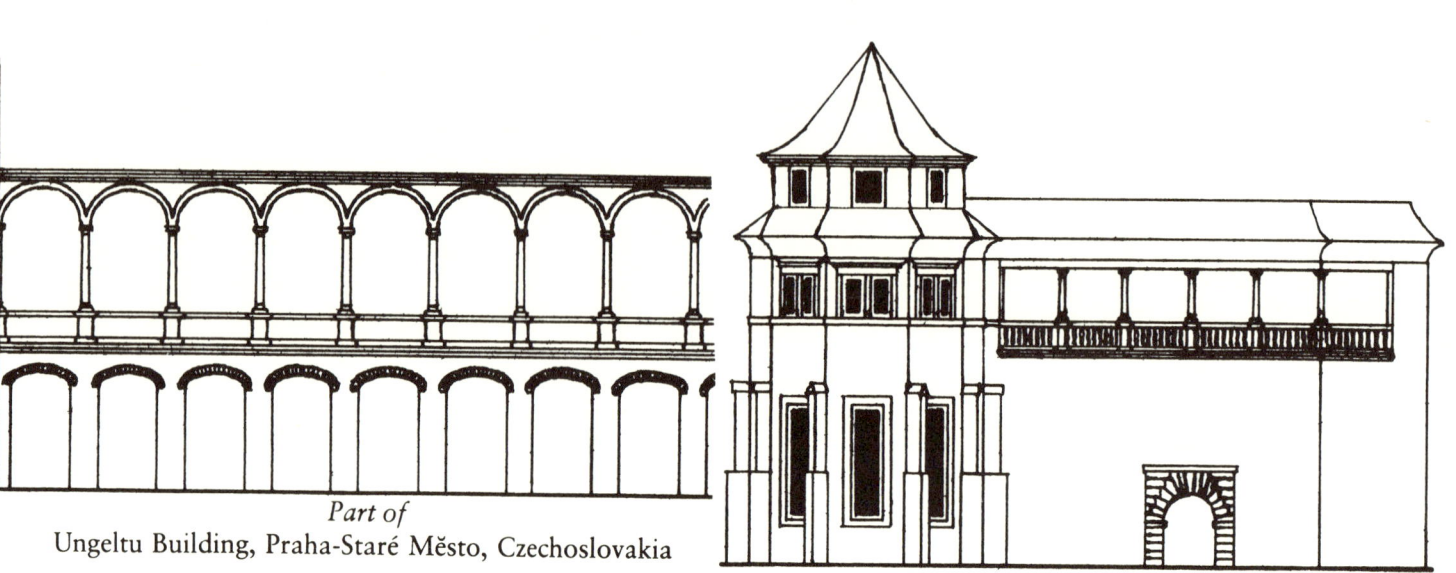

Part of
Ungeltu Building, Praha-Staré Město, Czechoslovakia

Part of Castle, Telč, Czechoslovakia

Part of 15-*bay loggia,* Castle, Telč, Czechoslovakia

PLATE 88

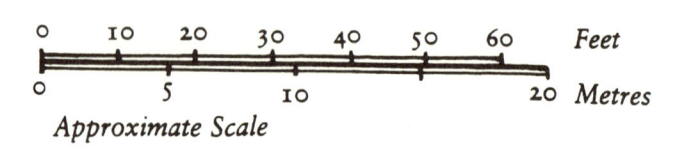

Approximate Scale

Summer Palace, Kratochvíle, Czechoslovakia

Courtyard, Castle, Jindřichův Hradek, Czechoslovakia

Courtyard Castle, Opočno, Czechoslovakia

floor has the appearance of a warehouse, and a single arcaded loggia on Tuscan columns stands above. The architect is anonymous and the date is about 1559. A top floor with windows may be a later addition.

Castle, Telč, Czechoslovakia PLATE 88

The castle at Telč has a few portions with classical details. Inside the Great Hall is some impressive trompe-l'oeil painting of architectural motifs in perspective; the interior of the chapel has a groined barrel-vaulted ceiling. The high-style work here is attributed to Baldassare Maggi and his associates in the period about 1560 to 1580. The complex contains two loggias, one a six-bay colonnade high on an almost blank wall connected to the chapel, and the other an independent fifteen-bay arcade in the garden.

Castle, Jindřichův Hradek, Czechoslovakia PLATE 88

Maggi and his team are also believed to have been responsible for the three-storey loggia at Jindřichův Hradek, Czechoslovakia, built about 1580. Ulrico Aostalli also worked on the castle in the late 1590s, as did Maggi and the rest of his team, which included the builders Antonio Cometta and Giovanni M. Faconi. One of the creations of the 1590s, although too late to be included in this book is an attractive round garden pavilion attached to long, single-storey garden loggias. The earliest loggia, the three-storey one, is ten bays wide, and supports its arches on Tuscan columns at each level, the columns of each stage becoming more and more attenuated.

Summer Palace, Kratochvíle, Czechoslovakia PLATE 88

Maggi designed a rather different building for the Summer Palace at Kratochvíle, near Netolice, Czechoslovakia, 1582–1589. This is a rectangular, two-storey building, nine bays wide, with a double-pile hipped roof (the present roof, a double-pile mansard, dates from 1762), and a small curvilinear gable over the center of the front. Architecturally, the design is simple, but it is complicated by trompe-l'oeil sgraffito work between the windows, indicating Tuscan columns and shell-headed niches (normally, this book does not show sgraffito work in the elevation drawings, but in this case it has been included). Around the villa are various dependency buildings a single storey in height and a tall entrance tower. Sgraffito work on some of the walls of these is designed to give the impression of diamond-cut stone blocks.

Maggi and his team worked at the castle of Český Krumlov, where they completed a handsome steeple on the Hrádek (Small Castle) in 1580 (not shown in this book), built for William of Rožmberk, the Lord High Burgrave or highest rank in the land after the king. Above a round tower is an arcaded loggia of arches on about 20 Tuscan columns, whose roof leads to a slightly narrower drum with round windows. Four dormers of almost baroque design stand on the steep roof of the drum, which leads to an octagonal cupola with an onion dome. This steeple is in the same class as the lighthouse of Louis de Foix at Cordouan, France, although it is most unlikely that de Foix ever saw Maggi's work or even a picture of it.

Castle, Opočno, Czechoslovakia PLATE 88

The Czech castle at Opočno contains a three-storey loggia on three sides of its open courtyard, built 1560–1567 by an anonymous architect. All the columns are Tuscan. The lower two storeys are formed of arcades, but the top floor is a colonnade of twice as many bays. Much of the rest of the castle was completed in a classical style considerably later than the period of the loggias.

Castle, Hustopeče, Czechoslovakia PLATE 89

The three-storey courtyard loggia at the Czech castle at Hustopeče, built in 1560 by an anonymous architect, is similar to the loggia at Opočno, except that the columns of the top floor lack the double-spacing found there.

Zielona Brama, Gdánsk, Poland PLATE 89

The magnificent three-storey Czech and Polish loggias were all the creations of imported Italians. However, classical forms appeared on the Baltic coast of northern Poland via German and Dutch architects. The strong emphasis on the vertical axis of these buildings points to northern Europeans as the designers. One such building is the Zieloma Brama (Green Gate) at Gdánsk. This was built in 1563 by a team, in which Regnier (no known first name) of Amsterdam was the architect and Bastian Kramer and his son Johann/Hans Kramer, who had been working at Dresden, were the masterbuilders. The building is divided into six bays, each containing two windows, except for three bays on the ground floor that have arches. If only the two central bays had arches, the façade would be symmetrical, but it would seem that the city authorities required three arches, one for pedestrians and one each for inbound and outbound vehicles. The bays are expressed by the application of pilasters and half-columns—rusticated Tuscan on the ground floor, banded Ionic on the next floor, and Corinthian and Composite on the three scrolled gables that stand across the main gabled roof.

Długa 45, Gdánsk, Poland PLATE 89 & Długa 35, "Lion's Castle," Gdánsk, Poland

Two other buildings in Gdánsk appear to have been designed by Regnier and built by Kramer, both on Długa Street. The smaller of the two, number 45, was built in 1563. It is three bays wide and three storeys high, plus a tall basement and a two-storey gable facing the street. Four of the storeys are articulated by Doric pilasters. The gable is trimmed with volutes and finials. The other building, number 35, was built in 1569, and is known as the Lion's Castle. Here, the three-bay façade is articulated with Tuscan, Ionic, Corinthian and Composite pilasters on the four principal storeys. A fifth

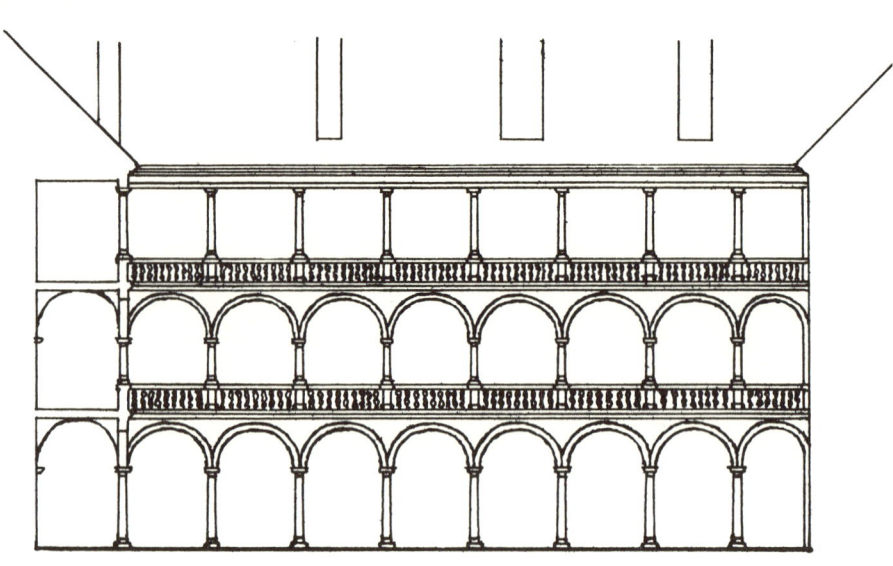

Courtyard   Castle, Hustopeče, Czechoslovakia

*Part of courtyard,
Turzo Castle, Nagybicese, Hungary*

*Turzo Castle, Betlanovec/Bethlenfalva,
Hungary*

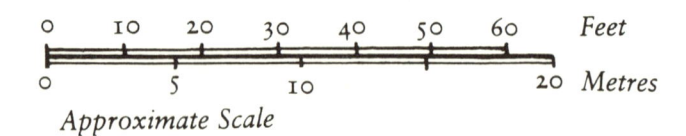

PLATE 89

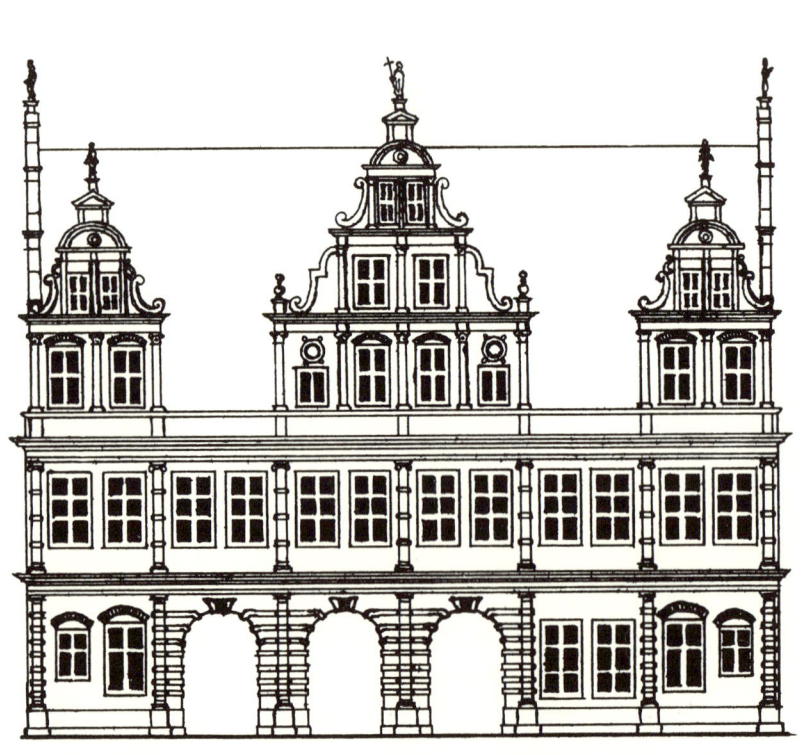

Harbor front,   Zielona Brama, Gdánsk, Poland

Długa 45, Gdánsk, Poland

*Długa 35, "Lion's Castle,"
Gdánsk, Poland*

*Stará Pošta, Nový Jičín,
Czechoslovakia*

160

storey is part of the gable, which, with its volutes, pinnacles and pediment, looks more classical than the gable on the house at number 45.

Turzo Castle, Betlanovec/Bethlenfalva, Hungary PLATE 89

Two Hungarian buildings were built in 1564 for the Turzo family, and they are remarkably different from each other. The castle at Betlanovec is a small, rectangular box, whose end elevation is shown here, four bays wide and two storeys tall. Above the cornice is a series of ornamental devices of the type already seen at the Cloth Hall at Krakow, here consisting of rectangles, semicircles and quarter-circles repeated for each bay, and a flared, circular Italian chimney at each corner. The building presently has a cantilevered balcony around it at the level of the upper floor, but the balcony is probably a later addition.

Turzo Castle, Nagybicese, Hungary PLATE 89

The other Turzo castle is at Nagybicese in Hungarian Slovakia. This was built by Kiliano Syröth de Mediolano, and its most significant feature is the two-decked arcaded loggia in the courtyard, standing only a short distance out from the walls behind it. The ground floor of the loggia has arches resting on piers with pilaster-strips attached to the front of the piers. The upper floor arches stand on diminutive Tuscan columns, whose axis is continued upwards to the cornice by further pilaster-strips, thus detracting from the natural rhythm otherwise produced by the arches themselves.

Stará Pošta, Nový Jičín, Czechoslovakia PLATE 89

Similar diminutive Tuscan columns support two floors of arcaded loggias above a warehouse-type ground floor in the three-bay Stará Pošta at Nový Jičín, Czechoslovakia, built by an anonymous architect about 1565. It looks as if it should be part of a much larger building that was for some reason never completed.

Castle, Bučovice, Czechoslovakia PLATE 90

At one time, one of the most impressive of the Czech renaissance castles was at Bucovice, and while it is still impressive today it has been altered above the cornice line, and its large pattern of formal dependencies has long since disappeared. It was built by Pietro Ferrabosco (who designed palaces in Vienna) and Pietro Gabri, 1567–1582. The forbidding exterior is superficially related to Ancy in that it has corner towers, but with nowhere near the grace. The corners are trimmed with quoins, and the windows are grouped in pairs under cornice-strips in three storeys, in which the piano nobile is much the tallest. Above the cornice is an attic storey with pairs of small round windows. The windows are all arranged symmetrically except for one bay on the south elevation, where windows at odd heights illuminate the staircase. The rooms of the castle are arranged on three sides of the courtyard, the fourth side being a wall with an arcaded loggia. The loggias run around three sides of the courtyard, leaving the east side plain. At first glance, these loggias look typical of many of the best Czech castle loggias, but they have some differences. The arches stand on columns of the Ionic, Corinthian and Composite orders, and the columns of the ground floor rest on bases rather than directly on the ground. The most notable achievement is that the loggias look correctly spaced and proportioned between the various floors, and yet the actual building has great variations in floor-heights, since it has a high piano nobile.

Castle, Račice, Czechoslovakia PLATE 90

Another three-storey loggia can be seen at the castle at Račice, Czechoslovakia, built by an anonymous architect in 1568. The arcades and top-floor colonnades have been filled in with windows at a later date, and the ground-floor columns appear to have been thickened at the same time. The orders throughout are Tuscan.

Monument to Count Albrecht, Kaliningrad, USSR PLATE 91

As noted above, the countries of the southern shore of the Baltic tended to receive their classical designs from the Dutch rather than from the Italians. In 1570, Cornelis Floris de Vriendt of Antwerp, who was primarily a sculptor, designed and executed a monument to Count Albrecht in what was then the East Prussian city of Königsberg, now Kaliningrad, U.S.S.R. The lower part of the monument takes the form of a wide Venetian arch with Corinthian columns, and a second storey of Composite columns stands atop the lower ones. Above their entablature is a central panel with pediment, and on either side of that is a roundel with finial. No confirmation was able to be obtained from Soviet authorities that the monument is still intact.

Castle, Jaroslavice, Czechoslovakia PLATE 91

The castle at Jaroslawice, Czechoslovakia, was built by an anonymous architect about 1570. Inside its courtyard are arcaded loggias on all four sides, nineteen bays by thirteen. However, perhaps the most unusual feature of this castle is that it also has an 11-bay arcade on tall Tuscan columns extending along part of the outside wall on the east side. The ground drops off sharply at this point, thus affording a good view from the loggia.

Castle, Plumlov, Czechoslovakia PLATE 91

One Czech castle that is very different from all the others is that of Plumlov, near Prostějov, built about 1570–1580. The carver was Michael Kramer, who had been working with the rest of his family at Dresden, and the builders were Gaspare Cuneo and Stanislas Ludwig, but it is not known if any of them served as architect. The castle sits atop a rocky eminence, and the side that faces out to the water is plain and undecorated; it has a gable roof and six storeys, alternating between regular windows and mezzanine windows. The landward side echoes the same window arrangements, but trims the

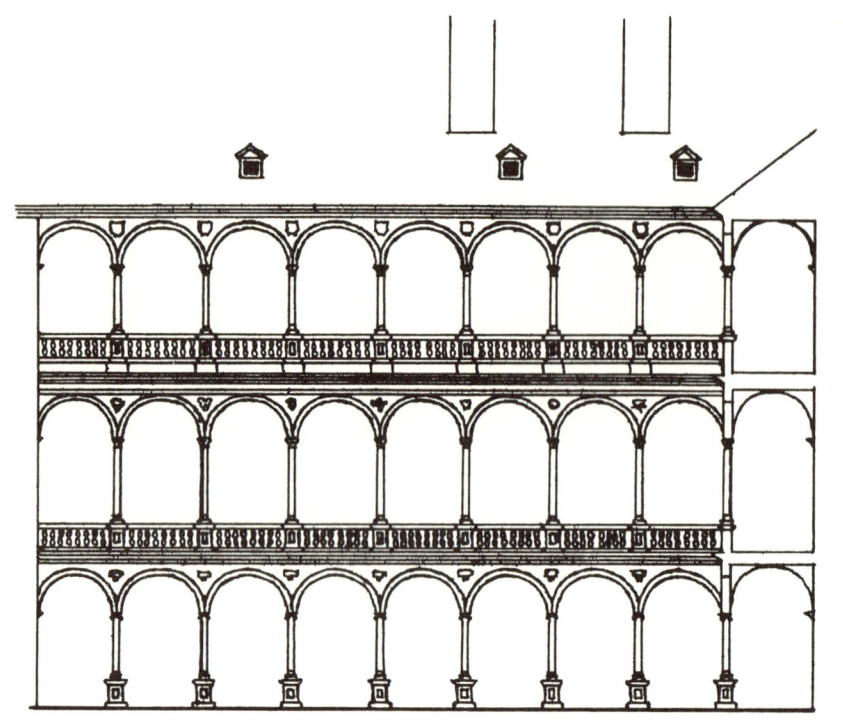

Courtyard,   Castle, Bučovice, Czechoslovakia

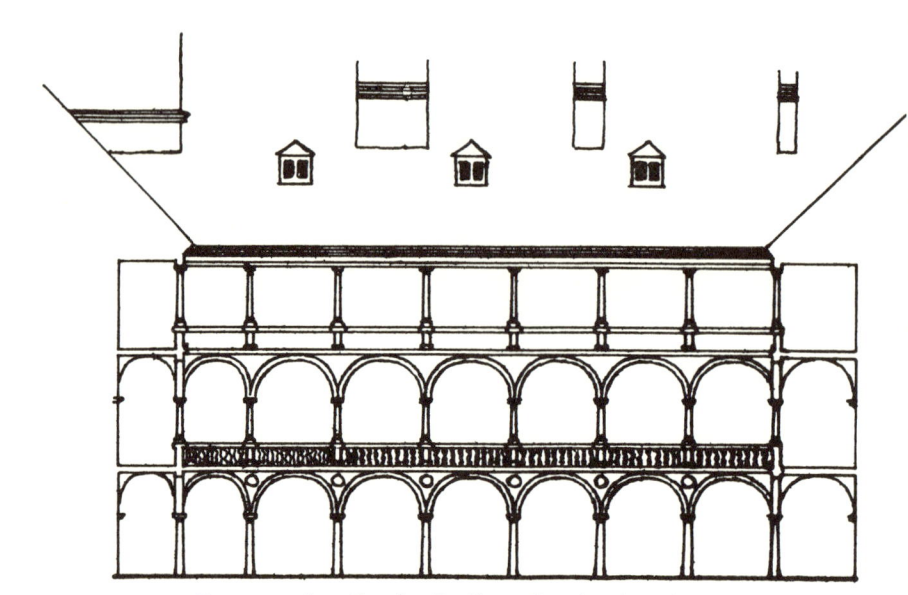

Courtyard   Castle, Račice, Czechoslovakia

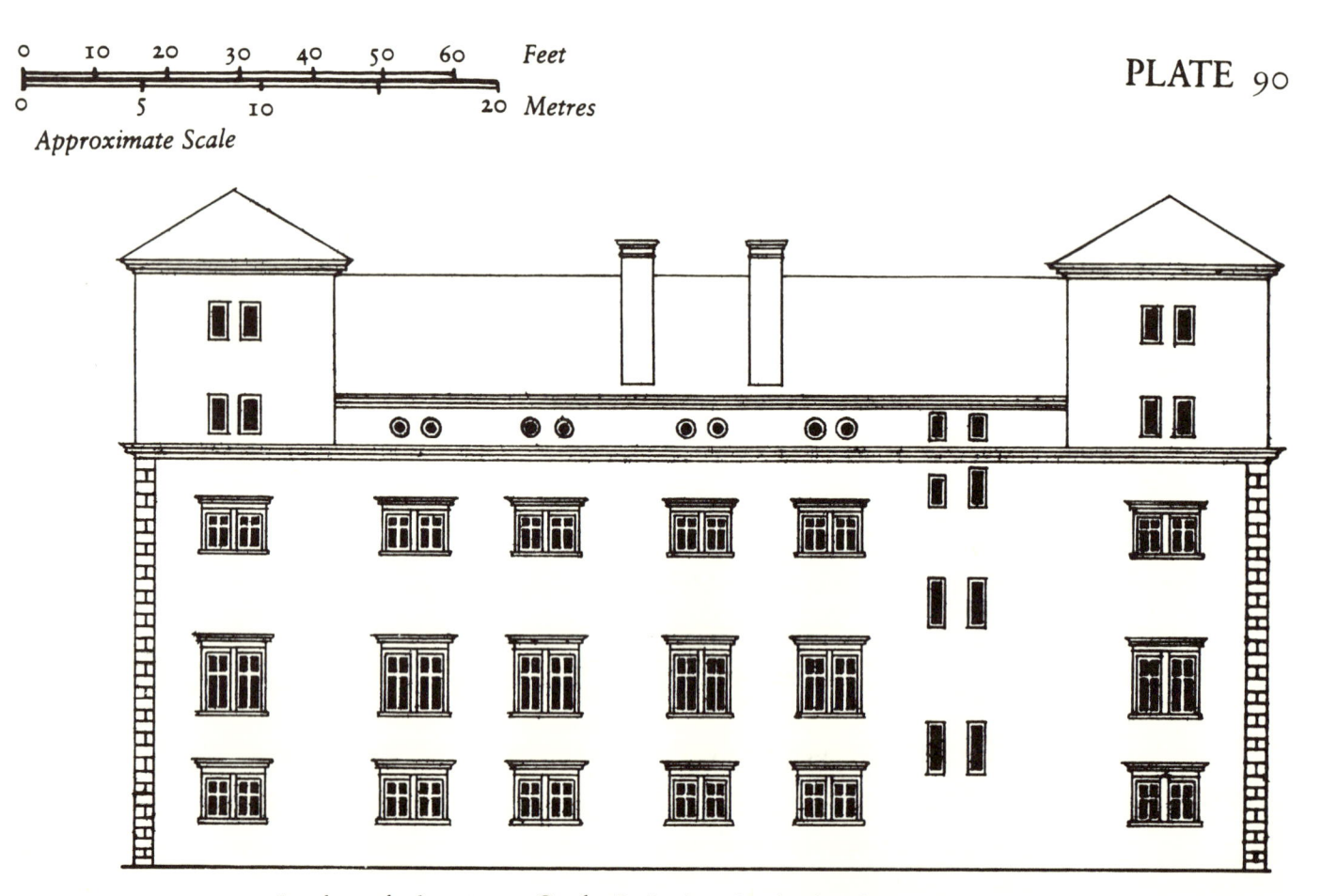

PLATE 90

South end elevation,   Castle, Bučovice, Czechoslovakia

External loggia, Castle, Jaroslavice, Czechoslovakia

Monument to Count Albrecht, Kaliningrad, USSR

Mydlářovský Building, Chrudim, Czechoslovakia

PLATE 91

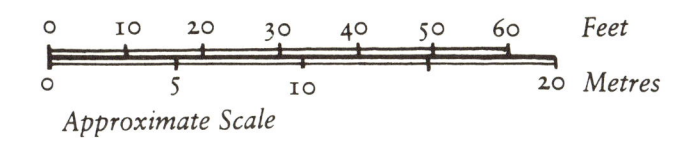

0 10 20 30 40 50 60 Feet
0 5 10 20 Metres
Approximate Scale

Section of Padniewski/Potocki Chapel, Cathedral, Krakow, Poland

Castle, Plumlov, Czechoslovakia

Edelmann Chapel, Church of Saint Moritz, Olomouc, Czechoslovakia

regular windows with both triangular and segmental pediments, and groups the windows into three apparent storeys by means of entablatures extending completely across the front. At every bay, the entablatures are brought forward to receive columns, Doric, Ionic and Corinthian; the columns are doubled at each end of the façade and one either side of the central bay. From a distance, this design appears excessively busy, similar to the defects in Palladio's project for rebuilding the Doge's Palace in Venice, but a closer view affords appreciation of the bold sculptural quality of the front (which the Doge's Palace project lacked).

Padniewski/Potocki Chapel, Cathedral, Krakow, Poland PLATE 91

The sculptor Jan Michałowicz of Urzędów built one of the many funerary chapels attached to the Wawel Cathedral at Krakow. This is the Padniewski Chapel of 1572–1575, since renamed the Potocki Chapel and redecorated in the neo-classical style of 1832–1840. Originally, this was a square building whose hipped roof was tapered so as to lead almost immediately into a hemispherical dome with lantern on top. The inside of the dome was coffered and appeared to rest on a band of columns, behind which were shell-headed niches; the columns and niches gave the illusion of a drum, which rested on pendentives over the four shallow arches of the bottom of the chapel.

Mydlářovský Building, Chrudim, Czechoslovakia PLATE 91

From this same period is an unusual version of the multi-storey arcaded loggia at the Mydlářovský building, Chrudim, Czechoslovakia. This was built by an anonymous architect in 1573–1577. What is unusual is that the arcades begin on the floor above the ground floor on a corbelled projection out over the sidewalk (for safety's sake, the structure is reinforced by posts to the street, a recent addition). The loggias must be heavy, for they are made of stone with Tuscan columns on each of two floors, plus a carved, panelled balustrade on the lower balcony and turned balusters on the upper balcony. At some later date, an extra storey was added above with wooden posts.

Edelmann Chapel, Church of Saint Moritz, Olomouc, Czechoslovakia PLATE 91

Also in Czechoslovakia is the Edelmann Chapel, attached to the church of Saint Moritz at Olomouc, and built in 1573. This diminutive building, by an anonymous architect, is of rusticated stone and has three arches across its front, which are trimmed by Corinthian half-columns. The frieze is rather larger than normal and is profusely decorated with carving.

"Italian Courtyard," Lvóv, USSR PLATE 92

Three buildings of importance appeared at this time in a city whose nationality has changed several times. At the time, it was Polish and was called Lwów, but it became German for a time under the name of Lemberg. It is now part of the U.S.S.R., and its name is Lvóv. The earliest of the three buildings, probably about 1570 (Soviet officials declined to provide any information about it), is the so-called Italian Courtyard loggia. The arches of the lower two floors stand on thick Tuscan columns, and the top floor arches stand on Ionic columns. An unusual feature here is that the columns stand directly on the entablatures below, rather on a base formed by the height of the balustrade. The architect is anonymous, but it may well have been Pietro di Barbona, who was given the Polish name of Crassowski; his Italian name may have been Grassi.

Dr. Anczowski's "Black House," Lvóv, USSR PLATE 92

Crassowski was definitely the architect of the four-storey house of Dr. Anczowski (known as the Black House) in the Market Place in Lvóv, built 1577. This asymmetrical, three-bay house is covered all over, including on its pilasters, with diamond-cut stonework, whose courses vary in height. Above the top cornice is a balustrade capped with volutes, finials and pinnacles. This house is not one of the most sophisticated examples of classicism—its pilasters, for example, are poorly proportioned and detailed—and it shows that the mere hiring of an Italian architect as late as the 1570s was not enough to ensure a classical result.

Church of the Benedictines, Lvóv, USSR PLATE 92

Crassowski was probably also the architect of the Benedictine Church in Lvóv, built in 1578, as it is similarly heavy in its detailing. The façade is divided into three bays by clusters of thick Corinthian pilasters, and the frieze above the capitals projects with ungainly blocks. The arched doorway, covered all over with carving, is related to the doorway at the Black House. The other two bays each contain a large compass-headed window. The low roof is pierced by three octagonal drums (the largest in the middle) with domes and cupolas reminiscent of Russian Orthodox churches. This small church is attached to a much larger one. Crassowski also built two church towers, one for the Walachian Church and one for the Armenian Cathedral (which burned down in 1778).

Castle, Vělke Losiny, Czechoslovakia PLATE 92

The castle at Vělke Losiny, built 1580–1589 by an anonymous architect, is an example of retardataire development, for among Czech castles with arcaded loggias it is far more primitive than most of those that preceded it by up to fifty years. The castle is arranged around three sides of a courtyard, the open ends being capped by scrolled gables. Part of the exterior is covered in sgraffito imitation of rusticated stonework. The three-storey arcaded loggias that extend around all three sides of the courtyard are heavy in detail, with short Tuscan

"Italian Courtyard," Lvóv, USSR

Dr. Anczowski's "Black House," Lvóv, USSR

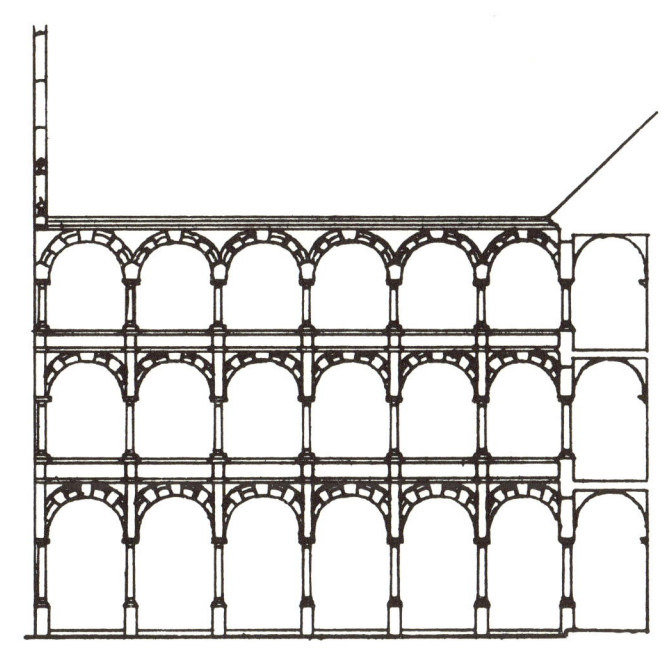

Courtyard, Castle, Vĕlke Losiny, Czechoslovakia

PLATE 92

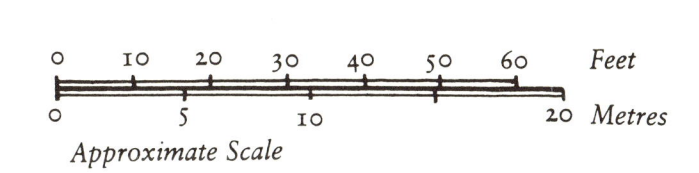

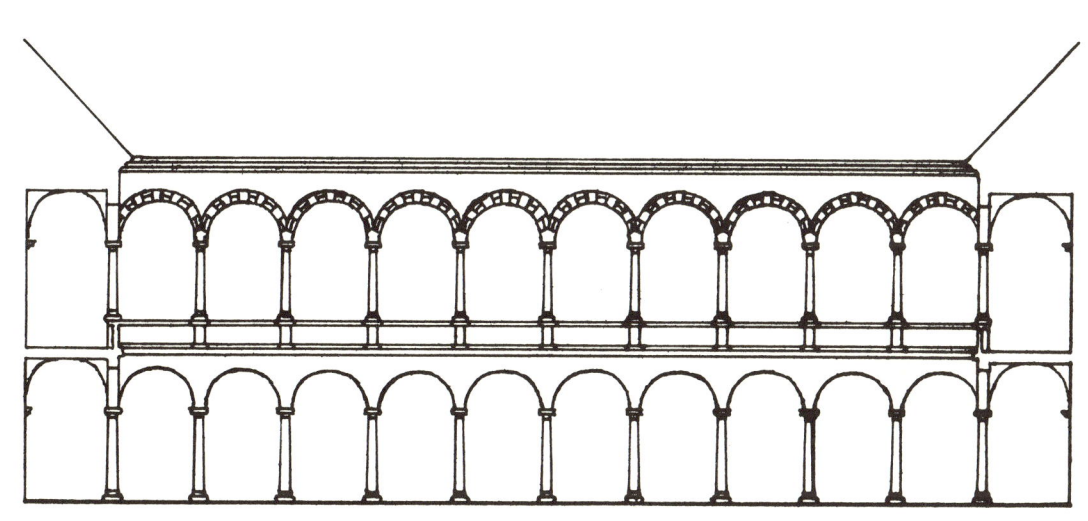

Courtyard, Castle, Koldštejn, Czechoslovakia

Church of the Benedictines, Lvóv, USSR

Part of courtyard, Castle, Oslavany, Czechoslovakia

165

columns supporting arches with pronounced voussoirs; in the case of the lower two storeys, the voussoirs are cut by pilaster-strips above the columns, a clumsy device that emphasizes unnecesarily the vertical axis.

Castle, Koldštejn, Czechoslovakia PLATE 92

The loggias at the Czech castle of Koldštejn (formerly Goldenstein) were built about 1580 by an anonymous architect, possibly the same man as at Vělke Losiny, since the voussoirs of the upper of the two storeys are pronounced. Once again, the courtyard is three-sided, but the two arms are of irregular length and at irregular angles to the main block. The lower arcades are plain, and both sets of arches stand on Tuscan columns.

Castle, Oslavany, Czechoslovakia PLATE 92

The final building in this section is the castle at Oslavany, Czechoslovakia, built by an anonymous architect about 1583. The courtyard loggia here is again only two storeys tall, and at one point a charming effect is obtained by a block of three bays which projects out one bay from the rest under a hipped roof with a pedimented dormer. Both sets of arches are supported by Tuscan columns, but the bases of the upper columns rest on brackets that intrude into the spandrels of the arches below.

The peak of perfection of classical design in Eastern Europe can be seen in a few domed chapels, in the Prague Belvedere and in the variety of multi-storey loggias found on many castles. Indeed, the finest of these are the equal of anything built in Italy of the same type in the same period, and in fact could be easily mistaken for Italian. Buildings in some other countries are sometimes the equal of their Italian counterparts, but they are seldom likely to be mistaken for being Italian. This last is perhaps the most significant achievement of Eastern European architecture in the Renaissance. However, particularly in the case of the loggias, the loggias themselves are usually the only parts of the buildings that achieve such a high level of classicism, and the exteriors of these buildings are often second-rate, which is a criticism that can fairly be levelled at much Eastern European architecture of the period.

Because the quality of architecture covered in this section appears to go downwards towards the end of the period, it should not be inferred that the downward slide continued. Shortly after the close of the period covered by this book, the architect Santi Gucci, among others, continued to build on the classical foundations laid by his many talented forerunners; this pattern was generally not seen in the rest of northern Europe, where a perverse form of mannerism took over for about two decades or longer.

For further reading, see the following:

Eberhard Hempel, *Baroque Art and Architecture in Central Europe,* Harmondsworth, Penguin Books, 1965.

Brian Knox, *The Architecture of Poland,* New York, Praeger, 1971.

Feuerné Tóth Rózsa, *Reneszánsz Épitészet Magyar-Országon,* Budapest, Magyar Helikon/Corvina, 1977.

Jan Białostocki, *The Art of the Renaissance in Eastern Europe,* Ithaca, NY, Cornell University Press, 1976.

Jiřina Hořejší, Jarmila Krcálová, Jaromír Neumann, Emanuel Poche and Jarmila Vacková, *Renaissance Art in Bohemia,* London, Hamlyn, 1979. Slobodan Ćurčić, *Art and Architecture in the Balkans,* Boston, G. K. Hall, 1984.

H. & S. Kozakiewicz, *The Renaissance in Poland,* Warsaw, 1976.

Balogh Jolán, *Az Erdélyi Renaissance,* Prague, Kolozvár, 1943.

August Prokop, *Die Markgrafschaft Mähren in Kunstgeschichtlicher Beziehung,* Vienna, 1904.

Eva Samánková, *Architektura České Renesance,* Prague, 1961.

Henry-Russell Hitchcock, *Netherlandish Scrolled Gables of the Sixteenth and Seventeenth Centuries,* New York, New York University Press, 1978.

SPAIN & PORTUGAL

Most people know that Ferdinand and Isabella sent Christopher Columbus on a maritime expedition in 1492 that resulted in Spain colonizing much of the New World, but few people know what other important event happened earlier that same year that made Columbus' voyages possible. Most of the Iberian Peninsula had at one time been conquered by the Muslim Moors (the same people who were called Turks when they conquered large parts of Eastern Europe), but gradually the Moors had been pushed back into North Africa. In January 1492 Ferdinand and Isabella reconquered the last Moorish stronghold on the peninsula: the province of Granada. With the Moors out of Spain, money and spirit could be freed for other things, such as voyages of exploration and conquest, and building great architecture.

People who follow the international news are aware that Spain is occasionally the victim of terrorist acts by a group known as the Basque Separatists. What they may not also know is that the apparently monolithic country of Spain was formed, in part by Ferdinand and Isabella, out of several different nations with names like Andalucia, Aragon, Murcia, Castilla, as well as a Basque homeland, and many of these countries had little in common with each other. One such country is Portugal, which was temporarily absorbed into Spain and managed to gain independence again several decades later. In terms of architecture, the story of Portugal is totally independent from the story of the Spanish provinces, and so the two are treated separately here. If one or other of the Spanish provinces had also gained independence from the rest in this period, would its architectural story have been different? Probably not to the extent of Portugal's architecture.

Colegio Santa Cruz, Valladolid PLATE 93

The first pretense at classicism in Spain came just before the final victory over the Moors. Lorenzo Vázquez and others built the Colegio of Santa Cruz (College of the Holy Cross) at Valladolid in 1487–1491. This large block is divided into five bays by buttresses that are disguised with classical details, such as pairs of Tuscan and Ionic columns and pilasters, but there was no disguising their gothic pinnacles that extend far above the rooftop balustrade and the heavy, elaborate classical cornice below the balustrade. A typically Spanish feature is the twisting of the corner buttresses to an angle of 45 degrees, thus permitting them to be a part of both the front and the end elevations. The central bay is rusticated. The windows of the piano nobile are in bracketed aedicules with alternating triangular and segmental pediments. The drawing shown here has been slightly regularized from the actual building, since it is probable that the architect drew the building regular and the local masons departed from the plans. It is possible that some of the classical details were not added until after 1500.

Medinaceli Palace, Cogolludo, Guadalajara PLATE 93

Also executed asymmetrically (but not regularized for this book) is the Medinaceli Palace at Cogolludo in Guadalajara, designed by Vázquez and built 1492–1495. This was undoubtedly influenced by Michelozzo's Medici Bank at Milan that was built about 30 years earlier. The exterior is covered all over with rustication under a classical cornice and carved balustrade. The lower storey has only a single opening in the front, a large Florentine doorway. The six windows of the upper story are detailed in gothic, and yet this remains essentially a classical building.

Cathedral, Plasencia PLATE 93

Some classicizing details were added to the cathedral at Plasencia by Juan de Alava and others from 1497 onwards. The north portal is the most interesting part. In this confection, it seems that the architect was anxious to demonstrate how much of the classical language he knew and in how many variations, but since he actually knew only a smattering of the language the design breaks many rules (of course, many later architects knew the rules and chose to break them, but it is clear that this is not such a case). Many of the details look similar to details that silversmiths were able to beat in relief into the surface of silver objects, and as a result the style is known broadly as "plateresque." This portal is the earliest example of plateresque with classical details. The ground-floor entrance arch is flanked by trios of engaged Ionic columns with shell-headed niches between them. The next storey contains a blind arch flanked by trios of short, clustered Ionic columns and pilasters, again with niches between them. The next storey has another blind arch flanked this time by trios of short, engaged square Tuscan pillars angled at 45 degrees, and again the niches. The top floor, taller than the rest, has a compass-headed window, flanked by trios of Corinthian columns on tall bases. The upper half of these columns, above a pronounced band, is fluted. Above the top entablature, a pediment sits on top of each trio of columns, and a weak, semicircular trophy sits between them.

Juan de Alava continued his work of using classical details in ways never imagined by their creators. One remarkable example is the church of San Estéban in Salamanca, begun 1524 (not shown in this book), where he played with the motif of giant carved shells on the entrance front of an otherwise gothic building.

Hospital de los Reyes Catolicos, Santiago de Compostela PLATE 93

The royal family became patrons of classical architecture at an early date by sponsoring the construction of three hospitals to the design of Enrique de Egas. Egas had been trained as a gothic architect, but he made a valiant try to employ classicism in at least parts of each building. The first of the hospitals was begun in 1501

Colegio Santa Cruz, Valladolid *(drawing regularized)*

PLATE 93

North entrance, Cathedral, Plasencia

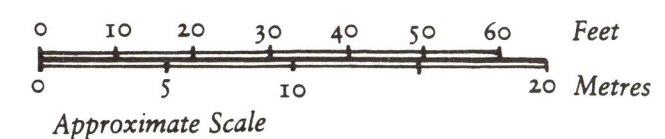

Approximate Scale

Medinaceli Palace, Cogolludo, Guadalajara

Unfinished courtyard, Hospital Real, Granada

Courtyard, Hospital de los Reyes Catolicos, Santiago de Compostela

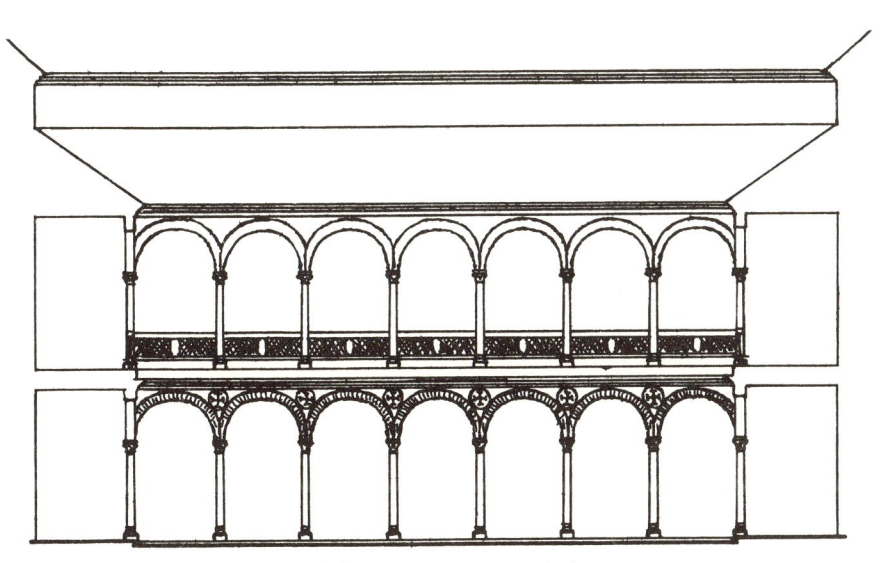

Courtyard, Hospital de Santa Cruz, Toledo

and completed in 1511, the Hospital Real (or, to give it its full name, the Hospital de los Reyes Catolicos—of the Catholic Kings) at Santiago da Compostela in the north. The large rectangle is divided by a cruciform range in the middle (which includes the chapel) into four courtyards or patios, of which the finest is shown here. The ground floor has a tall, arcaded loggia on Corinthian pillars with crossed archivolts. The arcade on the floor above has twice as many arches, divided from each other by pilaster strips. The design appears to be a crude copy of Bramante's Doric Cloister at San Ambrogio in Milan, built only a few years before.

Hospital de Santa Cruz, Toledo PLATE 93

The next hospital was Santa Cruz at Toledo, built 1504–1514. In the plan, the cruciform range in the middle was taken up entirely by the chapel, but only two of the patios were ever completed. The best patio design here was for a two-storey arcaded loggia with Corinthian columns supporting the arches on both floors; the upper columns rest on the entablature, not on the balustrade. Many Spanish loggias differed from their Italian prototypes in that the spaces between the arches and the walls had flat, beamed ceilings rather than vaults, and the patios at these three hospitals fall into that category.

Hospital Real, Granada PLATE 93

The third hospital, the Hospital Real at Granada, was begun in 1504, but little of it was ever built. Egas' son-in-law, Covarrubias, was hired to execute parts of it. Today, a single-storey arcade stands around the patio, roofless. It may once have been intended to have two storeys, but work was never completed. The tall columns are Corinthian, and above the arches is a particularly high entablature.

La Calahorra Castle, near Granada PLATE 94

About forty miles east of Granada is the village of Lacalahorra, where the Marquis del Zenete, Don Rodrigo de Mendoza, built himself a castle in 1508–1512. The interior contains a two-storey arcaded loggia completely around the courtyard, designed by Michele Carlone of Genoa with help from Vázquez. Although the carved details are somewhat crude, this is a purely Italian design. Both storeys have Corinthian columns, the upper set standing on the top of the balustrade. The arcades are backed by proper vaults not flat ceilings.

Tower of the Diputación, Valencia PLATE 94

Juan Montano designed the Diputación (House of Deputies) at Valencia beginning in 1518, despite its 1580-ish appearance. The three-bay tower is five storeys high, each storey being pierced by windows of different heights. The piano nobile has pediments over the windows and a balcony cantilevered completely across the front. Next comes a mezzanine and then a row of windows in aedicules. The top floor has another cantilevered balcony. The rooftop balustrade on top of a full entablature has pinnacles at the corners and finials on the newels. It is unfortunate that Montano appears not to have designed any other buildings in this style.

Cathedral, Granada PLATES 94 & 95

Enrique de Egas was engaged to design a new cathedral for Granada in 1523, but he had scarcely begun to lay the foundations before he was replaced by Diego de Siloé, who is the true architect of the building. While the cathedral has many gothic elements in its partly classical design, it is worth including here. Its chief glory is the plan of its enormous double ambulatory at the liturgical east end, the plan of which is shown in Plate 95. A high circular space trimmed with classical details is surrounded by a series of massive piers with a passageway cut through them. Further out is the main thoroughfare, from which access is obtained to the string of chapels and sacristies lodged between the piers of the outer wall. The piers of the nave are composed of clusters of fluted Corinthian columns on high, panelled bases. Above them are clustered flying entablatures supporting plinths, from which the aisle vaults spring. Since the nave vaults are much higher, pilaster-strips continue up the piers until they reach the imposts—clearly a gothic concept even if executed in classical forms, so that the ancient idea of triforium and clerestory could be retained. Gothic ribbed vaulting fans out from the piers.

Cathedral, Málaga
Cathedral, Guadix PLATE 94

Siloé repeated essentially the same pattern for the naves at the cathedrals at Málaga (begun 1538) and Guadix (begun 1541). The aisle vaults at Málaga are nearly the same height as the nave vault, and both have elegant saucer-domes. The column clusters are simpler. The nave and aisle vaults at Guadix are about of equal height, but much lower than at the other two churches, but gothic tracery has somehow managed to creep into this more classical design. The Málaga Cathedral was partly destroyed in an earthquake in 1680. The Guadix Cathedral was altered in the eighteenth century.

Palace of Charles V, Granada PLATE 96

Charles V, who was both King of Spain and Roman Emperor, wished to have an appropriate palace for his rank inside the Moorish Alhambra at Granada. The work, which was designed and supervised by a painter named Pedro Machuca and his son Luís from 1526 to 1568, remained uncompleted at Charles' death in 1558 and also when his son Philip II abandoned work on it a decade later. Its plan is a square with one corner clipped. Inside the clipped corner is a two-storey octagonal chapel intended to have a dome but, like the rest of the palace, never actually roofed. In the middle of the square is a two-storey colonnade (Doric below, Ionic above) in a large circle; a 1793 print suggests that a third storey with windows was intended. The parts of the exterior walls that were completed are divided into

La Calahorra Castle, near Granada

PLATE 94

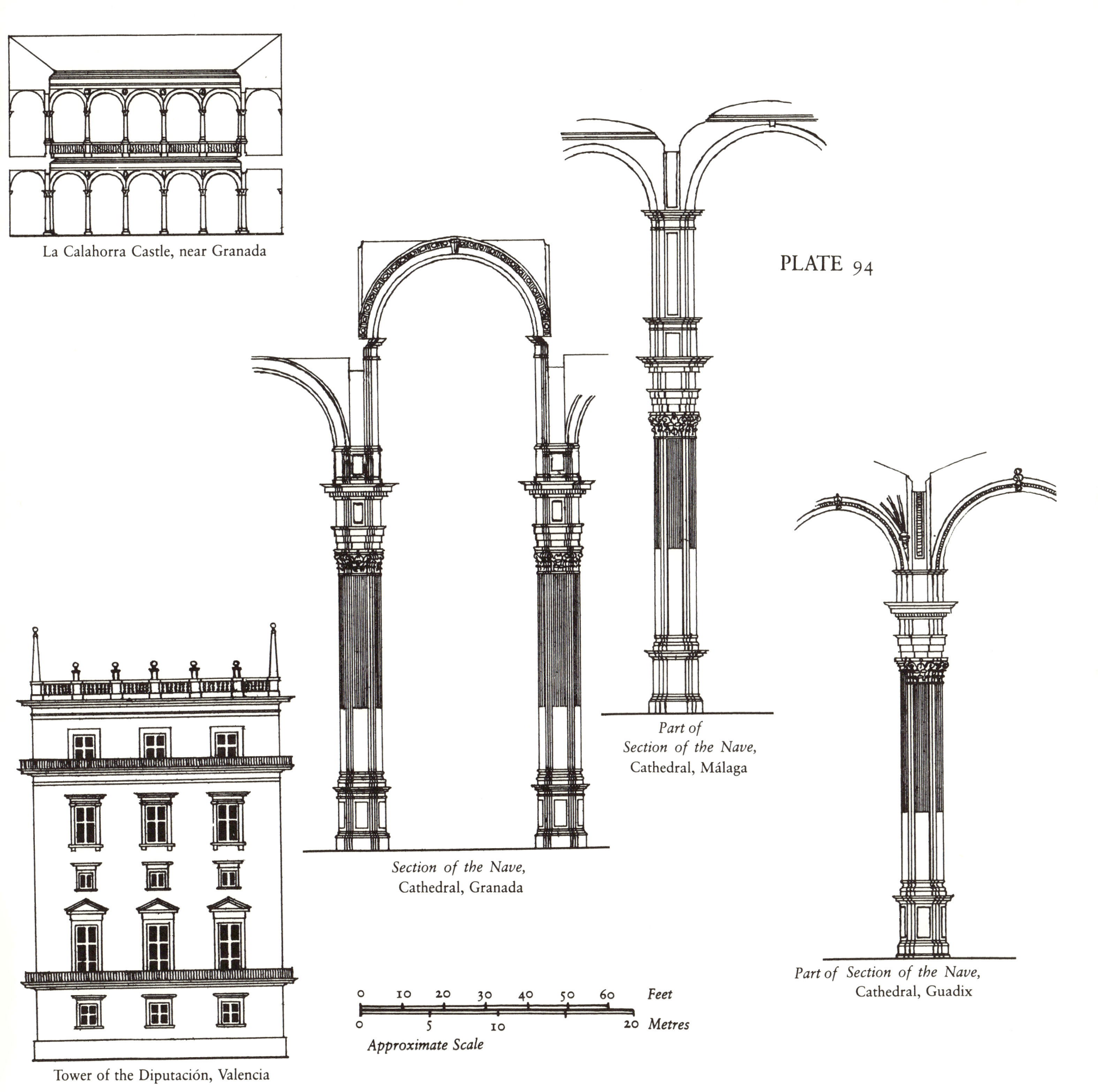

Part of Section of the Nave, Cathedral, Málaga

Section of the Nave, Cathedral, Granada

Part of Section of the Nave, Cathedral, Guadix

Tower of the Diputación, Valencia

0 10 20 30 40 50 60 Feet
0   5   10   20 Metres
Approximate Scale

171

PLATE 95

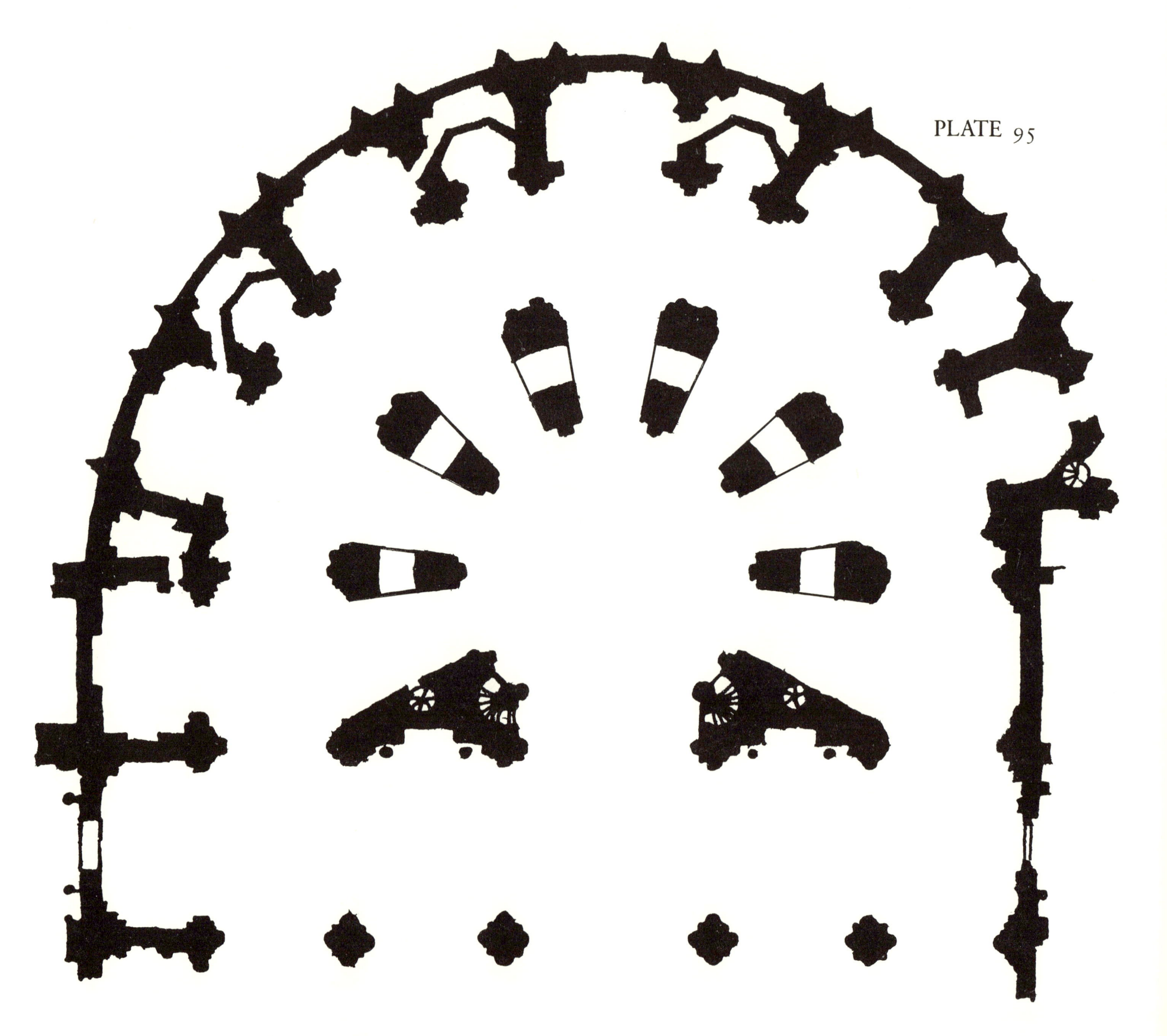

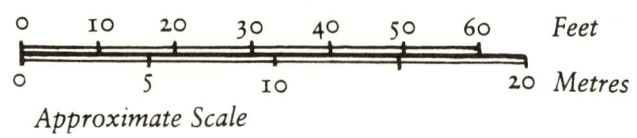

Altar end, plan, Cathedral, Granada

West elevation

South elevation, Palace of Charles V, Granada

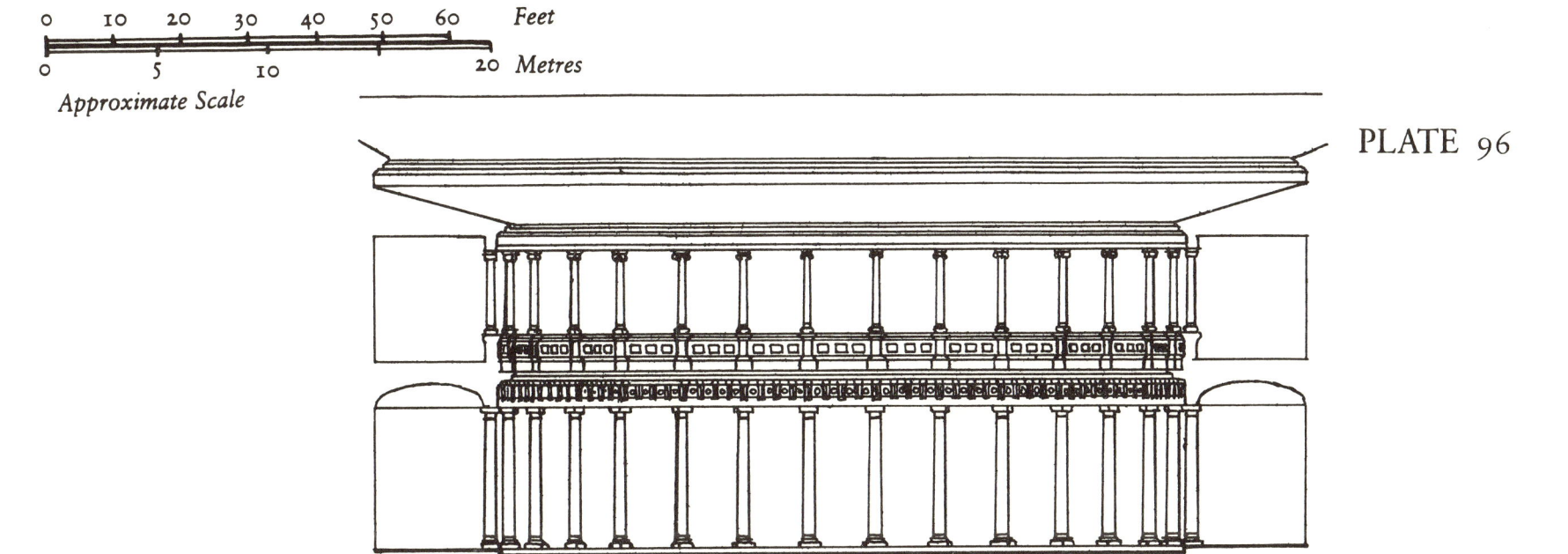

Approximate Scale

Circular courtyard, Palace of Charles V, Granada

PLATE 96

four storeys. The lower two are in rusticated stonework with rusticated pilasters marking the bays; the bottom windows are rectangular and the mezzanine windows are round or slightly oval. The top two storeys are of smooth stone, and Ionic and Corinthian pilasters on high bases separate the bays. The lower windows are capped with pediments on brackets alternating with cornice-strips on brackets with carving above, and the upper windows are round. Both the south and west fronts have monumental foci on the middle for an entrance, both apparently the result of refinement after trying other ideas first. The south front has a large door in a pedimented aedicule under a compass-headed window with small flanking windows; the smooth masonry in this section is trimmed with pairs of giant Ionic and Corinthian fluted pilasters. The west front forms its focus out of three bays with paired fluted pilasters, these being Doric and Ionic, and a print from 1793 suggests that an heroic pediment was intended to be placed over the three bays, while a balustrade with finials was to go over the rest of the façade (but the authority of the print is questionable, however attractive the result may seem). Pedro Machuca, with his training in Florence under Giuliano da San Gallo, emerges as by far the most competent classical architect to practise in Spain in the first half of the century.[1]

Casa Capitulares or Ayuntamiento, Sevilla PLATE 97

Spain in the sixteenth century saw many elaborate construction projects begun and never finished, possibly the result of the rivers of gold and silver that were already flowing back from Latin America and spurring inflation, so that buildings eventually cost many times what they were originally intended to cost. One such project was the Casa Capitulares or Ayuntamiento (Town Hall) at Sevilla, built 1527–1534 to designs by Diego de Riaño; construction ceased at his death with just over half the building completed. The original plan called for three blocks in a loose U, but only two were built, and when the building was eventually enlarged the new wing was in a different direction, although in the same style. The building was two storeys tall with a balustrade around the low roof (another storey has since been added to much of it). The bays are marked by panelled Corinthian pilasters at both levels, and many of the windows are set in aedicules. The entrance was to be through a great arch at the center, but the arch is now the last bay of the building. The pilasters and much of the outside walls are covered in carvings, which have been omitted from the drawing here for the sake of clarity.

Sacristy, Cathedral, Sevilla PLATE 97

The same sort of overall carvings can be found on parts of the inside of the sacristy of the Sevilla Cathedral, built about 1530–1543, so presumably Riaño was the architect. The Corinthian pilasters and half-columns that stand around the inside are all varied: panelled, fluted, twisted and plain. The plan is essentially a dome set in a square, set in a cross, with an extra room to one end. The angles of the cross are crowned with large scallop-shell motifs crammed into spaces ordinarily not suited for shells. It is possible that Siloé was hired to finish the work after the death of Riaño, but it is known that Martín de Gaínsa supervised construction of the dome.

Colegio del Arzobispo Fonseca/de los Nobles Irlandeses, Salamanca PLATE 97

In Salamanca, Archbishop Don Alfonso de Fonseca y Ulloa began construction of the Colegio de Santiago Apóstol about 1532, but shortly after its completion it was devoted for the use of Irish priests studying in Salamanca, so it has since been known as the Colegio de los Nobles Irlandeses. Its courtyard has a delightful two-storey arcaded loggia with flat ceilings. Fluted Corinthian half-columns stand in front of the piers of the ground floor, and smaller but similar columns with baluster-shaped shafts stand in front of the piers above. The upper arches are elliptical to save height. A finial stands over each column. The design of this building has been attributed, sometimes without apparent reason, to a variety of architects, including Juan de Alava, Alonso de Covarrubias, Diego de Siloé, Rodrigo Gil de Hontañon and Pedro Ibarra (who did not arrive on the scene until 1550), and the reader may choose between them.

Sacristy, Cathedral, Jaén PLATE 97

Andrés de Vandelvira, who was a disciple of Siloé, began work on the Cathedral at Jaén in 1532, work that continued for over two centuries. The clusters of fluted Corinthian columns in the interior are related to Siloé's work at Guadix, but the classical vaulted ceiling is probably later than Vandelvira; the handsome entrance front is also seventeenth-century. However, the sacristy is completely Vandelvira's work. It has a barrel-vaulted ceiling with a few small cross-vaults reflecting the arches on the walls below them. These arches are supported by pairs of fluted Corinthian columns, arranged so as to have three narrow bays alternating with two wide bays. It is altogether a handsome design.

Church of San Salvador, Úbeda PLATE 98

Andrés de Vandelvira and Siloé together are usually thought to have designed the church of El Salvador at Úbeda, beginning in 1536. The plan reflects the double-ambulatory at the cathedral at Granada, for the chancel is round with a coffered dome over it. Where the nave joins the chancel are vestigial transepts, in this case small side chapels with low, domed ceilings. The nave ceiling is a barrel-vault, intersected by the three arches on each side for the clerestory windows. A narrow, balustraded gallery goes completely along the nave and around the chancel at the level of the main cornice, just below the clerestory windows. Giant fluted Corinthian half-columns stand in front of the piers that support the arches leading to the aisles, which are in fact walled off as six side-chapels. The exterior, including the entrance

1. Earl Rosenthal, *The Palace of Charles V in Granada*, Princeton, Princeton University Press, 1985.

Casa Capitulares or Ayuntamiento, Sevilla

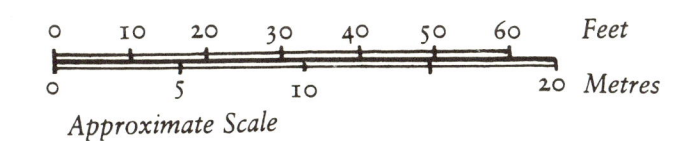

0 10 20 30 40 50 60 Feet
0   5   10   20 Metres
Approximate Scale

PLATE 97

Section, Sacristy, Cathedral, Sevilla

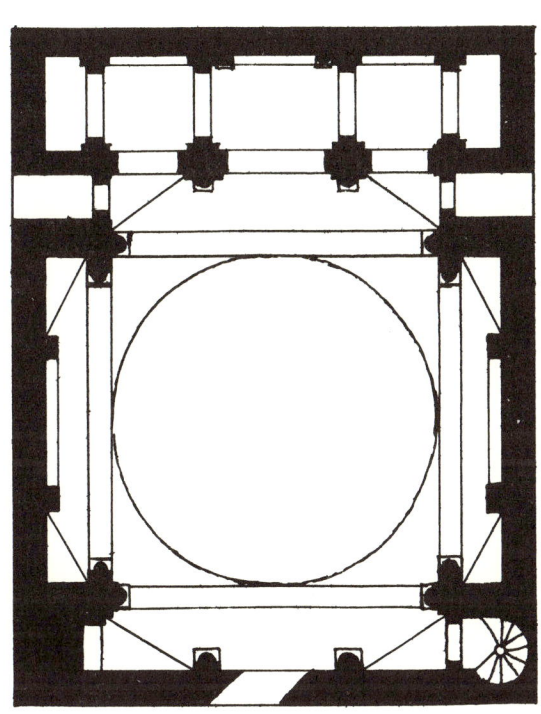

Plan, Sacristy, Cathedral, Sevilla

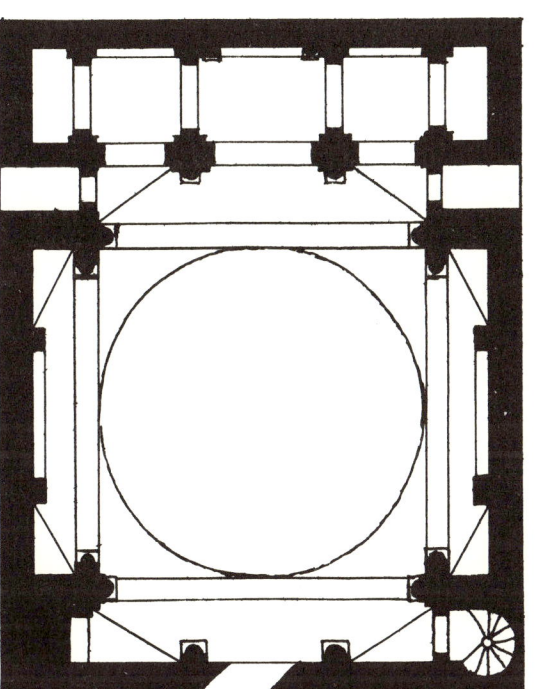

Courtyard, Colegio del Arzobispo Fonseca/de los Nobles Irlandeses, Salamanca

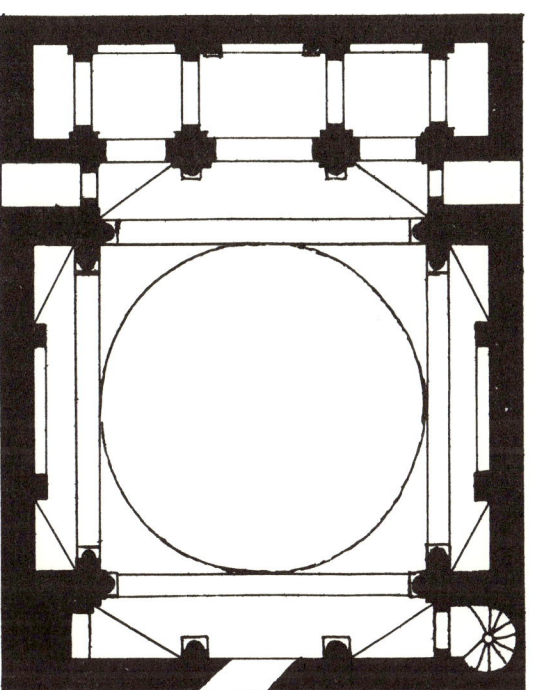

Sections, Sacristy, Cathedral, Jaén

175

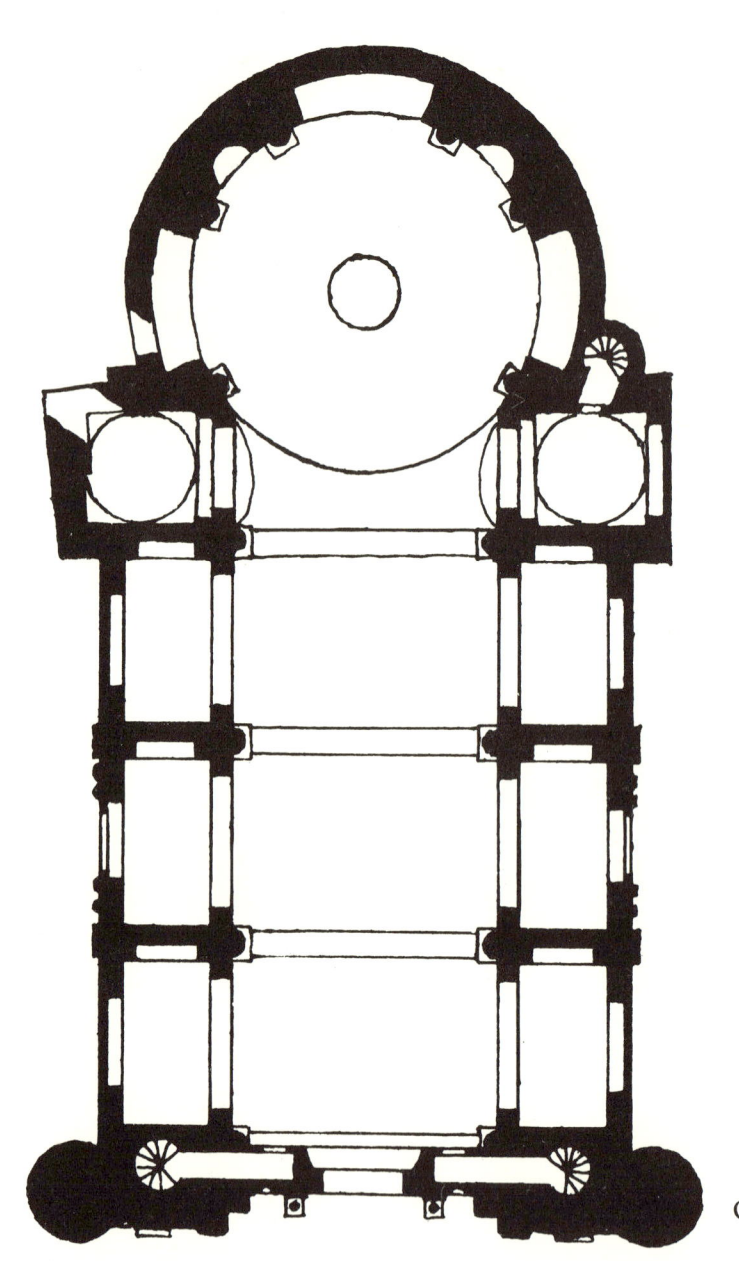

Plan,
Church of San Salvador, Úbeda

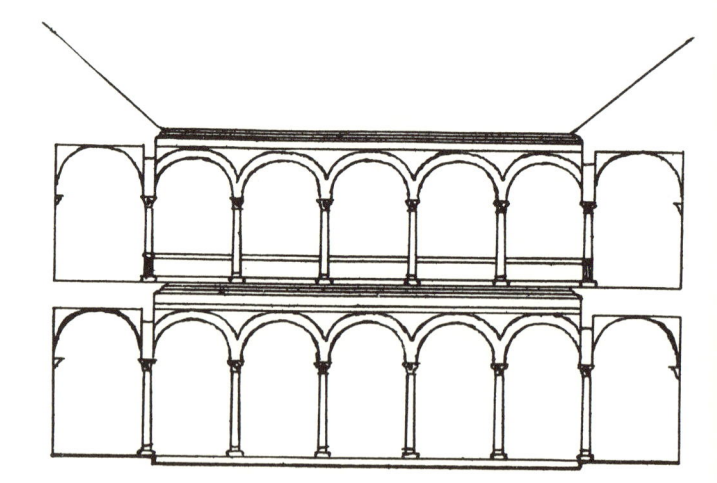

Palacio Vázquez de Molina, Úbeda

PLATE 98

Courtyard, Palacio Vázquez de Molina, Úbeda

Part of entrance front, Archbishop's Palace, Alcalá de Henares

176

front, is much inferior to the rich and reasonably "correct" interior.

Palacio Vázquez de Molina, Úbeda
PLATE 98

Much later in Vandelvira's career, he designed the palace of Vázquez de Molina at Úbeda, beginning in 1562. The front is seven bays wide and three storeys tall. The ground-floor bays are divided by panelled Corinthian pilasters, and, in an unusual reversal of classical rules, the middle floor's bays are divided by panelled Ionic pilasters. The top floor, lower in height like an attic storey, is divided by caryatids. The windows of the ground floor are enclosed in aedicules with flat tops and carving above and swags below, and the windows of the middle floor are in squat pedimented aedicules; the top-floor windows are oval. Inside the courtyard is a two-storey arcaded loggia, four bays by five, with Corinthian columns supporting the arches on both levels. The columns of the upper level stand on the entablature, after the Spanish fashion, but the ceilings are vaulted, after the Italian fashion.

Hospital de Santiago, Úbeda PLATE 99

Vandelvira's most elaborate plan was for the Hospital de Santiago at Úbeda, built 1562–1575. The hospital wards were sensibly arranged around a courtyard with loggias (five bays square), with the chapel taking up one side of the courtyard. The exterior elevations of the building are not up to the standard of the palace of Vázquez de Molina, but the interior of the chapel, with its panelled, barrel-vaulted ceiling, is of high quality; one may well wonder, however, why the nave of the chapel is constricted by a single narrow bay in the middle that supports small galleries above.

Archbishop's Palace, Alcalá de Henares
PLATE 98

Alonso Covarrubias, son-in-law of Egas, designed the Archbishop's Palace for Cardinal Tavera at Alcalá de Henares in 1534, the most notable feature of which is the grand staircase; this is framed by two storeys of elliptical arches standing on Corinthian columns. The courtyard loggias are inferior designs, with the upper entablature resting on typically-Spanish brackets on top of Ionic columns. Part of the main façade has interesting classical features. The rectangular ground-floor windows are capped with cornice-strips and carved cartouches, while the compass-headed windows of the floor above have a cornice-strip and a different carved design. However, above that is another storey with an arcaded loggia in front of it, two arches on Ionic columns to a bay as delineated by wide pilaster-strips, and the bays of the loggia fail to correspond in any way with the bays of the two storeys below—as if an entirely different architect had planned it to spite the architect of the lower portion. The palace burned down in 1940, and has been partially restored for use as a seminary.

Real Alcázar, Toledo PLATE 100

Covarrubias was appointed Maestro Mayor de las Obres Reales (Chief Master of the Royal Works), and Charles V ordered him to collaborate with Luis de Vega to rebuild both the Royal Alcázar at Madrid and the Royal Alcázar at Toledo in the 1540s. Later, when little had happened, Charles separated the two and awarded the Toledo building to Covarrubias and the Madrid building to de Vega. The principal entrance is on the north side of the Toledo Alcázar, which is three tall storeys high and nine bays wide between corner towers (the towers have been omitted from the drawing shown here). The windows of the piano nobile are enclosed in pedimented aedicules with finials on top. Above that is an open arcade of a gallery set in rusticated stonework. The gallery is reminiscent of the one at the Archbishop's Palace, in that it looks like an afterthought, but its bays at least correspond to the bays of the lower floors. The courtyard has a two-storey arcaded loggia, seven bays by nine, with Corinthian columns supporting the arches on both floors; the upper columns rest on the top of the balustrade of that floor, and another balustrade with ball finials stands atop the entablature. The ceilings of the loggias are properly vaulted. This is one of Spain's finest patios.

The University, Alcalá de Henares PLATE 101

Rodrigo Gil de Hontañon learned architecture by working with his father, who was a gothicist. Gil himself seems to have been but little interested in classical details, although he did aim at balance and symmetry. His most famous building is the University at Alcalá de Henares, built 1537–1553. The front of this building is divided into three large bays, the middle bay being decorated with three storeys of paired engaged columns, but disobeying many classical rules. For example, the ground floor Corinthian columns share an entablature with panelled Tuscan pilasters near the ends of the front, while the Corinthian columns of the middle storey share a Doric entablature with Ionic columns near the ends; the top-floor orders are Tuscan square pillars in the middle angled at 45 degrees, while Ionic pilasters stand as part of a buttress-like projection at 45 degrees on the ends, reminiscent of similar features on the Cathedral at Plasencia. Meanwhile, a series of engaged columns on high bases projects up into the main entablature of the top floor and stands in front of a loggia of five arches per side, whose placement is unrelated to the windows of the floors below. The ground-floor windows are enclosed in squat pedimented aedicules, and the three compass-headed windows of the middle storey are enveloped in complicated, double-decked aedicules with C-shaped volutes. Another building that should be seen at Alcalá de Henares is the renaissance courtyard at the Hostería with its loggia of elliptical arches (no date or architect given).

Palacio de Monterrey, Salamanca PLATE 101

Rodrigo Gil de Hontañon, assisted by Pedro Ibarra and others, designed the Monterrey Palace at Salamanca, beginning in 1539. The building, which is quite large as it is, was intended to be almost four times as large;

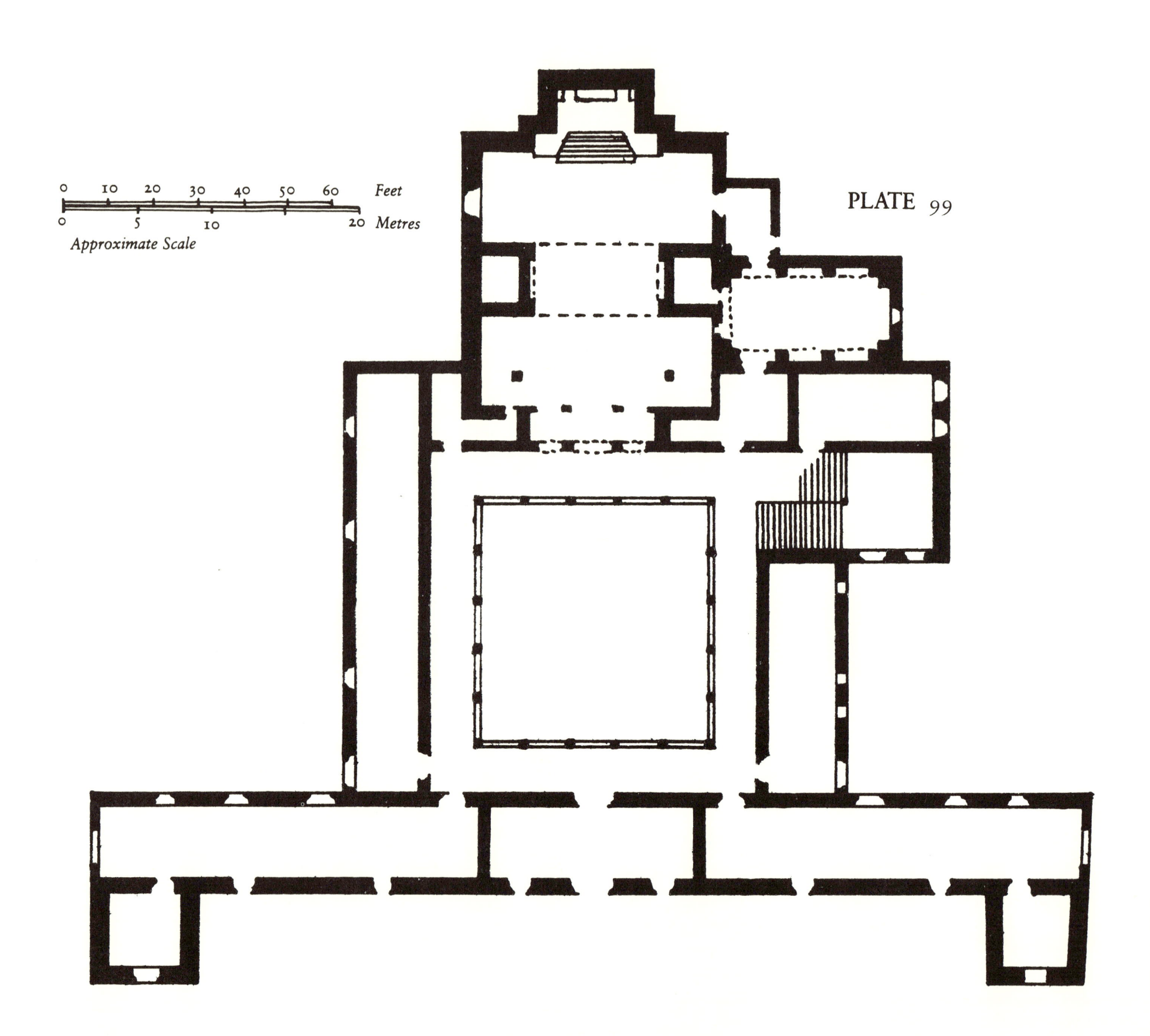

Plan, Hospital de Santiago, Úbeda

Part of North elevation, Real Alcázar, Toledo

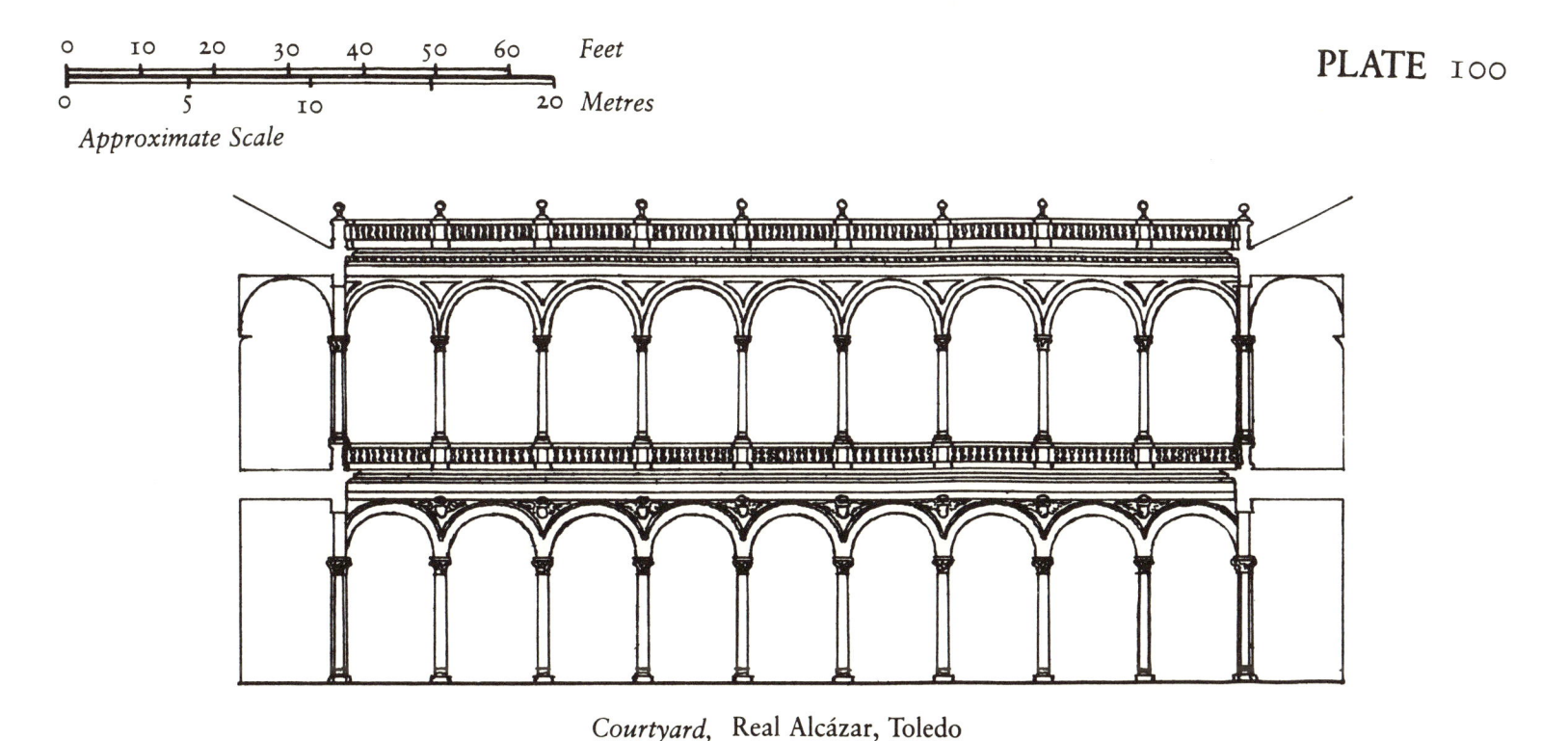

PLATE 100

Courtyard, Real Alcázar, Toledo

The University, Alcalá de Henares

Courtyard, University, Oñate

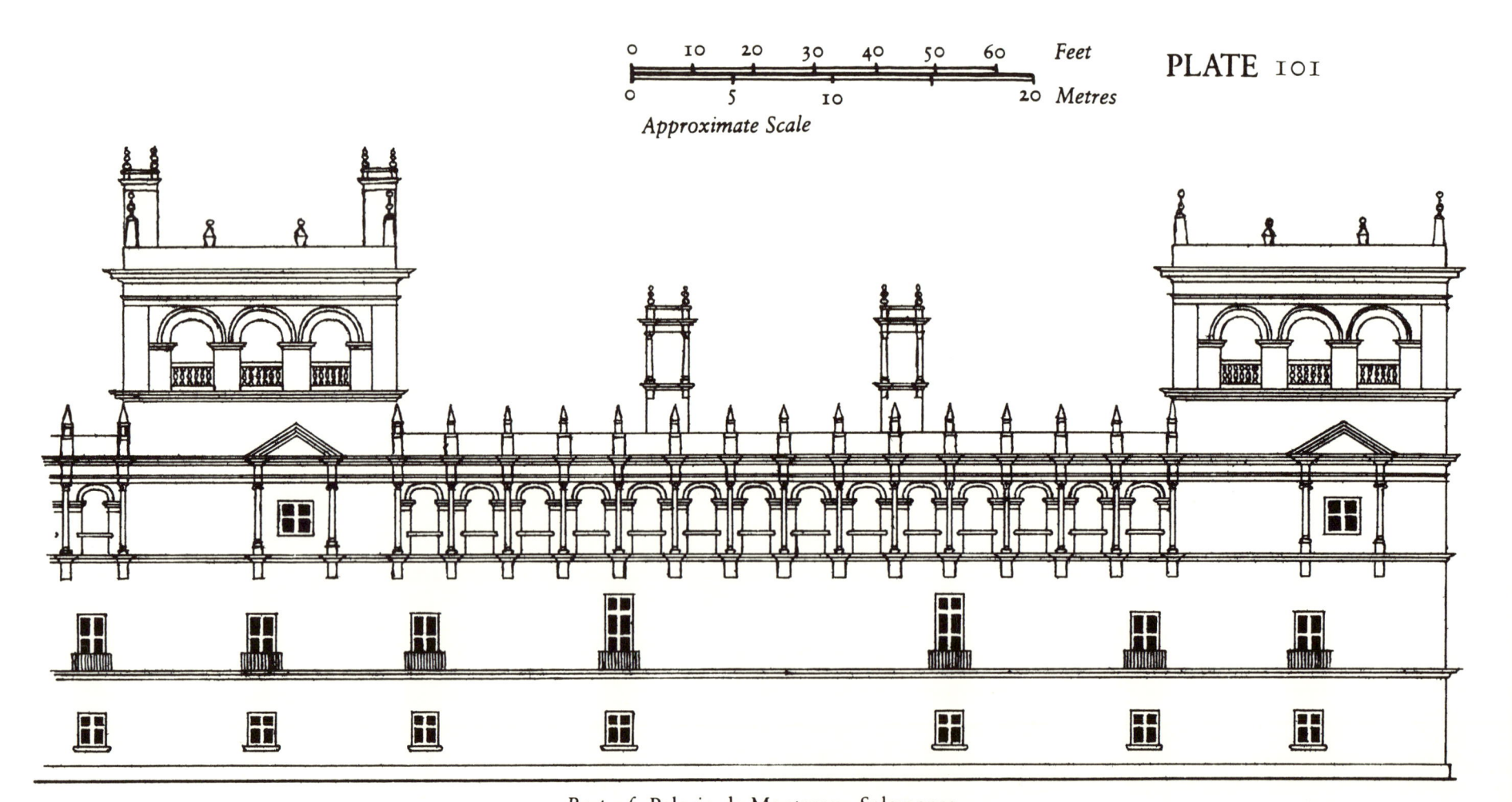

PLATE 101

Part of Palacio de Monterrey, Salamanca

only a portion of what was built will fit on the page of this book. The placement of windows seems to have little relation to the position of the other principal features, such as the towers, the pilastered chimneys and the top-floor arcaded loggia. A few classical details are employed, but not in a classical way.

University, Oñate PLATE 101

Beginning in 1548, Gil was engaged to design the University Building at Oñate. The exterior is for the most part plain, built of rough stone, but with a frontispiece around the entrance, and buttresses at 45 degrees at the corners clad in engaged columns and niches. The patio contains a two-storey arcaded loggia with Corinthian columns supporting the arches, but with flat ceilings inside the arcades, and the upper columns standing on the lower entablature.

Tavera "Afuera" Hospital of San Juan Bautista, Toledo PLATE 102

Cardinal Tavera, who was a prolific patron of architecture, commissioned Bartolomé Bustamente in 1541 to design the Hospital of San Juan Bautista at Toledo, a hospital that is often called by other names, such as Tavera (after the cardinal) and Afuera, which means "outside," for it was located outside the city. The building was never completed, but it has two arcaded courtyards of two storeys each, the range of loggias between them facing both ways. Tuscan columns support the lower arches, and Ionic columns, standing on the entablature, support the upper arches; the ceilings of the loggia are vaulted. The entrance front has been altered by the addition of a corner-tower, an attic storey, and a frontispiece. These additions have been removed for the drawing shown here, to reveal an extraordinarily severe design, more Italian than Spanish. Quoins and raised voussoirs surround all the windows and more quoins stand at the corners. The masonry of the ground floor is channeled to provide a contrast in texture. Bustamente became a Jesuit priest in 1552, and shortly afterwards relinquished his architectural activities, thus depriving Spain and the world of further fine designs in his style.

Palace of El Pardo, Madrid PLATE 103

Luís de Vega enjoyed considerable royal confidence for his skills as an architect, and he was engaged to design substantial royal buildings. He also designed buildings for other clients, such as the Palace of the Dueñas at Medina del Campo, begun about 1527, with its two-storey loggia of elliptical arcades in its courtyard (not shown in this book). About the same time, he worked at the Royal Palace at Valladolid that has a similar courtyard (also not shown here). In 1543, he was hired to build the Palace of El Pardo (pardo means dark or brown) as part of a new policy to make Madrid the capital of Spain. The north front was elegantly simple, with no obviously classical details, beyond quoins on the upper walls of the corner towers and cornice-strips over the windows of the piano nobile. Two rows of hipped dormers on the roof suggest that de Vega either knew of Flemish practices or left the building of the roof in the hands of Flemish builders—for Flanders, after all, was a part of the Spanish monarchy's dominions. El Pardo was substantially altered in the eighteenth century.

Alcázar Palace, Madrid PLATE 104

The rebuilding of the two Royal Alcázars at Toledo and Madrid had been jointly entrusted to de Vega and Covarrubias in the 1540s, but when no progress had been made at either place after a long time each architect was given one Alcázar to tackle separately. It is easy to see why little had been done in Madrid: the resulting building was enormous and thus required careful preparation before any obvious work could begin. Much of the task consisted in merely reinforcing ancient towers and walls, but the premiere palace of Spain would also need a modern entrance-front, so de Vega designed one three storeys tall over a high basement and 23 bays wide, stretched between a pair of three-bay corner towers. Each window was pedimented and had its own separate balcony, separated from its neighbor by a pilaster-strip. The three central bays were formed into a simple frontispiece with the royal arms on top. It was by no means a great design, but it served its purpose of suggesting grandeur while providing generous window area.

Royal Palace at Valsaín, near Segovia PLATE 105

De Vega was also retained to build a palace at Valsaín, near Segovia in the 1550s. It was almost finished when de Vega died in 1563, but it has since been totally destroyed by fire. Once again, the appearance of hipped dormers on high roofs and a pair of crow-step gables suggest the presence of Flemish builders, for these features were quite foreign to normal Spanish design. The plan was a confusing array of courtyards on asymmetrical axes with five sturdy towers and steeples and two roof-top steeples. It introduced an innovation for Spain: an arcaded loggia on the south external elevation, this in a country whose buildings were always arranged to face inwards and leave the exterior forbidding.

Colegio de San Matías/San Luís, Tortosa PLATE 106

A remarkably high standard of design was set by a certain Juan Anglés in mid-century, if attributions are to be believed. It is not known if this was actually an Englishman or his family name was merely Anglés. The earliest building attributed to him is the College of San Matías, since renamed San Luís, at Tortosa, begun in 1544. In the middle is a three-storey patio, five bays wide. The ground-floor arches are supported by Tuscan columns on bases, as are the arches of the middle floor at a slightly smaller scale. The top floor has a Tuscan colonnade at a still smaller scale, with two bays for every one below. The ceilings of the loggias are all flat, following the Spanish tradition.

Tavera "Afuera" Hospital of San Juan Bautista, Toledo

PLATE 102

Arcade between the two courtyards,
Tavera "Afuera" Hospital of San Juan Bautista, Toledo

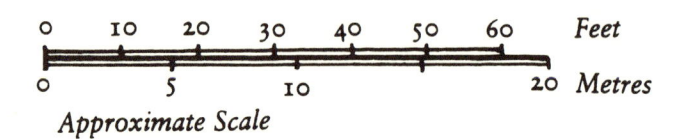

Approximate Scale

PLATE 103

North elevation,
Palace of El Pardo, Madrid

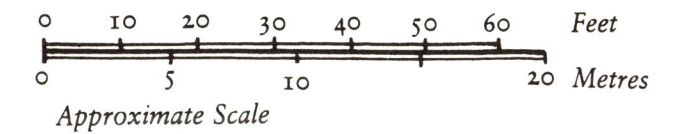

Approximate Scale

PLATE 104

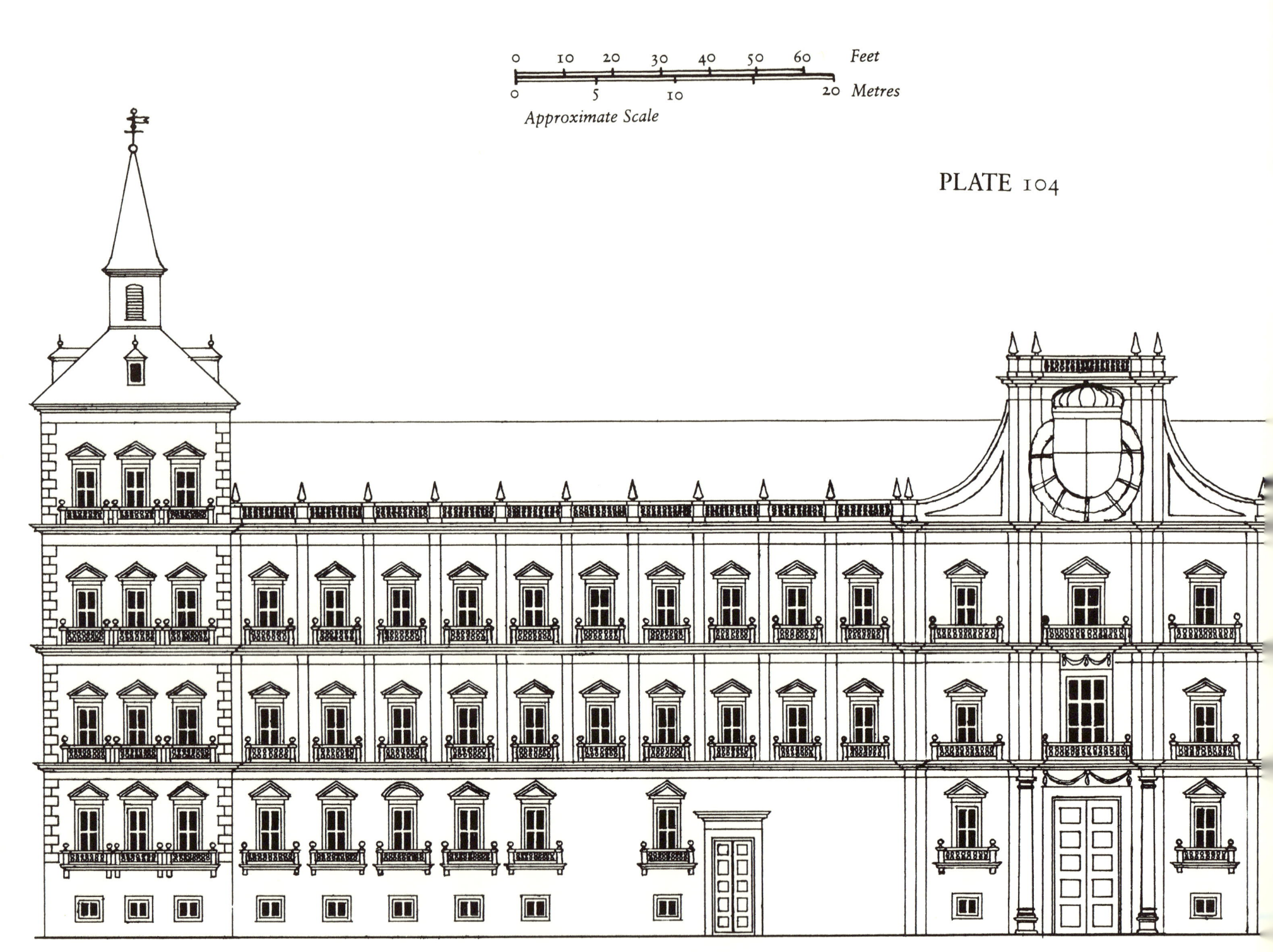

*Left and central portions, South elevation,
Alcázar Palace, Madrid*

PLATE 105

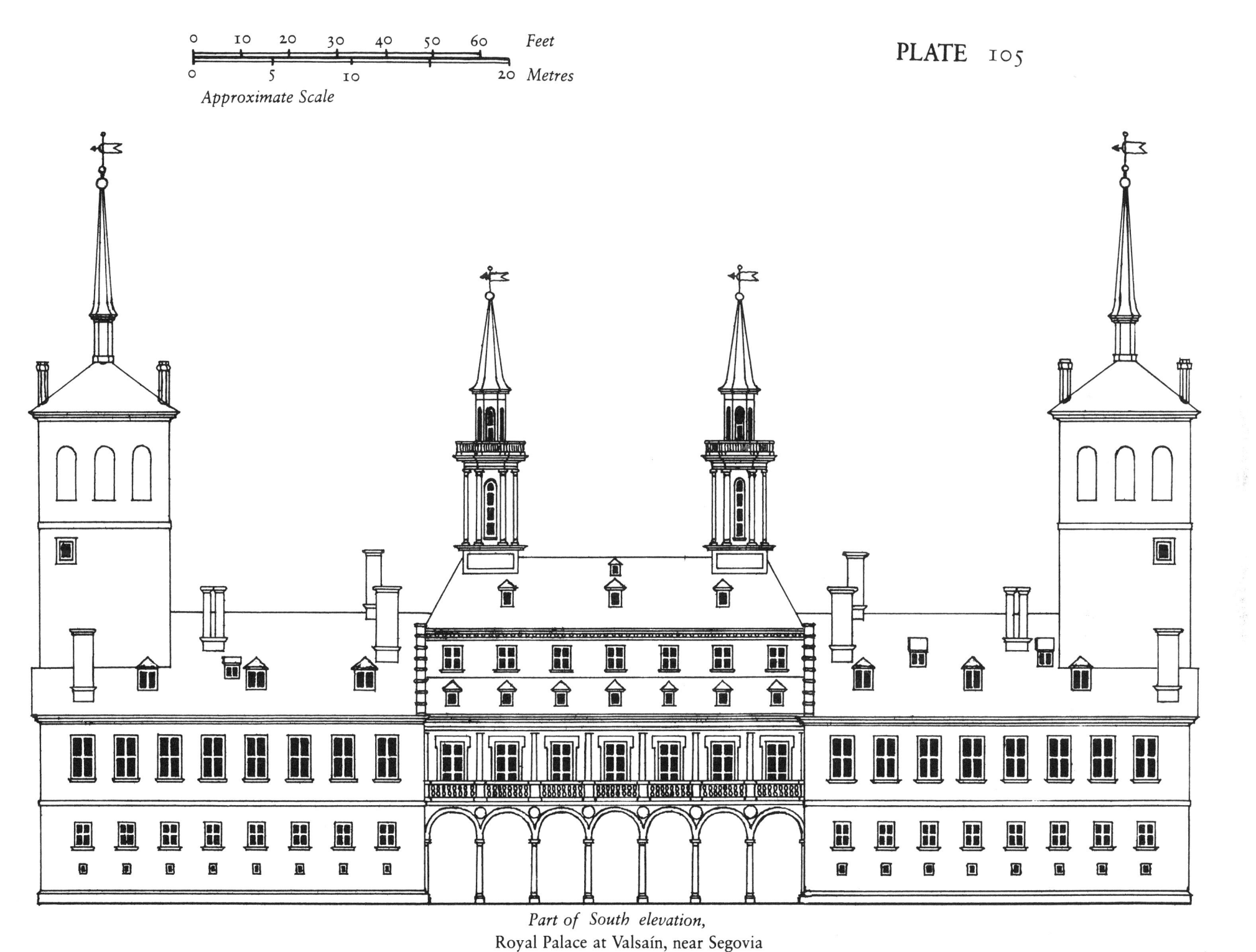

Part of South elevation,
Royal Palace at Valsaín, near Segovia

PLATE 106

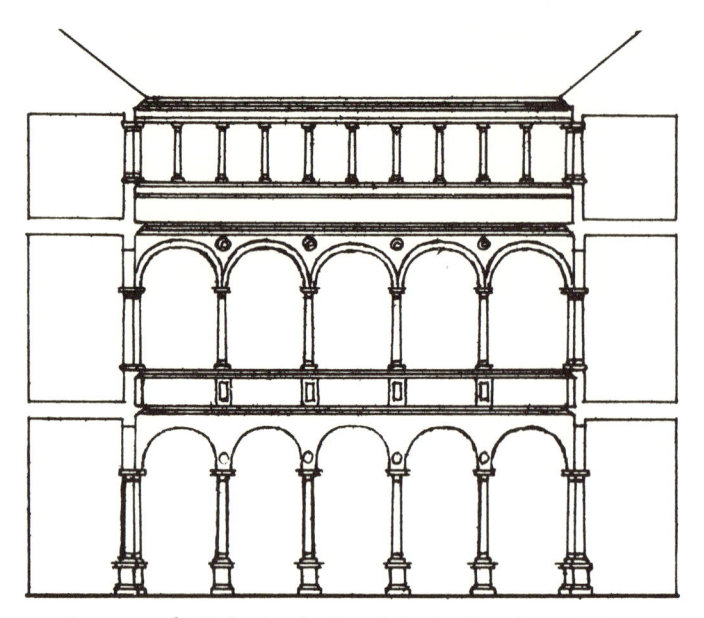

Courtyard, Colegio de San Matías/San Luís, Tortosa

Entrance, Church of Vistabella, Castellón

Main entrance, Convent of Santo Domingo, Orihuela

Chapel, Hospital Provincial de la Sangre, Sevilla

Old Cabildo, Jerez de la Frontera

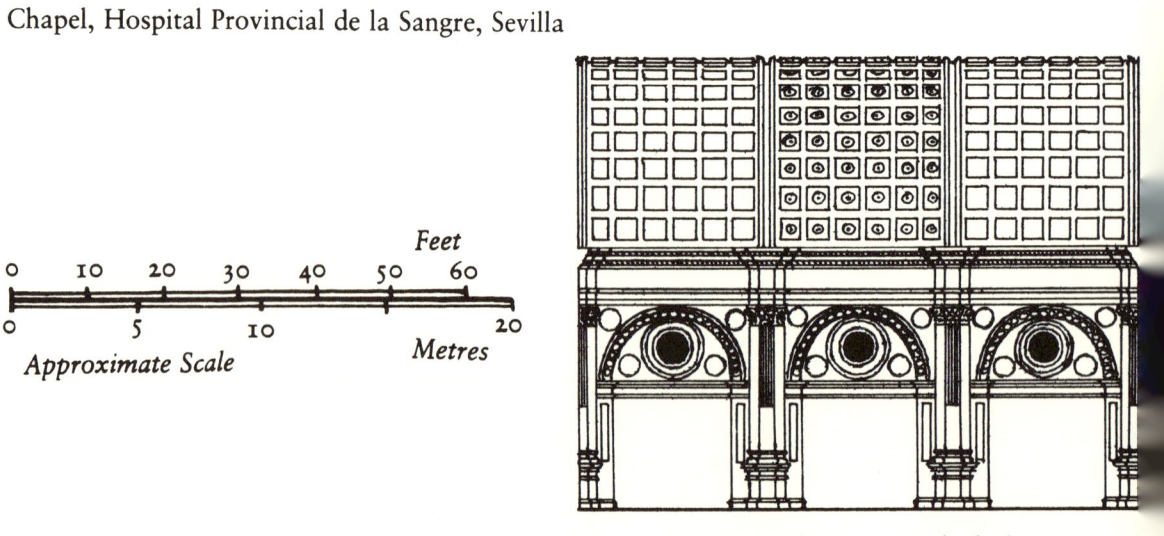

Section, Sacristy, Cathedral, Almería

186

Church of Vistabella, Castellón PLATE 106

It has been said that many Spanish and Spanish-American buildings of the classical period were nondescript barn-like structures that were given an impressive entrance-façade. The criticism seems to ring true in the case of the church at Vistabella, Castellón, built about 1550 presumably by local builders. Then an architect, believed to have been Anglés, was hired to add a frontispiece, and, like so many Spanish architects, he tried to use as many tricks as possible in this one façade. The ground floor is a Roman triumphal arch with four fluted Doric engaged columns guarding four niches. Above stand six twisted engaged Ionic columns, interspersed by five niches, and the top level has a pedimented aedicule with Corinthian columns, containing an arch and flanked by elaborate volutes. While this is, in effect, a "tower of the orders," it is a better composition than Delorme designed at Anet in that same field.

Convent of Santo Domingo, Orihuela PLATE 106

Also attributed to Anglés is the handsome portal at the Convent of Santo Domingo at Orihuela, added in 1568. This is a Roman triumphal arch with four fluted Corinthian columns and a pair of niches, surmounted with a pedimented aedicule containing a coat-of-arms. It is related to the portals to the college at Tortosa, and possibly also to the Cathedral of the Annunciation at Orihuela, sometimes also attributed to Jerónimo Quijano.

Chapel, Hospital Provincial de la Sangre, Sevilla PLATE 106

In 1546, Martín Gaínza began work at the gruesomely-named Hospital Provincial de la Sangre ("of the blood") at Sevilla. Like the royal hospitals of Egas, this had a cruciform range dividing a rectangle into four courtyards of larger size than the royal hospitals, but in this case the chapel was not part of the cross. Instead, the chapel was built in the middle of one of the courtyards. The chapel is on the plan of a Latin cross with short transepts. The nave is covered by three shallow domes under the hipped roof. The aisles are formed into side-chapels, four per side. On the outside, the walls are divided into three levels with Doric, Ionic and Corinthian pilasters. The lower two sections of the walls are otherwise blank, but the top level has substantial glassed area, including thermal windows. The main entrance and the two transept doorways are the only pieces of frivolity on the austere exterior; these are believed to have been carved by Pietro Torrigiani, son of the sculptor who came to London. Gaínsa died in 1555, and his place was taken by Hernán Ruiz, but how much the latter contributed to the design is unknown.

Old Cabildo, Jerez de la Frontera PLATE 106

The old Cabildo at Jerez de la Frontera (Jerez is the origin of the English word sherry, a drink that comes from that region) was built in 1575, somewhat in the style of Hernán Ruiz, but its architect is anonymous. Andrés de Ribera, Martín de Oliva and Bartolomé Sánchez were the constructors. The building takes the form of a Roman triumphal arch, minus the actual arch; it has four pairs of engaged Corinthian columns on bases, and a heavy balustrade above the entablature, decorated with urns and a frontispiece holding a coat-of-arms. The two flanking bays contain windows in pedimented aedicules and niches.

Sacristy, Cathedral, Almería PLATE 106

The cathedral at Almería was built in the gothic style with massive buttresses in the first half of the sixteenth century, but Juan de Orea was hired to work on it from 1550 to 1573, and he insisted on adding classical details, such as on the north and west portals. He also built a charming sacristy with a coffered barrel-vaulted ceiling. The fluted Corinthian half-columns that define its three bays stand under projecting pieces of entablature that have a semicircular section rather than the more usual rectangular section. Each bay encloses a deep, blind arch with a circular window in the upper part.

Church, Callosa de Segura PLATE 107

The church at Callosa de Segura was completed in 1553; Francisco Ripoll executed the work, but there is some question as to whether he was also the designer. The interior of the domed church is built around the rows of squat, fluted Corinthian columns that support the arches of the ceiling vaulting through heavy flying entablatures. The effect is all the more Roman by the placement of additional columns along the aisle walls instead of using pilasters.

Ayuntamiento & Prison, Baeza PLATE 107

The provincial town of Baeza contains some provincial impressions of classical design. One gable-roofed building (not shown in this book) actually has a pediment over one of its aedicules in which the slopes are pointing outwards after the ideas of Michelangelo. The ruins of the Convent of San Francisco have three-storey-tall fluted Corinthian columns enclosing shell-headed niches and flanking a giant blind arch, in which is placed the weak and dull portal—a clear case of bathos (not shown in this book). The most interesting building in Baeza is the combination of Town Hall (upstairs) and prison (downstairs) begun in 1559. Because of its function, the ground floor is almost windowless, but the upper floor has three large panels bordered by panelled pilasters and enclosing each a Venetian window, perhaps the earliest known in Spain. The architect is anonymous.

Palace, Escorial PLATES 107 - 110

In sharp contrast to the provincial designs of Baeza, the most familiar renaissance structure in Spain is without doubt the Escorial, or, to give it its full name, the Palace and Monastery of Saint Lawrence of the Escorial. This enormous building of austere grey granite was ordered by Philip II for three purposes: first, he wanted to celebrate his victory over the French at Saint-

Part of section of the Nave,
Church, Callosa de Segura

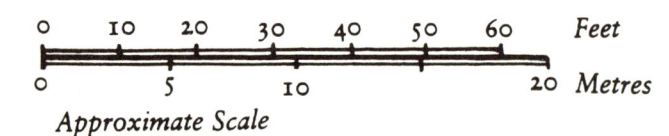

Ayuntamiento & Prison, Baeza

Tempietto & Fountain of the Evangelists, the Palace, Escorial

Main Cloister, the Palace, Escorial

PLATE 107

Monastery Cloister, the Palace, Escorial

South elevation, Sunshine Corridor, the Palace, Escorial

PLATE 108

One of two matching secondary entrances, The Palace, Escorial

West elevation, Church of San Lorenzo, the Palace, Escorial (drawn to 75% of regular scale)

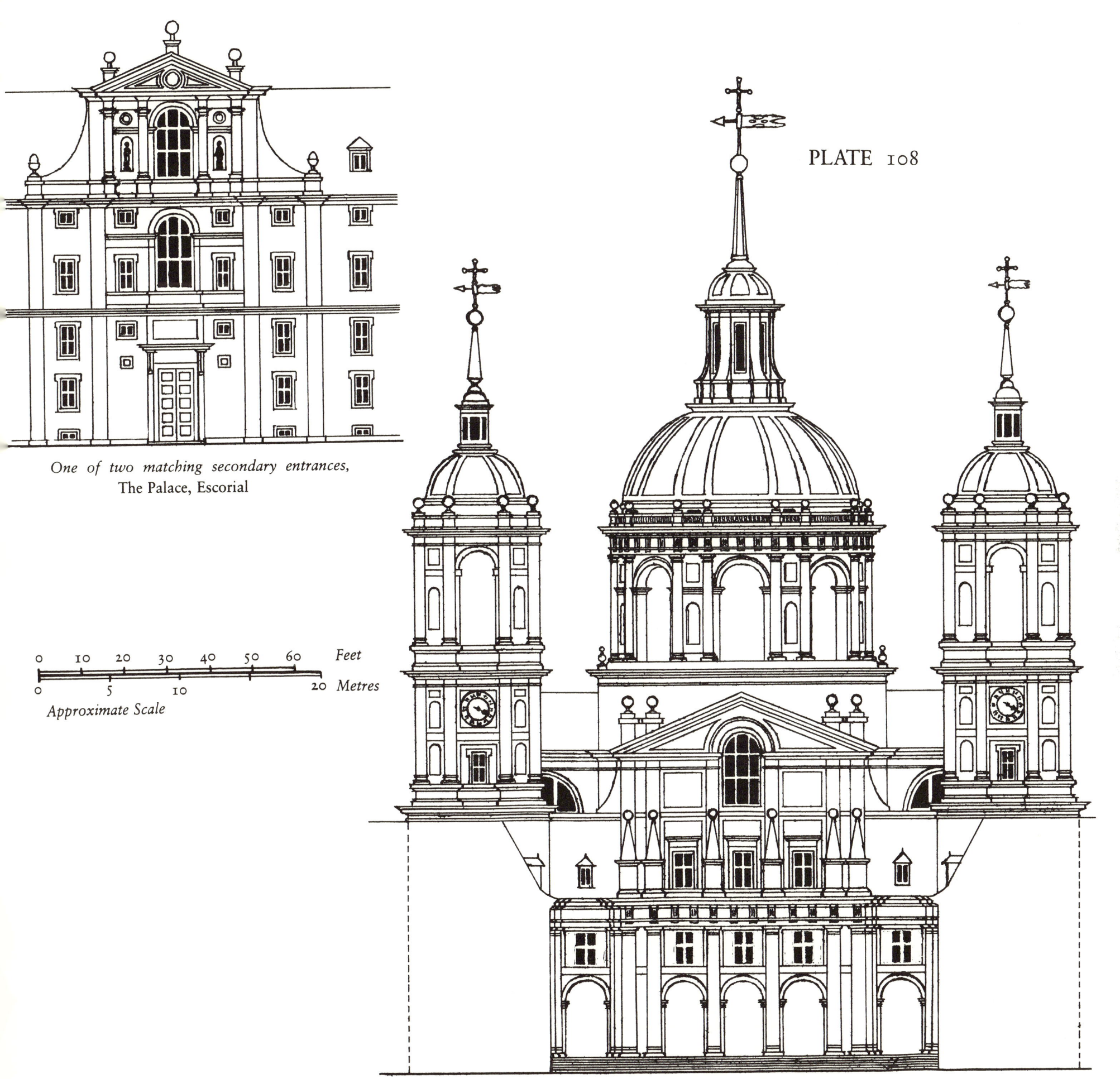

189

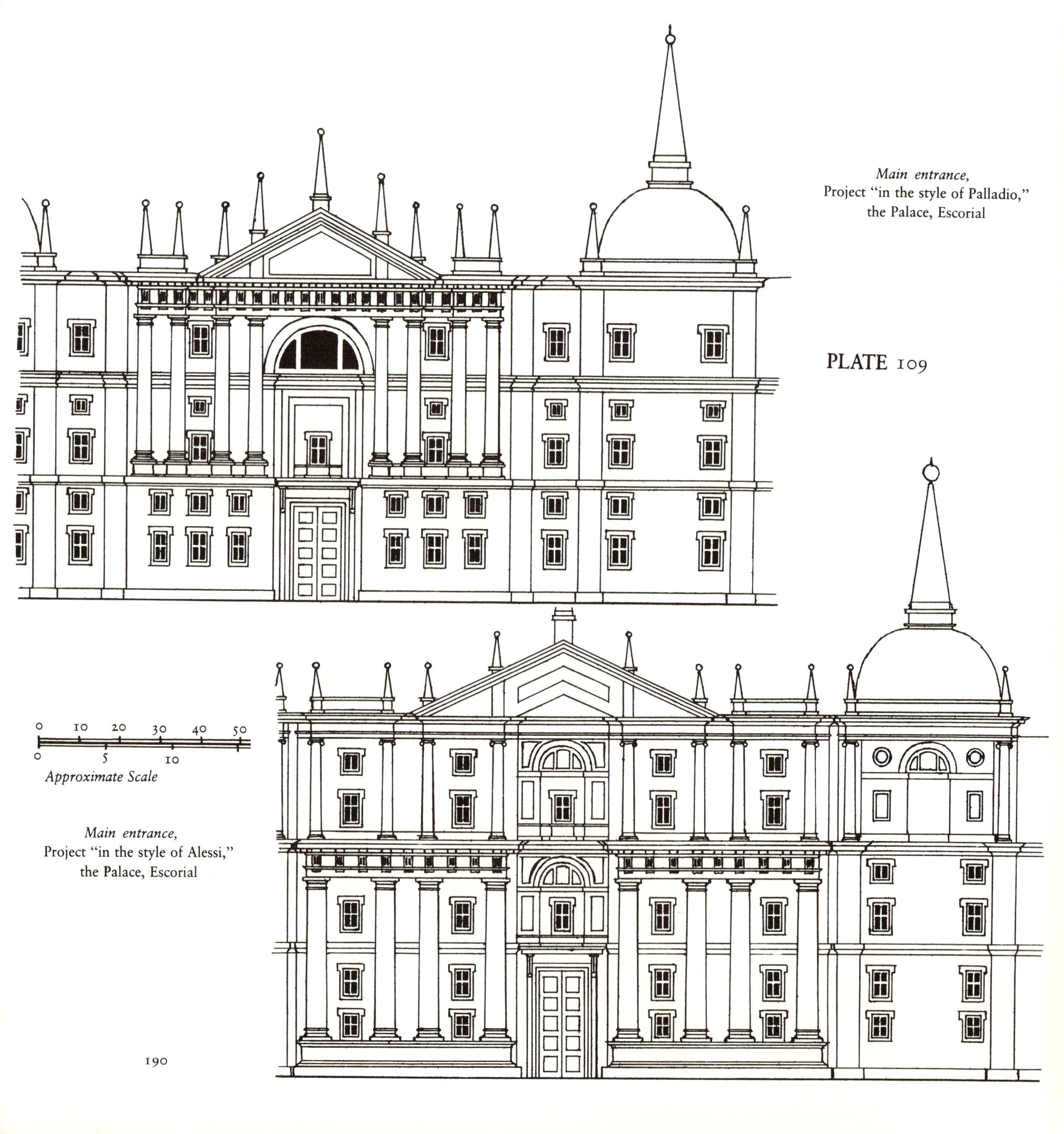

Main entrance,
Project "in the style of Palladio,"
the Palace, Escorial

PLATE 109

Main entrance,
Project "in the style of Alessi,"
the Palace, Escorial

PLATE 110

Main entrance, West elevation,
The Palace, Escorial

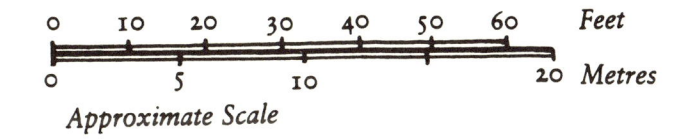

Quentin in 1557; second, he wanted to build a symbol for his intentions to make Spain the world's last bastion of Roman Catholicism and intolerance of any other faiths; finally, he had promised to replace a monastery dedicated to Saint Lawrence that had been destroyed in the late war, and to build a mausoleum for his family. The connection with Saint Lawrence governed the plan of the building: a gridiron like the one on which the saint had been martyred. The king decided not to employ any of the many architects already working in Spain proper, but instead summoned Juan Bautista de Toledo from Naples (then Spanish territory), where he had been working after having studied under Michelangelo. Bautista began work in 1562, supervising the levelling and draining of the land, and making a wooden model of the building. Bautista died in 1567, at which point Juan de Herrera, one of his assistants, was appointed to succeed him. Herrera was a nobleman and a member of the king's bodyguard, but he was widely travelled and was known to appreciate architecture, although his only real training in the field had come from watching Bautista at work. Nevertheless he learned his lessons well, for he subsequently designed many fine buildings on his own. The precise amount of the Escorial that can be ascribed to Bautista rather than to Herrera is not known; certainly not much had been finished by the time of his death. Many changes to Bautista's design were not only made but also earnestly solicited—according to one source, no fewer than twenty-two Italian architects, including Francesco Paciotto, submitted projects for the Escorial.

Like de Vega's designs at Madrid and Valsaín, the Escorial has a series of solid towers with steeples on top. The Escorial is so big that its many components can be treated as if they were separate buildings, which is the only way they can fit on the pages of this book at the normal scale. Many of the courtyard elevations include multi-storey loggias. The most impressive of these is that of the Main Cloister, which extends eleven bays on each side and is two storeys tall. The arches, which have since been filled with glass, rest on piers, in front of which stand Doric and Ionic half-columns. A balustrade with ball finials stands on top. The design of this loggia was later repeated almost exactly by Herrera in the five-bay Casa Lonja at Sevilla, and is directly inspired by Antonio de San Gallo II's Palazzo Farnese in Rome. In contrast to the rich detailing of the loggia in the Main Cloister, the Monastery Cloister is as simple as it can be while still retaining elegance. This three-storey, seven bay loggia consists modestly of identical arches on plain piers. A third loggia design is on the so-called Sunshine Corridor, which is actually outside the perimeter of the main building. This is an L-shaped structure with hipped dormers on its hipped roof. Its ground floor loggia uses Tuscan columns in an unusual rhythm: pairs of arches are separated from each other by a narrower, trabeated opening, and the same rhythm is repeated on the floor above with Ionic columns in a completely trabeated system—where the unusual spacing looks somewhat incongruous.

In the middle of the courtyard of the Main Cloister stands the Fountain of the Evangelists and its Tempietto. Although the plan of the Tempietto is cruciform and it is limited to eight Doric columns, it was undoubtedly an attempt to recall Bramante's Tempietto of San Pietro in Montorio, Rome. Above the entablature is a balustrade around the panelled drum, on top of which is a panelled dome and cupola. The dome, of course, can not help but echo and draw attention to the much larger dome on the Chapel adjacent to the cloister.

The Chapel is one of the most impressive church designs of the Renaissance in any country. Its plan is a rectangle but with emphasis on a Latin cross within it, and a Greek cross within that. The barrel-vaulted interior is lit primarily by thermal windows in the clerestory, and, as perhaps befits a monastery chapel, is but sparsely decorated except at the high altar. The entrance front is approached between two ranges of buildings, and entry is gained through arches standing under a giant Doric portico; the six pinnacles over the portico in Herrera's design were ordered by Philip to be replaced with large statues of biblical kings. On either side of the entrance are tall, domed campaniles decorated by pilaster-strips and niches. The Doric order reappears on pilasters in pairs around the drum of the main dome with arches and niches in a rhythm previously found at Bramante's loggia at the Vatican and Serlio's Ancy. Above the drum is a balustrade with ball finials, and then the panelled dome, leading to a large cupola. The general appearance of the dome—and of other aspects of the chapel—is strongly reminiscent of Alessi's Santa Maria in Carignano at Genoa, so it is perhaps not surprising to learn that Alessi had agreed to come by invitation to help with the design, but died in 1572 just as he was preparing for the journey.

The building material and the shortage of ornament, coupled with the immense size of the Escorial, give it an austere, forbidding aspect, especially on the exterior. However, the monotony of hundreds of windows in four storeys is relieved occasionally by a frontispiece. Two such matching designs are in the west wall. Their boundaries are marked in pilaster-strips, but the pedimented and buttressed gable on top is trimmed with Ionic pilasters. A large, compass-headed window in the gable is echoed in a duplicate that extends through the top two floors below. The frontispieces are, of course, intended to draw attention to secondary entrances.

For the principal entrance in the middle of the west wall, various projects were offered. Two of these were submitted, apparently by Bautista, in frank imitation of major Italian architects of the day. One, "in the style of Palladio," has a giant Doric portico of eight columns in three groups, standing on the bottom two floors as its base. Except for the thermal window in the middle of the portico and the strong impost moulding running behind the columns, the design does not look much like anything Palladio might have designed. The other, "in the style of Alessi," is less unified. It covers the lower two storeys plus high basement with four giant Doric half-columns and broken entablatures on each side of the doorway. The top two floors are decorated with Ionic half-columns, the central four of which support a strange pediment. Both the "Palladio" and "Alessi" projects are flanked with domed towers.

Herrera's eventual design for the main entrance is more successful and unified, and projects an air of brute strength mingled with dignity and reverence. The bulk of this part of the building is raised to six storeys under a hipped roof, instead of the four storeys of the rest of the outside, and the bottom four storeys are covered by a truly giant portico of eight Doric half-columns. Above the massive entablature, the line of the four central columns is carried up three more storeys by four giant Ionic half-columns to a pediment over an entablature with cushion frieze. Not by accident, the frontispiece as a whole is reminiscent of the west end of many Italian churches, in a variation of the same theme followed by the Gesù in Rome.

In spite of the Italian influences throughout the Escorial, enough Flemish builders were involved to see that the roofs followed the Flemish style of being tall and pierced by many dormers; the high roofs have a practical value, too, for central Spain receives occasional heavy snowfalls, and steep roofs shed the snow better than a low-pitched typical Spanish or Italian roof. In 1671, the entire interior of the Escorial was destroyed by a terrible fire, but it is a measure of the strength of its construction that it was able to be rebuilt with practically no repairs needed to the walls. The Escorial is now open to the public, and contains many of Spain's national treasures.[2]

Casa Lonja (Exchange), Sevilla PLATE 111

Sevilla was the city that more than any others ran Spain's pillaging of the gold and silver treasures of the New World. In the interdependent Europe of the Renaissance, the gold meant little unless it could be quickly exchanged in commerce, especially since Spain was spending the treasure faster than it could be imported, and loans for the purpose of prosecuting constant wars managed to pull Spain into ignominious bankruptcy twice in the sixteenth century. These financial requirements caused the merchants of Sevilla to order the construction of the Casa Lonja or Exchange, built to Herrera's designs in 1582–1599. The basic idea was patterned after Hans Hendrik van Paesschen's Royal Exchange in London, but it espoused a more up-to-date, if colder version of the classical style. In plan, the Casa Lonja is a large square with a square courtyard in the middle. The outside elevation, which seems deceptively low because it lacks a visible roof, is divided into two tall storeys. The windows of its eleven bays are separated by pilaster-strips on the ground floor and Tuscan pilasters on the floor above, sometimes in pairs. The windows are too short to fill the spaces allotted to them, so each has a panel above it. Tall, rusticated pinnacles stand at each corner of the building. The five-bay courtyard elevation is a duplication of the elevation of the larger Main Cloister at the Escorial, and both are copied from the Palazzo Farnese in Rome, designed by Antonio da San Gallo II. The arches have since been filled with glazing. The building now houses the valuable General Archives of the Indies.

Cathedral, Valladolid PLATE 113

From 1580 onwards, Herrera was engaged to build the new Cathedral at Valladolid. For its plan, he departed from anything that had ever been built in Spain before, and drew a rectangle with a dome in the middle, a tower at each of the four corners, and two aisles on each side (the other aisle being devoted to side chapels). Apparently, Riaño and Gil had slowly been trying to build a cathedral on that site, but Herrera had no use for their efforts and had the whole thing demolished before he would start. As a result, he himself died before construction was far advanced. Today the Cathedral remains unfinished, but it is further along than it was when Herrera died, thanks to the alterations made by various hands over the years. Nevertheless, both in the plan and in the lower half of the west elevation, which was all that was built to Herrera's plans, it is possible to see reflections of the Escorial, both of the chapel and of the main entrance on the west front. The west elevation of the Cathedral is, like the Escorial, sparing of detail, but it has a giant tetrastyle Doric portico at the entrance. It is much to be regretted that Herrera was unable to see the building completed to his designs, for he was of all the architects of the Renaissance the greatest master of scale. Inside the cathedral, the nave vaults spring from an entablature supported by giant Corinthian pilasters standing in front of massive square piers that support the aisle arches.

Royal Palace, Aranjuez PLATE 112

If Herrera was the master of scale, he may have faltered with the Royal Palace of Aranjuez, where he worked from about 1581 onwards. The plan was for a long front range with a square block behind it containing a courtyard. The central block of the front was three storeys high and sparing of windows. From it, a five-bay, two storey hyphen with high roof and two levels of dormers led to a two-bay corner-tower with a dome on each end. The detailing of the façade makes much use of a sort of pilaster strip, that are really pilasters minus their capitals, for they have elaborate bases and projecting sections of entablature. The total effect is fussy, and quite unlike the broad brush-strokes of the Escorial or the Valladolid Cathedral. The palace burned down and was rebuilt to a different design, yet retaining some features of Herrera's work.

a small palace, Plasencia PLATE 112

Two further buildings have been attributed to Herrera. One is a small section around the entrance of a small palace at Plasencia. This is most unlike his other designs,

2. George Kubler, *Building the Escorial*, Princeton, Princeton University Press, 1982, and Mary Cable, *El Escorial*, New York, Newsweek Books, 1971.

Casa Lonja (Exchange), Sevilla

PLATE III

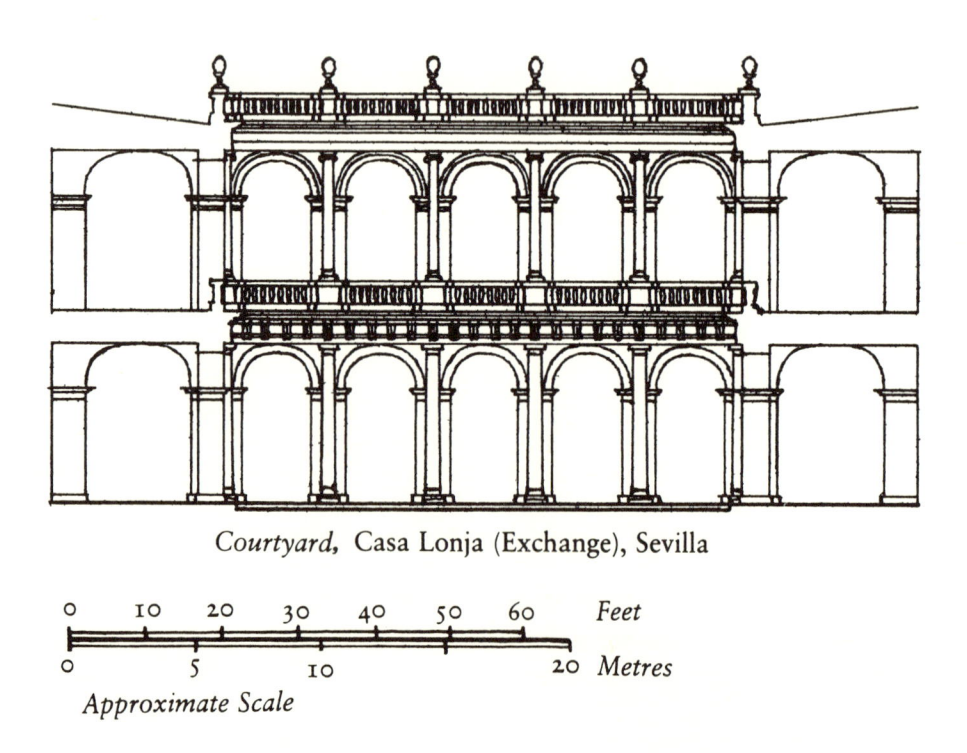

Courtyard, Casa Lonja (Exchange), Sevilla

```
0    10   20   30   40   50   60   Feet
0         5         10        20   Metres
Approximate Scale
```

Center of main front, Royal Palace, Aranjuez

Monastery between Escorial and Guadarrama

PLATE 112

Part of a small palace, Plasencia

Right wing of main front, Royal Palace, Aranjuez

195

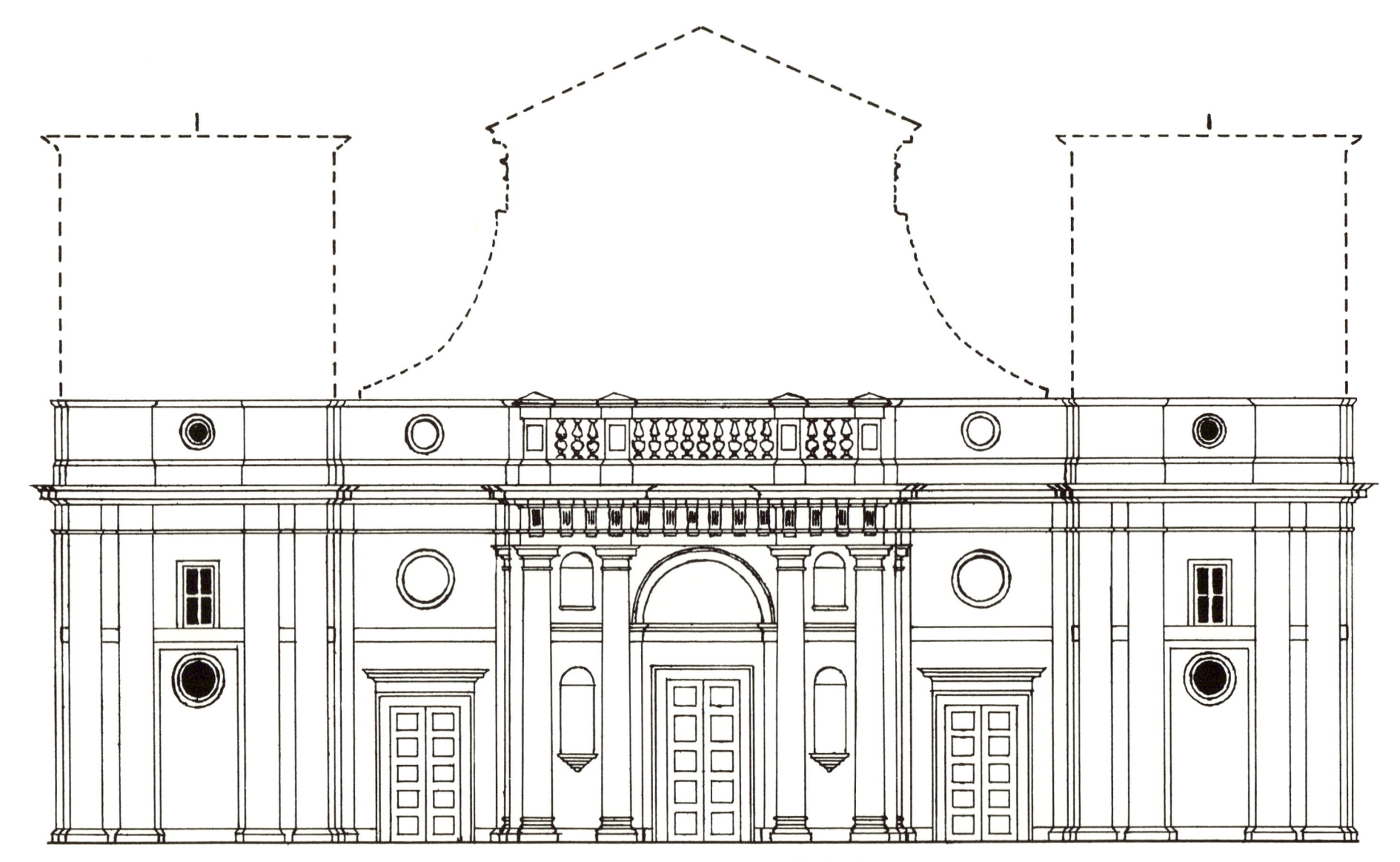

West elevation, Cathedral, Valladolid

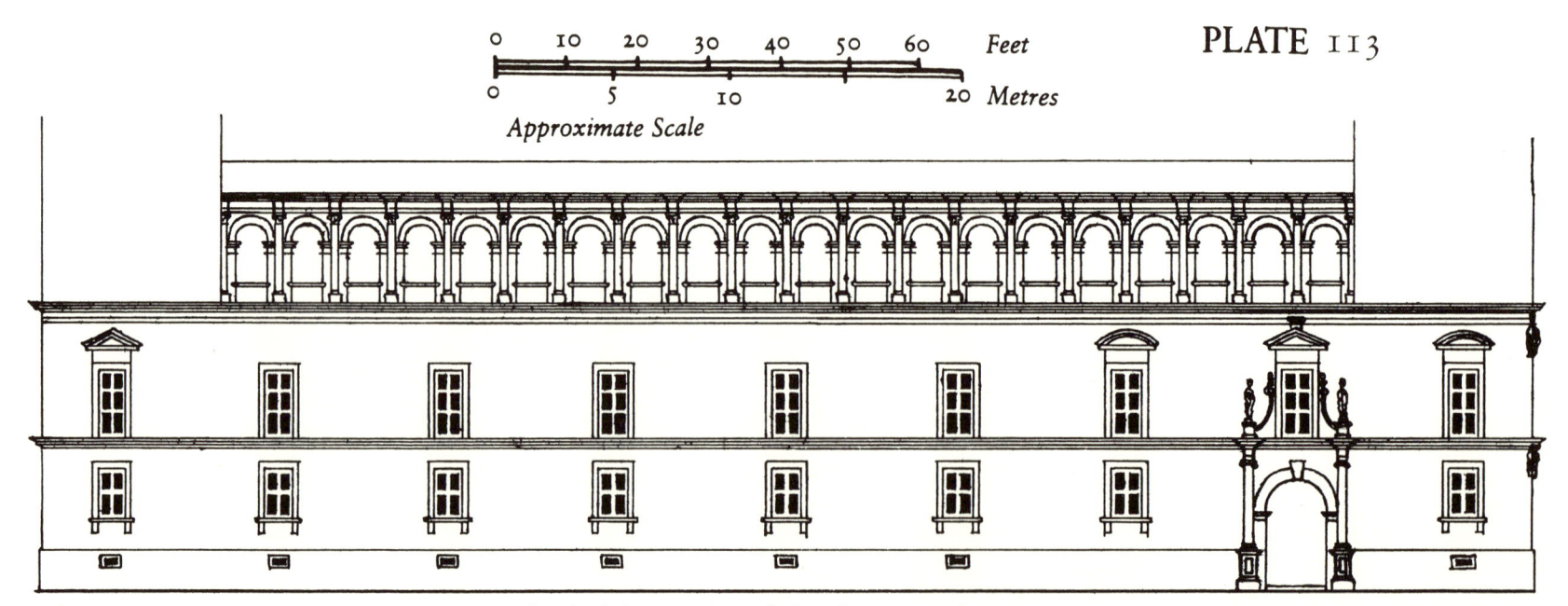

PLATE 113

Unfinished front, Casa de los Guzmanes, León

so the attribution may be viewed with skepticism. The three-storey entrance tower has its door in a Tuscan aedicule and the window above in an Ionic aedicule. The top floor has two small, plain windows. A balustrade stands atop the main entablature.

Monastery between Escorial and Guadarrama PLATE 112

The other attribution was more like Herrera's other works. This is a monastery between the Escorial and Guadarrama. The front elevation used an heroic pediment supported by a pilaster strip at each corner, but no entablature. The low roof, surprisingly, had two rows of hipped dormers. Each of the five plain windows of the upper floor had its own balustrade. The ground floor consisted of a loggia of five arches resting on piers. The building no longer stands, but is known both from an architectural drawing and an oil painting at the Museo Arqueologico, Madrid.

Casa de los Guzmanes, León PLATE 113

The Casa de los Guzmanes at Leon was begun by an anonymous architect around 1560, but never finished. The two lower floors have nine bays, the upper windows being larger than the lower ones, suggesting the concept of the piano nobile. The upper windows are for the most part plain, but four of them—three at one end and one at the other end—are capped by pediments, some segmental and some triangular. One might conclude that the other pediments were intended but never executed, but the alternation of segmental and triangular will not match with the one pediment at the left. In addition, the entrance is not in the middle but near the right-hand end. Had those defects been remedied, the building would have been able to fit into the mould that Palladio established. The designer then added a typical Spanish arcaded loggia as a third floor, stretching between the corner towers; at least in this case, the arches are related to the windows below them with a ratio of three to one.

Chapel of Mosén Rubín, Ávila PLATE 114

The Chapel of Mosén Rubín at Ávila is a gothic structure that was given a new façade in the classical style in about 1560. The architect(s) is referred to both as Pedro Valle and Pierre de Toulouse, and it is not certain whether this was the same man or two separate people who worked together. The Rubín family were converts from Judaism, and the addition of the new front may have been intended to show the suspicious Spanish authorities that the conversion was genuine. The façade is divided into five bays by giant Corinthian columns, grouped in pairs around the central bay. Oval windows in cartouches are placed above rectangular windows. The middle bay contains a large arch. Above the entablature is a balustrade with diminutive Ionic columns supporting a heavy entablature under the roof, a most unusual arrangement. Pedro Valle later worked at the Escorial. Had he (or Pierre) trained under Nicolas Bachelier at Toulouse?

Palacio del Marqués de Santa Cruz, Viso del Marqués, Ciudad Real PLATE 114

Three Italian architects were imported from Genoa from 1564 onwards to build the Palace of the Marqués de Santa Cruz at El Viso del Marqués, Ciudad Real. Giovanni Battista Prioli was the leader, the others being Domingo and Alberto Prioli. Much of the detailing, especially of the interior, is similar to work then being done in Genoa by Alessi and others, but the arcaded loggia in the courtyard prefigures the Main Cloister loggia at the Escorial and the loggia at the Casa Lonja at Sevilla in being a copy of the loggia at the Palazzo Farnese by Antonio da San Gallo II.

Philip II's Campillo, northeast of Escorial PLATE 114

Two small buildings built for the royal family as overnight stops for their more frequent journeys are depicted on oil paintings at the Museo Arqueologico, Madrid, attributed to the Italian painter Giuseppe Leonardo. Neither the dates nor the names of the architects are known, but both were built for Philip II, (who died in 1598, long after he had lost interest in travelling). The Campillo stood northeast of the Escorial on the road to Guadarrama. It was three bays wide and five storeys tall under a hipped roof with dormers. Most of the windows had relieving arches, and the corners of the house were trimmed with quoins.

Philip II's Casa de la Nieve, in the Pass of Fuenfria PLATE 114

The other house, the Casa de la Nieve (House of the Snow), stood in the Fuenfria Pass between Madrid and Segovia, not far from the Escorial. This had a piano nobile over a high basement, and two different levels for the main cornice provided an occasion for three interlocking hipped roofs.

Chancillería, Granada PLATE 114

The Chancillería at Granada is an example of the Spanish financial miscalculations in the face of unexpected inflation and national bankruptcy. It was begun by Siloé in 1546, but all he managed to complete was the lower storey of the arcaded loggia in the courtyard— a particularly graceful loggia on slender Tuscan columns. A second-rate upper loggia was placed above it by another hand at a later date. The entrance front was not finished until 1587 by an anonymous architect in a proto-baroque style that seems to owe something to Michelangelo's Capitol in Rome. Here, the indicated piano nobile is actually the third row of windows up from the ground, contained in aedicules with alternating triangular and segmental pediments; the central bay over the portal has a confection worthy of Michelangelo that combines both triangular and segmental pediments. The outside bay is enclosed in a slight projection marked with quoins. Above the balustrade that runs along the top of the main entablature are numerous fantastic finials and pinnacles, undoubtedly placed there to remind the viewer that he is in Spain, not in Italy after all.

Chapel of Mosén Rubín, Ávila

Philip II's Campillo, northeast of Escorial

Courtyard, Palacio del Marqués de Santa Cruz, Viso del Marqués, Ciudad Real

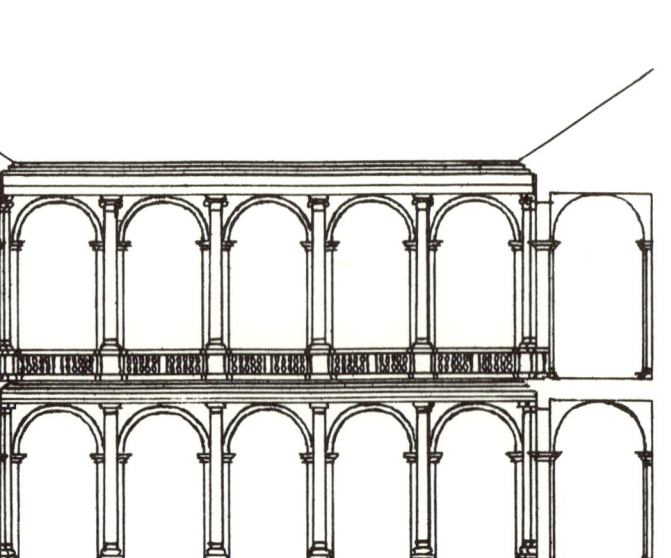

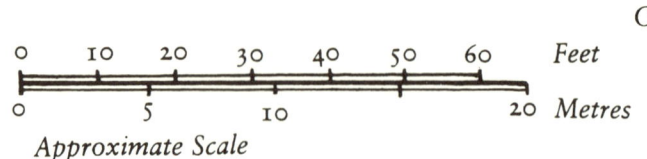

PLATE 114

Philip II's Casa de la Nieve, in the Pass of Fuenfría

Chancillería, Granada

PORTUGAL

Chapel of Nossa Senhora da Graça, Évora PLATE 115

Quite different in character is the renaissance architecture of Portugal. The earliest Portugese building to employ classical forms is the Chapel of Nossa Senhora de Graça at Évora, built from about 1530 onwards. The entrance is through a three-bay Tuscan colonnaded loggia. The two flanking bays of the upper storey are decorated with large rosettes, while in the middle stands a tall, Ionic aedicule containing a shell in high relief perched above a pair of smaller Ionic columns, whose entablature is bent to give the impression of deep perspective. The design is needlessly complicated by the addition of angled crenellations on top of the gable to link it with the higher plane of the pediment over the aedicule, and a subsequent hand has added oversized statues that look as if they were contemplating jumping to the ground. Much rebuilding of the rest of the structure was done at the end of the century. The architect is anonymous.

Devotional Fountain, Manga Cloister, Santa Cruz, Coimbra PLATE 115

The idea of the hemispherical dome caught on at an early date in Portugal, the first example being a devotional fountain built at the Manga Monastery, Santa Cruz, near Coimbra in 1533, probably by the Frenchman, Jean de Rouen (or Ruão in Portuguese). The details are full of mystic religious symbolism in an effort to reform the relaxed lives of the monks, but the basic design involves placing the central dome with cupola on eight Tuscan columns, and reinforcing it with flying-buttresses leading to four cylindrical towers with conical roofs and cupolas. George Kubler traces the influence of this design on the public Fountain at Chiapas, Mexico (1562) and the Fountain of the Evangelists at the Escorial (1580s).

Conceição Chapel, Tomar PLATE 115

Another early dome atop a square base stands over the crossing of the rectangular Conceição Chapel at Tomar, built about 1540, probably by João de Castilho (of Castilla). The dome on the exterior is largely cosmetic, because the interior coffered dome is easily contained within the square base, and so the external dome is solid masonry. In plan, the nave is almost square, three bays long; the crossing and transepts together are scarcely wider than the nave with its two aisles. Next, the chancel and its aisles add one bay to the length, before the church ends with a semicircular apse contained within the thick masonry of the straight end wall. The internal divisions are marked by Corinthian columns and entablatures under coffered barrel-vaults. On the outside, the rectangular windows are contained in shouldered architraves under bracketed pediments. Giant Ionic pilasters support a weak entablature, above which, on the west end, is a wide pediment with semicircular window.

Church of São Amaro, Lisbon (Alcantara) PLATE 115

The Church of São Amaro, Alcantara, Lisbon, built by an anonymous architect in 1549, has two internal domes covered with conical roofs. The plan for this church is extraordinary: the central core is a round space under the larger of the two coffered domes with its cupola, connected by an arch to a smaller round space under the smaller dome; the larger circle is the nave and the smaller circle is for the altar. Outside the nave, on the side away from the altar, is a large, semicircular ambulatory of seven bays, of which five contain arches leading to the outside. Additional rooms were built on either side of the altar for the sacristy and the priest's lodging. In spite of the sophistication of this daring design, the vaulting of the ambulatory is ribbed in gothic style.

Market & Misericórdia, Beja PLATE 115

Another classical façade in front of gothic, ribbed vaulting can be found at the building erected about 1550 to serve as a combination Misericórdia and Market Building at Beja. The anonymous architect gave the front three arches with rusticated voussoirs on rusticated piers and divided by rusticated pilasters, the end pilasters quite properly being wider than the middle pilasters. The parapet above the entablature supports ball finials over the pilasters.

Chapel of Bom Jesus de Valverde, Mitra PLATE 115

One of the most adventurous plans can be found at the diminutive Chapel of Bom Jesus de Valverde at Quinta da Mitra, near Évora. This was built 1550–1560, and is attributed to both Manuel Pires and Diogo de Torralva, perhaps working together. The building has no exterior elevation at all, since it is contained within the thick masonry walls of a larger building, so it can only be appreciated on the inside. The plan consists of five domed circles of eight columns each, in which each of the outer circles shares two columns with the central circle but none with any of the other outer circles. The result is a modified Greek cross. The Tuscan columns support the lower of two entablatures, which is broken on all the principal axes in order to permit the insertion of arches, thus forming many Venetian motifs. The upper entablature rests on top of the arches, and the four outer domes spring from that entablature. The central dome stands on an arcaded and pilastered drum, the chief source of light for the Chapel; other light is obtained through cupolas on top of all the domes.

Jesuit Church of Espírito Santo, Évora PLATE 115

Manuel Pires definitely designed the Jesuit Church of Espirito Santo at Évora, built 1566–1574. In contrast to many Jesuit churches elsewhere, this one is only sparsely decorated both inside and out. Entrance is gained through a one-storey, five-bay arcaded porch, and then

Chapel of Nossa Senhora da Graça, Évora

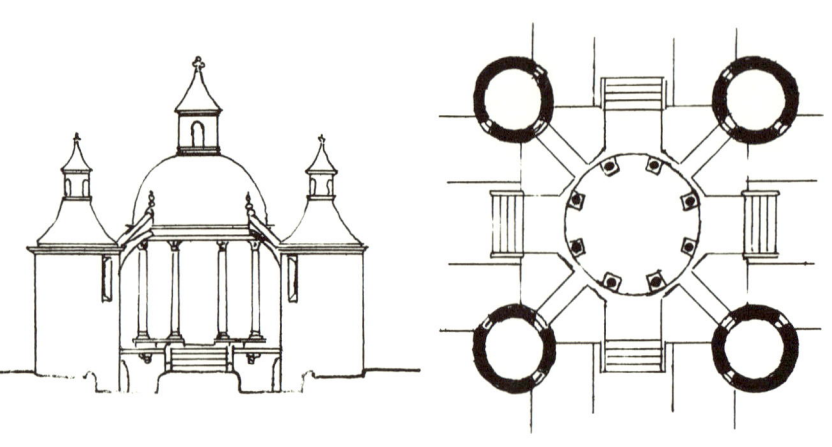

Plan & elevation,
Devotional Fountain, Manga Cloister, Santa Cruz, Coimbra

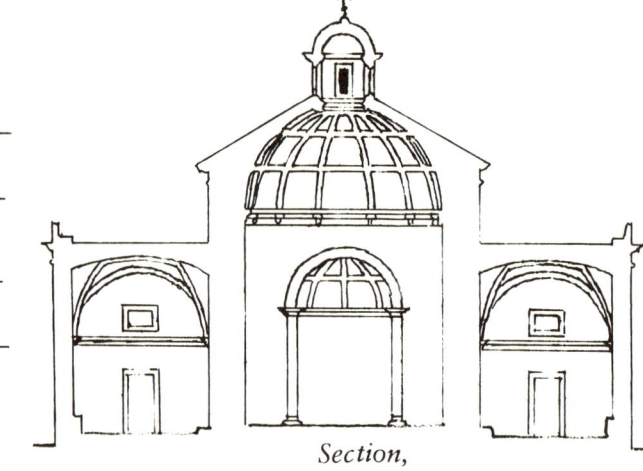

Section,
Church of São Amaro, Lisbon (Alcantara)

Main entrance,
Conceição Chapel, Tomar

Section, looking towards entrance,
Conceição Chapel, Tomar

Market & Misericórdia, Beja

Section,
Chapel of Bom Jesus de Valverde, Mitra

PLATE 115

Main entrance,
Jesuit Church of Espírito Santo, Évora

Section, looking towards entrance,
Jesuit Church of Espírito Santo, Évora

through a three-bay arcade that supports the rear gallery. The barrel-vaulted nave is separated from the side-chapels, that stand where the aisles would be, by a wall pierced by single-storey arches. Above the side-chapels is a gallery, which however is not organically a part of the same space as the nave, for it looks out on the nave only through window-like openings. A large round window high in the west wall helps to make up for otherwise inadequate fenestration.

Convent of Christ, Tomar PLATE 116

Almost certainly, the finest piece of renaissance architecture in Portugal is the square courtyard of the Convent of Christ at Tomar, built by Diogo de Torralva, 1554–1588. This two-storey loggia is derivative of many buildings Torralva may have seen in Italy. For example, the circular stair-towers in the corners are similar to those at Genga's Villa Imperiale at Pesaro, and the three-bay lower arcade seems to be a version of Bramante's loggia in the Vatican that Serlio also used at Ancy, although with wider arches. The engaged Doric columns of the lower loggia stand underneath Ionic columns that frame the upper loggia, but over the single arch of the lower loggia is a complete Venetian arch with small Ionic square pillars. João de Castilho had apparently drawn a plan for a Romanesque loggia in this courtyard, and it is fortunate that Torralva was hired to design something different. Unfortunately, the late-gothic church to which the cloister is attached did not require rebuilding by Torralva at the same time.

Church of São Mamede, Évora PLATE 116

The Venetian-arch motif appears several times in Portuguese renaissance architecture, including on the entrance-porch of the Church of São Mamede at Évora, built 1566–1568. Perhaps because of the arch, which is skilfully blended with a Tuscan aedicule, the porch, if not the rest of the building, is attributed to Diogo de Torralva, but it seems not to be up to his standards. The real designer may have been someone like Afonso Alvares. Two pilaster-strips support the main entablature and pediment, but the actual roof-line is above the pediment, so an angled parapet is clumsily placed above the pediment.

Jesuit Church of São Roque, Lisbon PLATE 116

The Jesuit Church of São Roque in Lisbon, built 1567–1586, would seem to be a better candidate for attribution to Torralva, and the usual attribution is indeed to him, with the assistance of Afonso Alvares. The plan is that of a rectangular hall-church well suited to the Jesuit specialty of preaching. In the place of aisles through the arches on both sides are the usual side-chapels, which are accommodated in spite of the fact that a corner had to be clipped off to allow for the awkward shape of the site. As if to emphasize the centrality of Jesuit preaching, not only is the pulpit in the middle of the south wall of the nave, but the altar is awarded no more than a shallow arched recess instead of a large chancel and apse. The main entablature contains a cornice whose heavy brackets—larger than modillions—intrude over the entire depth of the frieze, providing a strong unifying force for the room. Three of the exterior elevations are completely hidden by other buildings attached to the walls.

Church of Santa Catarina dos Livreiros, Lisbon PLATE 116

Afonso Alvares designed the Church of Santa Catarina dos Livreiros at Lisbon in 1572. The entrance façade, like so many Portuguese churches, sandwiches the nave between two bell-towers. A complete entablature runs around the church at the level of the eaves of the gable roof. Above the entablature, the building is less formal, with only pilaster-strips for trim. Below the entablature, the towers are edged with Tuscan pilasters, and the entrance is through a loggia made out of a Venetian arch. Inside, the ceiling is open to the roof. The aisles are divided from the nave by a series of arches on piers; the fourth arch, whose aisle space is cordonned off into a side-chapel, is framed with an aedicule.

Palace Chapel, Salvaterra de Magos, near Santarém PLATE 116

The Palace Chapel at Salvaterra de Magos, near Santarém, which is attributed to Miguel de Arruda in 1555, is another Portuguese building to use the Venetian-arch motif. The nave is contained in a square area in which is inserted an octagonal arcade on Tuscan columns with flying entablatures, and above the arcade sits a short octagonal drum and dome. The chancel, which is a rectangular extension of the nave's square, is divided from the nave by a Venetian arch. The flying entablatures of the octagon all face the same direction rather than being oriented to the radii of the dome.

Cathedral, Portalegre PLATE 117

The Cathedral at Portalegre, built by an anonymous architect in 1556–1590, is probably the first to set the standard for the front elevations of hundreds of churches built in Portugal and its overseas possessions (including Goa and Brazil) over the next two centuries or more. The front is divided into five bays by stocky Tuscan pilasters at three different levels. Nearly all the windows are capped by segmental pediments, although the central doorway and the window over it were replaced by a baroque confection at a later date. The twin towers project from the plane of the west wall and are crowned with spires. Reflecting the divisions expressed on the entrance front, the interior is divided into five parts, with the outer aisles walled to serve as side-chapels, except in the fifth bay, where transepts are indicated inside the rectangular building. The piers are clusters of Tuscan pilasters, but the vaults above them are all gothic with the exception of the dome over the crossing. Many Portuguese churches of this period had gothic vaulting in buildings that otherwise expressed a variant of the classical language. According to Kubler, the Spanish architect Herrera was in Portalegre in 1581,

Courtyard, Convent of Christ, Tomar

Church of São Mamede, Évora

Section & plan,
Palace Chapel, Salvaterra de Magos,
near Santarém

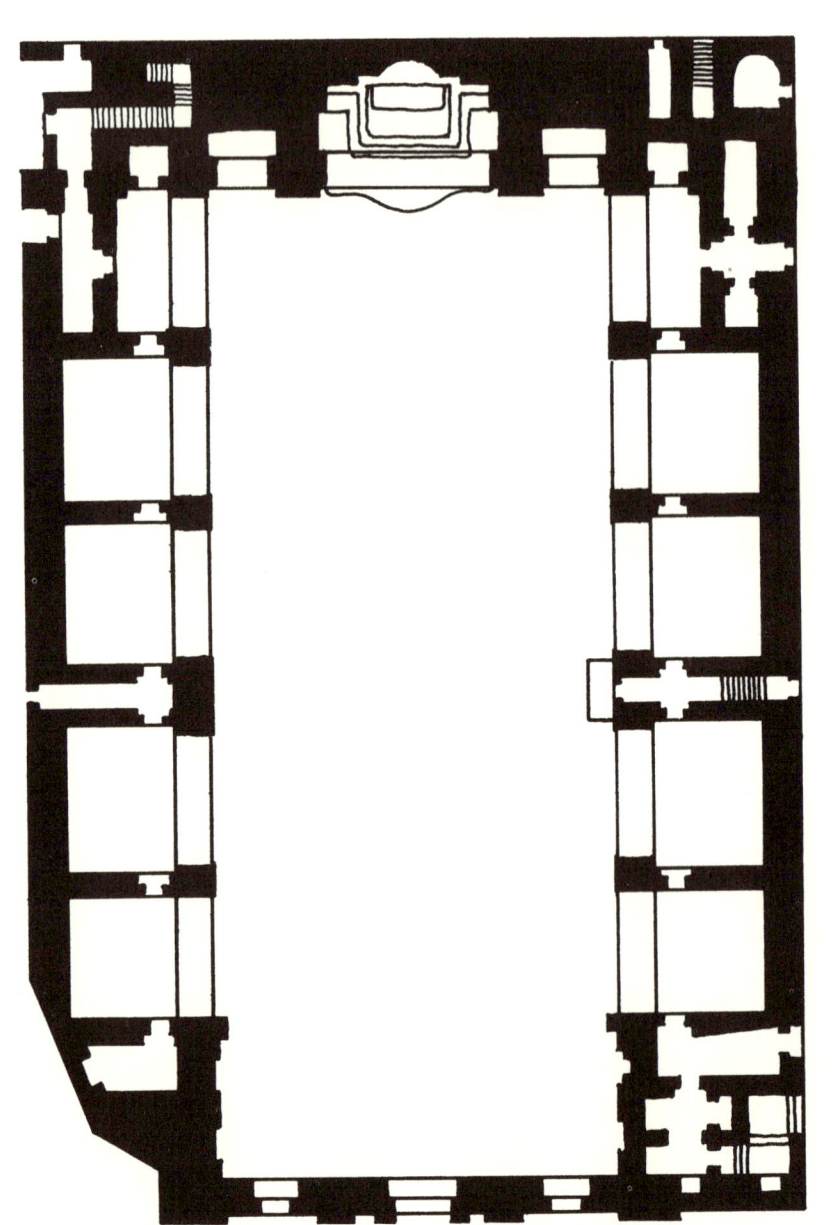

Plan, Jesuit Church of São Roque, Lisbon

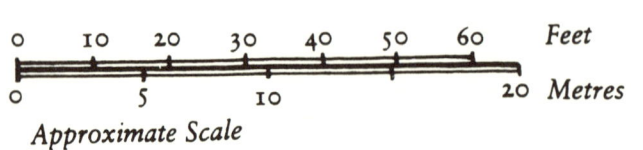

PLATE 116

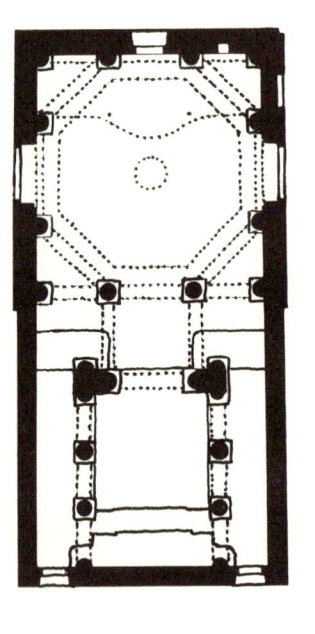

Church of Santa Catarina dos Livreiros, Lisbon

Cathedral, Portalegre

Church of Santa Maria da Graça, Setúbal

PLATE 117

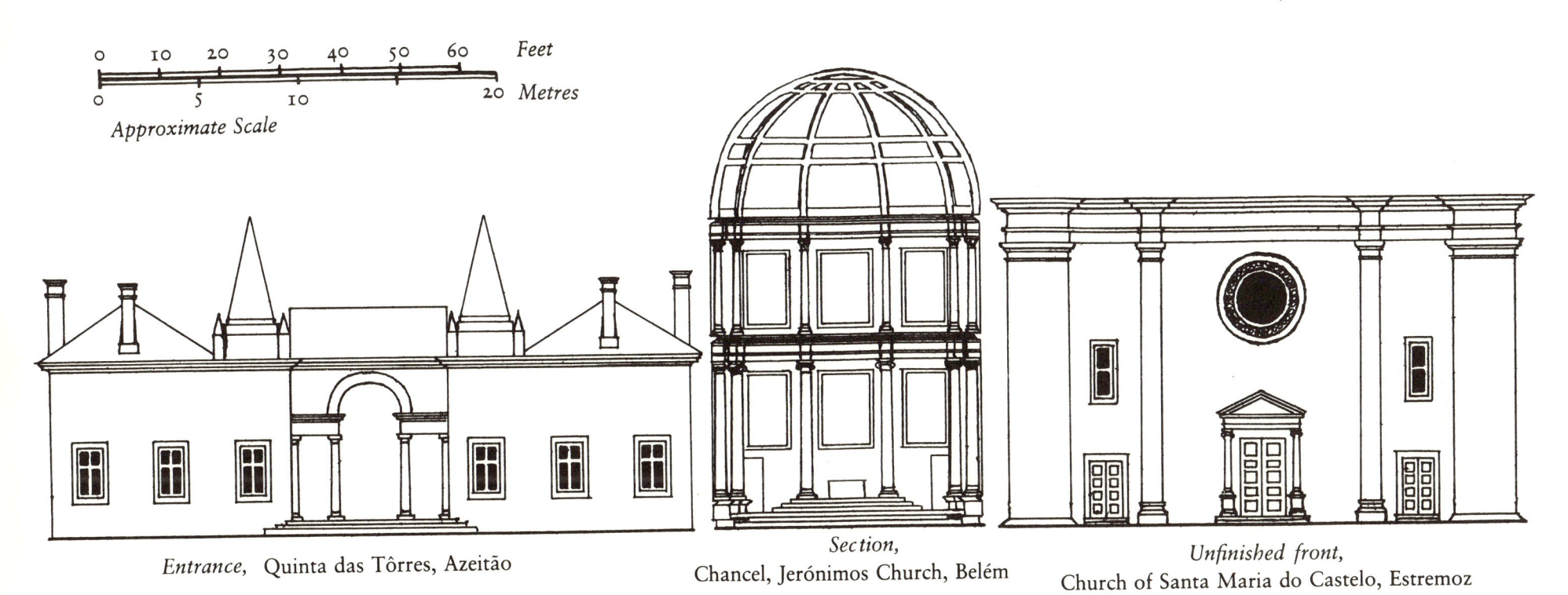

Entrance, Quinta das Tôrres, Azeitão

Section, Chancel, Jerónimos Church, Belém

Unfinished front, Church of Santa Maria do Castelo, Estremoz

but he was there on a political mission and presumably had nothing to do with any local architecture.

Church of Santa Maria do Castelo, Estremoz PLATE 117

The Church of Santa Maria do Castelo at Estremoz, built by Pero Gomez in 1559–1562 has gothic vaulting on top of Ionic columns that divide the square into nine parts (with an extra part added onto the east as a chancel). The entrance front was never completed, so it remains unknown whether the architect intended it to have an heroic pediment or a hipped roof. Slim giant Tuscan pilasters stand on either side of the main door, which has a rose window over it, and double-width Tuscan pilasters mark the corners of the building.

Quinta das Tôrres, Azeitão PLATE 117

Unusual for this period outside Italy on a secular building, a large Venetian arch forms a recessed entry-porch for the Quinta (meaning ranch or country house) das Tôrres at Azeitão. This was built by an anonymous architect about 1560. The entrance is flanked by a pair of short towers with pyramidal spires on top; these structures, coupled with the lack of a unified roof-plan, subtract from the otherwise Palladian aspect of the front elevation.

Chancel, Jerónimos Church, Belém PLATE 117

Jerónimo de Ruão, likely the son of Jean de Ruão/Rouen (who may have designed the Fountain at the Manga Cloister), designed the Jerónimos Church at Belém, Lisbon. The exterior, part of which looks more like a fortress than a church, can hardly be called classical, but the interior is classical in parts. Most of the interior dates from after the period covered in this book, but the chancel was built 1571–1572. This is two storeys high, and the aisle-arches of each bay are marked by pairs of Ionic columns. Pairs of Corinthian columns stand out from the wall on the upper storey. At both levels, the columns appear singly rather than in pairs to mark the five bays of the semicircular apse. The ceiling is ribbed and coffered.

Church of Santa Maria da Graça, Setúbal PLATE 117

The anonymous architect of the Church of Santa Maria da Graça at Setúbal (ca. 1572–1594) devised variations on classical themes developed at other Portuguese churches. The twin towers on either side of the entrance are decorated by two levels of squat Tuscan pilasters. The upper storey of each tower has two arches for the bells, and above this storey is a spire in the form of a banded trumpet. Between the bottom storeys of the towers is a porch with a Venetian arch for the entrance. Between the upper parts of the towers, and somewhat set back, is a screen with a single large window, behind which the gable of the roof is hidden.

Salvador Convent Church, Grijó PLATE 118

The front of the Convent Church of Salvador at Grijó, designed by Francisco Velasques from 1574 onwards, is markedly different from most other Portuguese churches of the period, and is somewhat reminiscent of work in northern Europe by Flemish architects. The three tall arches of the ground floor are separated by panelled Tuscan pilasters, which are doubled on the ends. The sections of frieze above them are also panelled. The next storey is articulated by partially-fluted Tuscan pilasters standing on high, decorated bases. The central bay is almost completely filled with a tall window, while the flanking bays each have a smaller window over a niche. The frieze in the tall entablature is again panelled. A balustrade stands on the cornice completely across the front, thus obscuring the bottom of the pediment. The pediment stops short of its normal apex, and, after a break, there comes a fragment of horizontal cornice. Six pointed finials in three pairs stand on top of the pediment. This front merely serves as the entrance porch, for the actual church is wider. The nave is three bays long with the aisles divided into side-chapels. After the transept comes a deep, narrow chancel.

Convent, Santa Maria de Serra do Pilar, Vila Nova da Gaia PLATE 118

The Convent of Santa Maria de Serra do Pilar at Vila Nova de Gaia has a remarkable cloister and chapel. The Chapel, divided into eight bays, is completely round. It is attached by a hyphen to a round cloister composed of a single storey of Ionic columns. Above the entablature is a high parapet, decorated with pointed finials and scrolled carvings. The architects, João Lopes and Jerónimo Luis, built this in 1576–1583, and probably had in mind Machuca's circular loggia at the Palace at Granada.

Church of Santa Maria da Atalaia, Fronteira PLATE 119

The Church of Santa Maria de Atalaia at Fronteira is another twin-towered church with Tuscan pilasters. The upper storey of each tower has two arched openings for bells and a simple dome for a roof. Between the towers is a two-storey screen-wall with a parapet over it; considerably behind the parapet can be seen the gable roof. The lower storey of the screen is an entrance porch with a Venetian arch, and above it is a single window to illuminate the choir gallery that looks out on the back of the nave through a screen of four pillars. The barrel-vaulted nave is separated from the aisles by high arches standing on square Tuscan pillars. This building was begun in 1577 by an anonymous architect.

Torreão Royal Palace, Lisbon PLATE 120

Filippo Terzi from Bologna, Italy was Portugal's contemporary with Herrera in Spain. He arrived in Portugal in 1576 to design buildings for the court, and when the two kingdoms were merged he was favored with the leading architectural commissions in Lisbon. The first of these was for the Royal Palace called Torreão on the Paço da Ribera in Lisbon in 1581. Much of the large building, which was intended to stretch back several hundred feet from the waterfront, was never completed.

Entrance,
Salvador Convent Church, Grijó

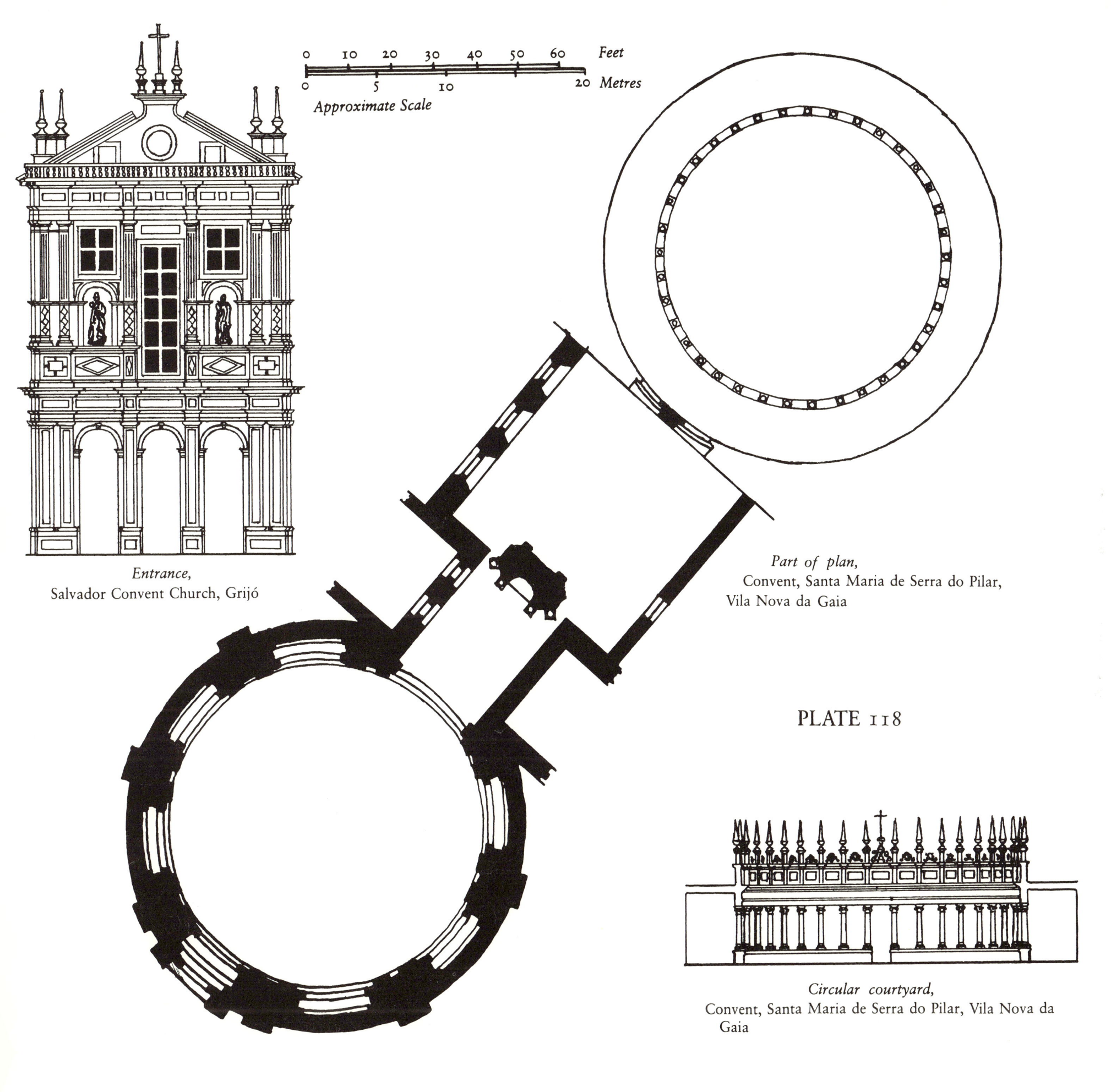

Part of plan,
Convent, Santa Maria de Serra do Pilar,
Vila Nova da Gaia

PLATE 118

Circular courtyard,
Convent, Santa Maria de Serra do Pilar, Vila Nova da Gaia

Church of Santa Maria da Atalaia, Fronteira

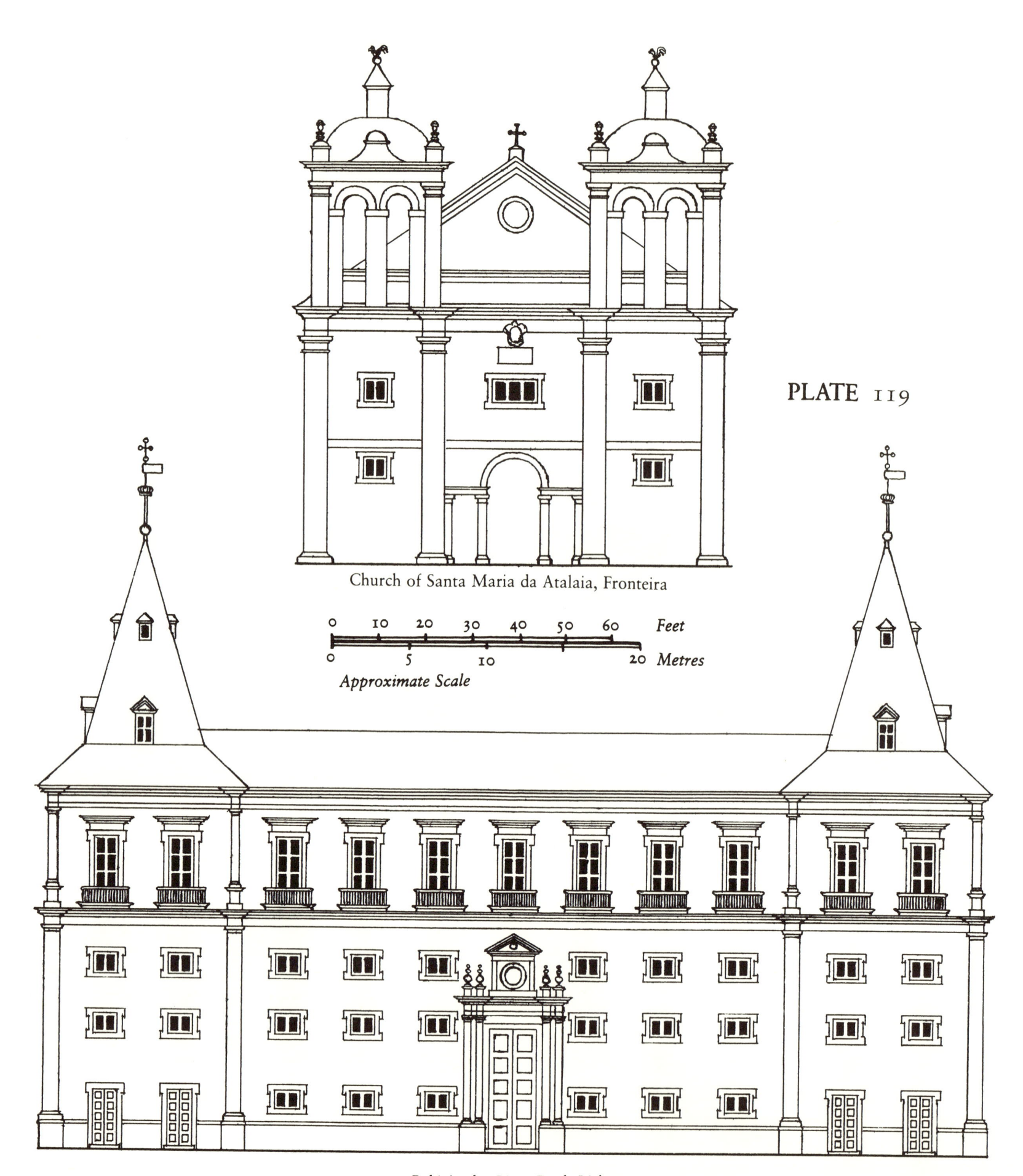

PLATE 119

Palácio do Côrte Real, Lisbon

The portion nearest to the water was the first part built. This was a square tower, five bays on a side. The walls of the bottom two storeys had quoins at the corners and sloped as if they were part of a fortification. Above that were two tall storeys whose windows had shouldered architraves and alternating triangular and segmental pediments on brackets. The bays were separated by Tuscan and Ionic pilasters, doubled at the ends. Above the entablature was a balustrade that was projected out from the plane of the building, hiding the base of a large octagonal dome that terminated in a cupola. At each corner of the roof stood a cupola or turret.

Church of São Vicente da Fora, Lisbon
PLATE 120

The most impressive church in Lisbon is São Vicente da Fora, built by Terzi, with some help from Baltasar Alvares, in 1582–1629. Like so many other Portuguese churches, it has twin towers and an arcaded loggia in the screen-wall between the towers, but in its details and proportions it is much more sophisticated. The lower part of the front is divided by giant Doric pilasters, which are doubled on the fronts of the towers. Above them are pilasters minus their capitals, leading to the main entablature with its balustrade. Pilaster-strips trim the bell-stage of the towers, which have a single arched opening for the bells. Above the entablature of the towers is another balustrade with finials in front of an octagonal dome with cupola. The principal windows of the front are enclosed in aedicules, and, like the seven niches also on the front, are capped with alternating triangular and segmental pediments. Like Herrera's churches, the interior is but sparsely ornamented. The nave ceiling is a panelled barrel-vault, standing on a massive Doric entablature. Under the entablature are pairs of giant pilasters of an order invented by Terzi. Between the pairs of pilasters are three large arches leading to the aisles, which are used as side-chapels. After the transepts (contained within the rectangular outline of the building), there comes a square chancel with no aisles. The exterior of the building extends with no change in appearance for some distance behind the high altar in order to enclose a variety of rooms. The original front steps, once arranged as a stepped pyramid, have since been made smaller, perhaps in order to accommodate modern traffic patterns.

Palácio do Côrte Real, Lisbon PLATE 119

Not far along the river bank from the Torreão Palace, Terzi was hired to design another royal palace in 1585, known as the Palácio do Côrte Real. This was vaguely reminiscent of de Vega's El Pardo Palace in Madrid. It had corner-towers with tall, pyramidal roofs on top. The large main doorway floated in a sea of three storeys of small windows. Above the first entablature was the piano nobile, which also happened to be the top floor below the hipped roof. The large windows here had individual cornice-strips above a shouldered architrave, and each window had its own private balcony. Tuscan pilasters were applied only to the corners of the towers, with giant pilasters for the lower three storeys and small pilasters on bases for the piano nobile. This palace, like the Torreão, has long since been destroyed.

Thus ends an interpretation of the story of the emergence and growth of classical architecture on the Iberian peninsula. It could be argued that the coverage should have been extended to include Spanish and Portuguese possessions overseas, such as the Atlantic Islands of the Azores, the Madeiras and the Canaries, and Latin America, but these areas will be covered in projected future books.

For further reading, see George Kubler & Martin Soria, *Art and Architecture in Spain and Portugal and their American Dominions 1500–1800*, Harmondsworth, Penguin Books, 1959.

Arthur Byne & Mildred Stapley, *Spanish Architecture of the Sixteenth Century*, New York, G. P. Putnam's Sons, 1917.

Fernando Chueca-Goitia, *Arquitectura del Siglo XVI*, Madrid, Editorial Plus-Ultra, 1953.

Francisco Iñiguez Almech, *Casas Reales y Jardines de Felipe II*, Madrid, Consejo Superior de Investigaciones Cientificas, 1952.

George Kubler, *Portuguese Plain Architecture*, Middletown, CT, Wesleyan University Press, 1972.

PLATE 120

Torreão Royal Palace, Lisbon

Church of São Vicente da Fora, Lisbon

A SELECTED BIBLIOGRAPHY OF SECONDARY SOURCES

ACKERMAN, James, *The Architecture of Michelangelo* (second edition), Cambridge, MA, MIT Press, 1985.

———, *Palladio*, Harmondsworth, Penguin Books, 1966.

ALMECH, Francisco Iñiguez, *Casas Reales y Jardines de Felipe II*, Madrid, Consejo Superior de Investigaciones Cientificas, 1952.

BECKETT, Francis, *Renaissancen og Kunstens Historie i Danmark*, Copenhagen, 1897.

———, *Uraniborg og Stjaerneborg*, Copenhagen, 1921.

BIAŁOSTOCKI, Jan, *The Art of the Renaissance in Eastern Europe*, Ithaca, NY, Cornell University Press, 1976.

BLOMFIELD, Reginald, *A History of French Architecture from the reign of Charles VIII till the death of Mazarin, 1494–1661*, 2 vols., London, 1911.

BLUNT, Anthony, *Art and Architecture in France 1500–1700*, Harmondsworth, Penguin Books, 1953 (rev. 1970).

———, *Baroque and Rococo*, New York, Harper & Row, 1978.

———, *Philibert de l'Orme*, London, Zwemmer, 1958.

BORSI, Stefano, *Giuliano da Sangallo: i disegni di architettura e dell antico*, Rome, Officina, 1985.

BOUDON, Françoise & BLÉCON, Jean, *Philibert Delorme et le château royal de Saint-Léger-en-Yvelines*, Paris, Picard, 1985.

BRISSAC, Philippe de Cossé, *Châteaux de France Disparus*, Paris, Éditions Tel, 1947.

BRUSCHI, Arnaldo, *Bramante Architetto*, Rome, ed. Lateran, 1969, republished, with alterations, in English as *Bramante*, New York, Thames & Hudson, 1977.

BYNE, Arthur and STAPLEY, Mildred, *Spanish Architecture of the Sixteenth Century*, New York, G. P. Putnam's Sons, 1917.

CABLE, Mary, *El Escorial*, New York, Newsweek Books, 1971.

CHUECA-GOITIA, Fernando, *Arquitectura del Siglo XVI*, Madrid, Editorial Plus-Ultra, 1953.

COLVIN, Howard and HARRIS, John, (ed.), *The Country Seat*, London, 1970.

ĆURČIĆ, Slobodan, *Art and Architecture in the Balkans*, Boston, G. K. Hall, 1984.

DIMIER, Louis, *Le Primatice*, Paris, 1928.

FANELLI, Giovanni, *Brunelleschi*, Florence, Becocai, 1977.

FRANKEN, Daniel, *L'Oeuvre Gravé des Van de Passe*, Amsterdam, 1881.

FROMMEL, Christoph L., *Raffaello Architetto*, Milan, Electa, 1984.

FUSCO, Renato de, *L'Architettura del Cinquecento*, Turin, UTET, 1981.

GANAY, Ernest de, *Châteaux de France*, many volumes, Paris, Éditions Tel, 1948ff.

GEBELIN, François, *Les Châteux de la Renaissance*, Paris, Les Beaux Arts, 1927.

GERSON, H. and ter KUILE, E. H., *Art and Architecture in Belgium 1600–1800*, Harmondsworth, Penguin Books, 1960.

GIROUARD, Mark, *Robert Smythson & the Elizabethan Country House*, New Haven, Yale University Press, 1983.

GOTCH, J. S., *Early Renaissance Architecture in England*, London, 1914 (second edition).

HAMILTON, George Heard, *The Art and Architecture of Russia*, Harmondsworth, Penguin Books, 1954 (rev. 1975).

HARTT, Frederick, *Giulio Romano*, Northford, CT, Elliots Books, 1958.

HAUTECOEUR, Louis, *Histoire de l'Architecture Classique en France*, vol. I, Paris, Picard, 1963.

HEDICKE, *Cornelis Floris*, Berlin, 1913.

HEMPEL, Eberhard, *Baroque Art and Architecture in Central Europe*, Harmondsworth, Penguin Books, 1965.

HEYDENREICH, Ludwig and LOTZ, Wolfgang, *Architecture in Italy 1400–1600*, Harmondsworth, Penguin Books, 1974.

HITCHCOCK, Henry-Russell, *German Renaissance Architecture*, Princeton, Princeton University Press, 1981.

———, *Netherlandish Scrolled Gables of the Sixteenth and Early Seventeenth Centuries*, New York, New York University Press, 1978.

HOŘEJŠÍ, Jirina, KRCÁLOVÁ, Jarmila, NEUMANN, Jaromír, POCHE, Emanuel & VACKACKOVÁ, Jarmila, *Renaissance Art in Bohemia*, London, Hamlyn, 1979.

HUGHES, Quentin, *The Building of Malta*, London, 1956.

JOLÁN, Balogh, *Az Erdélyi Renaissance*, Prague, Kolozvár, 1943.

KNOX, Brian, *The Architecture of Poland*, New York, Praeger, 1971.

KOZAKIEWICZ, H. & S., *The Renaissance in Poland*, Warsaw, 1976.

KUBLER, George, *Building the Escorial*, Princeton, Princeton University Press, 1982.

———, *Portuguese Plain Architecture*, Middletown, CT, Wesleyan University Press, 1972.

——— and SORIA, Martin, *Art and Architecture in Spain and Portugal and their American Dominions 1500–1800*, Harmondsworth, Penguin Books, 1959.

LIEB, Norbert, *Die Fugger und die Kunst*, Munich, Verlag Schnell & Steiner, 1952.

LOTZ, Wolfgang, *Studies in Italian Renaissance Architecture*, Cambridge, MA, MIT Press, 1977.

McANDREW, John, *Venetian Architecture of the Early Renaissance*, Cambridge, MA, MIT Press, 1980.

MURRAY, Linda, *Michaelangelo, His Life, Work and Times*, New York, Thames & Hudson, 1984.

MURRAY, Peter, *Renaissance Architecture*, New York, Harry Abrams, 1971.

NASIBOVA, Aida, *The Faceted Chamber in the Moscow Kremlin*, Leningrad, Art Publishers, 1978.

PEDRETTI, Carlo, *Leonardo Architect*, New York, Thames & Hudson, 1985.

———, *Leonardo da Vinci, the Royal Palace at Romorantin*, Cambridge, MA, Harvard/Belknap Press, 1972.

PORTOGHESI, Paolo, *Rome of the Renaissance*, New York, Phaidon, 1972.

PROKOP, August, *Die Markgravschaft Mähren in Kunstgeschilichtlicher Beziehung*, Vienna, 1904.

ROSENBERG, Jakob, SLIVE, Seymour and ter KUILE, E. H., *Dutch Art and Architecture 1600–1800*, Harmondsworth, Penguin Books, 1966 (rev. 1977).

ROSENFELD, Myra Nan, *Sebastiano Serlio on Domestic Architecture*, Cambridge, MA, MIT Press, 1978.

ROSENTHAL, Earl, *The Palace of Charles V in Granada*, Princeton, Princeton University Press, 1985.

RÓZSA, Feuerné Tóth, *Reneszánsz Épitészet Magyar-Országon*, Budapest, Magyar Helikon/Corvina, 1977.

SAINT-JOURS, M., *Cordouan*, Bordeaux, ca. 1900.

SAMÁNKOVÁ, Eva, *Architektura České Renesance*, Prague, 1961.

SARDUCCI, Guido, *A Few Columns from a Herm to a Caryatid: Why Cantilever Alone?*, Newport, RI, Gibson & Gibson, 1986.

SKOVGAARD, Joakim, *A King's Architecture*, London, Hugh Evelyn, 1973.

SLOTHOUWER, D. F., *Bouwkunst der Nederlandshe Renaissance in Danemarken*, Amsterdam, 1924.

STRONG, Roy, *The Renaissance Garden in England*, New York, Thames & Hudson, 1979.

SUMMERSON, Sir John, *Architecture in Britain 1530–1830*, Harmondsworth, Penguin Books, 1953 (rev. 1963).

———, *The Classical Language of Architecture*, Cambridge, MA, MIT Press, 1963.

TAFURI, Manfredo, *Architecture et Humanisme* (originally *Architettura dell' Umanesimo*), Paris, Dunod, 1981.

WARD, John, *Lives of the Professors of Gresham College*, London, 1740.

WITTKOWER, Rudolf, *Palladio and English Palladianism*, New York, Thames & Hudson, 1983.

APPENDIX

BIOGRAPHICAL INFORMATION ABOUT ARCHITECTS AND BUILDERS

AELST, PIETER COECKE VAN
see under COECKE.

ALAVA, JUAN DE   ca. 1465–1537.
Worked in Spain, rebuilding the Cathedral at Plasencia from 1497 onwards. His best-known work is the mannerist church of San Estéban, Salamanca with its giant carved shells (not shown in this book).

ALBERTI, LEON BATTISTA   1404–1472.
Born in Genoa in an exiled Florentine family. He studied ancient monuments in Rome 1432 and 1433. He wrote several books on art and architecture, of which the most important is the ten-volume set *De Re Aedificatoria* begun in 1452. He designed a number of unclassical buildings interspersed among his classical designs; the best of the latter are the Palazzo Rucellai, Florence, 1446; the Tempio Malatestiano, Rimini, 1446; the Benediction Loggia at the Vatican, ca. 1460; and the churches of San Sebastiano (ca. 1460) and Sant'Andrea (ca. 1470), both in Mantua. He died in Rome.

ALESSI, GALEAZZO   1512–1572.
Born in Perugia and taught by Antonio da San Gallo II and Baldassare Peruzzi. He is credited with reviving the Lombard style that had previously been eclipsed by Bramante and his followers. He worked in Genoa, where he built the Villa Cambiaso, 1548; the church of Santa Maria in Carignano, 1552; and the Palazzo Sauli, ca. 1555. He also worked in Milan before returning to Perugia shortly before his death.

ALEVISIO or ALOISIO (LAMBERTI DA
   MONTAGNANA)   fl. ca. 1500.
One of many Italians working in Moscow at the end of the fifteenth century and beginning of the sixteenth. He is sometimes known as Novyi, to distinguish him from an earlier Alevisio da Carcano in Moscow. He designed the Cathedral of Saint Michael Archangel in the Kremlin, known for its large and prominent carved shells.

ALLIO, DOMENICO DELL'   ?–1563.
An Italian who designed the Landhaus at Graz, Austria from 1557 onwards.

ALVARES, AFONSO   fl. 1569–1580.
The architect of the church of Santa Catarina dos Livreiros in Lisbon, Portugal in 1572; he may also have had a hand in the design of the Jesuit church of São Roque in Lisbon, 1567–1586.

AMATRICE, NICOLA DI FILOTESIO DALL'
fl. 1525.
A minor architect, who designed the church of San Bernardino at L'Aquila in Abruzzi in 1525.

ANDRESSEN, JAN   fl. 1581.
Worked in Groningen, the Netherlands, and Hamburg, Germany; he built the Exchange or Börse at Hamburg starting in 1577, and was described as being a resident of Amsterdam.

ANDROUET DUCERCEAU, JACQUES—
see under DUCERCEAU.

ANGLÉS, JUAN   15??–1593.
It is not known whether Anglés was the family name or whether it should be taken to mean that he was John, an Englishman resident in Spain. He is known to have designed the handsome entrance to the Convent of Santo Domingo at Oriheula, 1568, and various other works are attributed to him, such as the Colegio de San Matías (since renamed San Luis) at Tortosa beginning in 1544, and the entrance of the parish church at Vistabella, Castellon, ca. 1550.

AVOSTALIS DE SOLA (AOSTALLI),
   ULRICO   15??–1597.
Born near Lugano, Switzerland, died Czechoslovakia. Apprenticed to both Bonifaz Wohlmut and GIAN BATTISTA AVOSTALIS DE SOLA, he worked as mason on many prominent Czech buildings, such as the upper part of the Belvedere, Prague. He also worked with another relation, GIOVANNI BATTISTA MARIA AVOSTALIS DE SOLA, who died in 1575. He was appointed Imperial Architect in 1575, just as he finished building parts of the Castle at Litomyšl. Although he is known to have worked on many Czech buildings, the extent of his work is still unknown.

ARRUDA, MIGUEL DE   ?–1563.
To him is attributed the Palace Chapel, Salvaterra de Magos, near Santarém, Portugal, 1555.

BACHELIER, NICOLAS   ?–1556.
Born in Arras in northeastern France, he did most of his work in and around Toulouse in southwestern France. His best-known work is the Hôtel d'Assézat, Toulouse, 1552.

BARBONA, PIETRO CRASSOWSKI DI ?–1588.
An Italian whose Italian name may have been Grassi, who worked in Lvóv, Russia (then part of Poland); there he built the Anczowski House on the market Place in 1577, and may have built the so-called Italian building and the Benedictine Church (1578). He also built the later Wallachian Church Tower.

BAUTISTA, JUAN—see under TOLEDO

BEAUGRANT, GUYOT DE ?–1551.
A resident of Mechelin/Malines, Belgium, who worked in conjunction with Rombout Keldermans II on the Savoie Palace there, 1517–1526.

BERECCI, BARTOLOMEO fl. 1516–1537.
A Florentine who worked in Krakow, Poland. In company with Francesco Fiorentino he built the arcaded courtyard of the Wawel Castle (1507–1536) and by himself he built two chapels at the Cathedral, one in memory of Sigismund (1517–1533), and one for Bishop Tomicki (ca. 1530).

BERNABEI DA CORTONA, DOMENICO "BOCCADOR."—see under CORTONA.

BISENO, LEONARDO GAROVI DA—see under GAROVI.

BOCCADOR—see under CORTONA.

BONO, MARCO fl. 1532–1542.
Probably Venetian, for a large family of that name worked as builders in Venice, he came to Moscow to build the Ivan Veliki Bell Tower in the Kremlin, 1532–1542.

BRAMANTE, DONATO ca. 1444–1514.
Born near Urbino, considered one of the greatest architects of the Renaissance. Very little is known of his life even though his contemporaries and successors held him in high esteem. He was a poet and painter as well as an architect. His earliest works were in the Milan area, but by 1500 he had moved to Rome. He was the first to work on the plans for the new Saint Peter's Cathedral in Rome although his plans were considerably altered by others as construction slowly progressed—fortunately, because Bramante was unable to conceive of such a massive building other than in terms of the much smaller scale of design used hitherto in the Renaissance. Fifteen other buildings are covered in this book.

BROSSE, JEAN DE 15??–1584.
A Protestant French architect who married the daughter of Jacques Androuet Ducerceau. Their son Salomon became one of the major French architects of the seventeenth century. His most important work was the Château de Verneuil, Oise, ca. 1570.

BRUNELLESCHI, FILIPPO 1377–1446.
Born and died in Florence, the first classical architect of the Renaissance. A sculptor, he went many times to Rome to study ancient sculpture and in due course absorbed many aspects of ancient classical architecture. He was hired as an engineer to execute the dome on the Cathedral in Florence (whose general appearance had been set down on paper for years, but owing to its enormous span no builder had dared to attempt its execution). While engaged in this project he began to design other buildings in Florence, the first of which was the Ospedale degli Innocenti (Foundling Hospital), begun in 1419. The same year he was asked to build a sacristy for the church of San Lorenzo and then to build a new church of San Lorenzo. Shortly after, he was hired to build the Palazzo di Parte Guelfa, which was never finished. He built the Pazzi Chapel in 1430, the large church of Santo Spirito beginning in 1434, and the small church of Santa Maria degli Angeli (never completed) that same year. Brunelleschi had relatively little historical information available to him, so he accepted inspiration from such Romanesque structures as the church of San Miniato and the Cathedral Baptistery in the belief that they had been built almost 1000 years earlier than they had, but his instinct for classical design was nevertheless remarkable.

BULLANT, JEAN II ca. 1510/1520–1578.
Born at Amiens and died at Écouen, just north of Paris. He went to study in Rome about 1545. He wrote many books, of which the most important was *Reigle Générale d'Architecture des Cinq Manières de Colonnes*, 1564. From 1556 onwards he made classical additions to the late-gothic castle at Écouen. About 1570, he built a pavillion into Delorme's unfinished scheme of the Tuileries Palace in Paris, but it too was never completed. At the same time, he assisted Lescot with the work at the Valois Mausoleum at Saint-Denis that had remained unfinished at the death of Primaticcio.

BUONARROTI, MICHELANGELO—see under MICHELANGELO

BUSTAMENTE, BARTHOLOMÉ 1492–1570.
His chief work was the Tavera/Afuera Hospital of San Juan Bautista at Toledo, Spain (1541–1579) with its lovely arcaded courtyards.

BÜTTNER, CONRAD fl. 1570.
To him is attributed work at Schloss Isenburg from 1570 onwards.

CARLONE, MICHELE fl. 1490–1519.
A member of a large family of builders in the Genoa area, he worked at one time for Raphael. He and other members of his family came to install an arcaded courtyard inside the Castle of Lacalahorra, near Granada, Spain, 1508–1512.

CASSAR, GEROLAMO 1520–1586.
Born and died in Malta. He was a student of the Maltese engineer Evangelista della Menga and the Italian engineer Francesco Laparelli, and was given the most important commissions when the new city of Valletta was built. Most of his buildings have been destroyed or unrecognizably altered, but the Auberge d'Italie at Valletta (1574) although altered still reveals its original design.

CASTILHO, JOÃO DE fl. ca. 1540.
Born near Santander in northern Spain, he studied in Naples and later worked in Portugal. To him is attributed the Conceião Chapel at Tomar, ca. 1540.

CERCEAU, JACQUES ANDROUET DU—
see under DUCERCEAU.

CODUCCI, MAURO   ca. 1440–1504.
Born at Lentina, near Bergamo, and died at Venice, where he worked most of his life. He apparently worked at various times with Luciano Laurana and Giorgio Orsini da Sebenico, and may have spent time in the Italian colonies along the coast of Yugoslavia. Much of his work appears mannerist, but two classical works stand out, the church of San Michele in Isola, Venice, 1468, from the beginning of his career, and the Palazzo Loredan-Vendramin-Callergi in Venice, 1502, from the end of his career.

COECKE, PIETER VAN AELST   1502–1550.
Born at Aelst and died at Brussels. He collaborated with Floris and Vredeman in making triumphal arches and street scenery for the imperial visit to Antwerp in 1549; some of these are illustrated in his book *Le Triumphe d'Anvers,* 1550. He travelled widely, including to Constantinople.

COLIN, ALEXANDER   ca. 1527/9–1612.
Born Mechelin/Malines, Belgium and died Innsbruck, Austria. His chief work is said to be the Ottheinrichsbau at the Castle at Heidelberg, Germany, 1556.

CORBET, ROBERT   ?–1583.
An English diplomat who visited Italy, France and the Low Countries and thus had first-hand knowledge of classical architecture. He built, probably to his own designs, a new part of Moreton Corbet Castle, Shropshire. This remained unfinished at his death, was later altered and then pillaged so that it is presently in ruins.

CORTONA, DOMENICO "BOCCADOR"
BERNABEI DA   ca. 1470–1549.
Born at Cortona, he was a student of Giuliano da San Gallo. He first came to France in 1495. His two principal works there were designs (altered by others before execution) for the palace at Chambord, starting in 1519, and the Hôtel de Ville or Town Hall in Paris, begun in 1529; the latter was destroyed in 1871, but has been rebuilt in enlarged form.

COUR, JOIST DE LA   fl. 1560.
A French sculptor, trained by Jean Martin (who had translated Vitruvius into French) and possibly also by Jean Goujon. He could have worked at the Castle, Hovestadt, with Laurenz von Brachum, ca. 1563 and he is known to have worked at the Castle, Horst, with von Brachum and Arndt Johanssen in the 1560s. It is thought that he was responsible for the part of the castle shown in this book. He also worked with the Vernukkens.

COVARRUBIAS, ALONSO DE   1488–1570.
He designed the Palace of the Archbishop at Alcalá de Henares, Spain in 1534, and may have designed the Real Alcázar at Toledo, ca. 1537 onwards. He is also thought to have had a connection with the Colegio at Salamanca, built 1532 onwards. He was son-in-law to Egas.

CRASSOWSKI, PIETRO DI BARBONA—
see under BARBONA.

DALMATINAC, JURAJ—see under ORSINI

DELORME, PHILIBERT   ca. 1505/1510–1570.
Born at Lyon and died in Paris, France's first native-born architect to understand fully the classical forms of the Renaissance. He visited Rome 1533–1536 and published two books, of which the more important was *Le Premier Tôme de l'Architecture,* 1567. Ten of his best buildings are shown in the present book, of which the earliest was the Château of Saint-Maur-les-Fossés, just east of Paris in 1540. He fell out of royal favor in 1559, but was restored in 1563.

DIETTERLIN, WENDEL
(WENDLING GRAPP)   1550–1599.
Born at Pullendorf near Lake Constance, but lived most of his life at Strasbourg (then a German city, but now French). He was primarily a painter, but he is best known for his book *Architectura* that first began to appear in 1593 and was surprisingly popular. His illustrations in the book were mostly based on strapwork and fantasy, and were widely influential, although classical ideas occasionally shone through, as witness the design selected for this book.

DOMENICO DA CORTONA—
see under CORTONA.

DUCA, GIACOMO "JACOPO
SICILIANO" DEL   ca. 1520–1604.
Born Cefalù, Sicily. He became an assistant to Michelangelo and worked chiefly in Rome, where he designed the church of Santa Maria in Trivio, 1578.

DUCERCEAU, BAPTISTE ANDROUET
ca. 1540–1590.
The most talented son of Jacques I, he worked with his father. He designed on his own the Hôtel d'Angoulême or Lamoignon in Paris, 1584.

DUCERCEAU, JACQUES ANDROUET I
ca. 1515–1585.
A French Protestant who visited Italy in the 1530s, he was the head of a large family of architects and builders. He wrote many books, of which the most important is *Les Plus Excellents Bastiments de France,* 1576–1579. He built the royal Château de Charleval starting in 1570, but it remained unfinished after the king's death in 1574.

EGAS, ENRIQUE DE   ca. 1455–1534.
A Spanish architect of primarily late-gothic buildings. He occasionally flirted with the classical idiom, as witness the courtyards at the three royal hospitals at Santiago de Compostela (1501–1511), Toledo (1504–1514) and at Granada (1504ff). He was retained to design the Cathedral at Granada, but was dismissed in favor of Siloé when he had accomplished little more than placing the outer limits to the foundation.

FALCONETTO, GIOVANNI MARIA   1468–1535.
Born at Verona, died at Padua, where he had done most of his work. A follower of Bramante, he was instrumental in introducing the classical Roman style to parts of northern Italy. He built the Loggia Cornaro at Padua in 1524.

FERRABOSCO, PIETRO   ca. 1512/1513–ca. 1588.
Born at Como, Italy, he worked in Austria and Czechoslovakia. He is thought to have designed the Schweizerhof in Vienna in 1552, and he was the architect of both the Stallburg (1559ff) and the Amalienburg (1575ff) both in Vienna. In partnership with P. Gabri, he worked at the Castle, Bučovice, Czechoslovakia between 1567 and 1582.

FERRUCCI, ANDREA DI PIERO   1465–1526.
Born at Fiesole, near Florence, a member of a large family of builders there. He worked in Tuscany, Naples, possibly Rome and Hungary, where he designed the Bishop Bakócz Chapel at Estergom Cathedral at Gran in 1506.

FILARETE, ANTONIO AVERLINO
   ca. 1400–ca. 1470.
Born in Florence and worked as a sculptor in Rome. He worked for the Duke Sforza of Milan from 1447 onwards and later for the Medici family. He proposed to build an ideal city for Sforza, to be called Sforzinda, but nothing came of it beyond an influential treatise. He built the Ospedale Maggiore in Milan, 1456–1465, at the same time as he was writing 25 books called *Trattato di Architettura*.

FILOTESIO, NICOLA DI—see under AMATRICE.

FIORAVANTI, RIDOLFO
   "ARISTOTELE"   ?1415–?1486.
A celebrated Italian engineer, who worked in Milan, Bologna, Venice, Rome, Naples, Hungary and Moscow. In Moscow, he designed the Cathedral of the Dormition (Assumption) in the Kremlin (1475–1479) in the traditional Suzdal style that owed nothing to classical Renaissance ideas and is thus not shown in this book. However, he was among the first trained in the classical Italian style to work in Russia.

FIORENTINO, DOMENICO   fl. 1546.
A Florentine who worked in France. He designed the handsome Château Joinville, Haut-Marne in 1546.

FIORENTINO, FRANCESCO   14??–1516.
A Florentine who worked in Poland. He designed the Wawel Castle at Krakow.

FIORENTINO, NICCOLO   fl. 1445–1475.
A Florentine of the school of Filarete. He worked with Paolo Romano in Yugoslavia, where he built additions to the Cathedral at Trogir.

FLORIS DE VRIENDT, CORNELIS II   1514–1575.
Born at Antwerp he studied sculpture in Rome. He was a highly-regarded sculptor with commissions as far afield as Scandinavia and what is now Kaliningrad, USSR. He occasionally dabbled in architecture, as in providing the design for his brother's house in Antwerp (1563), but for major commissions on which he was consulted he apparently turned over actual design work to Hendrik van Paesschen, as in the cases of the Antwerp Raadhuis (1561) and the Hanseatenhuis there (1564).

FOIX, LOUIS DE   1535–1606.
Born in Paris. He provided the design and engineering for the remarkable Tour de Cordouan (1583ff), a much-needed lighthouse near Bordeaux. He had previously been an engineer at the Escorial in Spain as well as in France, and had taken part in the design competition for the Antwerp Raadhuis in 1561.

FRANCESCO DI GIORGIO MARTINI—
   see under GIORGIO MARTINI.

FRIASIN (Russian word for "Italian")—
   see under other name.

FRIES, HANS VREDEMAN DE—
   see under VREDEMAN DE FRIES.

GABRI, PIETRO   fl. 1567–1582.
An Italian who worked in Czechoslovakia. He worked, probably more as builder than designer, with Ferrabosco at Bučovice Castle, 1567ff.

GAÍNSA, MARTÍN   ?–1555.
Worked at the Hospital de la Sangre, Seville from 1546 onwards.

GALLI, AGOSTINO   fl. 1560.
Brought perhaps by Giovanni di Statio to Czechoslovakia from Massagno, near Lugano, he designed the Lobkovic-Švarcenberk Palace in Prague for John of Lobkovice.

GARDA, LEONARDO—
   see under GAROVI DA BISENO.

GAROVI DA BISENO, LEONARDO   fl. 1557–1578.
A member of a large Italian family of builders from Biseno. He is thought to have worked on the castles at Moravský Krumlov, Rosĭce and Náměšt'nad Oslavou in Czechoslovakia.

GENGA, GIROLAMO   1476–1551.
Born and died at Urbino, where he would have learned from Luciano Laurana and Francesco di Giorgio. He spent his whole working life building for the delle Rovere dukes, for whom he built the Villa Imperiale at Pesaro about 1530. He is thought to have taught the Portuguese architect Diogo da Torralva.

GIL DE HONTAÑON, RODRIGO
   ca. 1500–1577.
He designed the University Building at Alcalá de Henares, the Palace of Monterrey in Salamanca and the University Building at Oñate, Spain, and may have had something to do with the College at Salamanca.

GIORGIO MARTINI, FRANCESCO DI
   1439–1501.
Born and died at Siena. Trained as an engineer and artist, he moved to Urbino where he worked at the Palazzo Ducale. He wrote treatises on architecture and designed the church of Santa Maria delle Grazie al Calcinaio at Cortona in 1484. He is best known for his fortifications.

GIROLAMO TEDESCO—
   see under HIERONYMUS.

GIULIO ROMANO—see under ROMANO.

GOMES, PERO   fl. 1540–1560.
The builder of the church of Santa Maria do Castelo at Estremoz, Portugal in 1559.

GOUJON, JEAN   ca. 1510–ca. 1568.
Primarily a sculptor, he worked in France in partnership with Delorme and Lescot.

HAVEUS, THEODORE DE   ?–1573.
A resident of Cleves in northwest Germany, whose real name was probably HAVE. He came to England to design various buildings at Gonville & Caius College, Cambridge, of which the best is the Gate of Honour, 1572.

HERENGRAVE, HERMAN DE   fl. 1544–1569.
A builder at Nijmegen, the Netherlands, where he built the Raadhuis beginning in 1554.

HERRERA, JUAN DE   1530–1597.
Born in Santander and died in Madrid. A member of the nobility, he travelled to Italy, Germany and the Low Countries and entered the service of Philip II. Philip gave him certain supervisory duties at the Escorial where he became the chief architect upon the death of Juan Bautista de Toledo in 1567. He also designed the Palace of Aranjuez (1581ff), the Casa Lonja or Bourse at Seville (1572ff) and the unfinished Cathedral at Valladolid (1580ff) as well as various lesser buildings.

HIERONYMUS (called GIROLAMO TEDESCO in Italy)   fl. 1505.
A German who designed a building to be erected in Italy—the reverse of the usual pattern! He built the Fondaco dei Tedeschi or German Merchants' Palace in Venice in 1505. Little else is known of him.

HONTAÑON, RODRIGO GIL DE—
see under GIL DE HONTAÑON.

IBARRA, PEDRO I   fl. 1521–1539, and
PEDRO II   15??–1570.
A Spanish father-and-son team, believed to have worked at the College at Salamanca.

KELDERMANS, ROMBOUT II   ca. 1450–1531.
A Flemish builder who worked in Brussels, Gent and elsewhere. With Dominic de Waghemakere he built the influential Bourse at Antwerp in the gothic style, and with Guyot de Beaugrant he built parts of the Savoie Palace at Mechelin/Malines in 1517ff.

KIRBY, RICHARD   15??–1600.
He worked with the owner, Sir Thomas Smith, to build parts of Hill Hall, Theydon Mount, Essex, England in about 1568.

KNOTZ, HANS   fl. 1527–1538.
He worked at the German castle of Neuberg on the Danube.

KRAMER, BASTIAN   fl. 1560, and
JOHANN/HANS   15??–1577.
A German father-and-son team of builders. They executed designs in Gdánsk, Poland for Regnier, and the son worked at the Residenz Schloss at Dresden.

LAMBERTO SUAVIUS OF LOMBARDY—
see under SUSTRIS, LAMBERTO.

LAURANA, LUCIANO   ca. 1420/5–1479.
Born in Zara, Yugoslavia, died in Pesaro, Italy. His major work is parts of the Palazzo Ducale at Urbino, 1466ff.

LEBRETON, GILLES   ?1500–1553.
A mason who worked most of his life at the Palace at Fontainebleau. His chapel at Fontainebleau is a gem (1540–1550) although it may have been designed by another. He drastically altered Serlio's design for the Ballroom wing with unfortunate results. He worked until 1527 at Chambord with his father, and at Fleury with Lescot, just before his death.

LEONARDO DA VINCI   1452–1519.
A painter, sculptor and engineer born at Vinci, between Florence and Pisa, and died in France. He occasionally turned his hand to architecture. This book shows 11 of his designs in Italy and one in France. In 1506 he moved to France to serve Louis XII and later François I. Relatively few of his designs were actually built.

LESCOT, PIERRE   ca. 1510/5–1578.
Born in Paris of a noble family and died in Paris. He worked frequently in conjunction with the sculptor Goujon. He designed part of the Hôtel de Ligneris (now called Carnavalet) in Paris, ca. 1544; the southwest wing of the Cour Carrée at the Louvre, 1546ff; the Fountain of the Innocents, Paris, 1547; the Château of Fleury-en-Bière, Seine et Marne, ca. 1550, and the Château Vallery, Yonne, ca. 1550.

LOPES, JOÃO   fl. 1576–1583.
He worked with Jerónimo Luis at the Convent of Santa Maria da Serra do Pilar, Vila Nova de Gaia, Portugal.

LOSCHER, SEBASTIAN   ca. 1475–1548.
An early builder in Augsburg, south Germany. His career remains mostly unknown, but to him are attributed at least three works: the Fugger Chapel at the church of Saint Anna, 1509; the Damenhof at 36 Maximilienstrasse, 1512; and the church of Saint Katherine, 1516, all at Augsburg.

LUCCHESE, GIOVANNI   15??–1581.
Born at Lucca, Italy and died at Innsbruck, Austria. He worked in Czechoslovakia, particularly at Hvěsda Castle, near Prague, 1555.

LUIS, JERÓNIMO   fl. 1576–1583.
He worked with João Lopes at the Convent of Santa Maria da Serra do Pilar, Vila Nova de Gaia, Portugal.

LURAGO, ROCCO   1501–1590.
Born near Como and died at Genoa. A lesser architect building palaces in Genoa in the shadow of Alessi, he designed what is now the Palazzo Municipale for Nicolò Grimaldi in 1564.

MACHUCA, PEDRO   ?1485–1550, and
LUIS   fl. 1550.
A Spanish father-and-son team, based probably in Toledo. Pedro studied in Florence under Giuliano da San Gallo and was primarily a painter. However, he was hired by Charles V to build the palace at Granada starting in 1526. Luis took over the project after his father's death.

MAGENA, ONORATO   fl. 1538.
The builder of Cardinal Granvelle's Palace at Besançon.

MAGGI, BALDASSARE   fl. 1560–1589.
An Italian who worked in Czechoslovakia at such

castles as Jindřichův Hradec (ca. 1580), Kratochvíle (1582ff) and probably Telč (ca. 1560ff).

MAIANO, GIULIANO DA 1432–1490.
Born in Florence, brother of Benedetto, who was also an architect. He carved the portico of Brunelleschi's Pazzi Chapel. He designed the Medici villa or Palace of Poggio Reale in Naples for Prince Alfonso (1476–1485) which made a great impression on Serlio.

MANTOVANI, SIGISMONDO, ANTONIO and BERNARDO fl. 1536.
A family of builders from Mantua who had perhaps worked for Giulio Romano. They built the Residenz at Landshut, southern Germany.

MARTINI, FRANCESCO DI GIORGIO— see under GIORGIO MARTINI.

MASACCIO, TOMMASO GUIDI 1401–1428.
The first major Florentine painter of the Renaissance. Masaccio, incidentally, was his nickname, meaning "shiftless."

MAYNARD, ALAIN fl. 1560–1585.
A Frenchman working in England. He worked with Sir John Thynne and Robert Smythson at such country houses as Sherborne, Gloucestershire and Longleat, Wiltshire and he probably designed Chalcot House in Wiltshire. What relation he may have been to John Maynard who was given the title of King's Painter to Henry VII in 1505 is unknown.

MEDIOLANO, KILIANO SYROTH DE fl. 1564.
An Italian who worked in Hungary. He built the Turzo Castle at Nagybiccse.

MEER, GERHARDT VAN DER fl. 1567–1573.
To him is attributed the chapel of the Castle at Augustusburg, East Germany.

MICHAŁOWICZ of URZĘDÓW, JAN fl. 1570.
The builder of the Padniewski/Potocki Chapel at the Cathedral, Krakow, Poland, and a sculptor of note.

MICHELANGELO BUONARROTI 1475–1564.
Born in Caprese, near Arrezzo, brought up in Florence and died in Rome. He was already 45 when his first works of architecture were built, for he was primarily a sculptor. He was one of many who designed a façade for Brunelleschi's church of San Lorenzo in a competition in 1516, none of which was ever built. In Rome, his major work, other than parts of the Cathedral of Saint Peter, was the arrangement of three buildings atop the Capitoline Hill, of which the Palazzo dei Conservatori (1538–1561) is shown in this book.

MICHELOZZO DE BARTOLOMEO 1396–1472.
Born in Florence and trained as a metal-caster. In 1461 he moved to Dubrovnik (Ragusa), Yugoslavia. Many of his buildings were in the gothic and romanesque styles, but he learned from the example of Brunelleschi. He built the altar end of the church of Santissima Annunziata and the Palazzo Medici-Riccardi in Florence in 1444 and designed the Medici Bank in Milan about 1460 with some gothic details intruding on an otherwise classical building.

About 1452, Michelozzo designed the Church of Santa Maria delle Grazie at Pistoia. Using Brunelleschian details, he assembled a new plan of some ingenuity. The nave is a hall, separated from the crossing by an arch on columns. The crossing is capped with a small internal dome. The transepts and the chancel are of identical depth behind identical arches, the transepts being contained within the same width of walls as the nave. The church is not shown in this book.

MIJARES, JUAN fl. 1572–1598.
A Spanish builder who worked under Herrera at the Casa Lonja, Seville.

MONTANO, JUAN fl. 1501–1525.
The builder of the Diputación at Valencia, Spain, 1518ff.

MOSCA, GIOVANNI MARIA ?–ca. 1573.
An Italian architect and sculptor from Padua, who worked in Padua, Venice, Poland, Prague, and Dresden, East Germany. He designed the entrance of the chapel of the Residenz at Dresden, leaving the construction to be done by Johann Kramer and the carving by Hans Walther II. In Krakow, he may have designed the porch of the Cloth Hall, 1555–1560. He may have been the inventor of the parapet decorated with volutes that is now recognised as part of the Polish idiom of architecture.

NOORT, WILLEM VAN ?–1556.
The builder of the Raadhuis at Utrecht, the Netherlands, 1547.

NOVI—see under ALEVISIO.

NOYEN, SEBASTIAAN VAN ?1493–1557.
Born at Utrecht, died at Brussels. He designed parts of the Palace of Cardinal Granvelle at Brussels about 1550, following some ideas of Antonio da San Gallo II, with whom he may have studied.

OREA, JUAN DE 15??–1583.
He worked with the Machuca family building the Palace at Granada, and later designed the sacristy of the Cathedral at Almería, 1550–1573.

ORME, PHILIBERT DE L'—see under DELORME.

ORSINI DA SEBENICO GIORGIO (also called JURAJ DALMATINAC) ?–1475.
Born at Šibenik, Yugoslavia and died at Ancona. He worked with Laurana at Urbino and possibly with Coducci at Venice. He may have worked on the Cathedral at Šibenik.

PACIOTTI, FRANCESCO 1521–1591.
Born at Urbino and died there. He studied with Genga at Pesaro and worked in Italy, Spain and Flanders, chiefly on military fortifications, such as the Citadel at Antwerp (1569). The amount of his participation in the design of the Escorial in Spain is not known, although he was apparently responsible for part of it.

PAESSCHEN, HANS HENDRIK VAN ca. 1518–ca. 1582.
One of the more widely travelled of the Renaissance architects. He presumably studied in Italy. His home

was Antwerp, and he received some commissions there (such as the Raadhuis and the Hanseatenhuis) thanks to his friendship with Floris. He worked in England, Wales, Germany, Denmark, Sweden and Norway in addition to Flanders. This book contains up to twelve of his designs in Britain and another eleven on the Continent. He is known by a variety of spellings, such as Henryke, Henri de Pas, Hans Pascha, Paas, van de Passe, etc. Some of his children and grandchildren became distinguished artists. He also designed fortifications.

PALLADIO, ANDREA DI PIETRO   1508–1580.
Born at Padua and died at Vicenza. One of the greatest architects of the Renaissance, he started as a lowly stone mason. One of his patrons took him to Rome to study in 1545, and shortly afterwards he began designing buildings in northeastern Italy, especially in Vicenza and Venice. This book contains twelve of them. The impact of his style was furthered around the world by his writings and drawings, some of which are contained in *I Quattro Libri dell' Architettura*, 1570.

PAMBIO, GIOVANNI MARIA DEL   fl. 1555.
An Italian expert in marble who worked with Alessi at the church of Santa Maria in Genoa. He also worked at Hvězda Castle near Prague.

PARR, GIOVANNI BAPTISTA   fl. 1551.
One of a large Italian family of builders working in northern Europe. He built parts of the Castle at Brzeg, Poland. He came from Milan.

PAS, HENRI DE—see under PAESSCHEN.

PASQUALINI, ALESSANDRO   1485–1559.
Originally a painter from Bologna, Italy, he worked in the Netherlands and northern Germany. He is known to have designed the church bell-tower at Ijsselstein, ca. 1535, the Kasteel at Buren, ca. 1540 and the Zitadelle at Jülich, 1552, and may have designed part of Schloss Bedburg, Rheinland about 1550.

PERUZZI, BALDASSARE   1481–1536.
Born at Siena and died at Rome. He started as a painter but became one of Bramante's assistants in Rome in 1503. Two years later he was commissioned by the Chigi family to build the immense Villa Farnesina (not shown in this book), his greatest work. Ten years later he built the Chigi Villa near Siena at a more modest scale. He worked on Saint Peter's Cathedral in Rome for a time in partnership with Antonio da San Gallo II, and he taught both Serlio and Alessi. He was highly regarded as the greatest architect of his age and a universal man, a reputation that has not endured.

PHILANDRIER, GUILLAUME
   (also spelled PHILANDER)   1505–15??
Born at Châtillon-sur-Seine, France. He wrote commentaries on Vitruvius in 1543 that were widely praised. About 1559 he built the Loggia at Château Bournazel, Aveyron, and about 1562 he added a classical gable-end to the Cathedral at Rodez, Aveyron.

PIPPI, GIULIO—see under ROMANO, GIULIO.

PIRES, MANUEL   ?–1570.
He is believed to have worked on the chapel of Bom Jesus de Valverde at Quinta de Mitra, near Évora, Portugal, 1550–1560.

PORTA, GIACOMO DELLA   1531–1602.
Born at Porlessa, near Genoa and died at Rome. A sculptor, he learned architecture under Michelangelo and Vignola; he completed the former's plans for the dome of the Cathedral of Saint Peter, Rome, and he completed with alterations the latter's work on the church of the Gesù, Rome. He was particularly interested in building churches; he built the church of Santa Maria dei Monti, Rome in 1580, probably his best.

PRIMATICCIO, FRANCESCO   1504–1570.
Born at Bologna, Italy and died in Paris. He worked under Giulio Romano at the Palazzo del Té at Mantua, where he was a painter, 1525–1531. He came to Fontainebleau to execute the interior decorations of the Palace, but in the last decade of his life he designed a few buildings of high quality: the Mausoleum for the Valois Kings at Saint-Denis (begun about 1559), the Château of Montceaux-en-Brie near Meaux (about 1565) and the so-called Aile de la Belle Cheminée at Fontainebleau (1569).

PRIOLI, GIOVANNI BATTISTA   fl. 1564–1586.
One of a large family of builders from Genoa who came to build the Palace of the Marqués de Santa Cruz at El Viso de Marqués, Ciudad Real, Spain. Two other members of the family are known to have worked on the Palace, ALBERTO and DOMINGO, but GIOVANNI BATTISTA was apparently in charge. They were presumably influenced by Alessi.

QUADRO, GIOVANNI BATTISTA DI
   15??–1590/1.
From Lugano in southern Switzerland, near the Italian border. He worked in Poland and was appointed State Architect for the Poznán area in 1552. The following year, he commenced work on the Town Hall in Poznán.

RAFFAELLE SANZIO
   (often called RAPHAEL)   1483–1520.
Born at Urbino and died at Rome. He was primarily a painter, but like many other painters he found himself designing buildings occasionally. Among these are the Loggia at Monte Mario near Rome (about 1505), the Chigi Chapel at the church of Santa Maria del Popolo, Rome (1513) and the Palazzo Bresciano in Rome (1515). Bramante designated him as his successor at the Cathedral of Saint Peter in Rome, and it is probably due to Raphael that the plan was altered to a basilical one. Here he worked with Giuliano da San Gallo. He was the teacher of Giulio Romano.

REGNIER (no known first name)   ?–1572.
From Amsterdam; died in Gdánsk, Poland. He designed the Zieloma Brama or Green Gate there in 1563 for Bastian and Johann Kramer to execute, and presumably he also designed the houses a Długa 45 (1563) and Długa 35, "The Lion's Castle," 1569.

RIANO, DIEGO DE   14??–1534.
Died at Valladolid, Spain. His only known architectural work was in Seville, where he designed the Ayunta-

miento or Town Hall in 1527 and may have designed the Sacristy at the Cathedral in about 1530.

RIED, BENEDIKT VON LAUNA (also called BENEŠ REJT) 1454–1534.
Born in upper Austria and died in Bohemia, Czechoslovakia. The earliest reference to him in architecture is in 1489. He was primarily a builder in a late gothic style, but classical ideas appeared in the Ludvík Wing of Hradshin Castle, Prague (1500ff) and the Castle at Piotrkow (1511ff), Poland.

ROBIN, JAN II and GEORGE fl. 1563–1582.
Builders from Ypres, Belgium, they built the Juliusuniversität at Würzburg, Germany, 1582.

ROMANO, GIULIO PIPPI ca. 1492/9–1546.
Born at Rome and died at Mantua. He was trained as a painter by Raphael at a young age. Not long after Raphael's death he moved to Mantua to design buildings for the Gonzaga court. The most significant of these are the Palazzo del Té (1525), the much-altered Rustica courtyard at the Ducal Palace at Mantua (1538) and the Abbey Church of San Benedetto Po at Polirone (1539ff). He was invited by the Pope to take over the design work at Saint Peter's Cathedral in Rome, but died before reaching Rome. He employed Primaticcio and presumably taught him. He is considered to be a leading exponent of the Mannerist style.

ROMANO, PAOLO TACCONE DI MARIANO 14??–1477?.
From 1451 through the 1460s he is recorded as being in Rome where he produced statues and altars. Whether he actually designed any buildings is not known, although he worked with Niccolo Fiorentino at Trogir, Yugoslavia in alterations to the Cathedral there from 1468 onwards.

ROOMAN, JOOS fl. 1552–1581.
A builder in Gent, Belgium, he designed the excessively academic Bollaertskamer there in 1580.

ROSETTI, BIAGIO ?1447–1516.
Born and died at Ferrara. His most notable work is the Palazzo dei Diamanti at Ferrara, 1482ff.

ROSSELLINO, ANTONIO 1427–1479, BERNARDO 1409–1464
A family of several brothers born near Florence, of which two made notable careers in architecture. Bernardo, the elder and more famous, assisted Alberti at the Palazzo Rucellai, Florence, and later used a similar design for his Palazzo Piccolomini at Pienza. Antonio possibly had clearer classical instincts, as can be seen at his Chapel of the Cardinal of Portugal at the Church of San Miniato, Florence, 1461–1466.

ROUEN, JEAN DE fl. 1533.
A French builder in Portugal. To him is attributed the Manga Cloister of Santa Cruz at Coimbra.

RUÃO, JERÓNIMO DE fl. 1571.
Ruão being the Portuguese word for Rouen, it is likely that Jerónimo was the son of Jean de Rouen. He built the sanctuary of the Jerónimos Church at Belém, Portugal.

RUFFO, MARCO fl. 1490.
An Italian who worked in Moscow. In concert with Pietro Antonio Solario, he built the Granovitaya Palace (House of Facets) within the walls of the Kremlin, 1487–1491.

RUIZ, HERNÁN/FERNÁN, II ca. 1515–1606.
A Spanish builder who worked with Martín Gaínsa at the Hospital de la Sangre at Seville (1546ff) and may have built the Cabildo at Jerez de la Frontera (1575).

SAN GALLO, ANTONIO DA, I ca. 1453–1534.
Born and died in Florence, brother of Giuliano and uncle of Antonio II. His most important work was the church of the Madonna of San Biagio at Montepulciano (1518) that was never finished.

SAN GALLO, ANTONIO DA, II 1483–1546.
Born at Florence, and died at Rome. He learned architecture from his two uncles, Antonio I and Giuliano, and collaborated with Raphael and Peruzzi on projects in Rome, particularly the revisions to the designs for Saint Peter's Cathedral. His most significant design was the Palazzo Farnese in Rome; this remained unfinished at his death and was completed by Michelangelo with major changes. He taught Alessi.

SAN GALLO, GIULIANO DA ca. 1445–1516.
Born and died in Florence. He studied ancient monuments in Rome from 1465 onwards and while he was there designed the Palazzo Venezia (1469–1474). His best-known work is the small church of Santa Maria delle Carceri at Prato (1484), and his last work was an entry in the competition to design a new façade for the church of San Lorenzo in Florence (1516); none of the entries was ever executed. He trained Domenico da Cortona and Pedro Machuca and his own nephew Antonio II. At one point he visited France and presented a model for a new palace for the king of France at Lyon, but nothing came of it.

SAN MICHELI, MICHELE 1484–1559.
Born and died in Verona. He was an engineer, expert in building fortifications, which his various employers sent him to do in many parts of Italy and Yugoslavia and elsewhere. He was also talented at designing ordinary buildings; two of his finest are the Palazzo Canossa in Verona (ca. 1536) and the church of the Madonna di Campagna at Verona, begun the last year of his life.

SANSOVINO, JACOPO TATTI 1486–1570.
Born in Florence and died in Venice. He went to Rome in 1506 to study antiquities. Ten years later, he entered the competition to design the façade for the church of San Lorenzo in Florence. After the sack of Rome in 1527 he became chief architect of Venice, where he built La Zecca (the Mint) in 1535, the Library of San Marco (1537) and drew unexecuted plans for the church of Santa Maria della Misericordia. At the exact opposite corner of Italy he also built the church of San Geminiano at Palermo, Sicily in 1557.

SANZIO, RAFFAELLE—see under RAFFAELLE.

SCARINI, NICCOLO fl. 1560.
No reference about this Florentine appears either in

Thieme & Becker, *Allgemeines Lexikon der Bildenden Künstler,* or in the *Macmillan Encyclopedia of Architects.* Nevertheless, he submitted a project for building the Antwerp Raadhuis, the competition for which was under the direction of Cornelis Floris.

SEBENICO, GIORGIO ORSINI DA—
see under ORSINI.

SERLIO, SEBASTIANO 1475–1554.
Born at Bologna and died at Fontainebleau, France. After the sack of Rome in 1527, like Sansovino, he moved to Venice, where he designed some buildings of minor significance. In 1541 François I invited him to France, where he designed a number of buildings, of which ten are shown in this book. He also wrote about eight books on architecture, profusely illustrated with woodcuts of his designs. Not all of these books were published in his lifetime, but they exerted a tremendous influence on architecture in Europe and America for almost 250 years. The present work contains a further three of his designs in the chapter on Italy, taken from one of his earlier books. He was trained at various times by Bramante, Raphael and Peruzzi.

SHUTE, JOHN ?–1563.
An Englishman, sent to Italy to study architecture in 1550 by the Duke of Northumberland. At the end of his life, he published a small book that detailed the various orders, called *The First & Chief Groundes of Architecture,* in which he describes himself as a "paynter & archytecte" (the first time the word architect is known to have been used in English). Notwithstanding, no buildings are definitely known to have been designed by him, although it is possible that he designed parts of Newark Park, Gloucestershire, ca. 1560, and the unknown house of about the same date whose interior woodwork is displayed at the Victoria & Albert Museum, London.

SILOÉ, DIEGO DE ca. 1495–1563.
Born at Burgos and died at Granada. He received some early training in Naples. His greatest work is the Cathedral at Granada, whose foundations had been begun by Egas in 1523; he started work there in 1528. The Cathedral at Málaga, 1538ff, (partly destroyed in an earthquake of 1680) showed similar features refined, as did the Cathedral at Guadix, near Granada (1541ff). He is also one of five architects to whom is credited the College at Salamanca, 1532ff.

SIXDENIERS, CHRISTIAN fl. 1529–1545.
A Flemish builder, he worked with Wallot on the Griffie at Brugge.

SMITH, Sir THOMAS 1513–1577.
The English ambassador to France and kin to some of England's most powerful men—Gresham, Thynne and Cecil. He is recorded to have loaned an architectural book (possibly one of Serlio's) to Cecil. Working with builder Richard Kirby, he designed his manor house of Hill Hall, Theydon Mount, Essex about 1568.

SMYTHSON, ROBERT 1535–1614.
A member of an English family of masons. At such houses as Longleat, he merely executed the designs of others, but began to design for himself possibly at Corsham Court, near Bath (1575ff) and especially at Wollaton Hall, Nottinghamshire (1580ff). His later buildings showed a rejection of the classical vocabulary in favor of a development of English late gothic; the English climate encourages maximum area of glass, hence his masterpiece (1590ff) at Hardwick Hall, Derbyshire, "more glass than wall" (not shown in this book).

SOLARIO, PIETRO ANTONIO ca. 1450–1493.
An Italian who gravitated to Moscow. In partnership with Marco Ruffo, he built the Granovitaya Palace (House of Facets) within the Kremlin, 1487–1491.

STATIO, GIOVANNI DI fl. 1554–1559.
An Italian from Massagno who worked in Czechoslovakia. He built the Town Hall at Plzeň.

STELLA, PAOLO DELLA ?–1552.
An Italian who was working in Padua in 1529. He came to Prague, where he designed the Belvedere in 1538. This was not complete at his death, and Bonifaz Wohlmut finished it but apparently altered the design of the upper floor as he did so.

STICKELS, ROBERT
(also spelled STICKELLS) 15??–1620.
A mason, architect and engineer working in England, but perhaps Flemish in origin. For or with Sir Thomas Tresham he is believed to have built Rothwell Market House, Northamptonshire (1577). In 1595 he was described as "the excellent Artichect (sic) of our time."

STRADA, JACOPO 1507–1588.
Born at Mantua and died at Vienna. He was the publisher of some of Serlio's books, and had possibly studied under Serlio at one time. He designed the Antiquarium at the Residenz, Munich, about 1569.

SUAVIUS, LAMBERTO LOMBARDI—
see under SUSTRIS, LAMBERTO.

SUSTRIS, FRIEDRICH ca. 1540–1599.
Born in Italy and died in Munich, the son of Lamberto Sustris. Presumably he learned by working with his father. He is known for his buildings in the Munich area, such as the castle of Burg Trausnitz at Landshut (1578), the Grottenhof at the Residenz, Munich (1580) and the Jesuit College, Munich (1585). He worked in conjunction with Wolfgang Miller and Hans Krumpper on the Jesuit Church of Saint Michael, Munich, 1583ff.

SUSTRIS, LAMBERTO SUAVIUS LOMBARDI
ca. 1515/20–ca. 1565.
Born of an Italian family in Amsterdam and died at Padua, the father of Friedrich Sustris. He built the church of Saint-Jacques at Liège, Belgium (1558–1560) and was one of the contributors to the preliminary model design for the Raadhuis at Antwerp in 1561.

SYROTH, KILIANO DE MEDIOLANO—
see under MEDIOLANO.

TEDESCO Italian word meaning "German", so see under other name.

TERZI, FILIPPO   1529–1597.
Born at Bologna and studied briefly under Genga. He arrived in Portugal in 1576 to design for the royal court. When Portugal was joined to the Spanish crown, he was well placed to receive royal commissions, the first of which was the Torreão or Royal Palace on the Paço de Ribeira, Lisbon, 1581. He built the church of São Vicente de Fora, Lisbon starting in 1582, and the Palace do Côrte Real, Lisbon in 1585.

THYNNE, Sir JOHN   ?–1580.
An official of the English government to whom are attributed various buildings. The earliest of these was Old Somerset House, London (1547). Possibly in concert with Alain Maynard, he may have designed Sherborne House in Gloucestershire and Longleat in Wiltshire in the 1560s and 1570s.

TIBALDI, PELLEGRINO,
   Marchese DE VALSOLDA   1527–1596.
Born near Lugano, brought up in Bologna, influenced by Michelangelo and died at Milan. He worked briefly at Fontainebleau as a painter and later at the Escorial, but his chief output was in Milan. His best building was the Collegio Borromeo at Pavia, 1563ff.

TIROL, HANS   ca. 1505/6–ca. 1575/6.
A builder from Augsburg, Germany, who worked in Czechoslovakia. He worked at the castles at Kostelec nad Černými Lesy (1549ff) and Hvěsda (1555ff).

TOLEDO, JUAN BAUTISTA DE
   ALFONSIS DE   ?–1567.
A Spaniard who worked as an assistant to Michelangelo for a time. In 1559 he was entrusted with beginning the building of the Escorial, where he worked until his death. Some disagreement still exists as to how much of the Escorial was by him and how much by others.

TOLOSA, PEDRO DE—
   see under TOULOUSE, PIERRE DE.

TORRALVA, DIOGO DE   ?–1566.
A Portuguese architect who may have worked with Genga in Italy for a time. He designed the splendid Cloister of the Convent of Christ the King at Tomar (1554ff) and may have designed the portico of the church of São Mamede at Évora (1566) and the Jesuit church of São Roque in Lisbon (1567).

TORRIGIANO, PIETRO D'ANTONIO
   1472–1528.
Born in Florence and died in Seville. In 1512–1518 he was working on monuments in London, where he was called "Petir Torrysany." Carvings at the Hospital Provincial de la Sangre in Sevilla were executed by a son of the same name, for the Hospital was not begun until 18 years after Torrigiano's death. He died in Sevilla.

TOULOUSE, PIERRE DE   ?–1583.
A Spanish builder based in Salamanca. He is thought to have built the chapel of Mosén Rubén at Ávila about 1560, in concert with Pedro Valle, who could in fact be one and the same person.

TRESHAM, Sir THOMAS   ?1543–1605.
An English land-owner who caused a number of unusual buildings to be built. One of these, in a somewhat classical style, was the Rothwell Market House in Northamptonshire, 1577. It is not known whether Tresham himself designed it or whether a man named Stickels was responsible.

VALLE, PEDRO   fl. 1560.
A Spanish builder to whom is attributed some part in the building of the chapel of Mosén Rubén at Ávila, possibly in concert with Pierre de Toulouse, who could in fact be one and the same person.

VANDELVIRA, ANDRÉS DE   1509–1575.
A competent Spanish architect. He built the sacristy at the Cathedral at Jaén (1532ff), the Palace of Vázquez de Molina at Úbeda (1562) and the Hospital de Santiago at Úbeda (1562–1575). He is also thought to have worked with Siloé at the church of El Salvador at Úbeda.

VAN—see under other part of last name
   (Van NOYES, NOORT, PAESSCHEN).

VÁZQUEZ DE SEGOVIA, LORENZO
   fl. 1487–1512.
Born in Segovia. He was the Spanish architect who first introduced the Renaissance classical style to Spain, at the Colegio Mayor de Santa Cruz at Valladolid (1487ff), the Medinaceli Palace at Cogolludo in the province at Guadalajara (1492ff) and, in partnership with Michele Carlone of Genoa, the Castle of Lacalahorra, near Granada (1510ff). He seems to have been familiar with the work of Michelozzo in Milan about 1460, and may have studied under him.

VEGA, LUIS DE   ?–1562.
The official Spanish royal architect. He designed the Palace of El Pardo, Madrid (1543ff), the Alcázar at Madrid (1545ff) and the Palace of Valsaín, near Segovia (1552).

VELÁSQUEZ, FRANCISCO   fl. 1560.
A Spanish architect who worked in Portugal. He designed the church at the Salvador Convent at Grijo, 1574ff.

VERNUKKEN, WILHELM   15??–1607.
A mason and sculptor from the Netherlands who worked in Germany. He executed, with alterations, Floris' designs for the loggia in front of the Rathaus at Cologne, 1557–1573, but in most of his other works he avoided classical design.

VIGNOLA, GIACOMO BAROZZI DA
   1507–1573.
Born near Bologna and died at Rome. He was a painter at first. In 1541 he was brought to Fontainebleau with Serlio, having previously worked under both Peruzzi and Antonio da San Gallo II. He returned to Bologna in 1543 and inherited the patronage of the Farnese family. Late in his life, he was put in charge of the on-going works at the Cathedral of Saint Peter in Rome. His best works are the oval church of Sant'Andrea in Via Flaminia, Rome (1550), the Farnese Temple near Viterbo (1565), the gate to the Farnese gardens in Rome (1568), and the Gesù, mother-church of the Jesuit order in Rome (1568), which however was completed by Della

Porta to altered designs after Vignola's death.
 VINCI, LEONARDO DA—see under LEONARDO.
 VINCIDOR, TOMMASO DI ANDREA
  14??–ca. 1536.
A painter from Bologna who died at Breda, the Netherlands. He worked under Raphael and was sent to Flanders to supervise the making of Raphael's tapestries for the Sistine Chapel. While in the area, he designed the Salmon House at Mechelin/Malines, Belgium (ca. 1533) and the Kasteel at Breda (1536ff).
 VISSCHER, HERMANN II ca. 1486–1517.
A member of a large family of artists and builders at Nürnberg, Germany. In 1516 he designed the façade for a palace that was apparently never built, and a proposal for the Shrine of Saint Sebald that was rejected in favor of a gothic design by one of his relations.
 VREDEMAN DE FRIES, HANS/JAN 1526–1606.
Born at Leeuwarden, Friesland, the Netherlands. He travelled much and wrote many books; his first one, in 1554, was about grottoes and his next one, *Architectura,* was very influential in mannerist circles in northern Europe. He may have assisted Coecke and Floris with the street decorations for the celebrations at Antwerp in 1549.
 VRIENDT, CORNELIS FLORIS DE
  —see under FLORIS DE VRIENDT.
 VRIES, HANS VREDEMAN DE—
  see under VREDEMAN DE FRIES.
 WALLOT, JAN fl. 1534.
A Flemish architect who worked with builder Christian Sixdeniers at the Griffie at Brugge, Belgium (1534ff).
 WOHLMUT, BONIFAZ ?–1579.
Born at Überlingen, southern Germany, and died at Prague. He moved to Prague from Vienna in 1554, although he may have worked in Czechoslovakia before moving there. He took over work on the Belvedere, Prague upon the death of della Stella in 1552, and apparently altered the original design. This book shows at least six other buildings designed by him or attributed to him.

Glossary

Note: some of the terms contained in this glossary may not apply to architectural features covered in the book, but are relevant to the series of which this book is a part.

AEDICULE An opening in a wall, such as a window or a niche, framed by columns or pilasters and sometimes surmounted by a pediment (from Latin, "little temple").

AISLE Sections of a church, parallel to the nave and often separated from the nave by columns or piers.

ANTIS—see under PORTICO

APSE A projecting part of a building, usually semicircular or semi-elliptical in plan; it is most often found in churches, where it contains the principal altar.

ARCADE A series of arches of identical design.

ARCH
  a) Compass-headed or round-headed: a semicircular opening in a wall (rounded side upwards), usually part of a rectangular opening below.
  b) Elliptical: as in (a), but the shape being semi-elliptical.
  c) Basket (French "anse de panier"): as in (a) but flattened.
  d) Segmental: as in (a), but the base of the arch is a chord somewhat less in length than the diameter of the circle.
  e) Gothic: the top of the arch comes to a point.
  f) Blind: a wall surface decorated with the outline of an arch but not fully penetrated by it.
  g) Others: some arch variations, such as Venetian or Palladian are discussed under WINDOW.

ARCHITRAVE
  a) The lowest of the three divisions of an entablature (see under ENTABLATURE).
  b) The moulded frame surrounding a door or window.
  c) A shouldered architrave: in some cases, the architraves around doors or windows are formed into "ears" level with the top of the opening, projecting outwards; these ears are also occasionally found at the foot of the opening.

ARCHIVOLT An architrave moulding outlining an arch.

ASHLAR A facing of squared stone laid in regular courses, or (chiefly in eighteenth-century North America) wood channelled to resemble such stone.

-ASTYLE A Greek term denoting the number of columns contained in an architectural motif. The word "astylar" refers to motifs without columns or pilasters, while tetrastyle is a motif with four columns, hexastyle with six and octastyle with eight, etc.

BALUSTER One of the posts or supports, often richly turned, of a handrail, as on a staircase or balcony; a BALUSTRADE is a row of balusters and the rail they support.

BARLEY-SUGAR TURNING A column or baluster carved or turned so as to look as if it were twisted in a spiral similar to old-fashioned barley-sugar candy.

BAROQUE An architectural style that flourished between 1600 and 1750, characterized by ornate decoration, curved planes and other irregular deviations from the restrained classical language of the preceding

Renaissance (from the Portuguese "barrôco," a pearl prized because of its irregularity).

BASILICAL Describing a symmetrical church plan containing a high nave and at least two lower aisles.

BAY A subdivision of an external or internal wall, such as one window's worth, or that space between two pilasters or marked by a unit of vaulting.

BOLECTION MOULDING A convex moulding, originally of Italian design, popular in England and America from about 1660 to 1740, and used to frame panels and fireplaces; it always projects beyond the face of the panel.

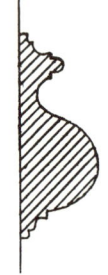

BOX PEWS In many churches seating for the congregation was provided in a series of boxes made of wood panelling, each pew having a door opening on the nearest aisle. This arrangement served at least three purposes: in an age before central heating it protected the occupants from cold draughts while helping to retain the heat from any foot-warmers; since the pews were sold or rented it provided a source of revenue for the church; and it helped to preserve social rankings.

BREAKFRONT A part of a façade projecting to give architectural emphasis, and usually crowned with a pediment; many writers refer to this motif as a pavilion, but since pavilion also means something quite different breakfront is the preferred term.

BRICKWORK When a brick is viewed from the side it is called a "stretcher," and from the end it is called a "header." Under certain circumstances of kiln-firing, some bricks will emerge covered in a greyish glaze, and these bricks are used to advantage to add texture to a wall by showing the glazed headers between unglazed stretchers. Since most brick walls are more than a single brick thick, bricks should be arranged in a "bond" by which certain bricks in a regular pattern are laid athwart the wall to connect two layers and thus presenting headers for the viewer. A row of bricks is called a "course" and one or more projecting rows (usually marking the levels of interior floors) are called "string courses" or "belt courses," while the projecting course at the top of the foundation is called the "drip course" or "water table." In copies of historic buildings the correct choice of brick bond is frequently neglected.

a) Running or Stretcher bond contains no headers.

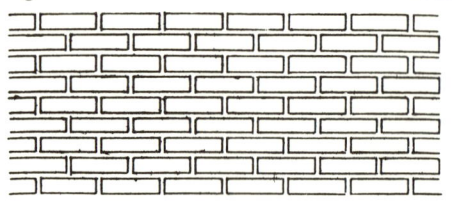

b) Common bond contains five courses of stretchers for every one course of headers.

c) English bond alternates single courses of stretchers with single courses of headers.

d) Flemish bond alternates headers and stretchers in each course, the strongest method of construction.

Glazed headers look their best in Flemish bond.

e) Dutch bond, similar to English bond, but with staggered stretchers.

224

f) Header bond (rarely seen) contains no stretchers.

g) Herringbone pattern (decorative) has bricks in a wall or in paving laid at 45 degrees to the straight, alternating with each other.

Most brick is moulded, whether in regular or special shapes, but some bricks, usually at corners of walls, and wall openings or serving as voussoirs and specially cut or ground after firing so as to make a snug fit; these are called "gauged" or "rubbed" brick.

CAMPANILE Italian word for church bell-tower, often detached from the church. The idea of a large bell hung in a tower for all to hear, rather than a bell-ringer going about the streets, came from Campania, Italy about 400 AD.

CAPITAL The crowning feature of a column, pillar or pilaster; see under ORDERS.

CARTOUCHE An ornamental plaque usually having a scrolled frame.

CHANCEL That part of a church plan closest to the principal altar.

CHOIR The arm of a cruciform church plan closest to the principal altar and often the area occupied by the singers of the choir.

CLAPBOARD Wooden external siding made of lapped horizontal boards. When such siding is used formally it is usually called "clapboarding" (the "p" is normally not pronounced) and when used informally it is called "weatherboarding."

CLERESTORY The upper storey of a church nave with windows looking out over the roofs of the aisles.

COLONNADE A row of columns supporting an entablature.

COLUMN A vertical shaft with moulded base and capital, used as a supporting member. A column is round in section, while a pillar is square in section. An "engaged" column appears to be elided with a wall, the maximum amount of elision thus producing a "half-column," and a column elided in the angle between two walls can be a "quarter-column." See under ORDERS.

CORBEL A supporting member projecting from the face of a wall (from the French "corbeille," a basket).

CORNICE A decorative feature found under the eaves of a roof or at the join between walls and ceiling in a room; also the uppermost of the three levels of an entablature. See under ENTABLATURE.

CORPS DE LOGIS The principal block of rooms in a large building or range of buildings.

COURSE A continuous horizontal row of brick or stone in a wall. See under BRICKWORK.

COVE A large concave moulding, sometimes taking the place of a cornice, hence a coved or "tray" ceiling.

CROSS PLAN Cruciform church plans are found in two regular forms: in a Greek cross, all four arms are of equal length, while in a Latin cross the nave is longer than the other three arms. The nave, usually to the west, is intended for the general congregation; the choir, usually to the east, is often reserved for clergy and singers; the other arms are called "transepts," and the area where all four arms meet is called the "crossing."

CUPOLA A small room, usually round, octagonal or hexagonal, atop a roof or crowning a done. It is sometimes referred to as a lantern or lanthorn.

DENTILS A series of small rectangular blocks spaced in a band to decorate a cornice.

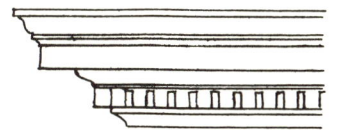

DOME An area of roof and/or ceiling generally hemispherical. Some domes are octagonal, hexagonal, or even square. A shallow interior dome, segmental in section, is called a "saucer-dome." It is generally agreed that a dome that looks well-proportioned on the exterior will appear too large on the interior, and one that fits well on the interior will be too small on the exterior. Many architects, among them notably Christopher Wren, therefore contrived to build one dome inside another to provide ideal proportions for both exterior and interior.

DORMER A window projecting from a roof. The most important kinds are gable-roofed dormer, hip-roofed dormer, shed-roofed dormer and Chippendale dormer.

gable-roofed dormer   hip-roofed dormer

shed-roofed dormer   Chippendale dormer.

ECLECTIC Architecture in which various elements are borrowed from different styles and periods.

EGG & DART MOULDING A band of alternating oval and pointed shapes applied to ovolo or quarter-round moulding.

ELL A wing, usually on the back of a building (from the French "aile," a wing of a bird).

ENTABLATURE An assembly of the top three parts of a Classical order, architrave, frieze and cornice, usually found on the top of a column, pillar or pilaster. A small block of entablature, often connecting a column with the foot of a number of arches, is called a "flying entablature." See under ORDERS.

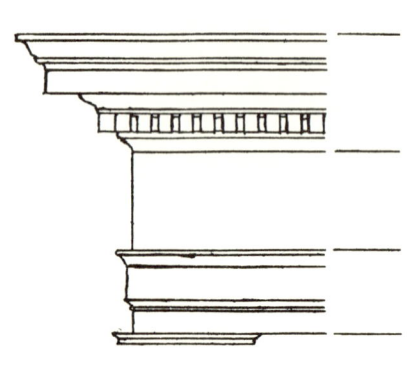

ENTASIS A slight swelling on the trunk of a column to counteract the optical illusion of concavity; a column with entasis is smaller in section at the top than at the bottom.

FAÇADE The principal face of a building.

FINIAL A decorative ornament, often urn-shaped, used to crown various architectural motifs.

FLUTING Concave, vertical grooves in the surface of a column, a pilaster or a pillar, often combined with smaller convex fillets inside each groove, and these are known as "reeding."

FORECOURT When a main building is formally related with some of its dependencies or out-buildings around a rectangular or curved area of ground, the area so enclosed is a forecourt. Palladio was one of the earliest architects to use this motif.

FRIEZE The middle of the three members of an entablature, sometimes plain but sometimes decorated with figures in relief. A convex band in place of the regular frieze (usually in connection with the Ionic order) is called a "cushion frieze" or "pulvinated frieze." See under ENTABLATURE.

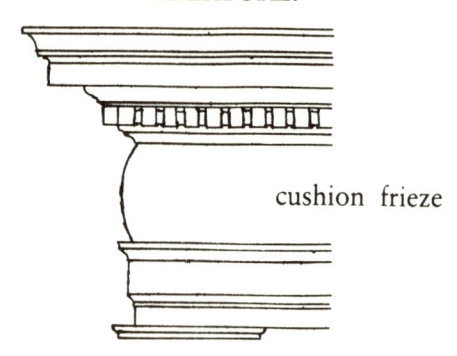

cushion frieze

GABLE The triangular portion of wall at the end of a gable roof (see under ROOF). A gable is occasionally decorated into different shapes, such as the crow-stepped gable and the curvilinear gable, both developed in the Low Countries.

GALLERY
a) A long room, principally in large houses of the sixteenth and seventeenth centuries, used for displaying art objects and for dancing longways country dances.
b) An upper storey or balcony in a church; across the back of the nave it is sometimes called a "tribune," and was often intended to hold the organ and the singers; over the aisles it was intended as additional space for the congregation, particularly for those people who could not afford to purchase pews on the ground floor.
c) Often spelled in the French manner, "galerie," a balustraded porch around one or more sides of the exterior of a building.

GAZEBO A small summer-house in a garden, often commanding an impressive view (from the French exclamation, "Que c'est beau!"—how beautiful it is!); sometimes called a belvedere.

GIBBSIAN SURROUND An arrangement in which windows and doors are dressed with heavy quoins and voussoirs, popularized by but not invented by James Gibbs.

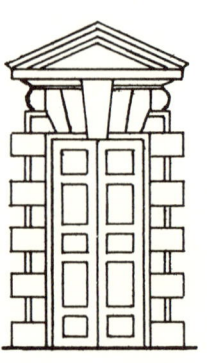

226

GOTHIC A relatively recent use of the word, meaning architecture of the pre-Renaissance style characterized by pointed arches. English architectural historians recognise three periods of Gothic, Early, Decorated and Perpendicular. An eighteenth-century style inspired by but not copied from Gothic was known as Gothick.

GREAT HOUSE The principal residence of a farm or plantation, not always a particularly great house.

HIGH-STYLE Architecture more or less up to date with the latest ideas of the leading architects, as opposed to VERNACULAR. Thus it can be assumed that nearly all high-style buildings were the work of architects or at least of architects working in collaboration with knowledgeable clients.

IMPOST The moulded member on which the ends of an arch rest.

JESUIT FAÇADE A church façade articulated as two storeys with columns and/or pilasters; the lower storey is wider than the upper, and the upper storey is usually flanked by a pair of volutes. This represents a solution to the problem of how to make a basilical church (essentially an idea developed in the pre-Renaissance period) look properly Classical on the exterior, and it was first achieved about 1500; Vignola and della Porta designed the Church of the Gesù in Rome in the late sixteenth century in this style, and since this was the headquarters for the Jesuits the style was exported around the world wherever Jesuit missionaries travelled.

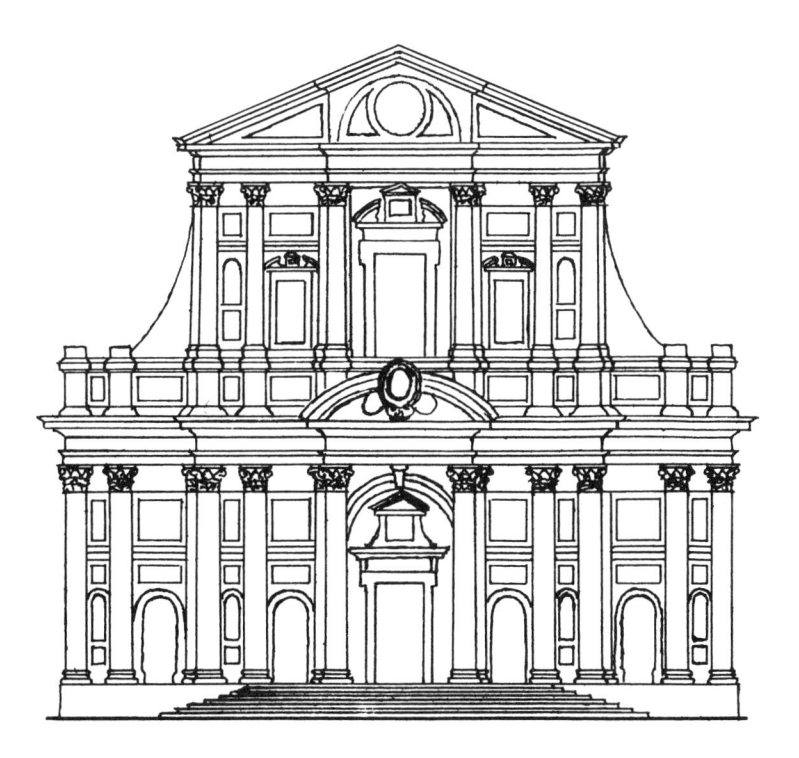

KEYSTONE A wedge-shaped stone in the crown of an arch or in the center of a lintel to lock the structure.

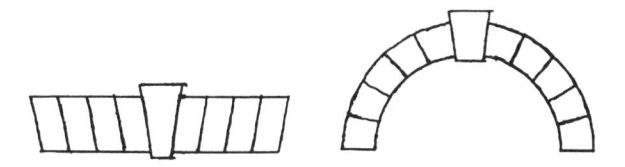

LINTEL The horizontal top piece of a window or door opening, requiring strength in order to support the wall above it.

LOGGIA A covered colonnade or arcade, open to the air on at least one side, sometimes ranging around a courtyard (an Italian word).

MANNERIST Two overlapping meanings of this word can be identified, and in an effort to keep them separate in this book, one sense of the word is capitalized and the other is not. A Mannerist architect is one who knows perfectly well how to assemble elements into a proper Classical design, but decides to deviate from Classical design for effect. A mannerist architect is one who is more or less acquainted with at least some Classical details, but demonstrates only a superficial knowledge of Classical style through an inability to assemble the details correctly.

METOPE The space between the triglyphs in a Doric frieze; this space may be plain or decorated with such devices as roundels and bulls' heads. See under ORDERS.

MEZZANINE An intermediate floor between two storeys.

MODILLION One of a series of rectangular or bracket-shaped blocks larger than dentils that are spaced in a band to decorate some cornices.

MULLION A vertical member forming major divisions in casement windows. See under TRANSOM and WINDOW.

MUNTIN A vertical or horizontal member forming lesser divisions in casement or sash windows.

NAVE The main body of a church; in a cruciform church, it extends from the main entrance (usually the west end) to the crossing.

NEWEL The principal post at the corner of a balustrade, as at the foot of a staircase or at the corners of landings.

ORDERS Categories of columns and entablatures (with or without pedestals). There are five main orders: Tuscan, Doric, Ionic, Corinthian and Composite, and of these Doric and Ionic are further divided into Greek and Roman Doric, and two-sided and four-sided Ionic. The proportions of each order may vary considerably at the whim of the architect, but generally Tuscan is the most massive, ranging in the order cited above to Composite as the most attenuated. Further attenuation can be achieved by contrasting a Tuscan column without pedestal or entablature with a Composite column on a pedestal and surmounted by a flying entablature. When different orders are to be used on different storeys of a building, the more massive order should always be placed below the more attenuated one, as in the order of the list cited above. A column that ranges over two or more storeys is known as a giant-order column. Everything about orders that applies to columns also applies to pillars (columns with square sections) and pilasters (portions of pillars protruding from walls).

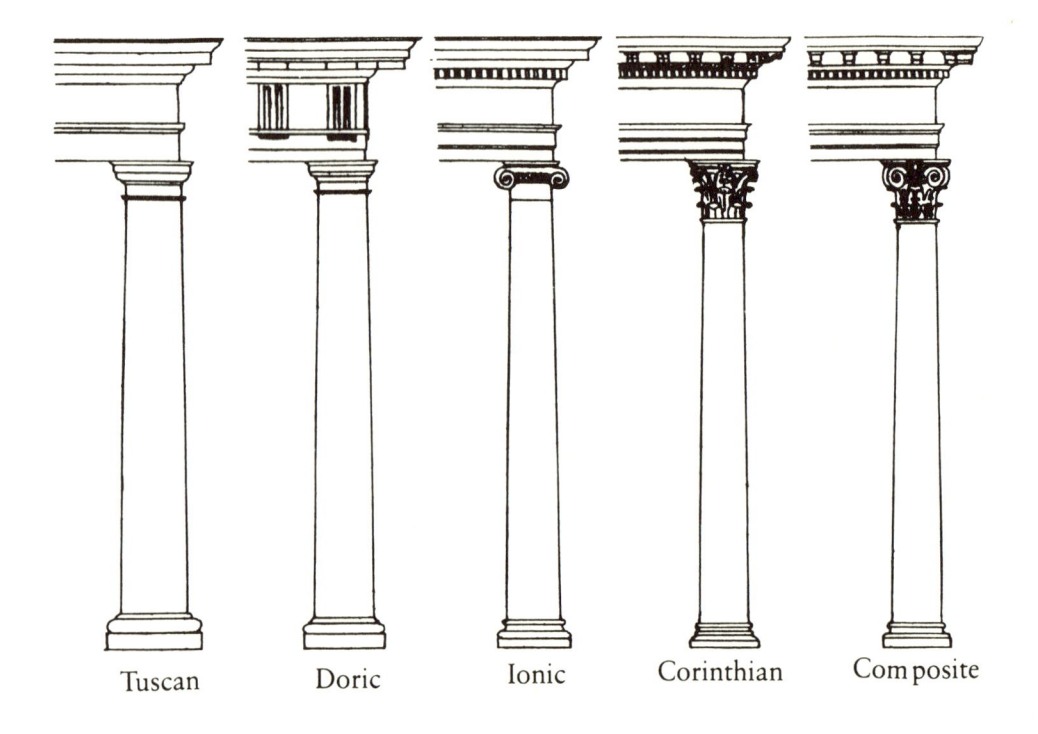

Tuscan   Doric   Ionic   Corinthian   Composite

Simple Tuscan Column; Composite Column with pedestal and flying entablature (same height; same size arch)

PALLADIAN Architecture in the style of Andrea Palladio, one of whose contributions was inventing a formal arrangement in plan and elevation for the dependency buildings of a farm with the main house. The popular motif of an arched opening flanked by a pair of smaller rectangular openings has frequently been called a Palladian arch, motif, door or window, but Palladio did not invent this form, which is more properly known as a Venetian arch, etc.; see under WINDOW.

PARAPET A low wall on a bridge or balcony or particularly above the cornice of a building; such a wall can be solid masonry or a row of balusters or other carvings. In most countries, the parapet was decorative, but in England from the late seventeenth century onwards it was intended to inhibit the spread of fires, while in the West Indies it was designed to prevent hurricanes from peeling off the roof covering. Parapets were dangerous in areas prone to earthquakes, and they caused leaks in the roofs of buildings in areas of heavy snowfall (such as North America), and so use in such areas was limited.

PAVILION A pleasure house, larger than a gazebo, in a park or garden, or a building attached to a main block by a wing. Some writers use this term to describe a projecting part of a façade, but to avoid confusion that feature is known as a BREAKFRONT in this book.

PEDESTAL A block that supports a column, statue, urn or finial; sometimes known as a plinth.

PEDIMENT A decorative feature, usually triangular but often segmental or occasionally ogee, found on gable ends, above porticoes, breakfronts, doors, windows or aedicules. The upper part of the pediment is formed by a cornice moulding. Some pediments are split to receive some ornament or finial in the center, and occasionally the open ends of the split segmental or ogee pediments are terminated in some form of scrolled block.

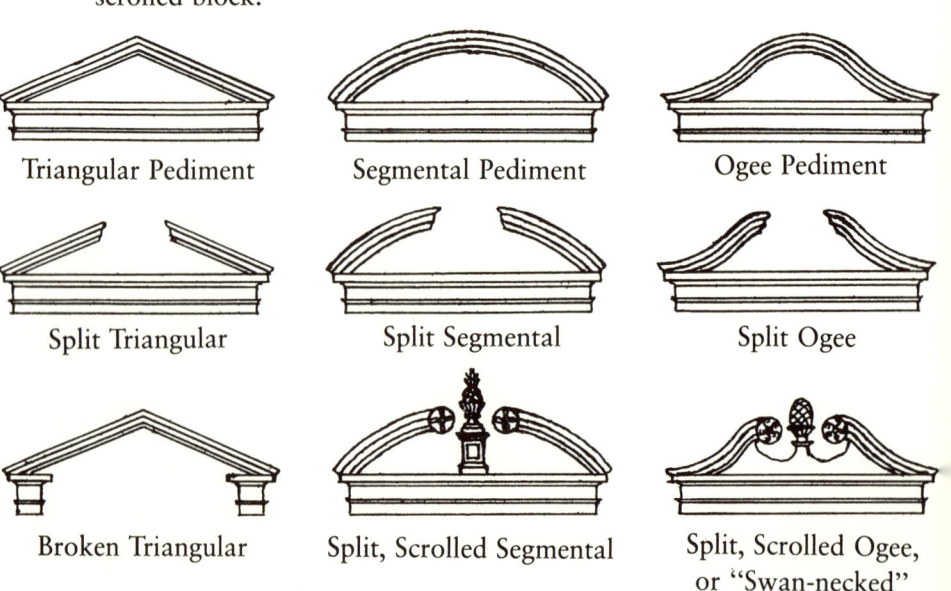

Triangular Pediment   Segmental Pediment   Ogee Pediment

Split Triangular   Split Segmental   Split Ogee

Broken Triangular   Split, Scrolled Segmental   Split, Scrolled Ogee, or "Swan-necked"

PENDENTIVE Each of the supporting concave triangles formed by intersecting arches under a dome.

PENT A cantilevered projection from the face of a masonry building at the level of a belt-course between storeys, covered by its own small roof. This device, which was presumably intended to inhibit masonry and the ends of the floor timbers behind it from becoming saturated by falling rain, was popular in the seventeenth and eighteenth centuries in the region around Philadelphia, and was imported from Germany.

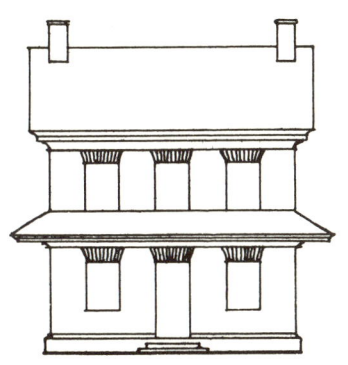

Small House with Pent

PERIODS Much of architectural history is characterized by the period of the design, and a number of standard terms are in use. The Italian terms Quattrocento (1400–1499), Cinquecento (1500–1599), Seicento (1600–1699), and Settecento (1700–1799) are commonly used, but some English and American terms are also appropriate. Strictly speaking, Tudor means from 1485 to 1603, but as an architectural term it is frequently taken to mean the same as Elizabethan (1558–1603). This is followed by the generic term Stuart (1603–1714), which can be broken down into Jacobean (1603–1660), Carolean (1660–1688), William & Mary (1688–1702) and Queen Anne (1702–1714). Next comes Georgian (1714–1820), which can be broken down into early, mid and late. In the United States, anything designed up to about 1790 can be called Colonial, slightly overlapping the Federal period, which began about 1783 and lasted about twenty years.

PIANO NOBILE In many historical buildings, when the principal storey containing the main reception rooms was above the ground floor, the Italians called it by this name. See under STOREY.

PIER A rectangular member used to support a beam, lintel or arch, and sometimes consisting of a cluster of columns or pilasters.

PILASTER (pronounced p'laster, not pyelaster) A flat, slightly raised form of a column or pillar projecting slightly from a wall. A PILASTER STRIP is like a pilaster but without a proper base or capital.

PILLAR Identical to a column, but with a square section rather than the round section of a column.

PINNACLE A pyramidal ornament or spike used as a finial.

PLINTH The projecting base for a building, a column or a finial, sometimes interchangeable with PEDESTAL.

PORTICO A covered, usually projecting colonnade (or occasionally arcade) at the entrance of a building, often crowned by a pediment. A PORTICO IN ANTIS is a recessed version.

POST In many situations, chiefly in but not limited to vernacular architecture, it is impractical to build in masonry. Historically, wooden architecture was approached in many different ways. The simplest was to sink the ends of a row of closely-spaced posts in the ground and caulk the interstices of the wall thus formed with mud or clay (French "bousillage entre poteaux"), but the wood in the ground was often quickly destroyed by rot and insects. A better method was to erect occasional vertical posts on wooden sills that sat above ground on a foundation; the interstices were filled either with wattle and daub or with bricks that were usually covered in plaster, a system known in England as half-timbering. In areas, such as New England, where wood was abundant, the spaces between the posts were partially filled with thinner vertical posts called studs, upon which were nailed horizontal sheathing on the outside and laths for plastering on the inside; the all-stud or balloon-frame construction was not invented until the nineteenth century. In late seventeenth-century New England, many posts were hewn so as to flare outwards near the top to give more support to the girts and plates resting on them, and these were known as gunstock posts. In parts of coastal Rhode Island and Massachusetts, many buildings were constructed without studs, simply nailing heavy oak vertical sheathing from sills to plates whose weight was borne by the corner posts; this was economical, strong, surprisingly weathertight (with the addition of clapboards and plaster) and less likely to suffer serious fires than studded buildings with their built-in air spaces, but the vertical sheathing tended to suck up moisture that promoted rot after many years.

PULPIT A raised and enclosed platform in churches from which sermons are preached. Pulpits were frequently located on the north side of the nave so that listeners would not have to look into the sun, but in many churches the pulpit stood in the center aisle in front of the altar, owing to the special emphasis placed on sermons after the Reformation. In the Anglican Church, a fully-developed pulpit had four features. The lowest level was the clerk's desk from which he led responses and singing; the next level was the reading desk, from which the bulk of the service and the scripture lessons were read; the next level was the actual pulpit for sermons; at the top level was a cantilevered or suspended canopy, known variously as a sounding-board, tester or type, whose purpose was to reflect the preacher's voice to the most distant pews. This kind of a pulpit is known as a three-decker.

QUOIN A squared stone, or similar arrangement of brick, stucco or wood, at the corner of a building or of other architectural features. Quoins are staggered so that on a given elevation one sees alternately headers and stretchers.

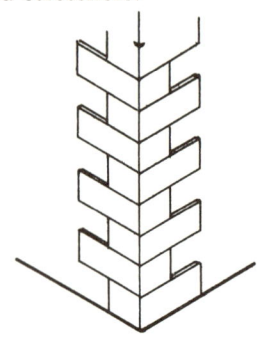

RESTORE, RESTORATION These terms have different meanings in Britain and America. In England, thanks to nineteenth-century men like Byron, Pugin, Ruskin and William Morris, a building that had been restored was one that had been altered, chiefly into the Gothic Revival style. In America, a restored building is one that has been repaired and brought back to the way it may once have looked at an earlier date. The American meaning is used exclusively in this book.

RÉTARDATAIRE Architecture newly-built in a style that is already out of date, or employing certain such features.

ROOF A covering over a building, made of thin pieces of stone, brick-like tiles, sheet metal or wood shingles. Roofs come in a surprising variety of shapes, some of which are shown here.

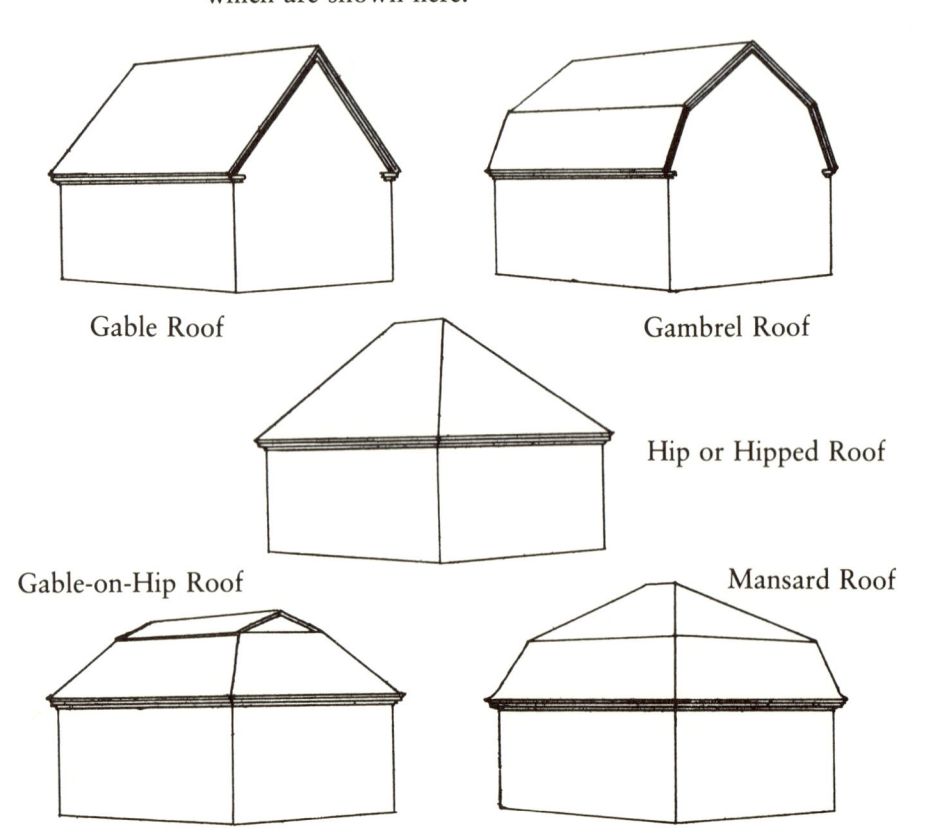

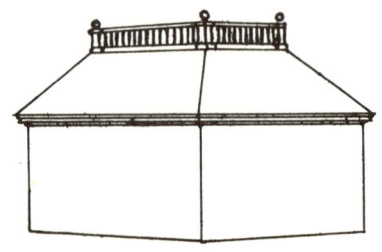

Gable Roof

Gambrel Roof

Hip or Hipped Roof

Gable-on-Hip Roof

Mansard Roof

Deck-on-Hip Roof

Clipped Gable or Jerkin-Head Roof

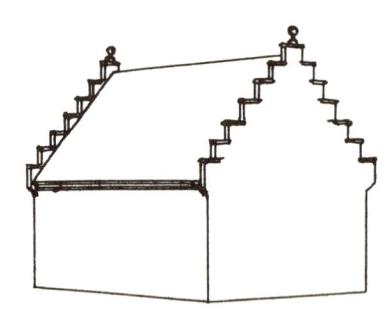

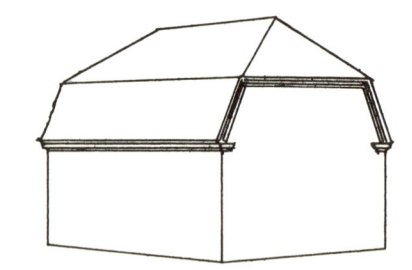

Stepped Gable

Clipped Gambrel Roof

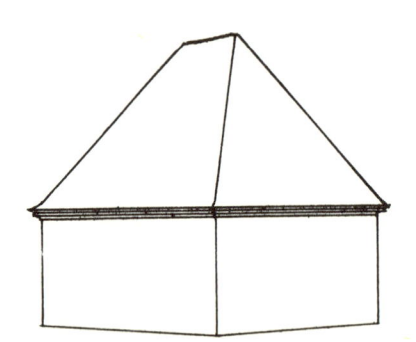

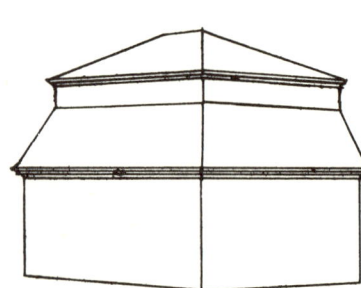

Pavilion-Hip Roof

Monitor Roof

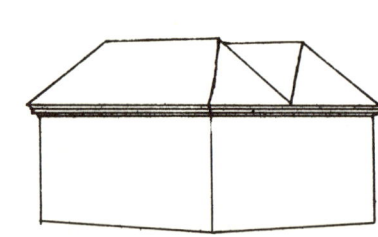

Multi (Double) Pile Hip Roof

Curvilinear Gable

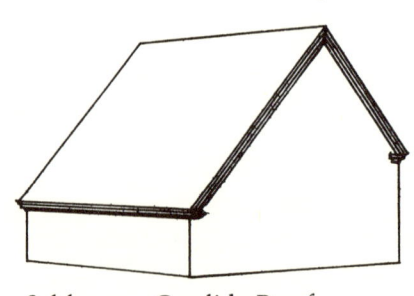

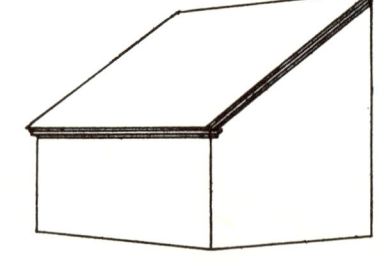

Saltbox or Catslide Roof

Shed Roof

230

RUSTICATION Horizontal and vertical channels cut into stonework to emphasize the joints. It was thought that country or "rustic" builders did not know how to cut stones closely enough to disguise the joints, and that such a "rustic," Mannerist treatment could actually create a desired textured effect. Rustication could also be applied to columns, pillars and pilasters, but in this case it means that the column was formed alternately of larger rough stones and smaller smooth stones. Peter Harrison, working in eighteenth-century New England, invented a system of carving wooden siding to look like rusticated stonework, a technique that achieved considerable popularity in America.

SCREEN As in choir-screen, chancel-screen, rood-screen or jubé, a division, sometimes elaborately architectural, placed between the altar area of many churches and the part containing the bulk of the congregation. In the early church the idea was that new converts should be allowed to hear but not see the mysteries celebrated at the altar by the priest and faithful, but by the Middle Ages it served to separate the great unwashed or "rude" from the clergy, choir and wealthy, for the majority of the people were expected only to attend services, not to receive Communion. Contrary to most dictionaries, the word rood in this instance derives from rude.

SHINGLES Thin, more or less rectangular pieces of wood used as roofing tiles, and as wall sheathing on some vernacular buildings. Unlike clapboards, whose grain runs horizontally, shingles' grain runs vertically.

SHUTTERS A solid or panelled or louvred wooden blind, usually used in pairs either inside or outside a window, sometimes to bar light and sometimes to inhibit intruders. In eighteenth-century America, the pattern of historical use was complicated. In the South, external shutters appeared only on wooden buildings, while masonry buildings had internal shutters. In the middle colonies, external shutters appeared exclusively on masonry buildings, while in New England only internal shutters were used.

SOFFIT The underside of an arch, lintel, cornice or balcony.

SPANDREL The roughly triangular area on each side of an arch or between two arches.

STEEPLE The complete assembly of tower, lantern and spire usually found on a church.

STOREY A complete horizontal division of a building, also called a floor. In counting the storeys of a building, British or European and American usages differ; Americans count the ground floor as the first floor, while the rest of the world holds that the first floor is the floor above the ground floor. This book attempts to avoid confusion by specifying the storeys in unambiguous ways. Three further terms should be defined: The PIANO NOBILE is the storey containing the principal reception rooms if those rooms are not found on the ground floor. A MEZZANINE is an intermediate floor between two storeys. An ATTIC STOREY is an additional complete, if short, storey above the main cornice in the place where a parapet might otherwise be found.

STRAPWORK A form of decoration invented by Rosso and other artists of the Fontainebleau school in the 1530s and later popular with mannerist architects and builders in the Low Countries, Germany and England. It simulated strips of leather or parchment cut into elaborate patterns.

STUCCO A special weather-proof plaster used for coating walls or for moulding into architectural decoration or sculpture.

TRABEATED Construction composed of horizontal lintels and vertical posts and employing no arches.

TRANSEPT Normally one of two side arms on the plan of a cruciform church.

TRANSOM An horizontal member making a major division in a window, as opposed to a MULLION which is a similar vertical member.

TRIFORIUM The section of a church corresponding to the attic space over the aisles, above the principal nave arches and below the CLERESTORY.

TRIGLYPH One of a series of rectangular blocks alternating with METOPES in a Doric frieze.

VAULT An arched roof or ceiling; a barrel vault is an uninterrupted vault of semicircular section, while a groined vault intersects with other vaults at right angles.

VERNACULAR A native or local style, usually conservative in comparison to that of metropolitan centers and the work of a builder or folk artist rather than an architect.

VOLUTE A spiral, scroll-like ornament found on Ionic capitals and some brackets. It is likely that the Ionic capital was initially inspired by the head and horns of a ram.

Obvious inspiration for Volutes on an Ionic Capital

VOUSSOIR One of a series of wedge-shaped stones or bricks used to form an arch, or wooden blocks in imitation of stone.

WINDOWS
1) Although glass had been invented before the birth of Christ, many of even the finest buildings of the

Renaissance had no glass in their windows.* Some windows had only solid shutters to keep out insects and draughts, while others used oiled parchment or thin panes of animal horn in place of glass. The typical window of the Renaissance was a CASEMENT, with one or more sections opening on hinges on a vertical axis. These sections were divided by vertical members called MULLIONS and horizontal members called TRANSOMS. The small pieces of glass were set into frames whose glazing bars are called MUNTINS.

2) Architectural historian Marcus Whiffen has found what appears to be a reference to a SASH window in William Horman's Vulgaria, published in England in 1519, but as far as is known sashes did not figure in Renaissance architecture; the first large-scale use of them in England was at Whitehall about 1685, and the first known use of them in America was in 1699 in Williamsburg. The sash is a window in which one or more sections open by sliding up or down, sometimes assisted by counterweights attached by cords over pulleys.

3) The casement and sash are the two basic types of windows, but windows can be found in an amazing variety of shapes other than the simple rectangle. Some have segmental soffits and are sometimes known as camber-headed.

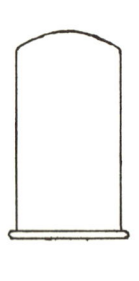

---

*"Their houses built of no slight matter, especially those which they call Palaces, are commonly more beautiful for the greatness of their structure than convenient for the use of the dwellers in them. They glitter with marble of divers kinds and sometimes with gold.... But where their walls do afford space for windows, there their houses doe lose somewhat from the lustre of the other building. For commonly eyther coorse linen or oyled paper doe cover those places which are ordained for letting in of light. Which thing as it is unsightly to the beholders, so it imprisons the eyes of the dwellers within the bounds of their Parlour or galery doores; farre from the comelinesse of the *French* or *Brittish* manner, where their windows are made of glasse..." (John Barclay, *The Mirrour of Mindes, or, Barclay's Icon Animorum*, London, 1631, pp. 194–199).

4) An arch-topped window is called compass-headed.

5) A compass-headed window with intersecting tracery is often called a Chippendale window.

6) A window that projects from the wall in a curve is known as a bow window.

7) One that projects from a wall with either squared or canted sides and which begins on the ground floor (but may go up through several storeys) is a bay window.

8) A bay window that begins at an upper storey and is supported on brackets or a corbel as an oriel.

9) An eyebrow window is a small opening peering from out of an entablature.

10) A round or oval window is known as a bullseye or oeil de boeuf.

11) A semicircular window is a lunette.

12) A large semicircular window divided into three sections by two mullions is called either a Diocletian or therm window, named after the Baths of Diocletian (ca. 300 AD), although the design is much older.

Diocletian or Therm/Thermal Window

13) A tri-partite design in which the central opening is compass-headed and springs from the entablature that rests on the smaller rectangular openings on each side is best known as a Venetian window, although it is often called a Palladian or Serlian window. The design can be traced at least as far back as the first century AD, and even in its Renaissance revival (Venice in 1488) it was far earlier than Serlio or Palladio, both of whom used the design.

14) Similar to the Venetian window is the rarer Ephesian window (Temple of Hadrian, Ephesus, ca. 150 AD) in which the entablature follows the curve of the central window. It was used by Giulio Romano, among others.

15) A tripartite window in which all three parts are rectangular and the same height, although the central opening is wider than the others, is known as a Wyatt window because it was popularized by James Wyatt in the late eighteenth century; it had been invented long before Wyatt's day, but was very rare.

16) The Nanto arch (from the high altar of the church at Nanto, Italy, ca. 1492), although it often contains a lunette window, is more properly described as a doorway, and yet since it is related to the Venetian and Ephesian arches it is shown here with them. Its unusual feature is that the archivolt is at the level of the capitals of the columns whose flying entablatures support a broken pediment. The Nanto doorway was particularly popular in North America in the second half of the eighteenth century.

INDEX

Adam, Robert & James, 133
Adrian (Pope), 96
Alava, Juan De, 168, 169, 174, 212
Alava, Juan De, 168, 169, 174, 212
Alba, Julia, see Gyulafehérvár
Alberti, Leon Battista, 2, 3, 4, 13–15, 19, 24, 212, 219
Albrecht, V, Duke of Bavaria, 112
Alcalá, De Henares: Archbishop's Palace, 176, 177, 214
Alcalá, De Henares: Hostería, 177
Alcalá De Henares: University, 177, 180, 215
Alessi, Galeazzo, 34, 39, 49–52, 190, 192, 193, 197, 212, 216, 218, 219
Alevisio, Novyi, 148, 149, 212
Alfonso, Prince of Naples, 19, 217
Allio, Domenico Dell, 100, 101, 212
Almería: Cathedral Sacristy, 186, 187, 217
Alveres, Afonso, 201, 202, 212
Alvares, Baltasar, 207, 208
Amatrice, Nicola Di Filotesio Daw, 36, 37, 212
Amsterdam: Exchange/Bourse, 130
Amsterdam: Paalhuis, 100, 101
Ancy-Le-Franc: Château, 19, 27, 69, 70–72, 103, 133, 192, 201
Andressen, Jan, 114, 115, 212
Anet: Château & Chapel, 48, 60–61, 78, 187
Anglés, Juan, 181, 186, 187, 212
Anne, Princess, 56
Annecy: Cathedral, 58
Antwerp: Arch, 92–94, 214, 222
Antwerp: Bourse, 130, 216
Antwerp: Citadel, 217
Antwerp: Frans Floris House, 94–95, 215
Antwerp: Gresham House, 105
Antwerp: Han Seatenhuis, 9, 94, 103, 104, 105, 112, 114, 128, 130, 215, 218
Antwerp: Raadhuis, 9, 84, 94, 95, 96, 100, 102, 103, 105, 112, 117, 215, 218, 220
Antwerp: Reviewing Stand, 92–94, 214
Aostalli, Giovanni Battista & Ulrico, 153, 154, 155, 156, 159, 212

L'Aquila: Church of San Bernardino, 36, 37, 212
Aranjuez: Royal Palace, 193, 195, 216
Arruda, Miguel De, 201, 202, 212
Augsburg, Church of Saint Katherine, 88, 89, 216
Augsburg: Damenhof, 88, 89, 216
Augsburg: Fuggerkapelle, 88, 89, 216
Augustusburg: Chapel & Schloss, 112, 113, 217
Ávila: Chapel of Mosén Rubín, 197, 198, 221
Azeitão: Quinta Das Tôrres, 203, 204

Bacciolini, Gian Francesco Poggio, 2
Bachecraig, vii, 128, 133, 134, 135
Bachelier, Nicolas, 78–79, 197, 212
Bacon, Sir Nicholas & Francis, 136, 138, 140
Baeza: Ayuntamiento & Prison, 187, 188
Baeza: Convent of San Francisco, 187
Bakhchisarat: Iron Gate, 148
Banco, Nanni Di, 3
Barbon, Nicholas, 133
Barbona, Pietro Grassi Di, 164, 165, 213
Barbaro, Daniele, 43, 48
Basel: Spieshof, 117, 118
Beaugrant, Guyot De, 88–90, 213, 216
Bedburg: Schloss, 91–92, 218
Beja: Market & Miseri Cordia, 199, 200
Belém: Jerónimos Church, 203, 204, 219
Belini, Nicolas, 122
Bellay, Cardinal Jean Du, 60
Berecci, Bartolomeo, 148, 150, 151, 213
Bernini, Giovanni Lorenzo, 65
Besançon: Granvelle Palace, 58, 59, 216
Betlanovec: Turzo Castle, 160, 161
Bisritza: Dealului Monastery, 151
Black, Prince, 84
Boccacco, Giovanni, 2

Boleyn, Anne, 123
Bologna: Church of San Petronio, 48
Bono, Marco, 151, 152, 213
Botticelli, Alessandro Filipepi, 3
Boulainvilliers, Philippe De, 84
Bouliers, Nicolas De, 75, 77, 78
Bournazel: Château, 81–82, 218
Brachum, Laurentz Von, 111, 112, 214
Brahe, Tycho, 110, 112
Bramante, Donato, 3, 4, 22, 24, 26–32, 34, 36, 41, 52, 69, 88, 103, 170, 192, 201, 213, 214, 218, 220
Brandýs: Castle, 153, 154
Breda: Kasteel, 90–91, 222
Brescia, Jacopo Da, 32
Brosse, Jean, 84, 85, 213
Brosse, Solomon De, 84, 213
Browne, Arthur, 130
Bruges, see Brugge,
Brugge: Griffie, 90–91, 220, 222
Brunelleschi, Filippo, 3, 4, 6–11, 13, 19, 24, 32, 130, 213, 217
Brussels: Palace of Cardinal Granvelle, 96, 97, 217
Brussels: Palace of Duc De Brabant, 105, 106
Brussels: Pigeon House, 96, 97
Brzég: Castle, 156, 157, 218
Bučovice: Castle, 161, 162, 215
Bull, John, 126
Bullant, Jean II, 63, 78–79, 213
Buren: Church, 90
Buren: Kasteel, 90–91, 218
Burghley House, 126, 128, 129, 136, 143
Bury: Château, 56, 57
Bustamente, Bartolomé, 181, 182, 213
Büttner, Conrad, 113, 114, 213

Caius, Dr. John, 142
Callosa De Segura, Church, 187, 188
Cambridge: Gonville & Caius College, 141, 142, 216
Cambridge: King's College Chapel, 3, 122
Cambridge: Trinity College Library, 39
Campillo of Philip II, 197, 198
Caprarola, Cola Di Matteuccio Da, 22, 23

Caprarola: Villa Farnese, 34, 48, 69
Carcano, Alevisio Da, 146
Carlone, Michele, 170, 171, 213, 221
Capri: Church of Santa Maria Detta Le Sagra, 30
Casa De La Nieve of Philip II, 197, 198
Cassar, Gerolamo, 52–53, 213
Castellón: Church of Vistabella, 186, 187, 212
Castiglione, Count Baldassare, 2
Castilho, João De, 199, 200, 201, 213
Cecil, Sir William, 126, 128, 130, 136, 140, 142, 220
Česky Krumlov: Castle, 159
Chalcot House, 139, 140, 217
Chambers, Sir William, 123, 133
Chambiges, Pierre, 75
Chambord: Château, 56–57, 214, 216
Charles V, 4, 50, 58, 92, 94, 170, 173, 174, 177
Charles VIII, 56
Charleval: Château, 81, 83, 142, 214
Chaucer, Geoffrey, 2
Chelmno: Town Hall, 156
Chiapas: Public Fountain, 199
Chicksands Priory, 126
Chigi, Agostino, 34, 218
Christian IV, 107
Chrudim: Mydlářovský Building, 163, 164
Clausse, Cosme, 75
Clough, Sir Richard, 133, 136, 142
Coducci, Mauro, 15, 18, 19, 30, 146, 148, 214, 217
Coecke, Pieter, 93, 94, 213, 222
Cogolludo: Medinaceli Palace, 13, 168, 169, 221
Colin, Alexander, 98, 100, 101, 214
Cologne: Rathaus, 94–95, 221
Columbus, Christoforo, 2, 168
Cometta, Antonio, 158, 159
Copenhagen: Kommunitetsbygningen, 112
Copthall, 128, 129, 133
Corbet, Robert, 142, 144, 214
Cordovan, Tour De, 84, 86, 215
Corsham Court, 139, 140, 220

Cortona, Church of Santa Maria Del Calcinaio, 21, 22, 215
Cortona, Domenico Bernabei "Boccador" Da, 56, 57, 58, 214, 219
Cosimo, Duke of Tuscany, 34
Coster, Laurens Janszoon, 4
Cour, Joist De La, 111, 112, 214
Covarrubias, Alonjo De, 170, 174, 176, 177, 181, 214
Covert, Richard, 142
Crassowski, Pietro, see Barbona
Crichton Castle, 143, 144
Cricoli: Villa Trissino, 32
Cromwell, Oliver, 136
Cuneo, Gaspare, 161, 163, 164
Curtea De Argash: Episcopal Buildings, 151

Dalmatinac, Juraj, see Orsini, Giorgio
Dance, George, 84
Delorme, Jean, 58, 59
Delorme, Philibert, 48, 59–65, 69, 78, 84, 92, 143, 187, 213, 214, 216
Denbigh: Church, 140, 142
Dietterlin, Wendel, 117, 119, 214
Donatello, Donato Di Batto Bardi, 3, 9
Dono, Paolo Uccello Di, 3
Dresden: Residenzschloss Chapel, 96, 98, 99, 112, 156, 159, 216, 217
Dubrovnik: Rector's Palace, 146
Duca, Giacomo Del, 52–53, 214
Ducerceau, Baptiste Androuet, 84, 86, 214
Ducerceau, Jacques Androuet, 60, 63, 65, 81, 83, 84, 138, 213, 214
Dudley, Robert, Earl of Leicester, 140, 142
Dufay, Guillaume, 2
Dunstable, John, 2
Dutton, Thomas, 138

Eastbury Manor, 136, 142
Echter, Bishop Julius, 117
Écouen: Château, 63, 78–79, 213
Edam: Weeshuis, 100, 101
Edward VI, 123
Egas, Enrique De, 168–170, 177, 187, 214, 220
Egckl, Wilhelm, 112, 113
Elizabeth I, 126, 128, 130, 136, 138, 140, 142, 143

Erasmus, Desidarius, 2
Eric XIV, 105, 107
Erfurt: Roter Ochse, 111, 112
Escorial, v, 52, 187–193, 197, 199, 215, 216, 217, 221
Este, Cardinal Ippolito D', 68, 69
Estremoz: Church of Santa Maria Do Castelo, 203, 204, 215
Évora: Chapel of Nossa Senhora Da Graça, 199, 200
Évora: Church of Espírito Santo, 199–201
Évora: Church of São Mamede, 201, 202, 221

Faconi, Giovanni M., 158, 159
Falconetto, Giovanni, 34, 35, 214
Falkland Palace, 123, 124
Faringdon: Market/Town Hall, 134, 136
Ferdinand & Isabella, 168
Ferdinand, Archduke of Austria, 92
Ferrabosco, Pietro, 96, 99, 161, 162, 215
Ferrara: Church of San Francisco, 19
Ferra: Palazzo Dei Diamanti, 19, 21, 154, 219
Ferrucci, Andrea, 148, 149, 215
Filarete, Antonio Averuno, 13, 15, 16, 17, 24, 215
Fioravanti, Ridolfo Aristotele, 146, 215
Fiorentino, Domenico, 75, 77, 215
Fiorentino, Francesco, 148, 150, 215
Fiorentino, Niccolo, 146, 147, 215, 219
Fleury-en-Bière: Château, 75, 77, 216
Florence: Barbadori Chapel, 6
Florence: Cathedral & Baptistery, 3, 9, 213
Florence: Chapel of Schiatta, 6
Florence: Church of San Lorenzo, 6–8, 9, 19, 20, 24, 25, 32–34, 36, 39, 213, 217, 219
Florence: Church of San Miniato, 9, 15, 213, 219
Florence: Church of Santa Annunziata, 9, 12, 13, 217
Florence: Church of Santa Croce, 6, 9
Florence: Church of Santa Maria Degli Angeli, 9, 10, 19, 213

Florence: Church of Santa Maria Novella, 3, 9, 13
Florence: Church of Santo Spirito, 9, 10, 213
Florence: Ospedale Degli Innocenti, 6, 7, 13, 213
Florence: Palazzo Di Parte Guelfa, 6, 8, 213
Florence: Palazzo Medici-Riccardi, 12, 13, 15, 217
Florence: Palazzo Pitti, 9, 11, 22
Florence: Palazzo Rucellai, 13, 14, 15, 212, 219
Florence: Pazzi Chapel, 6, 8, 9, 19, 128, 213, 217
Floris, Cornelis, 93, 94, 95, 103, 117, 126, 130, 136, 161, 163, 214, 215, 218, 220, 221, 222
Floris, Frans, 94, 95
Foix, Louis De, 84, 86, 94, 103, 159, 215
Fontainebleau: House of Cardinal D'Este, 68, 69
Fontainebleau: Palace, 52, 65, 68, 69, 78, 80–81, 122, 216, 218, 221
Francesca, Piero Della, 27
Francken, Frans II, 105
François, Gaten, 75
François I, 56, 60, 63, 65, 69, 123, 216
François II, 81
Frederik II, 107, 110
Fronteira: Church of Santa Maria, 204, 206

Gabri, Pietro, 161, 162, 215
Gadier, Pierre, 75
Gaínsa, Martín De, 174, 175, 186, 187, 215, 219
Galli, Agostino, 153, 154
Grand, see Gent
Gardiner, Bishop Stephen, Monument, 123, 125, 126, 138
Garovi Da Biseno, Leonardo, 156–158, 215
Garrett, Wendell, iii
Gdánsk: Długa 35 & 45, 159–161, 218
Gdánsk: Zielona Brama, 159, 160, 218
Genga, Girolamo, 36, 38, 39, 201, 215, 217, 221
Genoa: Church of Santa Maria in Carignano, 50–52, 192, 212, 218
Genoa: Palazzo Municipale, 51–53, 216

Genoa: Palazzo Sauli, 49, 50, 212
Genoa: Villa Cambiaso, 49, 50, 212
Gent: Bollaertskamer, 117, 118, 219
Gheeraerts, Marcus, 126
Ghiberti, Lorenzo, 3
Gibbs, James, 41, 226
Gil De Hontañon, Rodrigo, 174, 177, 180, 181, 193, 215
Giocondo, Fra Giovanni Da Verona, 56
Giorgio Martini, Francesco Di, 21, 22, 36, 215
Glover, Moses, 133
Gomez, Pero, 203, 204, 215
Gorges, Sir Thomas & Lady Helena, 143
Gorhambury Park, 135, 136, 138
Goujon, Jean, 75–77, 79, 214, 216
Gran: Bishop Bakócz Chapel, 148, 149, 215
Granada: Alhambra, 170
Granada: Cathedral, 170, 171, 172, 214, 220
Granada: Chancillería, 197, 198
Granada: Hospital Real, 169, 170, 214
Granada: Palace of Charles V, 170, 173, 174, 204, 216, 217
Granvelle, Antoine Cardinal, 58, 96, 97
Graz: Landhaus, 100, 101, 212
Gresham, Sir Thomas, 105, 126, 128, 130, 133, 136, 138, 140, 142, 220
Griespach, Florian, 151, 152
Grijó: Salvador Convent Church, 204, 205, 221
Grimaldi, Nicolò, 52, 216
Groningen: Kardinalshuis, 100, 101
Guadix: Cathedral, 170, 171, 220
Guise, Marie De, 123
Gutenberg, Johannes, 4
Gyulafehérvár: Lázói Janos Chapel, 150, 151

Hamburg: Börse, 114, 115, 212
Hampton Court Palace, 122
Hardwick Hall, 3, 90, 123, 140, 220
Harrison, Peter, iii, 231
Hatton, Sir Christopher, 136, 142, 143
Have, Theodore De, 141, 142, 216

Hawksmoor, Nicholas, 36
Haynes Grange, 126
Heidelberg: Ottheinrichsbau, 98, 100, 101, 156, 214
Helsingør: 76 Stengade, 107, 108
Heneage, Sir Thomas, 128, 130
Henri II, 60, 63, 65, 75, 78, 84
Henry VII (Henry Tudor), 2, 122, 217
Henry VIII, 4, 122, 123, 136
Herengrave, Herman Van, 96, 97, 216
Herrera, Juan De, 187–197, 201, 204, 207, 216, 217
Hieronymus, 32, 33, 88, 216
Hill Hall, 140, 141, 216, 220
Hillerød: Bath-House, 107, 109, 110
Hillerød: Fadeburslangen, 107, 109
Hofhaimer, Paulus, 2
Holt: Gresham School, 136, 142
Hoorn: Sint-Jansgasthuis Boterhal, 100
Horst: Schloss, 111, 112, 214
Hovestadt: Schloss, 214
Hus, John, 2
Hustopeče: Castle, 159, 160

Ibarra, Pedro. 174, 177, 216
Ijsselstein: Church, 90–91, 218
Intwood House, 129, 130
Isenburg: Schloss, 113, 114

Jaén: Cathedral Sacristy, 174, 175, 221
James V, 123
Jaroslavice: Castle, 161, 163
Jefferson, Thomas, 46
Jerez De La Frontera: Cabildo, 186, 187, 219
Jerman, Edward, 130
Jindřichuv Hradec: Castle, 158, 159, 217
Johanssen, Arndt, 214
Johnson, Dr. Samuel, 133
Joinville: Château, 75, 77, 215
Jones, Inigo, iv, 3, 41, 123, 136
Jülich: Zitadelle, 91–92, 218

Kačerov: Florian Griespach Castle, 151, 152
Kaliningrad: Count Albrecht Monument, 94, 161, 163
Kenilworth Castle, 140, 141
Keldermans, Rombout II, 88–90, 213, 216

Kepler, Johannes, 112
Keyser, Hendrik De, 130
Kirby Hall, 84, 136, 141, 142, 143
Kirby, Richard, 140, 141, 216, 220
Klagenfurt: Cathedral, 117, 118
Knotz, Hans, 89–90, 216
Koldštejn: Castle, 165, 166
Königsberg, see Kaliningrad
Kostelec: Castle, 153, 154, 221
Krakow: Cloth Hall, 156, 157, 161, 217
Krakow: Padniewski/Potocki Chapel, 163, 164, 217
Krakow: Royal Castle on Walsel Hill, 148, 150, 213, 215
Krakow: Sigismund Chapel, 148, 150, 213
Krakow: Tomicki Chapel, 150, 151, 213
Kralovice: Church of Saints Peter & Paul, 153, 154
Kramer, Johann & Bastian & Michael, 96, 98, 99, 159, 160, 161, 163, 164, 216, 217, 218
Kratochvíle: Summer Palace, 158, 159, 217
Kronborg Castle, 107, 108, 110
Krumpper, Hans, 114–117, 220

La Muette: Château, 75
La Rochefoucauld: Château, 58
Latour D'Aigues: Château, 75, 77, 78
Lacalahorra: Castle, 170, 171, 213, 221
Landshut: Burg Trausnitz, 114, 115, 220
Landshut: Stadtresidenz, 92–93, 217
Laparelli, Francesco, 213
Lastra A Signa: Hospital, 6
Laurana, Francesco, 148
Laurana, Luciano, 15, 18, 22, 24, 36, 146, 214, 215, 216, 217
Lebreton, Gilles, 65, 68, 75, 77, 216
Lemercier, Jacques, 81
Leo X (Pope), 34, 39
León: Casa De Los Guzmanes, 196, 197
Leonardo Da Vinci, iv, 21, 22, 23, 24, 39, 50, 56–57, 216
Leonardo, Giuseppe, 197
Lescot, Pierre, 69, 75–77, 78, 80, 143, 213, 216

Liège: Church of Saint-Jacques, 94, 96, 97, 220
Lippi, Fra Filippo, 3
Lisbon: Church of Santa Catarina Dos Livreiros, 201, 202, 212
Lisbon: Church of São Amaro, 199, 200
Lisbon: Church of São Roque, 201, 202, 212, 221
Lisbon: Church of São Vicente Da Fora, 207, 208, 221
Lisbon: Palácio Do Côrte Real, 206, 207, 221
Lisbon: Torreão Royal Palace, 204, 207, 208, 221
Litomyšl: Castle, 154–156, 212
Lloyd, John, 2
Lombardo, Pietro, 148
London: Church of Saint Leonard's Shoreditch, 84
London: Ely Place, 143
London: Gresham College/House, iii, iv, v, 126–128, 130, 143
London: Guildhall, 143
London: Royal Exchange, iv, 9, 103, 114, 128, 130–132, 133, 193
London: Somerset House, 123, 125, 126, 221
London: Steelyard, 128–130
London: Victoria & Albert Museum, 125, 126, 133, 220
Longford Castle, 143, 144
Longleat, 90, 123, 138, 139, 140, 142, 217, 220, 221
Lopes, João, 204, 205, 216
Loreto: Church of Santa Maria, 30, 31
Loscher, Sebastian, 88–89, 216
Louis XI, 56
Louis XII, 56, 216
Louis XIV, 65
Lübeck: Rathaus, 105, 106
Lucchese, Giovanni, 154, 155, 216
Ludwig, Stanislas, 161, 163, 164
Luis, Jerónimo, 204, 205, 216
Lumley, John, Lord, 143
Lund: Cathedral, 107
Lüneburg: 14 Lunertorstrasse, 112, 113
Lurago, Rocco, 51–53, 216
Lvóv: Anczowski "Black House", 164, 165, 213
Lvóv: Armenian Cathedral, 164
Lvóv: Church of the Benedictines, 164, 165, 213
Lvóv: "Italian" Courtyard, 164, 165, 213

Lvóv: Walachian Church, 164, 213
Lyon: Bourse, 65, 67
Lystrup Castle, 107
Lyttleton, Margaret, 4

Machiavelli, Niccolo Di Bernardo Dei, 2
Machsca, Pedro & Luís, 170, 173, 174, 204, 216, 217
Madrid: Palace of El Pardo, 181, 183, 192, 207, 221
Madrid: Real Alcázar, 177, 181, 184, 192, 221
Magena, Onorato, 58, 59, 216
Maggi, Baldassare, 158, 159, 216, 217
Maiano, Giuliano Da & Benedetto Da, 9, 19, 20, 217
Maire, Richare, 58, 59
Málaga: Cathedral, 170, 171, 220
Malines, see Mechelin
Manetti, Gianozzo, 2
Mansart, François & Jules-Hardovin, 81
Mantovani, Antonio, Bernardo & Sigismondo, 92–93, 217
Mantja: Cathedral, 36
Mantua: Church of San Sebastiano, 13, 14, 212
Mantua: Church of Sant'Andrea, 13, 14, 16, 212
Mantua: Citadel Gate, 36
Mantua: Palazzo Del Te, 35, 36, 37, 218, 219
Mantua: Palazzo Ducale, 36, 37, 219
Marseille: Chapel of Saint-Lazare, 148
Martin, Jean, 214
Mary Queen of Scots, 143
Mary Tudor, 123, 126, 130, 143
Masaccio, Tommaso Guidi, 3, 9, 10, 217
Maser: Tempietto Barbaro, 47, 48, 60
Maser: Villa Barbaro, 43, 45, 63
Masolino, Tommaso Di Cristoforo Fini, 3
Mavlnes-En-Tonnerois: Château, 69, 73–74, 84
Maynard, Alain, 81, 138, 139, 140, 217, 221
Maynard, John, 217
Mechelin: Salmon House, 90–91, 222
Mechelin: Savoie Palace, 88–90, 213, 216

Medici, Catherine, 60, 63, 81
Medici, Cosimo Di, 9
Medina Del Campo: Palace of the Dueñas, 181
Mediolano, Kiliano Syröth De, 160, 161, 217
Meer, Erhard Van Der, 112, 113, 217
Meledo: Villa Trissino, 46
Mendoza, Don Rodrigo De, 170
Menga, Evangelista Della, 213
Mesnières: Château, 58–59
Michałowicz, Jan, 163, 164
Michelangelo Buonarrot, 3, 30, 32, 33, 34, 36, 39, 52, 78, 187, 192, 197, 217, 218, 219, 221
Michelozzo De Bartolomeo, 9, 12, 13, 15, 146, 168, 217, 221
Midow, Herkules, 105
Milan: Church of Santa Maria Della Grazie, 3
Milan: Church of Santa Maria Presso San Satiro, 29, 30
Milan: Cloister of San Ambrogio, 24, 26, 170
Milan: Medici Bank, 12, 13, 168, 217
Milan: Ospedale Maggiore, 15, 17, 24, 215
Milan: Sforza Castle, 21, 22
Milan: Trivulsio Chapel, 24, 25
Milano, Ambrogio Barocci Da, 90
Miller, Wolfgang, 114–117, 220
Mitra: Chapel of Bom Jesus, 199, 200, 218
Montagnana, Alevisio Lamberti Da, see Alevisio Novyi
Montano, Juan, 170, 171, 217
Montceaux-En-Brie: Château, 81–82, 218
Montefeltro, Duke Federigo, 15
Montepulciano: Church of San Biagio, 34, 35, 50, 219
Montmorency, Anne De, 78
Moorfields: Villa, 125, 126
Moravský Krumlov: Castle, 156, 157, 215
Moreton Corbet Castle, 142, 144, 214
Mosca, Giovanni Maria, 96, 98, 99, 156, 217
Moscow: Cathedral of Saint Michael Archangel, 148, 149, 151, 212
Moscow: Dormition Cathedral, 146, 215
Moscow: Granovitaya Palace, 22, 146, 147, 219, 220

Moscow: Ivan Veliki Bell Tower, 148, 151, 152, 213
Moscow: Palace of Facets, see Granovitaya Palace
Moulins: Château, 56, 57
Munich: Church of Saint Michael, 114, 116, 117, 220
Munich: Jesuit College, 117, 118, 220
Munich: Residenz, 112, 113, 114, 115, 220

Nagybicese: Turzo Castle, 160, 161, 217
Náměšť: Castle, 156, 158, 215
Naples: Poggio Reale, 19, 20, 217
Napoleon, 60
Napoli, Pietro Di, 56
Nelahozeves: Florian Griespach Castle, 151, 152
Nemours, Due De, 84
Neuburg-on-the-Danube: Schloss, 89, 90, 216
Newark Park House, 125, 126, 220
Nijmegen: Raadhuis, 96, 97, 216
Nonsuch Palace, 122, 143, 144
Noort, Willem Van, 92–93, 217
Nový Jičín: Stara Pošta, 160, 161
Novyi, Alevisio, see Alevisio
Noyen, Sebastian Van, 93, 94, 96, 97, 217
Nürnberg: Church of Saint Rochus, 88
Nürnberg: Shrine of Saint Sebald, 88, 89, 222

Opbergen, Antonius Van, 107
Ockegen, Johannes, 2
Oliva, Martín De, 187
Olomovc: Edelmann Chapel, 163, 164
Oñate: University, 180, 181, 215
Opočno: Castle, 158, 159
Orea, Juan De, 186, 187, 217
Orihuela: Cathedral, 187
Orihuela: Convent of Santo Domingo, 186, 187, 212
Orihuela: Convent of Santo Domingo, 186, 187, 212
Orsini, Bishop John, 146
Oslavany: Castle, 165, 166
Osterley Park, 130, 132, 133, 134
Ottheinrich, Prince, 90, 98

Paciotto, Francesco, 192, 217
Padua: Loggia Cornaro, 34, 35, 214
Padua: Villa Pisani, 43, 44
Paesschen, Hans Hendrik Van, iv, 24, 93, 94, 100, 102–111, 126, 140, 143, 193, 215, 217, 218
Palermo: Church of San Geminiano, 39, 40, 219
Palladio, Andrea Di Pietro, iv, 4, 24, 30, 39, 41–48, 52, 60, 63, 75, 112, 133, 164, 190, 192, 193, 197, 204, 218, 228
Pambio, Giovanni Maria Del, 154, 155, 218
Pardubice: Castle, 155, 156
Paris: Basilica, 63
Paris: Château Madrid, 69, 75
Paris: Church of Saint-Elio, 63
Paris: Church of Saint-Nicolas-Des-Champs, 63
Paris: Convent of Notre Dame De Montmartre, 63, 65
Paris: École Des Beaux Arts, 60
Paris: Fountain of the Innocents, 75–76, 216
Paris: Hôtel Angoulême, 84, 86, 214
Paris: Hôtel Carnavalet, see: Hôtel De Ligneris
Paris: Hôtel Lamoignan, see Hôtel Angoulême
Paris: Hôtel De Ligneris, 75–76, 216
Paris: Hôtel De Ville (City Hall), 56–58, 214
Paris: Louvre Palace, 63, 65, 66–67, 75–76, 216
Paris: Tournelles Gate, 63, 64
Paris: Tuileries Palace, 63–64, 78–79, 213
Parr, Giovanni Battista, 156, 157, 218
Pasqualini, Alessandro, 90–92, 218
Passe, Crispin Van De, I, II, III, 100
Passe, Hans Hendrik Van De, see under Paesschen
Paul, III (Pope), 4
Paumann, Conrad, 2
Pavia: Certosa, 3
Pavia: Collegio Borromeo, 51–52, 221
Perrault, Claude, 65
Perrenot, Nicolas, Sieur De Granvelle, 58

Peruzzi, Baldassare, 19, 34, 35, 39, 48, 50, 69, 212, 218, 219, 220, 221
Pesaro: Villa Rovere/Imperiale, 36, 38, 39, 201, 215
Petrarcha, Francesco, 2
Philandrier, Guillaume, 78, 81–82, 218
Philip II, 58, 92, 94, 170, 187–193, 197, 216
Pienza: Palazzo Piccolomini, 13, 15, 219
Piotrków Castle, 147, 148, 219
Pires, Manuel, 199, 200, 201, 218
Pistoia: Church of Santa Maria Delle Grazie, 217
Plas Clough, 136, 142
Hatfield, 128, 136
Plas Mawr, 136, 142, 143, 144
Plasencia: Cathedral, 168, 169, 177, 212
Plasencia: Small Palace, 193, 195, 197
Plumlov: Castle, 161, 163, 164
Plzeň: Town Hall, 156, 157, 220
Poitiers, Diane De, 60
Polirone: Church of San Benedetto Po, 36, 37, 219
Porta, Giacomo Della, 34, 50, 52–53, 218, 221, 222, 227
Portalegre: Cathedral, 201, 203, 204
Poznán: Town Hall, 156, 157, 218
Prague: Belvedere, 151, 152, 212, 220, 222
Prague: Cathedral of Saint Vitus, 151, 152, 154
Prague: Chapel of Saint Adalbert, 153, 154
Prague: Church of Saint George, 146
Prague: Church of Sr. Trojice, 154
Prague: Hvĕsda Castle, 154, 155, 216, 218, 221
Prague: Lobkovic-Švarcemberk Palace, 153, 154, 215
Prague: Ludvík Wing, Hradshin Castle, 146, 147, 219
Prague: Royal Ball Court, 151, 153
Prague: Ungeltu Building, 156, 158, 159
Prato: Church of Santa Maria Delle Carceri, 19, 20, 219
Prez, Josquin Des, 2
Primaticcio, Francesco, 36, 48, 69, 75, 78–82, 213, 218, 219

Prioli, Giovanni Battista, Alberto & Domingo, 197, 198, 218
Protagoras, 2

Quadro, Giovanni Battista Di, 156, 157, 218
Quijano, Jerónimo, 187

Račice: Castle, 161, 162
Raffaelle Sanzio, 3, 26, 27, 31–32, 34, 36, 39, 41, 56, 58, 88, 156, 213, 218, 219, 220, 222
Regnier, 159, 160, 161, 216, 218
Rheydt: Schloss, 112, 113
Riaño, Diego De, 174, 175, 193, 218, 219
Ribera, Andrés De, 187
Richard III, 2
Ried, Benedikt, 146, 147, 148, 150, 219
Rimini: Tempco Malatestiano, 13, 14, 212
Ringshall, 130
Ripoll, Francisco, 187, 188
Robbia, Andrea Della & Luca Della, 3, 6
Robbia, Girolama Della, 75
Robertet, Florimond, 56
Robin, Jan II & George, 117, 119, 219
Roccaverano: Church, 29, 30
Rodez: Cathedral, 81–82, 218
Rodmister Lodge, 139, 140
Romano, Giulio Pippi, 35, 36, 37, 48, 69, 78, 92, 100, 151, 156, 217, 218, 219
Romano, Paolo, 146, 147, 215, 219
Rome: Belvedere, 27, 29, 30, 36, 69, 192, 201
Rome: Benediction Loggia, 13, 14, 19, 212
Rome: Cathedral of Saint Peter, v, 9, 22, 30, 31, 32, 34, 48, 52, 213, 217, 218, 219, 221
Rome: Chapel of San Biagio, 29, 30
Rome: Chigi Chapel, 31, 32, 41, 58, 218
Rome: Church of Il Gesù, 24, 49, 50, 52, 81, 114, 193, 218, 221, 227
Rome: Church of San Giovanni Dei Fiorentini, 34, 39
Rome: Church of Sant'Andrea in Via Flaminia, 48, 49, 221

Rome: Church of Santa Maria Dei Monti, 52–54, 218
Rome: Church of Santa Maria in Trivio, 52, 53, 214
Rome: Church of Santi Celso E Giuliano, 29, 30
Rome: Colosseum, 13, 39
Rome: Convent of Santa Maria Della Pace, 26, 27
Rome: Gate to Farnese Gardens, 48, 49, 50, 221
Rome: Loggia Di San Damaso, 27, 28
Rome: Palazzo Bresciano, 31, 32, 218
Rome: Palazzo Caprini, 26, 27
Rome: Palazzo Del Conservatori & Palazzo Capitolino, 33, 34, 217
Rome: Palazzo Della Cancellaria, 27, 28
Rome: Palazzo Farnese, 38, 39, 192, 193, 197, 219
Rome: Palazzo Senatorio, 34, 197, 217
Rome: Palazzo Venezia, 18, 19, 219
Rome: The Pantheon, 481
Rome: Porta Pia, 34
Rome: Sistine Chapel, 222
Rome: Tempietto of San Pietro in Montorio, 26, 27, 32, 41, 192
Rome: Villa Farnesina, 34, 218
Rome: Villa Madama, 31, 32
Romorantin: Royal Palace, 56–57
Rooman, Joos, 117, 118, 219
Rosice: Castle, 156, 157, 215
Rosmarino: Château, 69, 72
Rossellino, Antonio & Bernardo, 13, 15, 219
Rossetti, Biagio, 19, 21, 22
Rosso, Fiorentino, 3
Rothwell: Market House, 142, 144, 220, 221
Rouen, Jeande, 199, 200, 204, 219
Rožmberk, William of, 159
Ruão, Jerónimo De, 203, 204, 219
Rubens, Peter Paul, 50
Ruffo, Marco, 146, 147, 219
Ruiz, Hernán, 186, 187, 219
Ruthin: Clough Town House, 133, 134

Saint-André, Jacques De, 75
Saint-Ange: Château, 75

Saint-Denis: Valois Mausoleum, 78, 80, 81, 213, 218
Saint-Germain-En-Laye: Châteaux & Chapel, 62–63, 75
Saint-Léger: Château & Chapel, 60, 62
Saint-Maur-Les-Fossér: Château, 59–60, 65, 214
Salamanca: Church of San Estéban, 168, 212
Salamanca: Colegio Del Arzobispo Fonseca/De Los Nobles Irlandeses, 174, 175, 214, 215, 216, 220
Salamanca: Palacio De Monterrey, 177, 180, 181, 215
Salamanca, Gabriel Von Ortenberg De, 92
Salamanca/Porcia: Schloss, 92–93
Salvaterra De Magos: Palace Chapel, 201, 202, 212
San Gallo, Antonio Da, I, 34, 35, 39, 50, 219
San Gallo, Antonio Da, II, 34, 38, 39, 48, 50, 96, 192, 193, 197, 212, 217, 218, 219, 221
San Gallo, Giuliano da, 18, 19, 20, 34, 56, 174, 214, 216, 218, 219
San Micheli, Michele, 41, 42, 48, 219
Sánchez, Bartolomé, 187
Sansovino, Jacopo Tatti, 34, 38, 39, 40, 41, 43, 46, 48, 100, 219, 220
Santa Cruz: Manga Monastery, 199, 200, 219
Santi Gucci, 166
Santiago De Compostela: Royal Hospital (Hospital De Los Reyes Catolicos), 24, 168–170, 214
Scamozzi, Vincenzo, 46, 48
Scarini, Niccolo, 94, 103, 219
Schütz, Heinrich, 98
Sens: Archbishop's Palace, 59–60
Serlio, Sebastiano, iv, 19, 24, 27, 32, 34, 39–42, 48, 50, 65–74, 75, 81, 84, 88, 90, 103, 114, 128, 133, 140, 143, 192, 201, 217, 218, 220, 221
Setúbal: Church of Santa Maria Da Graça, 203, 204
Sevilla: Ayuntamiento (Casa Capitulares), 174, 175, 218, 219
Sevilla: Casa Lonja/General Archives of the Indies, 192, 193, 194, 197, 216, 217

Sevilla: Cathedral Sacristy, 174, 175, 219
Sevilla: Hospital Provincial De La Sangre, 186, 187, 215, 219, 221
Sforza, Bona, 148
Sforzinda, 15–17, 215
Sherborne House, 138, 139, 217, 221
Shute, John, 126, 220
Šibenik: Cathedral, 19, 146, 147, 217
Sienna: Villa Chigi Delle Volte, 19, 34, 35, 218
Sigismund I, 148
Siloé, Diego De, 170–172, 174, 176, 177, 214, 220, 221
Simontornya Castle, 148, 150
Sixdeniers, Christian, 90–91, 220, 222
Slaugham Place, 142, 144
Smith, Sir Thomas, 140, 141, 220
Smythson, Robert, 136, 138, 139, 140, 217, 220
Solario, Pietro Antonio, 146, 147, 219, 220
Somerset, Edward Seymour, Duke of, 123
Statio, Giovanni Di, 156, 157, 215, 220
Steenwinckel, Hans Van, 105, 112
Stella, Paolo Della, 151, 152, 220
Stewart, Francis Earl of Bothwell, 143
Stickels, Robert, 142, 144, 220
Stirling Castle, 123
Stjerneborg, 112
Strada, Jacopo, 112, 113, 220
Summerson, Sir John, 3
Sustris, Friedrich, 94, 112, 114–117, 220
Sustris, Lamberto, 94, 96, 97, 103, 114, 220
Suze-La-Rousse: Château, 78, 79
Talleyrand, Charles, 60
Tavera, Cardinal, 177, 181
Telč: Castle, 158, 159, 217
Terzi, Filippo, 204, 206–208, 221
Theobalds Park, 135–137
Thorpe, John, 136, 142, 143
Thynne, John, 123, 125, 138, 139, 140, 217, 220, 221
Tibaldi, Pellegrino, Marchese De Valsolda, 51, 52, 221
Tintoretto, Jacopo Robusti, 3
Tirol, Hans, 153, 154, 155, 221
Todi: Church of Santa Maria Della Consolazione, 22, 23
Tolbuzin, Prince Simyon, 146

Toledo: Hospital De Santa Cruz, 169–170, 214
Toledo, Juan Bautista De, 187–193, 216, 221
Toledo: Tavera "Afuera" Hospital De San Juan Bautista, 181, 182, 213
Toledo: Real Alcázar, 177, 179, 181, 214
Tomar: Conceiçao Chapel, 199, 200, 213
Tomar: Convent of Christ, 39, 201, 202, 221
Torralva, Diogo Da, 36, 39, 199, 200, 201, 202, 215, 221
Torrigiano, Pietro I & II, 122, 187, 221
Tortosa: Colegio De San Matías/San Luís, 181, 186, 187, 212
Toulouse: Hôtel D'Assézat, 78–79, 212
Toulouse, Pierre De, 197, 198, 221
Tour De Cordovan, 84, 86, 159
Tovačov Castle, 146, 147
Tresham, Sir Thomas, 142, 144, 220, 221
Trogir: Cathedral, 146, 147, 215, 219

Úbeda: Church of San Salvador, 174, 176, 177, 221
Úbeda: Hospital De Santiago, 177, 178, 221
Úbeda: Palacio Vázquel De Molina, 176, 177, 221
Unton, Sir Henry & Sir Edward, 136
Uraniborg, vi, 110–112, 143
Urbino, Palazzo Ducale, 15, 18, 22, 215, 216
Utrecht: Raadhuis, 92–93, 217
Uzès: Château, 84, 86
Uzès, Duc D', 69, 84

Valençay: Château, 59–60
Valencia: Diputación, 170, 171, 217
Valladolid: Cathedral, 193, 196, 216
Valladolid: Colegio Santa Cruz, 168, 169, 221
Valle, Pedro, 197, 198, 221
Vallery: Château, 75–76, 216
Valletta: Auberge D'Italie, 52–53, 213
Vallø Castle, 106, 107, 109
Valsaín: Royal Palace, 181, 185, 192, 221
Van—see under last name
Van Eyck, Hubert & Jan, 3, 4
Vandelvira, Andrés De, 174, 175, 176, 177, 178, 221
Vannes: Chapel of The Holy Sacrament, 58, 59
Vasari, Giorgio, 2, 3, 41
Vázguez, Lorenzo, 168, 169, 170, 221
Vega, Luís De, 177, 181, 183–185, 192, 207, 221
Vělke Losiny: Castle, 164–166
Veneziano, Domenico, 3
Venice: Church & Monastery of San Giorgio Maggiore, 43, 45, 46
Venice: Church of Il Redentore, 46
Venice: Church of San Francesco Della Vigna, 46
Venice, Church of San Michele in Isola, 15, 18, 30, 214
Venice: Church of San Nicola Di Tolentino, 48
Venice: Church of Santa Maria Dei Miracoli, 148
Venice: Church of Santa Maria Della Misericordia, 39, 40, 219
Venice: Convent of Santa Maria Della Carità, 43, 44
Venice: Ducal Palace, 46, 47, 48, 164
Venice: Fondaco Dei Tedeschi, 32, 33, 88, 216
Venice: Library of San Marco, 39, 40, 43, 219
Venice: Palazzo Loredan-Vendramin-Calergi, 18, 19, 214
Venice: Scuola Di San Marco, 148
Venice: La Zecca, 38, 39, 219
Verneil: Château, 84, 85, 213
Vernukken, Wilhelm, 94–95, 221
Verona: Church of Modonna Di Campagna, 41, 42, 219
Verona: Pellegrini Chapel, 41
Verona: Palazzo Canossa, 41, 42, 219
Verona: Palazzo Carnesali, 143
Vicenza: Basilica, 43, 44
Vicenza: Loggia Del Capitaniato, 45, 46
Vicenza: Palazzo Iseppo-Porto, 42, 43
Vicenza: Villa Rotonda/Capra/Almerico, 46, 47

Vicenza: Villa Saraceno, 41, 42
Vienna: Amalienburg, see Hofburg
Vienna: Hofburg Palace, 96, 99, 215
Vienna: Salvator Kapelle, 96
Vienna: Schweizertor, see Hofburg
Vienna: Stallburg, see Hofburg
Vignola, Giacomo Barozzi Da, 24, 34, 48–50, 52, 217, 221, 222, 227
Vila Nova Da Gaia: Convent of Santa Maria, 204, 205, 216
Villers-Cotterets: Château & Chapel, 60–61
Vinci, Leonarda Da, see under Leonardo
Vincidor, Tommaso, 90–91, 92, 222
Viso Del Marqués, Palace of Marqués De Santa Cruz, 197, 198, 218
Visscher, Hermann II, 88–89, 222
Viterbo: Church of Santa Maria Della Quercia, 90
Viterbo: Giulio Farnese Tempietto, 48, 49, 221
Vitruvius, 4, 214, 218
Vredeman De Fries, Hans, 93, 94, 100, 102, 117, 214, 222

Waghemakere, Dominic De, 216
Wallot, Jan, 90–91, 220, 222
Walther, Hans II, 96, 98, 99, 217
Westminster: Henry VII Chapel, 122, 221
Weyden, Rogier Van Der, 3
Whitehall Palace, 123, 124
Wilhelm V, Duke of Bavaria, 114
Wilhelm V, Duke of Cleve, 92
Willoughby, Sir Francis, 140
Winchester: Cathedral, 123, 126
Windsor: Queen's Loggia, 125, 126
Wohlmut, Bonifaz, 151, 152, 153, 154, 220, 222
Wola Justowska: Decius Villa, 153, 154
Wollaton Hall, 22, 140, 141, 220
Wolsey, Cardinal Thomas, 122, 123
Wren, Christopher, iv, 3, 39, 41, 126, 128, 143, 225
Wren, Bishop Matthew, 143
Würzburg: Julius Universität, 117, 119, 219

Wycliffe, John, 2
Wynn, Robert, 142

Thirteen Colonies Press
710 South Henry Street, Williamsburg, Virginia, 23185-4113   804-229-1775

ELIZABETHAN COUNTRY DANCES
by *John Fitzhugh Millar*

Historic background and dance instructions for 86 dances, the favorite recreation of 16th and 17th-century England and America, plus about 100 of the most delightful tunes from the Golden Age of English music. The dances, which include the first square-dances and contras, are graded from easy to difficult. The dances and the music are ideally suited for adding color and authenticity to historic re-enactments, anniversaries, Shakespeare plays, Renaissance Festivals, museums and schools—and for just plain fun.

LC 85-51583

| 0-934943-00-1 | sewn paperpack | $12.95 |
| 0-934943-03-6 | hard cover | $19.95 |

A COMPLETE LIFE OF CHRIST
compiled by *John Fitzhugh Millar*

A single narrative in modern English of the life of Christ compiled from the Four Gospels and other New Testament books plus other authentic documentary sources uncovered by archaeologists (rendered in *italic* type to distinguish from Biblical sources), such as the Abgar Letters, fragments of Peter's Gospel, the Koran, Josephus, etc.; none of the numerous false writings about Christ is included. Also an appendix on the latest scientific findings about the Shroud of Turin. Intended for committed Christians and non-believers alike.

LC 85-51584

| 0-934943-01-X | sewn paperback | $8.95 |
| 0-934943-04-4 | hard cover | $15.95 |

EARLY AMERICAN SHIPS
by *John Fitzhugh Millar*

Extensive information, including historical background, plans and period portraits of over 200 North American ships and boats built through 1790, including the world's largest ship of the day, the first wartime submarine, early steamboats, Franklin's swivel-sailed yacht, the "modern" Bermudan rig, John Paul Jones' ships, and 2 ca.1730 ships recently recovered by archaeologists. 64 early flags appear in full color, some never before published. Appendix has a surprising account of how the American Navy was founded in 1775. Appeals to readers interested in early American history or sailing, model-builders and marine artists from novice to expert.

LC 85-51585

| 0-934943-02-8 | sewn paperback | $22.95 |
| 0-934943-05-2 | hard cover | $34.95 |

1988

EARLY AMERICAN BAROQUE & CLASSICAL MUSIC
by *John Fitzhugh Millar*

Handel and Mozart may not have to lay aside their crowns, but Colonial America now appears to have had scores of highly competent composers—over 120 men & women in North America through 1790 who wrote oratorios, operas, cantatas, anthems, hymns, songs, symphonies, concerti, overtures, quintets, quartets, trios, duets, sonatas, minuets and country dances that, although almost unknown, in many cases rank with European contemporary work. This anthology provides examples of the work of most of these composers with biographies and historical background. Will appeal to readers of American history, choirs and both professional and amateur musicians.

BUILDING EARLY AMERICAN WARSHIPS
introduction by *John Fitzhugh Millar*

In this verbatim transcript, the account books of the committee to build the Continental Navy's 32-gun frigate *Warren* and 28-gun frigate *Providence* 1775-6 published for the first time reveal admirable efficiency coupled with massive fraud and war-profiteering. Intricate details of construction and rigging blend with evidence of personal greed and ambition and rum-soaked carpenters. Introduction gives context and historical background.

NEW ENGLAND COLONIAL DESIGNS BY PETER HARRISON
by *John Fitzhugh Millar*

Peter Harrison (1716-1775) was Colonial America's foremost architect, and one of the first to use the elegant neo-Palladian style. This book contains elevation and other drawings of 26 houses, 7 churches and 7 other public buildings from Connecticut to Nova Scotia believed to be by Harrison (many suitable for reproducing today), and explores European prototypes for Harrison's designs. Harrison's invention of rusticated wood siding has been widely copied, including by an impressed Washington at Mount Vernon. Appeals to readers of American history, novices and experts in art history, and people hoping to build in the Colonial style from simple to elaborate.

STEPHEN HOPKINS
by *John Fitzhugh Millar*

The first new biography of the remarkable Stephen Hopkins (1707-1785) in over 100 years. Hopkins, a practically-unknown giant in the American pantheon, was a Signer of the Declaration of Independence, the founder of the American Navy, of the Continental Congress, of the Committees of Correspondence, of the Stamp Act Congress, of the U.S. Post Office and of Brown University; he ordered the first shots of resistance fired against British authority in America in 1764, and served several distinguished terms as Governor and Chief Justice of Rhode Island. His exciting life was deeply involved in Rhode Island's smuggling industry. Washington, Jefferson, Franklin and Adams would agree that Hopkins deserves to be as well-known as they.

All our books are set in historic type styles, made of long-life paper and are offered in two forms: sewn paperbacks for best value, and hardcovers for the special needs of libraries. Libraries are invited to place a standing order.

shipping & handling $2 first book
.50 each additional